I CORINTHIANS

THE ANCHOR BIBLE is a fresh approach to the world's greatest classic. Its object is to make the Bible accessible to the modern reader; its method is to arrive at the meaning of biblical literature through exact translation and extended exposition, and to reconstruct the ancient setting of the biblical story, as well as the circumstances of its transcription and the characteristics of its transcribers.

THE ANCHOR BIBLE is a project of international and interfaith scope: Protestant, Catholic, and Jewish scholars from many countries contribute individual volumes. The project is not sponsored by any ecclesiastical organization and is not intended to reflect any particular theological doctrine. Prepared under our joint supervision, THE ANCHOR BIBLE is an effort to make available all the significant historical and linguistic knowledge which bears on the interpretation of the biblical record.

THE ANCHOR BIBLE is aimed at the general reader with no special formal training in biblical studies; yet, it is written with the most exacting standards of scholarship, reflecting the highest technical accomplishment.

This project marks the beginning of a new era of co-operation among scholars in biblical research, thus forming a common body of knowledge to be shared by all.

William Foxwell Albright
David Noel Freedman
GENERAL EDITORS

Following the death of senior editor W. F. Albright, The Anchor Bible Editorial Board was established to advise and assist David Noel Freedman in his continuing capacity as general editor. The three members of the Editorial Board are among the contributors to The Anchor Bible. They have been associated with the series for a number of years and are familiar with its methods and objectives. Each is a distinguished authority in his area of specialization, and in concert with the others, will provide counsel and judgment as the series continues.

EDITORIAL BOARD

Frank M. Cross	Old Testament
Raymond E. Brown	New Testament
Jonas C. Greenfield	Apocrypha

THE ANCHOR BIBLE

I CORINTHIANS

A NEW TRANSLATION

Introduction with a Study of
the Life of Paul, Notes, and
Commentary by
WILLIAM F. ORR
and
JAMES ARTHUR WALTHER

DOUBLEDAY & COMPANY, INC.
GARDEN CITY, NEW YORK
1976

Library of Congress Cataloging in Publication Data

Bible. N.T. 1 Corinthians. English. Orr-Walther.
   1976.
   I Corinthians: a new translation.

   (The Anchor Bible; v. 32)
   Bibliography: p. 133.
   Includes indexes.
      1. Bible. N.T. 1 Corinthians—Commentaries.
2. Paul, Saint, Apostle. I. Orr, William Fridell,
1907–   II. Walther, James Arthur, 1918–
III. Series.
BS192.2.A1 1964.G3   vol. 32   [BS2673]   220.6'6s
ISBN 0-385-02853-9   [227'.2'07]
Library of Congress Catalog Card Number 75–42441

PREFACE

This commentary began with a compendium of comments on First Corinthians prepared by Professor Orr for his classes on "the practical use of the New Testament." Anchor Bible general editor David Noel Freedman enlisted Dr. Walther to collaborate in the task of building from comments to commentary and suggested that this volume should also contain a study on the life of Paul. The resulting book presents approximately the following division of labor. The "Introduction with a Study of the Life of Paul" is mostly Professor Orr's work with editorial additions and notes by Dr. Walther. The Translation is a joint effort. Most of the NOTES were supplied by Dr. Walther and most of the COMMENTS by Dr. Orr. Dr. Walther provided all of the material on ch. 16 and revised the whole text for publication. Needless to say, both authors assume responsibility for the contents of the volume.

The literature on First Corinthians is full and rich. The "Selected Bibliography" lists the most noteworthy books, the NOTES supply other titles, and there are still other worthy works that can easily be found in a good library. This commentary aims at a middle course between exhaustive, research resource and simple, verse-by-verse interpretation. The Introduction and COMMENTS should be intelligible to diligent non-specialists. The NOTES provide necessary, technical data for careful, exegetical study. Some new directions are pursued, but the more common consensus is also explained.

It is perilous to try to modernize Paul (as H. J. Cadbury said of Jesus). If his life and message are to be meaningful today, the first task is precisely to discover the significance of his life and message for his own day. Only when this exegetical exercise has been rigorously and honestly carried out can we assess what the Apostle means for us now. This demands sympathetic and meticulous study of the linguistic, social, political, and religious milieus in which Paul lived and worked. Once these are clearly understood, it becomes possible to translate Paul, *mutatis mutandis,* into the twentieth century.

This interpretative procedure has a particular relationship to the translation of the text of a letter of Paul's. Accepted procedure requires that we first understand the idiom of the Greek (with the peculiar problems posed by Paul's Jewish background) and then try to express the intent of those idioms in acceptable, English idiom. This presents a difficulty peculiar to exegesis: the meaning of a passage sometimes is inextricably involved with the flavor of the Greek idiom. Accordingly, the translation here presented attempts to preserve particularities of Paul's language where this is considered to be important to the proper understanding of Paul's meaning. When this seems to jeopardize the English idiom, NOTES attempt to smooth the transition.

The authors record their debts. First, to the great company of saints and scholars who have provided insights into Paul's mind, heart, and correspondence. Second, to their families and to their colleagues, who have helped in ways too intimate and manifold to acknowledge. Also, to David Noel Freedman, without whose editorial wisdom this book would never have come to publication. To Arline Wylie and Ruth Davidson, whose secretarial skills made contributions only authors and editors can fully appreciate. To Richard H. Thames for his work as skilled graduate student assistant; and to Stephen R. Long, who prepared the indexes.

This commentary bears no formal dedication. It has been written for the church. The authors are certain that, if Paul's letter to the church in Corinth is studied with mind and heart open to the Spirit that inspired Paul, the message of the letter will be found to be addressed to God's people in Christ's church today.

WILLIAM F. ORR
JAMES ARTHUR WALTHER

CONTENTS

Preface VII
[The authors have chosen to forgo a list of Principal
Abbreviations. Those they use are economically
set forth in the Selected Bibliography. Ed.]

INTRODUCTION with A STUDY OF THE LIFE OF PAUL 1
    Paul's pre-Christian life 3
    From conversion to conference in Jerusalem 6
    From the Jerusalem conference to the ministry in
        Greece 13
    Mission to the Balkan and Aegean peninsulas 14
    Paul in chains 28
    Paul's life as described in The Acts of the Apostles 46
    Paul at Athens 71
    Mission at Corinth 81
    Mission in Ephesus and Asia 83
    Visit to Jerusalem and subsequent imprisonment 91
    Trip to Rome and imprisonment there 96
    Paul's authority as an apostle 101
    Paul, the law, and the gentiles 103
    What kind of man was Paul? 106
    Paul facing quarrels, scandals, and quandaries in
        Corinth 118
    APPENDIX: Order of events in Paul's life 124

SELECTED BIBLIOGRAPHY 133

TRANSLATION, NOTES, AND COMMENTS   139
   Introductory (1:1-9)   141
   A. Greetings (1:1-3)   141
   B. Thanksgiving (4-9)   143

I. Threat of schism from party quarrels and class rivalry
   (1:10-4:21)   147
   A. Parties derived from leadership authorities (1:10-17)   147
     1. Absurdity of the claims (10-13)   147
     2. Baptisms by Paul (14-16)   147
     3. Paul's mission to evangelize (17)   147
   B. The message of the cross vs. the wisdom of the world
     (1:18-2:16)   152
     1. Saving power and perishing folly (18-21)   152
     2. Jews, Greeks, and God (22-25)   153
     3. God's choice of the "nothings" (26-31)   153
     4. Paul's personal demonstration of God's
       paradoxical wisdom (2:1-8)   153
     5. The Spirit as revealer of God's wisdom (9-13)   154
     6. The spiritual person and the mind of Christ
       (14-16)   154
   C. Leadership and nurture in the church (3:1-23)   167
     1. Strife and immaturity (1-4)   167
     2. Cooperative roles of leadership (5-9)   168
     3. The church as God's building (10-17)   168
     4. Belonging to God (18-23)   168
   D. Stewardship of apostolic ministry (4:1-21)   176
     1. The Lord as judge (1-5)   176
     2. Standards of Christian living (6-13)   176
     3. Paul's authority in Corinth (14-21)   177

II. Scandals reported in the church (5:1-6:20)   184
   A. A case of incest (5:1-8)   184
     1. Toleration of one having his "father's wife"
       (1-2)   184

    2. Judgment pronounced by Paul (3-5) — 184

    3. Analogue: leaven and the Christ-passover (6-8) — 184

 B. Clarification of Paul's instruction regarding
association with immoral persons (5:9-13) — 190

 C. Lawsuits among church members (6:1-9a) — 193

    1. Scandal of appearing before heathen judges
(1-6) — 193

    2. Incongruity of injustice among brothers (7-9a) — 193

 D. Prostitution, a particular instance of immorality
(6:9b-20) — 198

    1. The kingdom of God and immorality (9b-11) — 198

    2. God and the limitations of legality (12-14) — 198

    3. The Christian body (15-20) — 198

       a. Not to be joined to a prostitute (15-18) — 198

       b. To glorify God as a temple of the Spirit
(19-20) — 199

III. First quandary from Corinth: concerning marriage
(7:1-40) — 205

 A. Sexual intercourse (7:1-7) — 205

    1. The mutuality of marriage (1-4) — 205

    2. Special instances of abstention (5-7) — 205

 B. Remarriage of widows and widowers (7:8-9) — 210

 C. Divorce (7:10-16) — 211

    1. The Lord's charge against ultimate separation
(10-11) — 211

    2. Paul's recommendation that believers not divorce
unbelievers (12-14) — 211

    3. Believers not bound by broken marriages with
unbelievers (15-16) — 211

 D. Excursus: Christians to remain in their
preconversion status (7:17-24) — 214

 E. Paul's opinion regarding the unmarried (7:25-35) — 217

    1. Marriage permissible but inadvisable because of
"the form of this world" (25-31) — 217

    2. Marriage as a potential distraction from devotion
to the Lord (32-35) — 218

F. The marriage of "virgins" (7:36-38)   222

G. Remarriage of widows (7:39-40)   225

IV. Second quandary: concerning idol-offerings
     (8:1 - 11:1)   227

     A. Love, not knowledge; the guiding principle
         (8:1-3)   227

     B. The question of eating food offered to idols
         (8:4-13)   230

         1. Idols nothing; God in Christ everything (4-6)   230

         2. Obligation of deference to the conscience of a
             weak brother (7-13)   230

     C. Excursus: Paul's exercise of his rights (9:1-27)   235

         1. His apostolic freedom (1-6)   235

         2. Traditional guarantee of support to God's
             workers (7-14)   236

         3. Paul's waiver of his rights (15-23)   236

             a. His compulsion to preach free (15-18)   236

             b. His adaptability for the gospel (19-23)   236

         4. An athletic analogue (24-27)   237

     D. A warning from the Exodus history (10:1-15)   244

         1. Advantages of the Israelite fathers (1-4)   244

         2. Their idolatry in the desert; its monitory function
             (5-10)   244

         3. The warning afforded and God's escape provided
             (11-15)   244

     E. The Lord's Supper and food offered to idols
         (10:16-22)   249

         1. An analogy provided (16-20a)   249

         2. Restriction against partaking of both
             (20b-22)   249

     F. Conscience and food offered to idols (10:23-29)   253

         1. When no question is raised (23-27)   253

         2. When another's conscience is concerned (28-29) 253

     G. Paul's Christian example (10:30 - 11:1)   256

V. Scandals in church services (11:2-34)   258
   A. Headdress of women and its significance (11:2-16)   258
   B. Faults at the Lord's Supper (11:17-34)   265
      1. Divisions existing at the Supper (17-22)   265
      2. The received tradition of the institution of the
         Supper (23-26)   265
      3. Judgment from unworthy participation in the
         Supper (27-32)   265
      4. Summary instruction (33-34)   266

VI. Third quandary: concerning spiritual gifts
    (12:1 - 14:40)   276
   A. The Spirit of God and spiritual gifts (12:1-3)   276
   B. Varieties of gifts, different persons, one Spirit
     (12:4-11)   279
   C. Analogue: the body and its parts (12:12-26)   283
      1. The nature of the body of Christ (12-13)   283
      2. Interrelationship of parts of the body (14-21) 283
      3. Harmonious function of the body (22-26)   283
   D. Functions of members in the church (12:27-31a)   287
   E. Excursus: Love, highest of the higher gifts
     (12:31b - 14:1a)   289
      1. Worthlessness of all gifts without love
        (12:31b - 13:3)   289
      2. Characteristics of love (4-7)   289
      3. Permanence of love (13:8 - 14:1a)   289
   F. Superiority of prophecy over speaking in tongues
     (14:1b-33a)   298
      1. Prophecy, tongues, and building up (1b-5)   298
      2. Tongues, interpretation, and building up (6-19) 298
      3. Tongues and unbelievers (20-25)   299
      4. Tongues, prophecy, and order (26-33a)   299
   G. Silence of wives in the church (14:33b-36)   311
   H. Injunction to proper order (14:37-40)   314

VII. Excursus: concerning the gospel of the resurrection
    (15:1-58)   316
  A. The received tradition about the resurrection
      (15:1-11)   316
      1. Covering statement (1-2)   316
      2. The saving career of Christ (3-4)   316
      3. First appearances following resurrection (5-7)   316
      4. Appearance to Paul and the sequel (8-11)   316
  B. Resurrection of Christ as evidence for resurrection
      of the dead (15:12-19)   323
  C. Consequences of Christ's resurrection (15:20-28)   327
      1. Christ the "first-fruits" of human resurrection
          (20-23)   327
      2. Consummation of Christ's reign (24-27a)   328
      3. God's ultimate supremacy (27b-28)   328
  D. Implications of the resurrection (15:29-34)   334
      1. Baptism "on behalf of the dead" (29)   334
      2. Meaning in Paul's perils (30-32)   335
      3. Summary exhortation (33-34)   335
  E. The nature of the resurrection body (15:35-49)   341
      1. Analogies (35-41)   341
      2. Scriptural and theological description (42-49)   341
  F. The "mystery" of the end (15:50-57)   349
  G. Exhortation (15:58)   353

VIII. Personal matters (16:1-24)   355
  A. Concerning the collection for Jerusalem saints
      (16:1-4)   355
  B. Travel plans (16:5-9)   357
  C. Recommendation of Timothy (16:10-11)   358
  D. Projected visit by Apollos (16:12)   360
  E. Concise exhortations (16:13-14)   361
  F. Appreciation and commendation of Corinthian
      leaders (16:15-18)   362

G. Greetings from Asian churches and leaders
    (16:19-20)   364
H. Paul's personal greeting, monition, and benediction
    (16:21-24)   365
Indexes   369
    Authors   371
    Subjects   373
    Scriptural and Other References   381
Key to the Text   392

INTRODUCTION
with
A Study of the Life of Paul

PAUL'S PRE-CHRISTIAN LIFE

Nowhere in the Epistles[1] does Paul refer to his birthplace, nor surprisingly, to the fact that he was a Roman citizen. In his numerous letters he never alludes to the name of a Greek philosopher, poet, or historian. If he received an education in the curriculum of Greek studies, no epistolary occasion arose of sufficient importance to prompt any mention of it. We perhaps may conclude from some technical terms and arguments about the ethical conscience of the gentiles (Rom 2:14-15,26) and the universal availability of the knowledge of God (Rom 1:19-23) that he was acquainted with the teachings of at least some of the popular schools of philosophy. But it is impossible to be very confident. Incidental references to his own past life are inserted in his letters to defend himself against derogatory remarks and efforts to subvert his position as a reliable Christian leader in the different churches.

When he warns the Philippians (Philip 3:2-7) against those who emphasize circumcision and the traditional requirements pertaining to the worship of God, Paul emphatically affirms that he has renounced any concern for externals that manifest themselves in the flesh, though these externals in his own life had furnished a powerful basis for the assumption of authority as a qualified Jewish religious teacher. He had been circumcised on the eighth day and belonged by race to the "tribe of Benjamin from the people of Israel." As a "Hebrew of the Hebrews" he had undoubtedly received full instruction in the Hebrew language as well as in Aramaic. This phrase may also indicate that he belonged to the more exclusive branch of the Israelite tradition rather than to those who were called Hellenists and who practiced assimilation to Greek customs.[2] He was a zealous member of the Pharisaic party and as such had received concentrated instruction in the Jewish law. This included thorough knowledge of the Hebrew Scriptures, especially the Code of Moses, and such parts of the oral tradition as had been accumulated up to the time of his youth.

Paul's training in the law was not confined to intelligent understanding of its requirements and detailed exegesis but also included the discipline of life. The typical Jewish instructor in the law observed the conduct of the

---

[1] I.e. both in Epistles generally acknowledged as Paul's and in those later attributed to him by Christian writers. The data in the book of Acts will be treated separately.
[2] Cf. I Macc 1:11-15,41*f*; II Macc 4:9-16; Acts 9:29.

students, who were expected to learn how to live by the law. These students memorized the law's precepts, assimilated the great decisions of the learned rabbis, and were steeped in stories and legends depicting the religious glories of the past. Living with their teachers, they performed much menial service for them and learned by observing the rabbis' behavior at home how they themselves should obey the law. Against this background of ethical and religious education Paul describes himself as "blameless" by the standard of the law. Thus he states publicly that, as a youthful pupil and an adult scholar, he had been able to master the teachings of the law, both in mind and conduct, so that the experts could find no flaw in his activities. As a result of his attainments in the law he became zealous for its authority and was very bitter against any movement which could weaken its hold on the loyalties of the Jewish people. This zeal led him into a career of persecuting the church. And indeed, to assume this prerogative required considerable authority in the law in order to command acceptance and respect as a prosecutor.

A fervent and pious Jew cherished such a character and position as one of the more valuable honors of this life. The description of Paul's past life, found in the third chapter of Philippians, is supplemented by the rather impassioned protest in II Cor 11:22-29. Here, in regard to certain people who insinuated that they had more basis for Christian authority than himself, he protests, "Are they Hebrews? I am also. Are they Israelites? I am also. Are they descendants of Abraham? Likewise am I."[3] Apparently some of Paul's contemporaries in the early church attached considerable prestige to a demonstrably Jewish lineage. There was also a belief among Jewish teachers that such racial ancestry guaranteed a favorable condition in eternity.[4] Paul's repetition of terms here seems to emphasize his point: he is an authentic Jew in every sense of the word. Though Paul affirms that when he became a follower of Christ he regarded all this as "refuse" and "loss," he reminds people who value these things that he had fallen short of none of them in his Jewish training and advancement.

Paul vigorously describes his mode of life in the Jewish religion in Gal 1:13-14, "You have heard of my conduct in Judaism at a former time in which I was fiercely persecuting the church of God and devastating it. I was more advanced in Judaism than many contemporaries in my race since I was exceptionally zealous for the 'traditions of the fathers.' In this passage Paul makes very clear that his loyalty to Judaism expressed itself

---

[3] "Hebrew is, a) the name of the people which the Israelites bear in distinction from the other people, and b) it is the title of Hebrew- or Aramaic-speaking Jews in contrast to the Jewish Hellenists that speak Greek. The name Israel, which was originally the honor-name of Jacob, characterized a) the entire Jewish people and b) particular Jews as members of the people of God." StB, III, 526.

[4] "All Israelites have a share in the world to come." Mishnah, Sanhedrin 10:1.

in a policy of persecuting and destroying the church. The Greek verbs indicate action repeated over a period of time. The word "devastate" points to the widespread havoc produced by repeated arrests, perhaps killings, and, certainly, crippling interruptions of group activities and meetings. This could only be carried out by someone who had a high legal position. Further, his experience and skill in the Jewish religion had exceeded that of many of the Jews his own age. This implies that he was a preeminent scholar, successful in mastering material that would furnish a severe test of memory for people of any civilization or age. Jewish students were notable for ability to absorb vast quantities of detail and for ingenious analysis and surprising arguments. Paul, more advanced than many of them, was thus a superior student. Excessively zealous for the traditions of the fathers, he was like the family of the Maccabees, who struck the agents of the Seleucid king to death when they tried to enforce sacrifices to pagan gods, and like many of the heroes of the Jewish nation described by Josephus as eager to defend the traditions of the fathers. It seems that the phrase "traditions of the fathers" was a stock term to refer to the law, the sacred history, and the customs built up during the ages on the basis of this law. Paul was himself, as he says, a zealot. Does he hereby hint that he was a member of the Zealots of first-century Judaism, committed to violence against the Roman authorities in defense of their national heritage? Whether he was a member of this revolutionary group or not, he certainly believed in using violence against the Christians who were posing a threat to the integrity of Judaism by claiming that Jesus' resurrection gave him commanding authority.

These statements comprise all the remarks that Paul makes about his life before his conversion, and the material is tantalizingly skimpy. A theological statement that he had been called by God to be an apostle from his mother's womb supplements these autobiographical remarks (Gal 1:15). Here Paul refers to himself after the manner of the story of Jeremiah's call by God to be a prophet: "Before I formed you in the womb I knew you, and before you came out of the womb I sanctified you. I appointed you as a prophet to the nations" (Jer 1:5). Like Jeremiah, Paul feels he was separated from his mother's womb by God and called to be a prophetic person or, as he would have it, an apostle. He seems to have been aware of a special call even as a young Jewish leader, but he learned later that God had a unique mission for him, to be Christ's apostle to the gentiles.

It may be significant that Paul never felt moved to mention any Greek education he may have received. But the thoroughness of his instruction in contemporary koine Greek is demonstrated by the fact that he could occasionally rise to true eloquence while using this language to express warm religious conviction and subtle points of doctrine and morals (e.g. I Cor 13,15; Rom 8,12; II Cor 3). It is hard to believe he could have mastered an alien language to this degree without having received considerable instruction in its literature, particularly that of the Hellenistic Greek communities, such as Alexandria or Tarsus. His description of his early life and instruction appears to include him among those Jews of the intellectual ghetto who had extensive knowledge of their own history and culture, but had completely cut themselves off from any knowledge of Greek or Roman paganism. However, the quality of the letters themselves leads us to believe that his experience somewhere and somehow enabled him to break out of this insularity.

As a Jew of the type thus described, Paul was a convinced believer in the invisible God who created the world, delivered his law to Moses, and chose the descendants of Abraham to be the means of blessing to the whole earth. This God had established among his people a line of kings, descendants of David, from whom the expected ideal king would come. It is a little strange that, though Paul's original name was Saul (according to Acts), he himself never refers to this name, nor does he mention the first king of Israel, from whom his name had been derived—and who was also a member of the tribe of Benjamin. Paul tells us nothing of the locations of his early life. We are not able to discover whether he was a Palestinian or a member of the diaspora. He neglects to mention any teacher or rabbi he may have had, or whether he visited Jerusalem on feast days if he were a member of the diaspora.

FROM CONVERSION TO CONFERENCE IN JERUSALEM

Paul's first reference to a locality connected with his life states that he "went into Arabia and again returned to Damascus" (after he had received a revelation of the Son of God [Gal 1:16-17]). Negatively, he states he did "not go up to Jerusalem to the apostles who were before" him. We therefore deduce (a) that the revelation occurred at or near Damascus, (b) that since the revelation included the disclosure that he was to preach Christ to the gentiles, his trip to Arabia took him to the first place where he preached the Christian gospel, and (c) that he assumed that the readers would connect him with Jerusalem, either because he had been there before, or because as a new Christian commissioned to preach in pioneering fashion to non-Jews, he should obtain the approval of the first apostles. But *neither* of these reasons impelled him to go to Jerusalem to get encouragement. So he began his Christian career on the basis of private experience of divine authorization by breaking with the most cherished convictions of Jewish exclusivism of the whole Christian church at first and of the most influential section of it later. This was a convulsive reversal of his religion and heritage.

An almost melodramatic event rounded off Paul's stay at Damascus. The local ruler, called an ethnarch, representing King Aretas, laid a plot to arrest Paul and watched the city gates with a guard. This attempt was foiled by the aid of faithful supporters who, through an opening in the wall,[5] let Paul down in a basket at night to the ground outside (II Cor 11:32-33). Mention of this event in the time of Aretas the king may furnish some information for dating Paul's ministry. At best, it is not very precise; but it demonstrates that his ministry had to be in the first half of the first century.[6]

The Galatians account goes on to say that Paul went up to Jerusalem three years later (1:18). This may mean three years after the revelation, or three years after he returned to Damascus. In the first case, he may have been in Arabia three years, and then have gone to Jerusalem immediately after returning to Damascus, or he may have gone to Arabia and returned to spend the greater part of the time in Damascus. In the second case there is no estimate of how long he was in Arabia, while he remained in Damascus three years after he returned. It is impossible from the language to decide which interpretation is correct. His trip to Jerusalem led to a stay of two weeks during which he conferred with Cephas, who is Peter. He then says he saw none of the other apostles except James the brother of the Lord (1:19). The language is ambiguous about whether (1) James is to be included among the apostles and thus the only one of the apostles besides Peter that Paul saw, or (2) belongs to an entirely different category as the brother of the Lord. Paul seems to mean that he saw no apostles except Cephas but also saw James the brother of the Lord. To make sure that these statements carry enough conviction he insists he is speaking the truth in the presence of God (1:20). This is a euphemistic oath. The vehemence of this assertion seems to justify the inference that his enemies had accused him of receiving all his authority from the early apostles to begin with, and later departing from their teachings. Against this charge he replies that he in no way depended upon them from the beginning, though his gospel was ultimately recognized by them as divinely authorized (1:11,12, 2:9).

When he left Jerusalem, Paul came "into the regions of Syria and Cilicia." Antioch was the great city of Syria, and the chief metropolis of Cilicia was Tarsus. Concerning this time Paul says, "I was unknown by

---

[5] The ancient wall survives. The opening was traditionally a window in a house built against the wall.

[6] The Nabataean king Aretas IV, originally Aeneas, ruled from about 9 B.C. to A.D. 40. We possess no knowledge of his temporary rule over Damascus, except that it must have been after A.D. 37.

face to the Christian churches of Judaea. They only kept hearing that the one who formerly was persecuting us is now preaching the faith which he devastated, and they were glorifying God by me" (Gal 1:21-24).

On the basis of this statement it has been affirmed that Paul had never appeared before Christian churches in Judaea; and it has even been questioned whether he had ever been in Jerusalem, thus making Paul here flatly contradict statements made about his career in the book of Acts.[7]

Separate sections *infra* will discuss the Acts account of Paul's life and its relation to his epistolary statements. Here we need only note that the verses quoted above designate Paul as the persecutor of the Christian churches of Judaea. Surely this means that the Christians of Jerusalem had been persecuted by Paul. While it is true that a considerable feeling of brotherhood extended throughout the ancient church, it is hard to imagine that Jerusalem or Judaean churches felt so closely akin to Christians in Damascus that they called the persecution of Damascene Christians "persecuting us." So when Paul says he was unknown by face to the churches in Judaea and then quotes them as saying, "the one who persecuted us is now preaching the gospel," it probably means he was unknown to them after his conversion, though he had persecuted them previously.[8] Some now in the churches had been youths during the time of the persecution, and some were later proselytes, neither of whom knew the post-conversion Paul. If this interpretation is correct, therefore, it merely affirms that, after two weeks' visit of Paul to Cephas and James, he did not go back to Jerusalem or Judaea during the time he says he was in Syria and Cilicia.

Then after fourteen years elapsed (Gal 2:1), Paul went up again to Jerusalem with Barnabas; and he also took Titus along. Did the fourteen years exclude or include the stay in Syria and Cilicia? Or does it mean fourteen years after the first visit to Jerusalem mentioned in Gal 1:17? Or again, does it refer back to the time of his own conversion? Either a chronology of fourteen years from the time of Paul's conversion to his second trip to Jerusalem or a longer chronology including at least seventeen years, either from the stay in Damascus or from his conversion, is possible. Chronological exactitude is also deficient owing to Jewish flexibility in the use of numbers whereby any fraction of a year could be counted as a year. Thus, "fourteen" years here might mean almost any period of time from twelve-plus to seventeen years.

In this Galatians passage Paul refers for the first time to both Barnabas and Titus—without informing us how he became allied with them, where they came from, and what was his official relation to them. The letter

---

[7] Haenchen, *Acts*, 332-336; Dibelius-Kümmel, *Paul*, 57, 126; von Loewenich, *Paul*, 49, et al.

[8] "By face" seems to suggest that they have not yet met personally one whom they have known already officially.

presupposes the reader knows about Barnabas and Titus as well as about Cephas and James. Present-day readers of this passage, familiar with the book of Acts, have a picture of Barnabas drawn from the Acts account which fills in the background of this statement of Paul. But the book of Acts never mentions Titus. In the letters of Paul which are accepted as genuine by most modern scholars, Titus is mentioned only in II Corinthians outside of this passage in Galatians. He is also referred to in II Tim 4:10 and is addressed as the recipient of the letter of Titus (1:4).

The trip to Jerusalem was undertaken because of a "revelation" (Gal 2:2). That is, by whatever means God communicated his will to Paul, he here instructed him to go to Jerusalem. This could have been by a vision, a strong intuitional feeling, or a persuasive injunction spoken by some respected disciple, prophet, or church group. The passage (2:1-10) does not enable us to choose among these options.[9] At Jerusalem Paul "delivered (or explained privately) to the ones who were held in high esteem" the gospel which he was preaching among the gentiles. This he did in order to prevent himself from "running in vain" or "having run in vain." The word we have translated "deliver" (anatithēmi) means to report facts or information to someone.[10] The clause "lest I am running or had run in vain" implies that the "esteemed persons" would be expected to react to the report in a manner that would critically affect Paul's own previous and present missionary policy. If they should disapprove what he had done, he would have run in vain. One might interpret this to mean that his entire message of salvation to the gentiles would be annulled, emptied of all authority, and canceled as untrue. This interpretation, however, is impossible. Paul says in Gal 1:8, "If we or an angel from heaven should preach to you anything beyond what we have preached to you, let him be anathema . . . and again now I say, if anyone preaches anything beyond what you have received, let him be anathema." Obviously, it would be a flat contradiction to understand that the "esteemed persons" in Jerusalem could render the gospel null and void, when any deviation from it would impose upon human authority or heavenly angels an anathema. So he must mean

---

[9] Another possibility is that the "revelation" is the signification of the prophet Agabus, Acts 11:27-28. This involves a shift in the assumed chronology; cf. *infra* p. 60.

[10] The only other place it is used in the New Testament is Acts 25:14: "Festus reported to the king the case of Paul." In this instance, Festus informed Agrippa about the fact that Paul had been arrested and detained as a prisoner for a long time by Felix and had finally made an appeal to Caesar after refusing to be taken back to Jerusalem for a further decision. Nothing in the account indicates that Festus was expecting Agrippa to pass judgment upon the procedure. Therefore the statement in AGB, 61b. that the word has "the added idea that the person to whom a thing is referred is asked for his opinion" is unsupported. This idea may be present in passages found outside the New Testament, but in itself, it appears to refer merely to an act of communicating something to someone.

that his communication of the gospel must be accepted by the "esteemed persons" so as to avoid a split in the church. Along with the Good News of justification for the gentiles, the gospel includes reconciliation between all classes of men, especially Jew and gentile. If he had been preaching the truth in such a way as to alienate the chief men in Jerusalem and they, in turn, had declined to allow their churches to have fellowship with the Christian gentiles, the second great purpose of the gospel would have been thwarted. This would not mean that Paul had been preaching a false gospel, but that either he or they had been conducting affairs in such a way that love was not effective. So with great care he explained this procedure in private to the esteemed persons in order to prevent a breach of unity in the church.

Intense feeling existed among nearly all religious Jews to the effect that gentiles were pagan, unclean, addicted to idols and various kinds of immoral corruption. Admission of gentiles to the Jewish community had to be effected with great care, and precautions had to be taken so that they would understand and accept fully the obligations of the law. Paul proclaimed that the gentiles have been justified by the grace of God and are called upon merely to believe God and accept their justification and not to be circumcised or to submit to other legalistic obligations of Judaism.[11] Paul knew that his gospel to the gentiles was authorized by God, but he also knew that he was not excused from the requirement to maintain and advance the unity of the Christian church, which to many Jewish Christians was threatened by the laxity of the gentiles. To jeopardize this unity would be to run in vain, even with the torch of the true gospel.

The statement that Titus (Gal 2:3), who was a Greek, was not compelled to be circumcised implies that some leaders were endeavoring to impose circumcision on gentile converts. But the leaders as a whole were sufficiently impressed with the validity of Paul's position in the gospel not to demand that he circumcise his companion Titus, whom he had brought along into the Holy City itself, and had presumably introduced to the church leaders.[12] That means that in principle they accepted the gentiles who were converted under the preaching of Paul into the full communion and fellowship of the church. However, the next statement (2:4), which is a broken sentence, hints that some serious obstacles still obstructed Paul's pathway: "because of certain false brothers who had been deceitfully introduced into the group for the sake of spying on the freedom which we have in Christ Jesus in order that they might enslave us. . . ." This mysterious clause indicates that, either in the group of the esteemed persons or

---

[11] So numerous passages; e.g. Rom 3:29-30. Cf. also next paragraph here.
[12] It remains an outside possibility that Titus did become circumcised and that the emphasis falls upon the absence of compulsion. Cf. Acts 16:1-3.

somewhere else, people had been introduced who appeared to be friendly and sincere in their fidelity to the gospel but whose real purpose was to spy on Paul. Since nothing in the verse gives us any clear hint about who these people were, we are left to conjecture. They may have been Pharisees who visited Antioch (according to Acts 15) under the pretense of friendship, but in actuality intended to destroy the authority of Paul and Barnabas and nullify their gospel. Nothing can disprove this identification as it has a high degree of plausibility. Yet it does seem to run counter to the saying in Acts 15 that these men from Jerusalem were teaching the brothers that unless they were circumcised they could not be saved. So it appears that these Pharisees were engaged more in open controversy with Paul than in spying upon him. This is not an overwhelming difficulty, for Paul might have regarded the very profession of faith in Christ as something that would make them false brothers if they did not accept the sufficiency of this faith for salvation. And it could be that their public arguments appeared like spying on Paul's liberty, but this hypothesis is a little strained. It seems that another explanation may be required. The false brothers must just then have been exposed in their true light as opponents while having previously appeared as brothers, either in Jerusalem or beforehand. It is possible that they were John Mark and some other companions. Mysteriously, according to the book of Acts, John Mark deserted Paul during the mission in Asia Minor. No reason is given for his desertion. It could very well be that he had been dismayed at the fact that Paul decided to go straight to the gentiles with the full gospel. As it dawned on Mark that this was Paul's intention, he may have decided not to take part in such a drastic innovation. It is also probable that he said nothing to Paul about the actual reasons for his departure. We may then further conjecture that as Paul appeared in Jerusalem, John Mark may have stood before the multitude of the whole church to protest, prematurely, that Paul and Barnabas were really welcoming gentiles into the Christian church without any of the normal precautions. In support of this Mark could relate what had happened in Cyprus and Pamphilia. If this were true, it would explain more clearly the later controversy between Paul and Barnabas about taking Mark with them on the second trip. Presumably, after the group in Jerusalem had heard the whole discussion, their decision to support Paul convinced Mark that Paul was probably right and made him willing to go along on further missions. Barnabas, a relative, was convinced of the genuineness of Mark's new loyalty, while Paul was very skeptical about it. Here then is real ground for the fierce controversy between Paul and Barnabas: Paul thought that Mark was still making a false appearance, while Barnabas believed in the genuineness of his change of heart. Later evidence proves that in this case Barnabas was right (Col 4:10).

Paul announces that he did not submit for one hour to these false brothers. The reason for his intransigence was his insistence that the truth of the gospel not be comprised for the gentile believers. A cryptic remark (Gal 2:5,6) about the highly esteemed persons and their reaction to Paul's determination has been disputed practically ever since he wrote this letter. The literal statement seems to mean that these highly esteemed persons did not consult him. Because of what appears to be a difficulty in this meaning the lexicons have suggested that it means they contributed nothing to Paul. Perhaps, however, Paul's meaning is that after hearing his report they felt no need for consultation including discussion and possible bargaining about future policy. The leaders in Jerusalem readily assented to his practice of receiving gentiles into the church. They were so enthusiastic about the success of his work and the apparent divine authorization of it that they conducted no further investigation, raised no more questions, and laid down no conditions, with the one exception that they asked him to remember the poor people in Jerusalem (2:7-10). The stress on the poverty of the people in Jerusalem shows that the Christians there had a relatively hard time and may have been excluded from normal society. In addition, Jerusalem as a whole may have been confronted with stringent economic difficulties, both by reason of famine and by continuous trouble with the Roman authorities. Rather they immediately gave Paul the right hand of fellowship because they saw that just as Peter had a commission to the Jews God had entrusted Paul with the gospel to the uncircumcised.

The highly esteemed persons, now called "pillars," are identified as James, Cephas, and John. It is certain that this is James the brother of the Lord, and Cephas is Peter. The clear result of the conversation was authoritative recognition of the rightness or validity of Paul's preaching along with full encouragement to continue to press his work as far as possible.

In this report Paul relates that Barnabas accompanied him to Jerusalem and that the pillars gave them the right hand of fellowship. Therefore Barnabas had been associated with Paul in his work for some time previous to this Jerusalem meeting. It was expected that he would continue to work with Paul. Paul also alludes to his association with Barnabas in I Cor 9:6, "Do only Barnabas and I not have the right of freedom from physical work?" This question implies that Paul and Barnabas had been work partners and had earned their own living. Based solely on the information in Paul's letters it could be concluded that Barnabas was with Paul in Corinth.

FROM THE JERUSALEM CONFERENCE TO
THE MINISTRY IN GREECE

After the Jerusalem meeting Paul went to Antioch accompanied by Barnabas (Gal 2:11). Peter also came to Antioch, where he practiced full table fellowship with the gentiles. After some emissaries from James arrived, however, Peter withdrew from free and open communion at meals because (according to Paul) he was afraid of Jews who kept the kosher laws. The other Jewish Christians in Antioch withdrew with him; and even Barnabas joined their number, to the consternation of Paul, who considered this hypocritical. (This action of Barnabas may have been a factor in the dissension between Paul and Barnabas cited in Acts.) Paul refused to be intimidated by the decision of his friends. He told Peter, in effect, that his conduct amounted to a denial of the gospel itself, that he was imposing on gentiles adherence to a law which the apostles themselves had found ineffectual for spiritual justification. Peter apparently saw how radical the position of Paul was: Jewish identity within the Christian community would end if all distinctive practices of Jews were abandoned.

The account in Galatians includes the portentous event in Jerusalem and its sequel in Antioch but gives no information about Paul's missionary activities immediately after he was in Syria and Cilicia. It clearly indicates, however, that he had already received numbers of gentiles into the Christian community and was afraid that there might be a split in the church if he and the leaders in Jerusalem did not come to an early understanding. Apparently the disagreement in Antioch stemmed from a failure in communication: James, Peter, and then Barnabas were still convinced that Jewish Christians could eat openly with gentiles only if they observed Jewish dietary laws; they were either unaware of Paul's position or not inclined to take it seriously. Paul understood that the acceptance of gentiles without circumcision meant freedom from any limitations on full fellowship, whereas the original disciples seem to have felt that gentiles must be required to eat only kosher food and to abstain absolutely from blood, as well as from any food that had been offered to idols. This suggestion may explain serious difficulties that arise out of apparent discrepancies of Paul's account of this meeting with the account in Acts 15.[13]

This letter "to the churches of Galatia" proves that Paul had established congregations in Galatia. He reminds them of the fact that they had received a portrait of Jesus as one who had been crucified, and that when they heard the gospel, they received the Spirit (Gal 3:1-2). It is clear that

[13] Cf. pp. 63-65.

the one who thus presented Christ to them was Paul himself; for he reminds them in 4:13-14 that they had accepted him when he preached the gospel to them at first "because of weakness" and that they did not in any way despise the test that his "flesh" provided for them. Rather, they received him "as an angel (or messenger) of God . . . as Christ Jesus" himself; and if they had been able, they would have "dug out" their eyes and given them to him. This could mean that he had some kind of eye trouble and perhaps some other repulsive bodily deformity or lesion as well. But instead of turning with disgust against him, they had received him whole-heartedly and were so loyal to him that they would have done anything to help him.

In this pathetic description of his own weakness and their warm reception of him, Paul does not inform us by his letter just who the Galatians really were. All we know is that the name Galatia was sometimes used to describe the territory in Asia Minor to which Gauls had migrated in the third century B.C. This territory was in the central part of the country where Ankara is now located. But Paul may have used the name of the Roman province, Galatia, which included the southern regions of Lystra, Iconium, and Derbe. If these were the Galatians, he had preached to them, according to Acts, on his first missionary journey. Many scholars incline to this view, but it is not absolutely proved. (These arguments will be discussed later.) If the reference is to the gentile Galatia, then there is no way to be sure when it was that Paul preached to them; but it is probable that the ministry which occurred before the meeting in Jerusalem included a mission to Asia Minor.

MISSION TO THE BALKAN AND AEGEAN PENINSULAS

The epistle of I Thessalonians informs us in the very first verse that there was a church in Thessalonica. We deduce from I Thess 1:5 that Paul was the first to proclaim the gospel in Thessalonica since he says, "Our gospel did not become powerful only in words toward you but also was full of energy and the Holy Spirit, just as you know what kind of persons we were in your midst." He further reminds them that they had become imitators of Paul when they received the word and had endured much pressure. The word translated "pressure" may mean affliction or persecution. Further the report of their reception of the gospel had been echoed in Macedonia and Achaea (Greece). They had, in fact, become an example to all the believers in these two provinces. Hence we learn that, before this letter was written, Paul had been to Thessalonica, had won converts, and had been persecuted to some degree, and that there were believers in the province of Macedonia as a whole as well as in Achaea, the central cities of which were Athens and Corinth. So he had preached in the Aegean lands.

The first element of his preaching is indicated by his statement that they had turned to God from idols, and were awaiting his Son from the heavens, whom God had raised from the dead, and who would deliver them from the coming wrath. Thus Paul continued the work of Jewish missionaries who had propagated monotheism all over the Roman empire and had proclaimed a coming judgment upon mankind. But he added the message that God had raised his Son from the dead into the heavens. From there he would come to receive those who were waiting for him, and would deliver them from the judgment. Thus, Paul's message included an announcement of delivery from the danger of eternal punishment and of the coming manifestation of Jesus Christ who has been raised from the dead (I Thess 1:1-10).

In the following paragraph he reminds them that he had suffered beforehand and had been insulted in Philippi and that, when he appeared to them in Thessalonica, they already knew about this. But despite that previous misfortune and mistreatment, he had preached boldly in Thessalonica and they had received his message. In none of this preaching did he employ such human tricks[14] as flattering the ears or minds of his hearers, but had declared the full message of God with sincerity and truthfulness (2:1-7). After he left Thessalonica he was tense and anxious because he knew the converts were being subjected to the same kind of treatment by their countrymen as the Christian Jews in Jerusalem were receiving from their authorities. In addition, Paul was nervously eager to discover whether during this pressure the Thessalonians would weaken or remain loyal to the faith. He intensely desired to visit them again but "Satan hindered him" (2:18). He says that he had been deprived of association with his Macedonian converts, hence had decided to send Timothy to them while he remained alone at Athens. Since he mentions no other locality, we may conclude that Athens was the first place in Achaea that he reached. How Satan hindered him from returning to Macedonia we do not know unless Paul was a marked man, prohibited by authorities from coming back to the Macedonian province. The participle we translate "deprived of" (aporphanisthentes, "having been made an orphan," vs. 17) implies that he had been banished from the province.

Timothy was commissioned to encourage them not to be swept away from the faith by their sufferings and then to report back to Paul. At the time of this letter Timothy has returned and shared the delightful news that they would maintain their faith and continue to display their love.

---

14 Cf. H. D. Betz, *Der Apostel Paulus und die sokratische Tradition* (Tübingen, 1972), 57-69.

While the account gives no hint of the length of Timothy's absence, it must have been long enough for him to make a return trip of about 350 miles from Athens to Thessalonica. Under ancient conditions he would have spent no less than three weeks on the journey.[15] Timothy must have stayed at Thessalonica an additional week or more. Paul therefore was in Athens for more than a month. He neglects to tell us anything about what he did there or what kind of church, if any, was established.

Paul says in I Cor 1:14, "I baptized none of you except Crispus and Gaius." He goes on, "I did baptize also the household of Stephanas." The household of Stephanas, therefore, is an exception, along with Crispus and Gaius, to the statement "I baptized none of you." This seems to mean that "the household of Stephanas" was a Corinthian family. In I Cor 16:15 we read "you know the household of Stephanas, that it is a first fruits of Achaea." The "first fruits" means the first person in Achaea converted to the gospel. Since this household was Corinthian, and since they were the first in the province to be converted, it appears necessary to conclude that there were no converts made in Athens during the time of Paul's stay there. Thus the stay in Athens was ineffective in establishing a church and Paul probably left as soon as Timothy made his favorable report about conditions in Thessalonica.[16]

It was at Corinth that Paul succeeded in establishing the first functioning congregation in Achaea. Evidence for his activity in this city is furnished in great abundance by the two letters to the Corinthians. The letter to the Romans was written from Corinth,[17] and thus the three great epistles of the New Testament were written either to or from Corinth.

Paul remarks, "I came to you, brothers, . . . without any excellency of speech or wisdom as I was proclaiming the mystery of God" (I Cor 2:1). He does not tell where he came from, but he does indicate that he came for an evangelistic objective. He goes on to describe himself as appearing with weakness, fear, and much trembling, though his proclamation was accompanied by a display of great spiritual power. The measure of this power was probably the number of converts and the quality of their church life. Except for Onesimus (in Philemon) the people named in the letter as having been baptized by Paul in Corinth are the only persons whom Paul mentions specifically in any letter as his personal converts. These few names are noted in connection with a protest that it was not his policy to baptize; if there were others, he has now forgotten. He gives us clearly to

[15] For travel data, cf. Ogg, *Chronology*, 123-126.

[16] See pp. 80-81 for discussion of the difference between Paul's account and that in Acts 17:34.

[17] Or possibly from Cenchreae, the harbor town, a conjecture based upon Rom 16:1. The Corinthian origin is discussed by Manson, *Studies in the Gospels and Epistles*, 225-241.

understand that he preached only the message of the cross, that is, of Jesus Christ who has been crucified. By so proclaiming Christ he laid the only foundation which could be laid, and he planted the church (I Cor 3:5-11). As the founder of the church he claims to be its father (I Cor 4:15). During his stay at Corinth he taught them the facts about Jesus' death and resurrection (I Cor 15:1). As a result of his preaching and teaching they had received spiritual grace (I Cor 1:4,7) and apparently were inspired with a high degree of religious excitement. (Such fruits as these, rather than baptism itself, were primary objectives of Paul's mission.)

After an unspecified interval Paul left Corinth. Apollos then appeared in the city and built on the foundation that Paul had laid, watering the plant that Paul had sown (I Cor 3:5-6). Unfortunately, one result of this double leadership was that some people began to gravitate to one or the other of these preachers. At the same time, still others professed to be loyal to Cephas. This fact may suggest that Cephas had also been to Corinth. Since Paul repeatedly refers to the work of Apollos and himself together and does not mention Cephas except as a name to which one of the groups was attaching itself, it is more probable that he was known not from a visit, but from widespread reputation. This is confirmed by a statement in Gal 2:7 that Peter had been entrusted with the gospel of the circumcision, which seems to mean preaching to the Jews of Palestine and Syria.

A gap yawns before us in the letters of Paul which precludes knowledge of what he did when he left Corinth. In the first epistle itself, he informs us that at the time of writing (which is obviously a time considerably later than his stay in Corinth), he is in Ephesus. Here he has had some rugged experiences, such as running in danger every hour, and, in a human fashion, fighting with wild beasts (I Cor 15:30-32).[18] At the same time a number of people known to the Corinthians have moved to Ephesus or have come to visit Paul there. These are Stephanas, Fortunatus, and Achaicus (I Cor 16:17), who have come to bring some sort of greeting and perhaps a gift from Corinth. Aquila and Priscilla are in Ephesus as residents who have a church in their house. The fact that Aquila and Priscilla are mentioned as sending greetings to the church in Corinth means that the Corinthians knew them and that they had probably either lived in or visited Corinth. Despite the adverse conditions that Paul had to face, he wanted to remain at Ephesus until Pentecost, "for a great and productive door has opened to me, and adversaries are many" (16:8,9). In Ephesus he then began to find that people were becoming interested in his message, and he had every expectation of establishing a powerful church. Nothing in his remarks about the situation in Ephesus reveals whether any Chris-

---

[18] Cf. commentary ad loc.

tians had been there before he arrived. Though he makes no claim to have founded the church or to be its father, Paul's remark indicates that he probably had encountered the type of hostility usually stirred up by the spokesman of a new religion. The opposition and its aftermath appeared to create a magnificent new opportunity. Paul may well have been the first properly equipped apostle of Christ in Ephesus.

His experiences as an apostle included all sorts of hardships, humiliations, physical needs like hunger and thirst, nakedness, endurance of public abuse and violence, and being treated as the trash of mankind (I Cor 4:9-13). At the time he wrote I Corinthians, he sent Timothy to Corinth to remind them of Paul's manner of life and teaching. Expecting that Timothy would be mistreated by some, Paul urged them to receive Timothy with respect and obedience (4:18-20). Before this dispatch of Timothy numerous rumors had reached Paul about a split in the church (1:18-4:13), about a scandalous case of incest (5:1-8), and about lawsuits entered by some Corinthian Christians against others (6:1-11).

Before this he had written them not to associate with sexually immoral people (I Cor 5:9). In the meantime a letter had arrived from the Corinthian church to Paul which raised questions about marriage, divorce, and mixed marriages (I Corinthians 7), about idol-offerings (8:1-10:33), about spiritual gifts (12-14), about a collection to be taken up for the saints in Jerusalem (16:1-4), and about a visit to Corinth which they wanted Apollos to make (16:12). In addition to these issues Paul has been informed about disorderly conduct in the church by some married women (11:2-16)[19] and about abuses in the celebration of the Lord's Supper (11:17-34). Finally, he was greatly agitated by information that some were denying the resurrection of deceased believers (ch. 15).

The economic conditions of the believers in Jerusalem aroused a serious concern in Paul's mind. The first people he enlisted in this concern were the members of the churches in Galatia, whom he directed to collect the funds that would be used for the relief of the saints in the Holy City (I Cor 16:1). He ordered them to collect money every first day of the week. Likewise he urged the people in Corinth who had already heard about the collection to follow the same procedure. He emphasized that they should store the gifts according to the prosperity of the givers. The collection once completed he would come to Corinth. At that time he would send the collection to Jerusalem with those whom the church has appointed. If it should be providentially possible, he would also go along.

He says that he intends to make this visit after he goes through Macedonia. Apparently they had hoped he would come to them in Corinth first and then go to Macedonia. Here, however, he protests that it would

---

[19] Cf. the exegesis of this passage, pp. 258-264.

be better for him to go to Corinth last since he could make a more permanent stay with them throughout the winter, and thus his visit would not be a hurried side event. From Corinth they could send him wherever he should go.

The course of Paul's life traceable from statements in II Corinthians presents new problems. Just before the writing of this letter he has been subject to a great "pressure" (*thlipsis*) (II Cor 1:8) which brought him suffering and feelings of depression and despair. It occurred in Asia, probably in Ephesus. So severe was the pressure that at one point he despaired of his life; fortunately he was delivered from death by "God who raises the dead" (1:9). No more detail is given about this affliction, which could be either an attack directly against Paul by the people of Asia or some desperate sickness. But in view of the fact that he thanks God for consoling him so that he, in turn, may console them in similar sufferings, we may suppose that he was talking about riots or attacks of the populace against him.[20]

He states that he had intended or wished to come to them in order that they might get a "second gift" (II Cor 1:15). This implies that he had intended a second visit to Corinth. Presumably, then, he had not returned to Corinth with pleasure and harmony. Thus he did not carry out his intent (I Cor 16:5) to visit them after he went through Macedonia and receive the collection at Corinth at the end of the winter, and then be sent on perhaps to Jerusalem or perhaps somewhere else. Now he states that he was wishing to come to Corinth, then go to Macedonia, come back to Corinth again, and definitely to be sent to Judaea. The announcement of this wish had resulted in a charge of lightness or frivolity against him. This is due either to the fact that this plan amounted to a change of his first plan or that he had failed to carry out this second plan. With great stress and pathos he insists that he did not shift from one plan to another, that he does not say "Yes" one time and "No" the next, but that he has a consistent purpose: the proclamation of God's promises in Jesus Christ, which is God's "Yes" to all people. Then he explains that the reason he had not come to Corinth was to spare them grief (1:16-2:1).

Hereby we are informed that real dissension had broken out between Paul and the people of Corinth so that a second visit in grief would be extremely disturbing. This may imply an earlier "grief visit." Paul has grieved along with the rest of the church, from whom he has a right to expect encouragement. Their grief was caused by a letter he had written "with many tears" (2:4) concerning a man who had been an occasion of

[20] By the language employed Paul seems to be describing something they hadn't heard of before and which, therefore, is not the same as the daily danger and the fighting with wild beasts mentioned in I Cor 15:30.

sorrow, not only to Paul but at least partially to all the people in Corinth. Because of this letter Paul decided not to visit Corinth at that time. He hastens to assure them that he had heard that this person had been sufficiently rebuked, so he now should receive love. He states that he wrote the letter to discover how they might pass the test of his rebuke and be true to the interpretation of the gospel. Since they have forgiven the man, Paul is ready to forgive him also (2:5-11).

The report of the good effect of the letter was brought to Paul by Titus, the brother mentioned already in Galatians.[21] Here we are not informed about where Titus was sent or what connection this visit of Titus had with that of Timothy described in I Corinthians. Nor are we informed about what brought him to Troas, or from where.[22] Because of Paul's unmanageable anxiety about the effect of his letter, he left Troas where a great and open door awaited him, to go on to Macedonia in the hope of finding Titus, who would presumably tell him what had happened (2:12,13). Fortunately God comforted Paul in Macedonia by the appearance of Titus, who was able to report that the church had manifested grief, repentance, and an acceptance of whatever Paul had suggested. They had shown zeal and readiness for defense, a certain indignation and fear, and zealous desire to carry out Paul's instructions as well as to impose ecclesiastical discipline. Paul's relief at this report was so great that he says he was delighted not so much at the repentance of the man who had committed an injustice, or by the reparation made to the one who was injured, but at the display of their zeal on behalf of God and his apostle. Likewise, Paul was delighted that they had received Titus with such honor and brotherly affection. Their conduct had justified all the praise that Paul had used in describing them to Titus.

Critical scholars have long been divided about the identity of this letter written "through many tears." The traditional opinion is that it is I Corinthians, which described the man who had committed incest and demanded severe punishment, even excommunication.[23] Others think that the tone of the whole letter of I Corinthians could not be described as a letter written "through many tears," and even the section where Paul is dealing with the matter of incest breathes an air of indignation and severity rather than one of sorrow. While Paul is agitated in other chapters of I Corinthians about the problems in Corinth, there is no suspicion that its recipients would be distressed by his letter or incited to rebellion by it. Es-

---

21 Cf. 8-9.
22 Apparently this was Titus' first visit to Corinth, for Paul says he had boasted to Titus about the people in Corinth before he sent him (II Cor 7:14). He would hardly have needed to praise them to Titus if he had already been there and had known their qualities himself.
23 Cf. Meyer, Hand-Book, 441-443.

pecially in recent years leading scholars have identified the "tearful letter" with the contents of II Corinthians 10-13, which they think was originally a separate letter.[24]

The principal argument for regarding chs. 10-13 as separate from the rest of II Corinthians is that these chapters are written in a sharp polemic tone which treats his readers either (a) as members of a group misled by persons who claim to be apostles or to have the authority of apostles, while as a matter of fact they are "false apostles, deceitful workers, who like Satan have been transformed into apostles of Christ" (11:13,14), or (b) as those who have been ready to put up with this group and to tolerate sharp and destructive attacks on the authority of Paul. Along with this they have been willing to receive another gospel which is different from the one Paul proclaimed to them. He also fears that when he visits them he will find "contention, jealousy, anger, party strife, slanders, whisperings, and riotings among them" (12:20). All of this, as these chapters are now arranged, comes after parts of a letter in which Paul is almost ecstatic with joy over the recent repentance, care, and anxiety for his feelings shown by the church of Corinth, a demonstration that they have been pure and sincere in their policy, and that, in the case of the man who has committed an injury, they have rebuked him and then forgiven him, both of which actions Paul highly approves. After this remarkable reconciliation between the apostle and the church, and after some very careful plans are described for the raising of a collection for the saints in Jerusalem (ch. 9), it is hard to see how he could, without any transition, immediately launch into such a vicious attack on them as is found in the last four chapters (10-13). As a result of these considerations perhaps the majority of critical scholars since the time of Johannes Weiss have concluded that these last chapters were originally an independent letter which Paul refers to as "the letter written with tears." When the Corinthian correspondence was finally published, the publishers appended this letter to the first nine chapters of II Corinthians which up until then had been a complete letter. In order to give this composite letter some literary unity, the introduction of the second part had to be eliminated.

This is a neat explanation and does help answer some perplexing difficulties, but a few questions are raised by the solution. (a) Why would an editor append this letter at a place so unsuitable for it without explanation? (b) How could he be willing to detach the introduction completely, as well as remove the conclusion of the previous letter? (c) Since the alleged separate letter is directed against a group or multitude of individuals, how can we identify it with the letter written with tears that was directed

---

[24] Cf. Plummer, *Second Corinthians*, 50-51; Héring, *Second Corinthians*, 11-13; and the list of protagonists in Feine-Behm-Kümmel, *Introduction*, 212.

against a man who had committed an offense and referred to another person who was injured by this offense (7:12)?

Many scholars have not been convinced by the critical argument that the last chapters composed a separate letter, but most admit that the present position of these chapters is difficult to explain, and it is hard to see how Paul could be writing to the same people in ch. 7 as in chs. 12 and 13. In ch. 7 everything looks serene, and Paul is delighted with the situation Titus has described. If the later chapters are in their right place, then we have to assume that, after Paul had been reassured about Corinth from Titus, he received news about a recent visit of unidentified (to us) people who agitated the church anew and stirred up a dangerous anti-Pauline movement.

Here we must postulate that the new report arrived while Paul was writing the letter which described his joy at Titus' recent good news, and Titus' forthcoming collection trip. Therefore, soon after Titus' return from Corinth which had so consoled Paul, the other report arrived to plunge him into a new frenzy of wrath that inspired his composition of chs. 10-13, which he appended to the previous chapters.

Some critical scholars say this theory is so absurd as to be self-refuting.[25] But given volatile circumstances like those enveloping the church in Corinth which, even in the time of Clement of Rome (A.D. 95) was still engaged in disturbances and agitation,[26] we cannot be sure that any condition of serenity could be counted on to last more than a few days. We might also note that Paul had expected to meet Titus in Troas (II Cor 2: 13) but had not found him there and had gone on to Macedonia to see if he could find him there. This implies that Titus had not come to the expected place as fast as Paul hoped, thus threatening a considerable delay. He may have spent some time in Macedonia. Therefore, there could be time after his departure from Corinth and his reunion with Paul for hypothetical reporters to come bringing news of the outbreak of a new disturbance. We can easily understand how, if Paul were immediately cast down from a state of delight to one of new apprehension and indignation, he would rush into a denunciation without alluding to the previous report or compose any transitional niceties. He knows that his intended readers understand his situation and would expect him to be agitated by the news. We need see no absurdity in this possibility. We would have to conclude that he decided to send the first part of the letter with the new denunciation, both to reveal how elated he had been, and to exercise some influence on them in their present condition. There is no reason to suppose that, though he was indignant and perplexed, he was at the same time in

---

[25] E.g. Plummer, *Second Corinthians*, 35; M. S. Enslin, *Christian Beginnings* (New York, 1938), 257.
[26] Cf. I Clement 1-8.

despair. It is also to be noted that even in the last four chapters, along with indignation, there are many expressions of affection and hope for the future of the church. His sharpest attack is against certain persons who had come into the church to subvert his apostolic position (10:7-11, 11: 4-5,13-15,20,22, 12:11).[27]

There is no doubt that either one person or several from the outside have come to Corinth and stirred up the church: "If the one who comes preaches another Jesus whom we did not preach, or you receive another spirit which you did not receive, or another gospel which you did not obtain, you put up with it very well. For I consider that I have fallen in no way short of the superlative apostles" (11:4f). The cause, then, of the agitation was an entry of outside emissaries. That these are more than one is proved by 11:13: "For such kinds are false apostles, deceitful workers, transformed into apostles of Christ." That these are not members of the local church is demonstrated by the fact that they are called "false apostles" which means messengers, ambassadors, or missionaries coming from another place.

The question immediately arises whether the letter "written with tears" concerned the visitation of outsiders and subsequent subversion of the church, for he indicates in 2:2 that the one who was grieved by him is the one who should cause him rejoicing. This is not the kind of statement one would make about a false apostle coming to a place. Moreover he says, "If anyone has caused grief, he has not grieved me alone but all of you in part" (2:5). This would mean an action performed by an individual which was really upsetting to all the members of the church. It is hardly the thing that would be said about visitors claiming to represent authority higher than Paul. Hence the statement that the majority has rebuked such a person and forgiven him indicates that he was a regular member of the church subject to its admonition and rewelcome. Paul confirms their forgiveness and wants to avoid casting this man into an excess of grief, which indicates that the man should be understood to be under Paul's jurisdiction and liable to great grief without a reconciliation. This again does not appear to be a description of the kind of persons castigated in chs. 11 and 12.

Titus is referred to in 12:18 as one whom he had urged to go to the people of Corinth. In the description of this dispatch of Titus, Paul asks the question which presupposes a negative answer, "Did Titus take advantage of you?" Paul raises this question to defend himself against any charge of craftiness. He refuses to take financial support from the Corinthian church. Clearly the conduct of Titus, Paul's emissary to this

---

[27] Such mercurial change of disposition also seems to be present in the letter to the Galatians, a document of the genuine Paul. Cf. also R. M. Grant, *Historical Introduction to the New Testament* (New York, 1963), 180-181.

church, was such as to refute finally the accusation that Paul and he were
engaged in a subtle policy of gaining control over the church by pious
fraud. This implies that the visit of Titus to the church was a very happy
one and should have convinced the people in Corinth once and for all that
Paul himself was sincere in seeking their welfare in the gospel. It seems
highly probable that the visit must have been the one mentioned in 7:7-8
where Titus received such a welcome and assurance of the church's loyalty
to Paul. If we assume that these latter chapters, 10-13, are identical with
the letter written in tears, there must have been a visit of Titus before the
visit of reconciliation; and thus we have to multiply Titus' visits. It is better to assume that the last chapters of II Corinthians were written after the
return of Titus from that happy visit, and consequently that they belong in
the place they now occupy.[28]

So we conclude that, after I Corinthians was completed, Timothy returned to Ephesus from carrying the epistle of I Corinthians to Corinth
with a disheartened report that the Corinthians were unwilling to do anything about the man condemned in ch. 5. Paul immediately made a hurried
trip to Corinth to try to get them to understand his view. They paid no
heed while some members heaped abuse on him. He then left and wrote
the "tearful letter" which has now been lost. He sent this letter by Titus,
whose return he awaited with such fearful anxiety, described in II Cor
7:5f. When he found Titus in Macedonia, he was raised to such heights of
joy that he wrote the first nine chapters of our present letter. Then people
came to tell him about the recent disturbance stimulated by outsiders
which cause dhim to dash off the last four chapters and attach them to the
ones already written. Presumably, since the letters to the Corinthians were
preserved in Corinth, Paul's communications had a beneficial effect and he
was acknowledged by the church as a true apostle.

In the middle of this Corinthian agitation Paul was also disturbed about
completing the offering which he was trying to raise to relieve the poor
Christians in Jerusalem. As we have already seen, he previously gave initial instructions to the Corinthian church in I Corinthians 16. There he informs us that he had laid down directions to the churches of Galatia which
he expects the people of Corinth to follow. Now in II Corinthians he again
broaches the question of the collection by referring to the fact that the
churches of Macedonia, which were suffering from great distress and poverty, have shown remarkable generosity and devotion by giving themselves
and their money to a degree which greatly exceeds any normal expectation
of their ability to sacrifice. He now urges the people in Corinth to get busy
in this good cause with which they had been engaged for at least a year.
We thus are informed that the time of ch. 8 is about a year later than the

[28] Cf. Munck, *Paul and the Salvation of Mankind*, 168-171.

first reference to the collection in I Cor 16. In II Cor 8 Paul informs us he had dispatched Titus to Corinth to urge them to complete the offering which they had begun at least a year earlier. Did he send Titus for this purpose at the same time that he sent him with the letter written in tears, or is he now sending Titus with the letter he is writing after Titus' return from Corinth with the good report? Against the idea that he is sending him back is the fact that he doesn't say "I am sending him again now to work on the offering." Neither does he refer in the offering discussion to the conditions previously existing in Corinth. In fact, it is possible to infer that Titus is going to Corinth for the first time to organize the campaign according to what Paul has told him about this church.

Yet assuming that Titus has just returned from a very successful mission in getting the people reconciled to Paul, Paul may now have filled Titus with a new enthusiasm to go back to capitalize on the present situation and to take the congratulatory letter with its urgent recommendation that they proceed to complete the offering. Since they know that Titus has returned and since Titus knows that he had been there, there is no need for Paul to jot down the fact that this is Titus' second visit to Corinth. Since he says he has sent Titus with brothers who accompanied him, it is clear that he was also sending the present letter with Titus, for the letter about Titus was written for the sake of having them receive and cooperate with them in the collection. If so, it also follows that Titus brought the whole letter with the last chapters appended.

From Rom 15:25 we learn that Paul is going to Jerusalem to serve the saints: "For Macedonia and Achaea have been pleased to take a common share in aiding the poor saints in Jerusalem." This proves that the effort of Paul through Titus was successful and that he went with the offering to Jerusalem. The Roman letter, according to all the evidence, was written from Corinth. So we learn that Paul did make another visit to Corinth after he wrote the two Corinthian letters, and that a sufficiently large collection was made to justify his going to Jerusalem.

From the letters to Corinth we learn that Paul refused to receive any support for himself in Corinth. During the time he was there, however, people from Macedonian churches brought him gifts (II Cor 11:8,9). When Paul was in Thessalonica, and presumably in other parts of Macedonia, he supported himself: "You yourselves know that we did not eat bread without paying for it in anybody's house, but we worked in hard labor and wretchedness night and day in order to lay no burden on any one of you. Not that we didn't have the right, but in order that we might give you an example to imitate us; for when we were with you, we commanded you as follows: 'Any one who does not wish to work, neither let him eat'" (II Thess 3:7-10). So his policy of not receiving physical support from a church he was establishing was followed both in Macedonia and Achaea. The kindly concern of the Thessalonians for Paul while he was in Corinth was matched by the generosity of the Philippians when Paul was in chains. "You did well when you shared in my affliction; for you know, Philippians, that in the beginning of the gospel when I came out from Macedonia, no church shared in the matter of giving and receiving except you alone because you sent once and twice to my need when I was in Thessalonica" (Philip 4:4-16). Of the Macedonians the Philippians were probably the most thoughtful for Paul's physical needs.

By the time of writing the last chapters of II Corinthians Paul had extended his work beyond Corinth. His policy was to enter places where no one else had preached. Against the charge that he was overreaching himself by coming as far as Corinth, he replies that he acted in accordance with the rule which God had laid down for him, according to which he did not enter places where other men had already founded churches. Under the rules he accepted, no place would be too near or too far if it had not had a chance to hear the gospel (II Cor 10:13-16). According to Rom 15:19 Paul's work had extended from Jerusalem in a circle as far as Illyricum. Illyricum was located north of Macedonia on the west coast of the Balkan Peninsula. He thus went much farther on the west coast of Greece than any place mentioned either in Acts or the other epistles. So when he tells us in II Corinthians that his mission under the rule of God led him beyond Corinth, he meant much more than simply a trip to the next city or town.

In the course of these extensive travels on behalf of the gospel Paul endured almost unspeakable hardships. Five times he was beaten with the thirty-nine stripes imposed by the Jews according to the law. From rabbinical sources we discover that the lashes were imposed by men who would leap off the ground when they delivered the blows. Many times the victims were left insensible, sometimes even killed when they were weak to begin with. Five such beatings during a career would be incredible suffering for anyone to endure. In addition to this, he was beaten by the Romans three times. On one occasion he was stoned, and three times he was shipwrecked; during one shipwreck he spent a day and night in the water. All this occurred to Paul in addition to the anxieties and fears produced by the dangerous conditions of travel and by threats from gentiles, his own people the Jews, rioting mobs, and false brothers within the Christian community. He was worn down by labor and distress, by sleepless nights, by hunger and thirst, and by freezing cold. Throughout it all, he carried the anxieties and care for all the churches, feeling full and personal responsibility for the weaknesses, dissensions, and scandals that might arise in them (II Cor 11:23-28).

Fourteen years before the time of these last chapters of II Corinthians he had been snatched by a vision into the third heaven (II Cor 12:2-5).[29] This was some kind of ecstatic experience which "enabled him to hear words which it is not lawful for a man to speak." The glory of this experience, however, was balanced by some mysterious counterblow by Satan which he calls a "thorn" or a "stake in the flesh." This consisted of "a messenger of Satan" who was to beat him in order that he not be distended with too much pride. This passage (II Cor 12:1-8) indicates that Paul felt he had been granted not only the original revelation of the gospel which commissioned him but also other revelations that were designed to encourage him and display something of the glory of the divine paradise. Experiences of this kind amply compensated for the hardships, physical sufferings, and mental anguish he had to endure in his work. But God was concerned that his faithful follower be not overinflated with egotism and allowed the messenger of Satan to abuse Paul. All sorts of suggestions have been offered to explain what this experience really was: some think serious illness, disease of the eyes, epileptic fits, periodic persecutions, or constant harassment by opponents within the church.[30] One may suggest still another possibility: that the messenger of Satan might have been something like an accusing inner voice raising doubts about his authority to deviate so much from Judaism and the position of some of the leaders of the Jerusalem church, while at the same time accusing him as being unworthy of serving Christ and suggesting that his troubles may be signs of God's disapproval of his actions. In the passages of these last chapters the term "flesh" is employed to designate the complex of characteristics, achievements, and credentials that constitute eminent status in Judaism and in the segment of the church opposed to Paul. He had demonstrated that he was not lacking in qualifications that provide such status in the flesh (II Cor 11:18-23); and so when he refers to being buffeted by the messenger of Satan with a stake in the flesh, he may be referring to periodic attacks of depression and inner doubt about his own worthiness before God. This would make his experience somewhat parallel to Luther's bouts with the devil who was constantly attacking his self-confidence in the gospel.

We may note that this description of Paul's experiences shows clearly that the book of Acts was not guilty of exaggerating the hardships Paul went through. Acts mentions no beatings by the Jews before his arrest in Jerusalem. It mentions no shipwreck until the last one on the trip to Rome, long after the events of this epistle. It mentions one beating by the

---

[29] Assuming that the use of the third person singular is a rhetorical device to sublimate his "boasting."

[30] Cf. Héring, *II Corinthians*, 92-93; also Calvin's remarks ad loc.

Roman authorities in Philippi and alludes to riotings in Lystra, Thessalonica, and Ephesus. No attempt is made to portray the dangers of his travels nor to dramatize his inner feelings in connection with all the problems that emerged.

PAUL IN CHAINS

Since many Pauline scholars question the authenticity of Ephesians, and a smaller number Colossians, and a few Philippians, perhaps the discussion of Paul's internment had better begin with information derived from a letter which no one doubts is genuinely from Paul's hand: the letter to Philemon. When Paul wrote this letter, he was a prisoner on behalf of Jesus Christ: "Paul, a prisoner of Christ Jesus, and Timothy our brother, To Philemon our beloved fellow worker." This is not a figurative term to indicate that he had been taken captive into the service of Christ. He describes himself "as being such a person as Paul, the old man, but also now a prisoner of Jesus Christ."[31] From this it may be inferred that when he wrote this letter, Paul must have been at least fifty years old and had already been imprisoned. The charge directed against him had something to do with his proclamation of the gospel of Christ, for it was in Christ's service that he ran afoul of the authorities. During his confinement in chains he had met a runaway slave named Onesimus, "whom I begot in my chains" (Philem vs. 10). The verb "begot" is a technical term which Paul uses to describe converting a person to Christ. If he begets someone, as a result of his preaching or conversation, that person has become a Christian and has professed the faith. Therefore whatever the nature of his confinement in chains, Paul was able to converse with an escaped slave so as to evangelize him. That means he was not locked up in some jail to which outsiders would not have access; or, if he was in jail, people could visit him freely.

While Onesimus, the converted slave, was present with Paul, he had become so useful that Paul kept wishing to retain him in order that he continue to render service to him "in the chains of the gospel" (vs. 13). Hence, Paul's confinement did not prevent people from helping him by domestic service. Further, he was allowed to write letters; for he says he is writing this letter with his own hand (vs. 19). He affirms emphatically that, if Onesimus owes Philemon anything, he himself will repay the amount. Paul either had some money or felt he would be able to earn some. Perhaps his jailers did not confiscate all his possessions, or Paul ex-

---

[31] Philem vs. 9. On the conjectural *presbeutēs*, "ambassador," see Metzger, *Textual Commentary*, 657.

pected that in the foreseeable future he would be able to engage in gainful employment.[32] The letter calls Philemon a "beloved brother and fellow worker" of Paul and Timothy. It appears clear that Paul had been the human agent by whom Philemon himself had been converted to Christ. "Not to say that you owe your very self to me" (vs. 19) emphasizes that Philemon owed his Christian status, personality, and salvation to the ministry of Paul. The statement "you owe your very self to me" means either "it is on account of me that you have become what you are," or "because of my relation to you, you are under obligation to give me everything, up to your life." Either interpretation requires the assumption that Philemon's Christian existence was due to Paul. Some time after his conversion Philemon became a co-worker in promoting the gospel (vs. 2).

Onesimus, the slave on behalf of whom Paul drafted the beautiful letter, is mentioned in one other passage of the New Testament, Col 4:9. In this passage Paul informs the Christians in Colossae that he has sent Tychicus "along with Onesimus, the faithful and beloved brother who is from you." This letter written to Colossae proves that Onesimus had come from Colossae. There is no indication in this allusion that he is a runaway slave and a recent convert to Christianity. On the face of it the passage implies that Onesimus had been a member of the Christian group in Colossae. If this is so, he had run away even though a Christian. In such a case, when he appeared before Paul, he was already a Christian. But Paul's statement "I begot him in my chains" demonstrates that he had not been a Christian before. The only possible conclusion is that Onesimus came from the city of Colossae, and Paul mentions this fact to inform them, the Colossian group, of it. Thus the inference is turned around to the opposite, namely, that the *Christians* in Colossae had not known Onesimus and now were enlightened about his origin in their city.

At the time of writing Paul was surrounded by friends. He mentions Epaphras as a fellow prisoner in Jesus Christ; so we learn that he had at least one companion in captivity who was arraigned under the same accusation as Paul. Also some co-workers or partners of Paul were present: Mark, Aristarchus, Demas, and Luke. These all joined Paul in greetings to Philemon, which demonstrates they were acquainted with him (vss. 24, 25). So they had either been with Paul when he made Philemon's acquaintance or been in the locality where Philemon lived. Mark must be John Mark, who in Col 4:10 is called the kinsman or cousin of Barnabas. His inclusion among the companions of Paul demonstrates that he is acceptable to Paul at this time. Aristarchus is called a "fellow captive" of Paul in Col 4:10. Demas is mentioned together with Luke in Col 4:14 as

---

[32] The possibility is also open that Paul is employing a conscious *tour de force* and the second half of vs. 19 means he did not expect to be called to make good his generous offer.

joining in the greeting.[33] Epaphras is mentioned twice: in Col 1:7, "as you learn from Epaphras my beloved fellow slave," and 4:12, "Epaphras, who is from you, a slave of Jesus Christ, greets you." This informs us that Epaphras is likewise from Colossae, perhaps known to the Christians there, or like Onesimus, a fellow citizen, but one who had been converted later. Since he was "always contesting in the prayers on behalf of" the Christians in Colossae, Laodicea, and Hierapolis, we may suppose that he had been a Christian in fellowship with these churches in Asia Minor.

The joint mention of all these persons in Philemon and Colossians proves either (1) that Paul wrote both letters, probably at the same time, and sent them by Tychicus and Onesimus, or (2) that the person or persons who formulated the Colossians letter and attributed it to Paul had excellent information about the persons who were with him when he wrote the letter to Philemon. Thus (a) the unknown author had independent knowledge of Paul's circumstances in confinement, and hence the other biographical details in Colossians are reliable items we may use to round out our picture of Paul's circumstances, or (b) the author had access to the letter to Philemon. Since the letter to Philemon was a private one, the author of Colossians must have known Philemon or his descendants. Then he would also know of other persons and details connected with the work at Colossae. Credibility is stretched beyond reasonable limits when it is argued that a man could be as well acquainted with the details found in the Philemon letter as is this author, yet at the same time would have to depend on invention for other material concerning the Colossian church. For our purposes, consequently, it makes no practical difference whether Paul wrote the letter to Colossians or not; for if he did not, the actual author had to be well acquainted with Paul's situation, and thus we can use his statements as those of an original source.

Since Colossians refers to another letter to be brought to the Christians in Laodicea, the spurious author produced not only Colossians, but another letter to the Laodiceans at the same time. It is often supposed, perhaps correctly, that what we call the epistle to the Ephesians is this Laodicean letter. That supposition goes back to Marcion, Tertullian, and Origen, who did not find the phrase "in Ephesus" in the manuscripts available to them. This phrase, in fact, is omitted from the earliest manuscripts we have: P[46], the original of Sinaiticus, and original Vaticanus. Thus, manuscript evidence makes very doubtful the reading "in Ephesus." Since the epistle to the Ephesians is so closely akin to the Colossians, the conclusion that the two letters were written at the same time is a very weighty one. If we grant that Paul wrote Colossians, he also wrote another letter to

---

[33] Demas is referred to as a defector in II Tim 4:10, and Mark and Luke are mentioned in the next verse. These personal references may be an authentic Pauline passage.

the Laodiceans. If he wrote Colossians but not Ephesians, Ephesians is not the letter to the Laodiceans. However, it is conceivable that he wrote a letter to the Laodiceans, parts of which were inserted into the letter to the Ephesians in various places. One has to grant that the Ephesian letter is written in a very unique style and has some points of view that appear to be different from those expressed elsewhere in Paul's letters, while at the same time it is filled with phrases that are found scattered throughout the letters of Paul. Goodspeed thinks these facts point to the production of Ephesians as a covering essay written by an editor; as an introduction, he compiled a standard letter, gathering Pauline phrases from the whole of Pauline literature.[34] But a major difficulty with this theory is the fact that the editor, so-called, appears to have made extensive use of Colossians. Three-fourths of the material found in Colossians is found also in Ephesians. No other letter of Paul assimilates so closely to another as Ephesians to Colossians. The hypothetical editor must have been fascinated particularly with the epistle to the Colossians.[35]

The Colossians letter indicates that Paul is in a condition of suffering and of affliction: "I am now rejoicing in my sufferings on behalf of you and I am filling up the things that were lacking in the afflictions of Christ in my flesh" (1:24). It also notes that Paul has been bound for the sake of, or because of, speaking "the mystery of Christ" (4:3). At the time the letter is written, he asks the Colossians to pray "that God may open up to us a door for the message in order to speak the mystery of Christ" (4:3). According to this, his constraint is such that he is not as free to proclaim the mystery of Christ as he desires. Whether this is due to the conditions of the confinement or to the unreceptiveness of people with whom he converses, we do not know.

Paul intends to send Mark to Asia Minor and he requests that the Colossians receive him. Mark is to be received as an official representative of Paul. He further states that Mark and Justus "who are from the circumcision"—that is, who are Jews—are partners with Paul for the sake of the kingdom of God and have become a real comfort to him (4:10-11). Luke is identified as "the beloved physician" (4:14). Greeting is sent to certain persons who belong to the church in Laodicea,[36] to Nympha with the church in her house, and to Archippus. In Philemon, Archippus is mentioned along with Apphia as persons to whom the letter is written in addition to Philemon himself.

---

[34] E. J. Goodspeed, *New Solutions of New Testament Problems* (Chicago, 1927), 11-20; repeated with some added details in later publications.

[35] For other objections see E. F. Harrison, *Introduction to the New Testament* (Grand Rapids, 1964), 316-318. The relationship of Colossians and Ephesians will be treated in detail by M. Barth in AB, vol. 34B.

[36] Knox, *Philemon Among the Letters of Paul*, 45-55, argues strongly for the identification of Philemon with "The letter from Laodicea" (Col 4:16).

During this period of confinement and suffering Paul relied on messengers to report his condition to the churches ("Tychicus will make known to you all my affairs" [4:7]). Delegates from the churches gave Paul up-to-date information about their condition ("Epaphras, who also revealed to us your love in the Spirit" [1:8]). By correspondence and the interchange of couriers Paul kept in contact with his widespread ecclesiastical empire throughout the time of his imprisonment. He takes the same kind of care of his Christian converts as he had when he was free. He never allows anxiety about his own personal difficulties to interfere with management of all his churches at a distance.

From his references to Laodicea and Hierapolis it is not completely clear whether Paul had been there in person. He knew Nympha in Laodicea and was closely enough acquainted with the situation to know that she had a church in her house (4:15). He was somewhat jittery about Archippus, who he felt should be advised to look after the ministry to which he had been commissioned so as to fulfill it (4:17). These personal details could hardly refer to persons in Colossae later than the time of Paul. A pseudonymous letter writer would hardly compose a letter to the Colossians a decade or two later than the supposed time and refer to conditions and persons extant at the time of his letter and mix them with persons and details from the time of Paul, who lived twenty years earlier. He should be inserting remarks about persons who flourished at the time when Paul was supposed to have written the letter, and thus all these personal remarks would be either historical statements about the real past or fictional touches. This is another argument confirming the hypothesis that the purported letter writer, if indeed it was not Paul himself, did some historical research; and we can rely on his allusions as if they had come from Paul himself. Fictional greetings and directives have a very low probability.[37]

On this point of authorship of Colossians we may add that the hypothetical forger was adroit enough to attach the statement "This greeting is by my own hand, Paul's. Remember my bonds. Grace be with you" (4:18). At the conclusion of Galatians Paul adds a paragraph in his own handwriting. At the end of I Corinthians he adds the greeting "in my own hand—Paul's" (16:21). Word for word this statement is identical with the statement in Colossians. Rom 16:22 introduces Tertius, who inserts his greeting, as he says he was the scribe who wrote the letter. Thus the supposed forger was perfectly familiar with Paul's custom of attaching a short statement in his own handwriting, and here he avoids the trap of imitating other conclusions too closely for he adds only "grace be with you." In other letters the benediction of grace is qualified by "of the Lord Jesus

---

[37] A further argument for the Paulinity of these details may stem from the relative unimportance of Colossae. Cf. Knox, *Philemon.*

Christ" (Gal 6:18) or "of the Lord Jesus Christ and the love of God and the fellowship of the Holy Spirit" (II Cor 13:14); Colossians is the only place where the greeting is confined to the bare benediction. Could any forger have restrained himself from imitating Paul a little more convincingly? The abbreviated formula seems to be a watermark of Paul's own freedom of style.

One wonders whether refined criticism based on the comparative anatomy of theological ideas or systems and on subtle qualities of style may not have become a jungle of hypotheses which should be cleared up by the machete of common sense. A rational supposition about the original publication of Paul's letters may assume that the editor was convinced these were actually addressed by Paul to the people of the churches named. The best explanation for this is that he got the letters from these churches. Then the assumption of pseudonymity implies that the churches were willing to accept as authentic letters those written in Paul's name.

Reading through an epistle like Colossians makes it difficult to see what sort of motive could induce anyone to expend such skillful labor in imitating Paul. There were, of course, some kinds of theological enemies of Paul's position who are excoriated, and these could have been circulating in the churches decades later; but in that case, one would suppose that the author of the letter would have identified them much more directly than he does and have aimed much heavier theological firepower against them. It seems when everything is added together, the best conclusion is the traditional belief that Colossians was written by Paul.

Philippians is the other letter that appears as a product of Paul's hand when in chains. "I wish you to know, brothers, that my affairs have turned out for the advancement of the gospel so that my chains have become public in Christ throughout the entire praetorium and among all the rest" (Philip 1:12-13). Despite the prosperity of the gospel proclamation associated with Paul's imprisonment, he complains here that some people are preaching the gospel from envy and strife (1:15). This fact is an irritation, but Paul rejoices that the gospel is being preached from whatever motive (1:18). He is in doubt as to whether his confinement will result in life or death (1:20). He expects, if he is freed, to see the Philippians again (1:27). This expectation raises two questions: (a) was Paul imprisoned at Rome? (b) had he changed his intention of going from Rome to Spain (see Rom 15:24)? It has been argued that Paul's imprisonment from which he wrote the "prison letters" was either at Ephesus or Caesarea rather than Rome.[38] Several details drawn from Colossians and Ephesians support this supposition, such as the number of people from

[38] The information pointing to Ephesus is fully marshaled by George Duncan, *St. Paul's Ephesian Ministry* (New York, 1930), 59-143. For details about Caesarea cf. Feine-Behm-Kümmel, *Introduction*, 229-235.

Asia Minor who are referred to in the letters, and allusions to the conditions in the region around Ephesus. But this can be fully explained by the fact that the references to persons and conditions in Asia Minor would naturally be found in the letters to people in churches of Asia Minor. On the other hand, Philippians refers to conditions and people in Macedonia. If we had a letter written from prison to Athens or Corinth, undoubtedly it would reflect conditions in these cities. We know so little about what happened to Paul while he was in chains that we cannot exclude the possibility that he decided either to postpone or forgo his long-hoped-for trip to Spain. It is perfectly possible that his experience in prison along with things that may have happened in the eastern churches convinced him that he should revisit them when he got out. A strong argument for Rome rests on the unanimous tradition that he was a prisoner in Rome and on the references to Caesar's household and to the "praetorium" guard in Philippians. Admittedly, this argument does not extend to the other three letters, Ephesians, Colossians, and Philemon; and it is not conclusive even for Philippians since references to "Caesar's household" might be used of a proconsul's palace and the "praetorium" used of his court (cf. John 18:33, "Pilate therefore entered again into the praetorium"). Yet we have no other reference to Caesar's household in the New Testament.

Arguments against the authenticity of Philippians appear overstrained and hypercritical. The same kind of arguments presented in the case of Colossians obtains here. In addition the style of the letter fits in with what we know of the style of Paul so that we feel safe in assuming that Paul wrote it. Whether he wrote it before or after Philemon and/or Colossians is not clear. He does not seem to be experiencing the same constraint that required him in Colossians to pray that the door might be open for the gospel. He now glories in its progress, and his feeling that the choice between death and life is imminent indicates that he thinks he is at the last stage of his imprisonment. Without any compelling arguments to the contrary, we may therefore suppose that this is the last of the "prison epistles." The ever faithful Timothy is with Paul to join him in addressing the letter to the Philippians. Paul intends to send Timothy to Philippi very quickly so that he may discover the situation there and report back. Timothy is now the only one really close enough to Paul to join him completely in his concern for the Philippians. Paul complains that all the others are seeking their own interests, not the things of Jesus Christ (2:19-21). This indicates either that the people referred to in the other letters as faithful supporters have departed for other localities or have developed some unfortunate tendencies that aroused Paul's disapproval. Apparently all was not well in Camelot.

From Philippi a very good brother, partner, and fellow soldier named Epaphroditus had arrived to serve Paul's needs. This man, during his stay with Paul, had fallen so sick that there was despair for his life, but with the aid of the Lord he had been restored to health. Now Paul hopes to send him also to Philippi so that he may in person reveal the marvelous nature of his cure (2:25-30). During Paul's confinement the people of Philippi had "revived their personal thoughtfulness on his behalf though they hadn't had an opportunity to carry out what they planned" (4:10). This seems to indicate that Paul heard they had planned earlier to send him support but had been thwarted. He then recalls the repeated times the Philippians in earlier days had sent aid to him after he left Macedonia. Finally now, they have succeeded in sending him something by Epaphroditus (4:18). While Paul alludes to brothers and saints who are with him, he mentions no names of associates except Epaphroditus, Timothy, and Clement. He does urge a person in Philippi called "my sincere yokefellow" to assist Euodia and Syntyche as persons who have struggled along with Paul in behalf of the gospel, together with Clement and other partners. At the same time he urges both women to compose themselves and "think the same thing in the Lord" (4:2-3). This hints that, like other Christians, the two had somehow become irritated with each other over some ethical or doctrinal issue. Incidentally, this furnishes a bit of proof that women even in Pauline churches were actively engaged in evangelism and public advocacy of the Christian religion. Paul was no such anti-feminist as many women have feared and many theologians argued.

From the "prison letters" we can conclude that Paul was bound in chains and kept in some kind of confinement and restraint for a considerable time. The balance of probability is in favor of the old opinion that he was bound in Rome, though this cannot be affirmed as a certainty from material in his letters. His imprisonment was caused by his faithfulness to the gospel. Since he never mentioned either those who arrested him or his jailers it is probable that the confinement was imposed by Roman authorities, possibly at the instigation of the Jews, or possibly because of some riot among the gentiles. Paul never castigates Roman authorities openly, except in I Corinthians 6, where he upbraids Christians who take lawsuits before "unrighteous judges." So indifferent is Paul to what happens to him personally that he neglects to describe the indictment, the stages of the legal process, any facts about his personal treatment, and the nature of his defense or arguments which might be used to clear him. He shows no zeal for a martyr's death, nor does he demonstrate any great eagerness for freedom. How different this is from the attitude of Ignatius of Antioch whose letters are filled with eager anticipation of his future execution as a martyr.[39] With fierce dignity Paul awaits the outcome,

---

[39] E.g. *Trallians* 4:2; *Romans, passim; Smyrnaeans* 4:2. Ignatius died about A.D. 115.

concerned only that everything would turn out for the advancement of the gospel on earth.[40]

The so-called Pastoral epistles, I and II Timothy and Titus, have been supposed, traditionally, to have been written after Paul's release from the Roman imprisonment. If these letters were written by Paul—which is doubted by a large number of modern students—questions must be resolved about their chronological relation to the other letters, and about how to fit items in them into the life of Paul as pieced out from the other epistles. An examination of I Timothy does not disclose any sure details which demonstrate certainty about the time of the letter, the place from which it was written, or how it may be related chronologically to the other letters. It is addressed to Timothy, who is mentioned in Romans, I and II Corinthians, I Thessalonians, Philippians, and Colossians. In those references he is characterized as a fellow worker of Paul, a trusted emissary to the church at Corinth, a brother presumably of the apostle and of the church (II Corinthians), a fellow slave of Christ with Paul (Philip 1:1), and the messenger to whom Paul commits his most serious interests (Philip 2:19). From these allusions it may be inferred that Timothy was a very close associate of Paul from the time of his correspondence with Corinth down through his imprisonment. This should cover a span of four or five years at least. There is no precise evidence concerning the age of Timothy at the end of this period, but supposedly he is a mature man, at least in his late twenties.

In I Timothy, on the other hand, Paul[41] addressed his partner as "my sincere child in the faith" (1:2). Paul advises Timothy, "let no one despise your youth" (4:12). At the time of the letter, Timothy was so young that people might be inclined to have reservations about, even contempt for, his authority or responsibility as a sound Christian leader. Both these references appear to be more fitting for an immature person than for one who has had considerable experience in close association with the apostle and has been used to carrying out delicate missions and handling difficult crises in the churches. The author refers to the fact that he had left Timothy at Ephesus when he himself was going to Macedonia. If this letter is written after the imprisonment of Paul, then he had gone to Ephesus and from there proceeded to Macedonia, leaving Timothy in charge of affairs in Ephesus. The letter seems to be written for the sake of instructing Timothy how to handle the situation in Ephesus with reference to persons who are addicted to complicated disputes and genealogies, and at the same time are interested along with others in emphasizing the law. Paul appar-

---

[40] E.g. Philip 2:12-18.
[41] To avoid the awkward necessity of consistently referring to the possible pseudonymity of the author, the name of Paul is used—without intention of prejudicing the literary decision.

ently had already "handed over to Satan" such offenders as Hymenaeus and Alexander, about whose vices we know nothing more (1:3-20). The church would require from Timothy decisions about the conduct of husbands and wives (2:8-15), choice of "bishops" (men occupying supervisory offices), and deacons or servants (3:1-13). Timothy is given instruction on how best to deal with these officials, and then about how to manage the enrollment of widows and the kind of life style and conduct to be expected of widows in the church. In addition, he is advised about slaves and their masters. Paul also urges Timothy personally to avoid those who teach doctrines alien from those of the apostles and exhorts him to be loyal to the faith and true piety (5:1-10). Paul indicates that he hopes to come to meet Timothy very quickly, even though there may be some delay (3:14-15). Presumably this means that after he has completed a circuit through Macedonia, he intends to return to Ephesus.

These details raise a genuine question about the time of this epistle in the life of Paul. Does it fit the period before the Roman imprisonment or after? The letter nowhere mentions any imprisonment or release or informs about the period of Paul's life into which it falls. It does indicate that Paul had been a persecutor and insulter of the churches (1:13), that he was converted and had become a leader of those who were about to believe in Christ for life eternal (1:16), and that he had left Ephesus and was proceeding to Macedonia, already seen (1:3), and that Paul has had for some time a policy of preventing wives from teaching (2:11). The letter shows that the church has already reached a stage of organization in which there were overseers and deacons, along with a regular class of widows who were being supported by the church; and this church was now confronted with a group of false teachers, opposed to marriage, refusing to eat different kinds of meats, seeming to be fascinated with teachings about demons.[42] Many have concluded that these features of the church situation justify the belief that I Timothy was written late in the first century or early in the second. In either case, it was not written by Paul but by someone taking his name in the later period of the early church. This hypothetical personage addressed a letter in the name of Paul to Timothy when he was supposedly young, and he transferred the conditions of the church of his own time back into the time when Paul started missionary activity from Ephesus.[43] If this theory is correct, probably no historical weight may be assigned to the details about Paul or Timothy.

Arguments based on the development of organization or on the charac-

---

[42] These demons need not be evil spirits as in the Gospels, but might be some supernatural entities such as the aeons of the Gnostics.

[43] For an adequate summary of the relevant arguments, cf. Dibelius and Conzelmann, *The Pastoral Epistles*, 1-10.

teristic of the heresies in the church do not force the conclusion that the letter was too late for Paul. It has been pointed out that the society of the Essenes described in the Dead Sea scrolls was organized very much along the same lines as this church in I Timothy.[44] Such organization could easily have appeared any time in the first century. Paul refers to the "one who rules" (Rom 12:8) and to service, *diakonia* (Rom 12:7). In Philippians he refers to bishops (*episkopoi*) and deacons (1:1). The word *episkopos* means someone who supervises, and it could be employed for any person who has an official responsibility in an organization. The description of the qualifications of these officials in I Timothy does not imply that they composed a class that had been entirely unknown before the end of the first century. It might be concluded that the stereotype into which widows have been cast in this letter represents an advanced development over the status of widows who are described in I Corinthians 7 since the widows in I Timothy are on a list kept by the church and are to be supported by it. They have evidently existed as such long enough for certain abuses to creep in which Paul hopes Timothy will correct; but aside from the fact that Acts implies widows were supported by the church from the earliest days in Jerusalem (6:1), we may assume that the Old Testament's concern for widows and orphans was never absent from the church.[45]

It is hard to say (a) whether the internal features of I Timothy point to a letter written to Timothy when Paul was going from Ephesus to Macedonia concurrently with his writing I Corinthians, or (b) whether Paul wrote to Timothy after being released from prison and going back to the regions of his early missionary activity, or (c) whether some later Paulinist composed the letter in Paul's name after Paul and Timothy were both dead. The only usable conclusion is that, if the letter is genuine, it supplies very little information about the life of Paul either before or after his imprisonment to supplement what is in the other letters. If option (b) is correct, it does indicate that he was in Ephesus and Macedonia after being released from prison. If either of the other two options is correct, it supplies no certain information about a post-prison activity of Paul. Perhaps the best conclusion is to leave the question undecided. If Paul wrote I Timothy, the letter would preferably have a provenance around Ephesus before rather than after Paul left prison, this based on Timothy's youth and the lack of a reference to Paul's having been released from jail.

In contrast to I Timothy, II Timothy appears to presuppose that Paul is in prison at the time he wrote it. "Do not be ashamed of the testimony of

[44] Kelly, *The Pastoral Epistles*, 73-74; Bo Reicke, in *The Scrolls and the New Testament*, ed. K. Stendahl (New York, 1957), 152; M. Burrows, *More Light on the Dead Sea Scrolls* (New York, 1958), 113-114.
[45] The Gospels record Jesus' condemnation of those who oppressed widows and his praise of the poor widow's "mite" (Mark 12:40-44, par.).

our Lord, nor of me, his prisoner" (1:8). "May the Lord give mercy to the house of Onesiphoros because many times he refreshed me and was not ashamed of my chain" (1:16). "I am suffering evil even to the extent of bonds as a criminal" (2:9). These citations imply that Paul is being constrained by fetters. It is, however, the type of imprisonment which allows visitations from friends who may seek to help him. The same situation is described in Philippians and Philemon. In II Timothy the information is given for the first and only time that the imprisonment was in Rome (1:17). A single detail appears partially inconsistent with the supposition that Paul was in prison at Rome when the letter was written: "I left Trophimus sick at Miletus" (4:20). Since Miletus is situated on the coast of Asia Minor, the statement "I left Trophimus there" appears to imply that Paul had recently been in Miletus. According to Acts at least two years elapsed between the time when Paul was at Miletus and when he was in Rome. Because of this time problem Beza conjectured this should be read *Melitē*, which is the name in Acts for the island of Malta on which the victims of the shipwreck were cast by the wind as Paul was being taken prisoner to Rome.[46] If II Timothy was written within a reasonable time after Paul arrived in Rome, reference to having left Trophimus at Malta would be perfectly consistent. Otherwise it would be perhaps necessary to suppose that Paul's location as he writes the letter is meant to be somewhere in the East, probably close to Ephesus after he was released from prison. This possibility agrees with option (b) which was mentioned above (p. 38) in connection with the writing of I Timothy. However the quotations referring to his bondage appear to presuppose that the bondage is now in force.

This conclusion may very well be confirmed by Paul's complaint, "No one was present with me at my first defense" (4:16). Paul had to make a first appearance on a certain occasion, and this leads to the conclusion that later he made a second appearance. On this first occasion, though, he was abandoned by all his friends; he was delivered by the Lord "from the mouth of the lion" (4:17). This cryptic statement could mean that he had been acquitted and released.[47] On the other hand, it could mean he was not condemned on this first occasion as he feared he would be, but was held over for further appearances. Since Paul does not say he had been released but affirms, "The Lord will deliver me from every evil work and will save me for his heavenly kingdom" (4:18), we may conclude that he still had to face further hazards and was in no way free from jeopardy in Rome.

---

[46] Cf. Nestle's apparatus. But also Dibelius and Conzelmann, *The Pastoral Epistles*, ad loc.

[47] The "lion" could conceivably be a literal reference—which raises the insoluble question of when arena torture was first meted out to Christians. The "lion" could be a figurative expression for Roman imperial power (cf. Rev 13:2). Finally, it could be simply a literary figure of speech.

The "first defense" could, however, be his appearance before the Roman governor in Caesarea when the Jews, led by their spokesman Tertullus, indicted Paul for disturbing the peace in Jerusalem and demanded that he be sent back to Jerusalem for trial before the Sanhedrin. On this occasion the request of the Jewish embassy was denied. Paul thereby escaped almost certain death at Jerusalem. If this is the case, the setting of II Timothy is all the more surely at Rome.

According to II Tim 3:10-11 Timothy had shared with Paul in his preaching and in the persecution and sufferings which had happened to him in the localities described in Acts 13:14-14:28. According to the Acts account Paul was harassed by persecution in Pisidean Antioch and at Iconium. He had to flee an attack of both Jews and gentiles, and at Lystra he was stoned and left for dead. This account agrees with II Timothy as regards persecutions and sufferings; but in Acts Timothy was not with Paul since Timothy was converted only when Paul went through this region for the *second* time (16:1). Several possibilities may be suggested for reconciling these two sources: (a) that the conversion of Timothy actually took place when Paul first went through these towns, (b) that the persecutions actually took place during Paul's second visit to this area; (c) that during the second visit Paul was persecuted again; (d) that Timothy's presence during the persecutions is a fiction of the pseudonymous author of the epistle, who extracted the sufferings from Acts but failed to notice that Timothy had not yet become Paul's associate; (e) that there could have been a floating tradition about Paul's work and sufferings in southern Asia Minor which was drawn upon by the authors of Acts and II Timothy independently of each other.[48] The second and third possibilities would have to be maintained despite a lack of any mention in Acts of such troubles during Paul's second journey through the region; 16:5 merely remarks that "the churches were being strengthened in the faith and were increasing in number daily." If Paul wrote II Timothy, then there is a presumption of accurate memory in favor of the details there; and Acts would have to be harmonized, presumably in the direction of the first possibility.

Contrary to the prevailing tendency of present-day scholarship, no overwhelming evidence forces a denial of Pauline authorship of II Timothy even though the letter shares stylistic peculiarities only with I Timothy and its details do not easily fit into a plausible picture of Paul's imprisonment. This last consideration is certainly not determinative since little is known about what happened in Paul's Roman imprisonment, and the scheme into which such details would have to fit is not clear.

However one deals with all this, the statements that are made about

---

[48] The relationship of this tradition to II Cor 11:23-27 is a possible part of this suggestion.

Paul's situation are as follows. He is writing, according to the letter, in a condition of loneliness because "those in Asia have all left me" (II Timothy 1:15). "Demas forsook me since he loved the present age and went to Thessalonica. Crescens went to Galatia, Titus to Dalmatia. Luke alone is with me . . . I sent Tychicus to Ephesus" (4:10-12). "All forsook me in my first defense" (4:16). It is strange that, despite this loneliness Paul complains of, he does mention four people who joined with him in greeting Timothy: "Eubulus and Pudens, Linus, and Claudia." Besides these, he says, "All the brothers greet you" (4:21). How he is bereft of all companions except Luke when these other persons join with him in extending greetings, one can only conjecture. Perhaps he distinguishes between resident members of the local congregation and persons who have been more closely associated with his mission.

The associates who had surrounded Paul have thus disbanded of their own accord or have been dispatched to various localities in the East. Two of them were on the Balkan Peninsula, Demas in Thessalonica, Titus in Dalmatia; Erastus was in Corinth; while Crescens was in Galatia and Tychicus was in Ephesus. "I already am being offered up, and the moment of my demise is upon me. I have struggled in a good contest, I have finished the race, I have kept the faith. As for what is left, the crown of righteousness is awaiting me" (4:6-8). This indicates that Paul was expecting an early death, looking forward to meeting Christ and receiving the mark of victory. He can still be interested in having Timothy bring to him an overcoat which he left at Troas with "the books and especially the parchments" (4:13). Thus he anticipates living long enough to receive a visit from Timothy, who at the time seems to be at Ephesus (Rom 1:18). To add to Paul's feeling of desertion and anxiety about future dangers (however mitigated by his confidence in the Lord) he is troubled by certain evils which have been committed against him by Alexander, the bronze worker. The only other Alexanders mentioned in the New Testament are the member of the high priestly family (Acts 4:6), the Jewish speaker when the mob was stirred up by the silver worker Demetrius in Ephesus (Acts 19:33), and an unknown apostate from the faith, whom, along with Hymanaeus, Paul had "turned over to Satan" (I Tim 1:20). It is possible that this last Alexander is identical with Alexander the bronze worker, though, of course, we cannot be sure. From all this it appears that, while it was possible for Paul to be visited by friends in his imprisonment and even to have them stay for a period of time, most of them felt that association with him was perilous. They, like the disciples at the time of Jesus' trial, had an irresistible impulse to depart for distant regions when Paul was to make his first defense before the authorities. Paul regards this desertion as something he hopes would not be charged against them in the divine reckoning. This wish is reminiscent of Jesus' prayer, "Father forgive them," and of Stephen's cry, "May this sin not be charged against them" (Acts 7:60).

As we summarize these allusions to persons and to the situation of the prisoner in this letter, the impression is strong that this comes from Paul's pen rather than from some writer imagining what Paul would have written a generation earlier. There are persons like Phygelus, Hermogenes, Philetus, Crescens, Carpus, Eubulus, Pudens, Linus, and Claudia, nine who do not have stock names which would readily have come to mind (except for Claudia, and perhaps Philetus). This miscellany of names which must have been drawn from real people certainly argues for the fact that they are named as persons remembered. This impression is increased by the fact that none has any theological or historical significance. In addition to these names the letter mentions other persons who are known from other books of the New Testament. Demas joined Paul in greeting the people at Colossae (Col. 4:14). Titus is known from several places in Paul's letters. Luke was mentioned along with Demas in Col 4:14 and with Philemon in Philem vs. 24. Mark is mentioned in several letters as well as in the book of Acts, and so is Tychicus, an Asian, who had been sent by Paul to the region of Ephesus. Alexander could possibly be the brother of Rufus mentioned in Mark 15:21 or the partner in crime of Hymanaeus mentioned in I Tim 1:20—we do not know. Prisca and Aquila (II Tim 4:19) are the same pair mentioned several times in Acts and alluded to in Rom 16:3 and I Cor 16:19. In Acts and I Corinthians they are associated with Ephesus, while in Romans, if the sixteenth chapter is genuine, they seem to be at least temporarily in Rome. Here on the assumption that Timothy is in Ephesus, the request in II Tim 4:19 implies that they are now in Ephesus again. Erastus was the steward of the city mentioned in Rom 16:23, and he was coupled with Timothy in Acts 19:22 as a pair of Paul's servants who had been sent into Macedonia. Here (II Tim 4:20) it is stated that he remained in Corinth.

If II Timothy was pseudonymously written after all the recollection of the personages around Paul had faded, the author would have made use of the book of Acts and the published letters of Paul to cull out these names. In this case it would be necessary for him to write after the book of Acts and the letters of Paul had been published, and perhaps after Paul's letters had been gathered into an initial collection. But it is hard to believe that, if this were the case, he would have included no facts found in the other sources about these persons to identify them more specifically. The way they are mentioned here presents a high degree of probability that Paul is recalling them for the purposes of this letter, without feeling impelled to harmonize the details with statements in other letters he has written.[49]

---

[49] Contrast the concern for corroborative detail in II Peter 1:12-14,16-18, 3:1-2, 15-16. Also cf. Kelly, *The Pastoral Epistles*, 8-9.

Thus the list and character of the names mentioned as well as such statements as are made about them seem to carry the same force as that of the names mentioned in Colossians. These names prove either that Paul wrote the whole letter, or that a later letter writer had fragments of a letter of Paul in which all these names are referred to. In either case, this letter supplies valuable information about Paul's circumstances when he was in prison.

The last epistle of the Pastoral triad is Titus. Titus is not mentioned in Acts but is referred to eight times in II Corinthians and twice in Galatians. In Galatians he is a Greek whom the authorities in Jerusalem did not compel Paul to circumcise (2:3), whereas in II Corinthians he is the trusted emissary of Paul who brought back good news from Corinth and who was appointed by the apostle to collect the funds in Corinth to be used for the relief of the saints in Jerusalem (7:6-7, 8:6). Titus had unquestionably made an excellent impression upon the people in Corinth which Paul uses as a kind of reflex commendation of himself since he is guided by the same spirit and follows the same policy as Titus (II Cor 12:18). This person who received the spotlight in II Corinthians disappears totally from sight until he emerges as the ostensible recipient of a letter from Paul. Paul addresses Titus as his "beloved"[50] child (Titus 1:4). He delegates to him the authority to appoint elders according to certain qualifications (1:5-9). As a leader in the church, Titus is instructed how to regulate the lives of the old men and the old women, the young men, the young women, slaves and masters (2:1-10). He is commanded to secure from the people of the church obedience to the political authorities and to turn them away from complicated disputes and arguments about genealogy and laws (3:1-11).

According to the contents and style, the letter belongs in the same category as I and II Timothy. Some phrases are common to all three letters, and both Timothy and Titus occupy similar positions as appointees of the apostle in charge of the churches in a certain territory. Whatever arguments are used against the genuineness of the epistles to Timothy likewise hold against the epistle to Titus. Titus presents some additional difficulties. The greatest of these is the fact that Paul says he left him in Crete. No place can be found in the outline of Paul's life covered in Acts for a sojourn on the island of Crete before his arrival at Rome. It is true that the ship which was conveying Paul along with freight to Rome sailed "under Crete by Salome and it landed in a certain place called Fair Havens" (Acts 27:7-8). Paul urged the captain of the boat to winter in this harbor, but the owners of the boat decided to head for another harbor of Crete which could better withstand storms. The story goes on to relate how they were unable to reach another port in Crete and had to set sail for

---

[50] *gnēsios*, not a common word, used also at I Tim 1:2 and with somewhat different import at II Cor 8:8 and Philip 4:3. At II Tim 1:2 *agapētos* is used.

the middle of the Mediterranean because of the storm that finally wrecked them on the coast of Malta. It is possible that Titus, who is not mentioned in the book of Acts, was one of the companions of Paul on this trip, and that Paul had left him in Crete to establish churches. However the letter does not indicate that Titus was to establish churches, but rather was to regulate and straighten out those already existing. If Paul left Titus in Crete on his trip to Rome, then churches had already been formed by some other preachers; and Paul was assuming the prerogative of setting Titus over them. It is hardly likely that the short stay of the ship in Fair Havens would have given Paul time to travel over Crete and establish churches. Since there are so many gaps in our knowledge of the founding of early churches, the possibility cannot be ruled out that churches were in existence on Crete at this time and that they had appealed to Paul to help them regulate their affairs; and thus he would have been acting in due order in delegating this responsibility to Titus.

It has been proposed that Paul may have been released from captivity in Rome and then gone to the East as we find hinted in I Timothy.[51] During this hypothetical trip he may have visited Crete along with Titus and established churches himself. When he left, he placed the churches under Titus' charge.

Admittedly these possibilities suffer under a degree of improbability. In the first place Acts makes no mention of any preaching activity of Paul during his stay in Fair Havens and gives no indication whatever that there were Christians on the island. Paul's other letters, likewise, give no hint of any time he spent in Crete. For him to send Titus to a country or territory that other people had evangelized and thus correct their abuses and straighten out their laxities would appear to contradict the policy he himself asserts, "in order that I may not build on another's foundation" (Rom 15:20).

The letter delineates some ungracious characteristics of the people in Crete: "insubordinate, addicted to empty speeches, and deceived in mind, especially those from the circumcision" who were "subverting households and teaching for shameful profit things they should not" (Titus 1:10-12). Such description suggests that the writer had definite knowledge of the people in the churches of this island, either from letters about them or from his own experience. He seems to be telling what he had seen. Usually indictments based on communications would refer to the source of information. If the description implies personal contact with these churches, it must have extended over some time so that he could become aware of their tendencies and qualities. The suggestion of a rapid tour while Paul's ship waited to leave Fair Havens does not allow this time.

Since nothing definite is known about what happened to Paul in Rome,

---

[51] 3:14f. Cf. Kelly, *The Pastoral Epistles*, 9-10.

one cannot say, on the other hand, that he did not ultimately get released, nor that he did not return to the East. Such possibilities are complicated by the fact that Clement of Rome, writing at the close of the first century, says that Paul, after giving his testimony at "the limits of the West," departed this life and went to "the holy place" (I Clement 5:7). This passage has been universally understood to mean that Paul was in Rome, though it is possible that "the limits of the West" might refer to the Pillars of Hercules at the Strait of Gibraltar.[52] No hint is given in this reference to a release of Paul nor to a trip back to the East. If Clement's statement affirms that Paul was killed in Rome, the only way a trip to the East after his imprisonment could be provided for would be to assume that he was released after a first imprisonment, then left for the East, and was arrested again and imprisoned a second time in Rome, at the close of which imprisonment he was killed. This supposition, though possible, is against probabilities; for there is no hint in first-century literature that Paul was imprisoned in Rome a second time.

One detail in this letter appears out of character for Paul, that is, the famous Cretan paradox. Paul quotes a certain prophet of theirs who said, "Cretans are always liars, evil beasts, idle gluttons." Paul says, "This testimony is true" (Titus 1:12-13). It is hardly within the province of a mind of ordinary generosity to indict a whole nation of people as always liars, beasts, and gluttons. In view of the record of Paul's delicate sensitivity toward the feelings of others and his unfailing courtesy in showing appreciation of their good qualities first and foremost, it is hard to think he was so completely annoyed with any one group of ancient Christians as to categorize them all with such abusive language. This would be all the more difficult if he described them merely on the basis of letters he had received.[53] Since Paul was very much opposed to passing condemnatory judgments and was trying to unite humanity by the elimination of ethnic, national, and linguistic distinctions, it is hard to believe that he would have put his apostolic imprimatur on this Cretan statement. While nobody can say that Paul could not have, in a fit of impatience or even with a certain wry humor, approved such a quotation as a pardonable exaggeration, it is still not the kind of language he employed elsewhere[54]; and one may hesitate to assign it to Paul here. For these and other reasons, an overwhelming majority of commentators admit doubts about Paul's composition of Titus, at least in all its parts.[55] We therefore need not attach much cred-

---

[52] Cf. Richardson's note in *The Early Christian Fathers*, 46, n. 28.

[53] This quotation of the so-called prophet has been used in logic books down through the ages as an example of a trick syllogism. "All Cretans are always liars"— the author of this was a Cretan; therefore he was a liar, for he said all Cretans are liars. So the argument goes *ad infinitum*.

[54] With the possible exception of Gal 5:12.

[55] Cf. R. H. Fuller, *A Critical Introduction to the New Testament* (London, 1966), 133-144.

ibility to the proposition that Paul conducted a ministry in Crete, either before or after his imprisonment. Apart from mention of Crete and its peoples the letter gives little information about Paul's life or any of the people who were with him. It makes no mention of an imprisonment or release. The location of the writer seems to be Nicopolis, a city in Thrace. The letter states that Paul is sending Artemas or Tychicus to see Titus. Tychicus has already been introduced in Ephesians and Colossians, but Artemas is unknown elsewhere. The author asks Titus to send on Zenas the lawyer, about whom we have no further information, and Apollos, who may be the famous Apollos of the book of Acts and I Corinthians. Since the two unknowns, Artemas and Zenas are very common names, they give no basis for argument about the genuineness of the information. Conclusions are uncertain. Paul may have made a trip to the East after the Roman imprisonment; he may have established churches on Crete; he may have appointed Titus as a subordinate to look after the churches following his own departure. Perhaps the strongest point in favor of some authenticity is the very difficulty of connecting the details with other information accepted about Paul: it would seem strange if spurious items were left so cryptic. No decision supplies the data for a reliable reconstruction of the story.

PAUL'S LIFE AS DESCRIBED IN THE ACTS OF THE APOSTLES

In the last fifty years a great shift of opinion with reference to the book of Acts leads most present-day interpreters to assign relatively little historical value to many parts of it. Bornkamm, in a recent book on Paul, evaluates the book of Acts as possessing little historical value and believes we should rely almost exclusively on the epistles for information about Paul's life. Only with great reserve should information be accepted from Acts.[56] Perhaps less total in his dissatisfaction of it as a historic source, but still ruthless in rejecting large segments, is Haenchen, a representative form critic who has written the outstanding modern commentary on Acts.[57] Like the majority of form critics, Haenchen values Luke as a creative theologian, but not as a historian.[58]

[56] Bornkamm, *Paul,* xv-xxi.
[57] Haenchen, *Acts.* The fourteenth German edition, from which the English edition was prepared, is one of the venerable Meyer commentaries.
[58] Haenchen subjects every passage in the book to a rigorous critical analysis, making use of form-critical criteria, the predilections of the author, detailed comparisons with the Pauline material, and exhaustive coverage of information to be derived from ancient non-scriptural sources and archaeology. His book is a masterpiece of comprehensive scholarship written in remarkably clear style, characterized by sly humor.

Since such writers spatter their books with jibes against old-time theologians eager to demonstrate that faith is supported both by reason and the historical accuracy of the original sources and thus were so biased that they could not face the obvious inaccuracies and non-historical features in books like Acts and the Gospels, we may not be altogether unfair in pointing out that the present-day theological attitude seems almost relieved to find that accounts previously thought to be historical are really not so and thus the faith is cleansed of all contamination with extraneous historical concerns. We seem to face a new bias today which takes it as a theological advantage to discover that canonical sources are riddled with unhistoric items. The more the events recounted are proved to be unhistorical, the more reliable is the faith which is exhibited by the author in presenting these stories. Faith is actually aided by destroying its human supports.

Surely, however, one should attempt to avoid either kind of bias. Certainly theological dogmatism must not inhibit the kind of free examination that checks the statements of sources against any information available from any quarter. If a story, even in the most sacred book, contradicts another story in the same book or is not in accord with reliable information to be gained elsewhere, no doctrinal position can justify overlooking these difficulties; nor does it justify misinterpreting passages in order to fit them in with other passages or information. On the other hand, it appears equally true that a theological position which, for various reasons, connects faith in God with some sort of transcendental event of revelation

---

The result of the analysis is to elevate the reputation of Luke as a creative theologian at the expense of his historical accuracy. One almost gains the impression that Haenchen feels that the kind of theological competence exhibited by the author of Acts need not be hampered by scrupulosity about historical truth. He shows repeatedly that Luke shades his account of the events to prove some theological position. The question seems never to be raised whether a theological position proved by altering the story or by creating stories out of nothing is worth anything: Haenchen, like many other representatives of the present-day form-critical school appears to feel it is woodenheadedness to be concerned about historical accuracy in connection with a book like Acts. Instead we should try to understand the theological truth to which the book witnesses and to analyze the Christian message conveyed by this truth. A sophisticated theologian does not expect ancient theologians to manifest critical historical rigor. Equally he does not value any less their theological convictions. One questions such a sharp separation between the value of a theology and the accuracy of the history upon which the ancient theologian thought he was basing his theology. If, as has been widely asserted even by the form-critical school, it is true that Christianity is a historical religion, professing faith in God's revelation in history over against myth or fiction, one wonders how the advocates of this position can be so debonair in their unconcern for the historical reliability of most of the ancient Christian sources. Of course, many modern theologians have followed Kierkegaard in the denial that any historical study could support a conviction of faith. Conversely, faith which rests upon any sort of support, either of reason or history, is not faith but some sort of intellectual conclusion. Therefore many advocates of this modern position seem to feel that their Christian convictions are strengthened by the demonstration that they are independent of rational proof or historic actuality.

through "the Word" should not cause a student to find contradictions where they really do not exist, nor should it justify assuming that a writer who has theological beliefs is, in the nature of the case, bound to shade, omit, or distort the events which he is describing. It may be true that, in some instances, he does this; but this should not be assumed in advance. When there are discrepancies between one writing and another, such as between the book of Acts and the letters of Paul, we at least ought to leave open the possibility that in some cases what appears like contradiction could be cleared up if we had more information from other sources. In Haenchen's book and in others as well, if Acts and Paul differ in recording what seems to be the same event, the difference is taken as a contradiction when it may very well be that both descriptions are true.[59]

Haenchen makes very vigorous assertions to the effect that Paul's doctrine about his own apostleship was radically different from that exhibited in the book of Acts—that, in fact, Acts regards the apostles as consisting of the Twelve, while Paul, the hero of two-thirds of the book, is not an apostle. The fact that Paul and Barnabas are called apostles, even *"the apostles"* in Acts 14:4 and 14, is discounted as having no significance with reference to Luke's conception of the Twelve as the genuine apostles.[60] Why we should say that these passages have no significance is hard to understand since at least once they show that Luke calls Barnabas and Paul apostles, and his failure to do so elsewhere may have been due to stylistic considerations. Paul, while affirming that he is an apostle in the introduction to most of his epistles, and while insisting upon his apostleship in I and II Corinthians and Galatians where he has been attacked, makes little of the fact that he is an apostle in his other letters. Likewise Paul clearly makes a distinction between himself and the Twelve in I Cor 15:5-9: Jesus "appeared to Cephas, then to the Twelve. . . . next to all the apostles. And last of all, as if to the one untimely born, he appeared also to me. For I am the least of the apostles, who am not fit to be called an apostle. . . ." Here Paul acknowledges the existence of a group called "the Twelve" and another large group called "the apostles" to which latter group he himself belongs, and he even acknowledges that his previous life casts legitimate doubts on whether he is strictly an apostle. Luke in Acts never casts any doubt on the apostleship of Paul. He never hints that he was in any way unworthy, and he revealed Paul as exercising in his life's work all the prerogatives and powers that a strict apostle belonging to the Twelve ever exhibited. When Haenchen argues strenuously that Luke could not have been a companion of Paul and could not have known directly Paul's doctrine of his own place in the church since Luke does not include Paul in the twelve apostles, he overstates the difference between

---

[59] Bornkamm's remarks about Luke as historian are apropos.
[60] Haenchen, *Acts,* ad loc., also pp. 122-125, 157-165, 411, n. 2.

Acts and Paul to an excessive degree. A careful study of Paul's letters indicates the same kind of respect for the Twelve that Luke exhibits.

Haenchen likewise sees a profound difference between Paul's doctrine of justification by faith and the impossibility of justification by works as gleaned from his epistles and the description of that doctrine found in Peter's speech at the Jerusalem Council and in Paul's speech in Antioch of Pisidia.[61] The difference, however, is hard to discover even after Haenchen's explanation of it. Theologians up through the nineteenth century, moreover, were not aware of such contradictory differences in these two statements, even those sensitive to the most finely drawn distinctions.

The author of Acts is discovered to be a convinced Christian. He endeavors to present the original Christian leaders in as favorable light as possible and to show that they were violating no imperial law, were not irresponsible leaders of a worthless rabble, but were serious missionaries of a divinely revealed religion. This does not in and of itself prove that he will misconceive or misrepresent every incident he describes. If the Christian religion is divinely revealed, it may very well be true that the kind of picture given of the first leaders in Acts is a faithful representation of what they did and said, even though one may agree that, like all historical books, it may contain inaccuracies. The question should at least be left open whether the statements as they stand bear a fair interpretation which can be reconciled with information obtained elsewhere.

Haenchen is aware that some details in Acts formerly deemed inaccurate have been vindicated by more recent discoveries. A considerable amount of evidence, for example, has turned up regarding Sergius Paulus, proconsul of Cyprus.[62] Similarly, corroborative evidence is now available for Gallio's proconsulate in Corinth as indicated by Acts.[63] There also is reason to believe that Acts describes accurately the official titles of the government personnel of the cities where Paul had contact with them, such as the Asiarchs in Ephesus, the *Stratēgoi* or Generals in Philippi, and the Politarchs in Thessalonica.[64] Luke seemed to be concerned with accuracy about official titles at least. If he was writing to a learned Roman, he would feel impelled to be precise in his allusions to politicians and statesmen. Would he not also desire to stick close to the truth in describing the things which Paul did in the various cities whose officials are so carefully labeled? There are, to be sure, some discrepancies between the statements in Acts and those of Paul which cannot now be cleared up. For example, according to Acts 9:23f the Jews laid an ambush against Paul at Damascus and were watching the gate night and day to kill him. Paul,

[61] Ibid., 415-418, 462-472.
[62] Ibid., 64. Cf. Ogg, *Chronology*, 60-65.
[63] Haenchen, *Acts*, 66-67. Cf. *Beginnings*, V, 460-464.
[64] Cf. Haenchen, *Acts*, 574, n. 1, 496, 507f.

however, states in II Cor 11:32-33, "In Damascus the ethnarch of Aretas the king was guarding the city of the Damascenes in order to arrest me, and I was let down in a basket by a window through the wall and escaped his hands." This may be a clear contradiction, and perhaps Luke made a mistake in assigning the responsibility to the Jews. One could say that this is due to a tendency of Luke to clear government officials as far as possible from any complicity in the attacks and plots against Paul and also to lay most if not all the blame on the Jews.[65] Nevertheless, it should be remembered that the term "ethnarch" means "the head of a tribal or national group"[66]; and we may infer that Paul is here indicating the head of the Jewish group of Damascus, who was appointed by Aretas. If this is possible, both accounts were different and yet can be literally true. Paul mentions the ethnic leader, while Acts refers to the people he used in guarding the city. Since there were leaders of different nationalities in various provinces, there is no overwhelming reason to reject Luke's account offhand as contradicting Paul. And so also in several other places.

Johannes Munck, on the whole, has considerably more respect for Acts as a historical source than has Haenchen; but he also thinks that it is unreliable as our primary source of information about Paul.[67] He accepts the position which we have likewise accepted methodologically, that information about Paul should be garnered from his epistles, treating them as the original sources of information and Acts as a secondary source. In his study of the epistles[68] Munck finds a particular view which Paul had of his ministry and a conception which he had of the enemies in the localities of Galatia and Corinth. In sum, Paul conceives himself as appointed by God to be the apostle to the gentiles, to win them over and thereby stir up the Jews to jealousy in order that the Jews would accept the Christian religion also. His purpose was ultimately directed to the salvation of the Jews. At the same time, Munck rejects definitely the idea that so-called Judaizers in Galatia represented any church group in Judaea or that they agreed with the position of the apostles in Jerusalem. Thus Paul's account of the meeting with the apostles in Jerusalem which indicates no doctrinal difference between them whatsoever is to be accepted, and it is rightly to be concluded that nobody in the official circles in Jerusalem had any opposition to what Paul was doing among the gentiles, and certainly no one felt that the gentiles should be circumcised. Acts indicates, even though with some reserve, that there were Judaizers in Judaea, that there was tension be-

---

[65] As in "tendency-criticism" of years past; e.g. Weiss, noted by Haenchen, *Acts*, 23-24.

[66] This etymology is readily confirmed in Liddell and Scott's *Lexicon*. AGB, 217a, notes different meanings but assigns "governor" for this passage.

[67] Munck, AB, LXVI-LXX and *passim*.

[68] Munck, *Paul and the Salvation of Mankind*.

tween Paul and the Jerusalem authorities to some degree even from the beginning, and that a circumcision party in Judaea that included nearly all the members of the church at Jerusalem was very much disturbed by Paul's activities (Acts 21:20-21) though the passage exempts James and the elders from hostility to Paul. According to Munck, Acts is wrong about this tension.[69]

Munck argues that Luke, or the tradition as he received it, varies from the original event of the apostolic council and the last visit of Paul to Jerusalem so as to make the accounts conform to conditions as they were experienced in the latter part of the first century. According to present-day understanding of the circumstances at the end of the first century, Jewish Christians had been separated from gentile Christians largely because of the effects of the Jewish War. This meant that the Jewish Christians became encysted within a hard shell of Judaism by requiring their members to practice Jewish law, including circumcision. Luke retrojected the contemporary situation into the earler decades of Paul's career. Thus he concluded that there was in the church in Jerusalem and Judaea a considerable party that demanded circumcision of gentiles. Munck had convinced himself by his interpretation of the epistle to the Galatians that the church people who were demanding circumcision of the gentiles were not Jewish Christians at all, but were gentile believers who had been impressed by Paul's own preaching, and with the fact that Christianity was the proper product of the divinely authorized revelation to the Jews described in the Old Testament. This led the new converts to study the Old Testament with great zeal. In it they found that the people of God were to keep circumcision as a sign for all eternity. And they inferred from its teaching about the proselytes that all those who were to be included among the people of God must accept the provisions laid down in the Old Testament for proselytes. Also Paul himself had insisted that the Jews were the people who had received the oracles, and who belonged to the native stock of the tree, whereas the gentiles were branches grafted on. So these zealous new believers felt that they should go beyond the requirements of Paul and accept the yoke of circumcision.

Munck thinks that Luke misunderstood the real source of Judaistic agitation in the Pauline churches and transferred it to Judaea as he made the believing Pharisees in Jerusalem the first agitators for imposing circumcision on the gentiles. There really was no great difference between Paul and the Jewish Christians in Jerusalem and Judaea. Basically two arguments are used by Munck to sustain his position. First, in Gal 6:13 the "present" participle "those who are being circumcised" has to mean that the people who are agitating for this requirement are people who are being

---

[69] Cf. the excursus in Munck, AB, COMMENT on Acts 15:35-41.

circumcised themselves and thus are gentiles.[70] Consequently, there is no need of postulating outsiders coming from Judaea into Galatia and insisting that the gentiles had to be circumcised in order to be good Christians. It rather means that some of the gentile Christians convinced themselves that they should come under the Jewish sign of the covenant. This interpretation is very ingenious and is worth consideration. It is possible, however, to understand the participle to mean *those who are circumcised,* thus indicating a state rather than a continuing or repeated act. In addition, Munck has to set aside the passages in Acts which show that a group existed in Judaea which contended that circumcision was necessary for Christians. But it is somewhat difficult to believe that Luke was either so careless or ill-informed as to make this mistake.

The other basis for Munck's position is furnished by his discovery that Acts, in its present form, gives us an impossible picture of James and the Jerusalem church in ch. 21. According to Acts when Paul arrived at Jerusalem, he was received gladly by the brothers and was invited to report about what he had done among the gentiles with the aid of God. Then James and the elders who were hearing this report said, "You see, brother, how many myriads of believers there are among the Judaeans; and all are zealots for the law. They have been informed that you are teaching all the Jews among the gentiles to desert Moses and not to circumcise their children or to observe the customs" (21:20*f*). Munck thinks that the position of James and the elders is portrayed as unworthy of true Christian leaders; for while they themselves accepted Paul's position, they were afraid of the attitudes of the main body of believers who were bound by rigorous Jewish ideas and who persisted in accepting false reports about Paul. James and the elders were either unable or afraid to correct the membership of the churches, and they advised Paul to make a demonstration of his loyalty to Judaism by sponsoring a ceremony of purification for four returning pilgrims. In this manner he could prove by action that he was not teaching Jews to depart from Moses. But why could James and his elders themselves not announce authoritatively to their members that Paul's Christian program was no different from their own and that the information they had accepted was false? In view of this, Munck suggests that the text be altered by striking out the phrase *who have believed* from vs. 20, thus making the verse read "You see, brother, how many tens of thousands . . . among the Jews . . . are all devoted to the Law." Thus the enemies of Paul in Jerusalem would be unbelieving Jews rather than Jewish Christians. Again, Munck's reasoning is fairly sharp; but he resorts to a drastic emendation of the text without any manuscript evidence to support it.[71] Those who

---

[70] Munck, *Paul and the Salvation of Mankind,* 87-89.

[71] Munck, AB, 211. The Byzantine reading is "of Judaeans"; but if the Alexandrian reading is accepted, the genitive of the altered form suggests the genitives "of [those who] have believed" are firmly part of the text.

have had modern experience with the laity of the churches do not find it hard to believe that a gap can stretch between leaders and membership, especially in case of questions that involve accepting people of other races and nationalities on an absolutely equal basis.

In the first century the Jews felt obligated by the law to maintain ritualistic purity and to restrict relations with the gentiles to an absolute minimum. Those who accepted Jesus as the Messiah and who were convinced that he had come primarily to save his people Israel had no tendency to relax the requirements of Judaism. Since it took a heavenly vision to convince Peter that he should receive a gentile into the church, it is not hard to believe that many of the Jewish Christians, even after Peter's experience, felt bound by their old religious habits. (In our day we have observed that when elements of denominational leadership endeavor to move in an ecumenical direction, conservatives still insist on retaining their old ways.) It is easy to suppose that James should have been able to make a declaration about Paul and his work that would pacify the conservative elements in Judaea. We may argue that he had such authority that all would accept what he said, but there is no reason to suppose that first-century Christians were free from the human tendency to resist the leaders who tried to impel them to accept the full logic of Christianity. On Munck's own theory, some new converts in Galatia who had received Paul "as an angel of God, as Jesus Christ"[72] nevertheless decided from their own reading of the Old Testament that they had to accept circumcision despite Paul's teaching. If new converts, whose knowledge of Christianity was obtained solely from their great apostle, could revolt against his fundamental doctrine, why should we suppose that Jewish Christians could not have resisted urgings of James with reference to Paul, especially when they were merely retaining habits and beliefs inherited from past generations and apparently unchallenged by Jesus Christ himself? It seems more logical to suppose that Acts has good reason to indicate that a fairly considerable party in the church in Judaea believed that gentiles should accept the requirements for Jewish proselytes when they entered the church. It would require a sociological miracle taxing the resources even of the Holy Spirit to produce a community that unanimously agreed with its leaders in adopting an entirely new idea and in accepting new relationships with gentiles when this not only went against the grain of their own feelings but aroused tremendous hostility from their non-Christian Jewish compatriots.

Munck seems also to reject obvious implications of some statements made by Paul. In Gal 2:11-13 Paul refers to the fact that "some came from James" to Antioch and frightened Peter and Barnabas into with-

[72] Gal 4:14.

drawing from table fellowship with the gentiles. This certainly shows that followers of James, if not James himself, were anxious about free acceptance of gentile Christians even after James, Peter, and John had accepted Paul as the true missionary to the gentiles. This surely supports the conclusion that in Jerusalem there were some Christians who felt unhappy about Paul's free and easy acceptance of new gentiles into full brotherhood. Likewise II Cor 11:22 indicates that opponents of Paul in Corinth were "Hebrews" belonging to the seed of Abraham and were Israelites and servants of Christ. This set of characteristics could properly pertain only to Jewish Christians.[73] The same people seem to have presented themselves as apostles since Paul calls them "false apostles and deceitful workers having changed their external form into apostles of Christ" (11:13). These statements do not say in precise words that these people were from Judaea, but they imply beyond possibility of doubt that they were Jewish Christians. We cannot assign as high a degree of probability to the implication that they were from the apostles in Jerusalem, but Paul's statement about their being false apostles appearing in the form of apostles of Christ would certainly suggest that some basis existed to make this claim credible to the people in the church at Corinth. So we conclude that opponents of Paul in Corinth were Jewish Christians who claimed the authority of the apostles for their position and who therefore most likely had come from Palestine. This does not in any way mean that Paul's statement implicates the apostles in the heresy of these emissaries any more than we conclude that James himself was in sympathy with "the people from James" who intimidated Peter.

All of this indicates that in describing the life and doctrine of Paul we may supplement information derived from his letters by information derived from Acts. Admittedly some features of the story in Acts present insuperable difficulties; it is impossible to take all parts of the book exactly as they stand. It seems, however, that with a minimum of accommodation the account in Acts furnishes reliable sources for our study.

In its main outline the book of Acts portrays the earliest disciples as a group of Christians led by the twelve Galileans, who remained in Jerusalem after the resurrection of Christ and there witnessed the ascension and received the Holy Spirit. They were pious Jews going to pray at the temple daily and observing all the dietary laws and purificatory rites that were binding on other Jews. They were proclaiming the gospel to Jews and urging that they accept the salvation which was being offered to Israel. As a result of their preaching (aided, perhaps, by other agents) a vigorous church flourished in Jerusalem. Two groups were apparently separating out in this church, one called the Hellenists and the other the He-

---

[73] Schmithals, *Gnosticism in Corinth*, 115, 127, identifies them as Jewish Gnostics who only loosely qualify as Christians.

brews (Acts 6:1). Unfortunately, Luke does not inform us about any beliefs or practices which distinguish these groups except that in the daily distribution of food the Hellenists claimed that their widows were being overlooked.[74] It is hard to understand how this could happen if these widows were mingling together in one common assembly. But if they were in separate conventicles, just as there were separate synagogues for the people from Cyrene, Alexandria, Cilicia, and Asia (5:9), it is conceivable that the food distributors neglected to go around to where these widows were meeting. According to Acts the apostles decided to solve the problem by having men appointed to look after the distribution. At their suggestion seven men were chosen who were "full of spirit and wisdom" (6:3) and all of whom had Greek names. The story as it stands displays the paradox that the men who were chosen to look after the distribution of the food immediately embarked on theological disputes, preaching, and performance of miracles among the people in Jerusalem (6:8,9). In turn they were strongly opposed by the people from the above-mentioned synagogues. The fact that seven men existed in the church, all with Greek names, and that two of them, at least—Stephen and Philip—were engaged in disputation and evangelism suggests that they were more than stewards of food and drink. When they were resisted by Jews from these special synagogues composed of people from prominent cities of the Mediterranean, it does not require too much imagination to conclude that Stephen and his group were carrying on Christian propaganda among Jews from the provinces of the empire who had returned to Jerusalem.

The resisters stirred up such an agitation that charges were brought against Stephen, before the elders and scribes of the Jewish people as a whole. The opponents of Stephen accused him of saying that Jesus would destroy "this place" (probably the temple) and would change the customs which Moses delivered to them (6:13-14). In his long defense (7:2-53) Stephen shows that the people of Israel from time to time had repelled the men sent to them by God and had proceeded without authorization from God to set up a temple in Jerusalem, which was in reality more in the succession of the worshipers of the golden calf in the wilderness than of devotees of the tent of testimony, which Moses had constructed in the desert. Worship in the temple overlooks the fact that God "does not dwell in handmade buildings," and an insistence upon the temple with its cognate practices is a continuation of stubborn opposition to the Holy Spirit which the Israelites had been in the habit of extending to God. While Munck argues that there is nothing unique about the position of Stephen in this speech and that the charges made against him as

---

[74] For an entirely different approach to this material, cf. Appendices v and vi in Munck, AB. We reject Mann's declaration (on p. 301) that the interpretation there is "beyond question," but this is not the place to take up the problem as it does not materially affect the analysis offered here.

well as the statements he made could have been attributed to Jesus,[75] it remains an undeniable fact that such statements were never made by the spokesman of the Twelve, according to Acts, and neither is anything like this found in the epistles of Paul. Since a persecution arose against the followers of Stephen after Stephen himself was stoned, and since the twelve apostles were not attacked by the persecution, it seems indubitable that Stephen and the Seven headed a movement in the church which was different in emphasis from that of the twelve apostles and was recognized as different by the authorities. Since the temple was the center of gravity for Jewish patriotism, we may suppose that the party of the Seven in attacking it were moving in the direction of a more universalistic type of Christianity than that so far advocated by the Twelve. This impression is fortified by the stories that Philip evangelized Samaria, that he converted an Ethiopian eunuch, and that those who were scattered by the persecution directed against Stephen were preaching outside of Jerusalem, at first only to Jews, but in time some of them from Cyprus and Cyrene also to Greeks. In fact Barnabas was sent from Jerusalem to Antioch where these people had been preaching to the Greeks in order to investigate and to see what had happened. Because he was a good man, he delighted in what he found and exhorted all of them to remain faithful to the Lord.[76]

Since Paul (who was at that time known as Saul) continued to persecute the Christians following the inquisition against Stephen, it may be inferred that he was acquainted with the anti-temple section of the church and directed his opposition to it. The book of Acts has a tendency to identify those who were persecuted as "the church." Yet it acknowledges that at first the Twelve were not persecuted (8:1). The tolerance must have embraced not only the Twelve but those who belonged to their group. It is contrary to the usual practice of persecution to attack members of a group and exempt the leaders. Conversely, if the leaders are left untouched, the followers are ignored also.

According to Acts 9:1-2, Saul secured letters to some authorities in Damascus so that he might arrest and harass the Christians there. A considerable amount of skepticism has been directed to the statement that letters from the Jerusalem high priests would give him authority to apprehend the Christians in Damascus and bring them back to Jerusalem. But often in ancient times arrangements were made between the Roman authorities and different ethnic groups, especially the Jews, according to which the Romans would acknowledge the authority of the high priests over the Jews in other provinces. The role of the ethnarch of Aretas is

[75] Munck, AB, 59, 148-154.
[76] This datum is in ch. 8 and 11:19-24. It is important for the possible influence upon Paul's thinking.

questionable. There is no sure evidence that Roman authority was not in control. So the statement of the book that Paul went to arrest Jewish Christians in Damascus is not unlikely.[77]

On the trip to Damascus, Saul heard the words which changed the course of his whole life. Up until this time, Luke's narrative has identified Saul as a young man at whose feet the witnesses, presumably against Stephen, have laid Stephen's garments; and has Saul approving of Stephen's death (7:58, 8:1). After this, Saul was maltreating the church, going from house to house and dragging out men and women to deliver them into jail (8:3). These statements tell us little except that he was a person of fierce convictions with enough authority to enforce his convictions against Christian victims. Much later, in an address to a crowd at Jerusalem after his apprehension, Paul states that he was born in Tarsus, educated in Jerusalem at the feet of Gamaliel, and had been such a zealot for the law as to persecute "this way" unto death (22:3-5).

The vision which he received outside Damascus took the form of an intense light which was accompanied by a voice that said "Saul, Saul, why do you persecute me?" To his astounded question, "Who are you, Lord?" the answer came, "I am Jesus whom you are persecuting." Saul was further instructed to get up and go into the city, so that he might be informed what he would have to do in the future (9:3-6). Apparently it was the light which struck him blind, for he remained three days without being able to see. It is impossible to determine the physical or metaphysical nature of this event. What was the nature of the light? Did the voice which he heard actually produce sounds audible to the physical ear? Apparently, the tradition was that the people with him "heard the voice" (or "sound"), which would mean it produced audible sounds. But they "saw no one," which implies that whatever Saul saw was private. The verb "to hear" may, of course, be followed by either the genitive or accusative case. In vs. 4 the accusative *phōnēn* occurs; in vs. 7 the genitive *phōnēs*. This precise differentiation seems to convey the idea that Paul heard an intelligible communication while the people perceived a sound without understanding what it said. Paul received the revelation that the "speaker" was Jesus, whom he was persecuting; but his fellow travelers heard only a strange sound. While it is beyond our range of understanding to explain what kind of experience this actually was, we do know that it changed Saul from a persecutor of Christians to a most amazing and impressive preacher and missionary of Christ.

In Damascus Saul was met by a Christian disciple named Ananias. The Lord had revealed to Ananias that Saul had received instructions in a

---

[77] Munck, AB, ad loc., is not inclined to question the high-priestly authority, but he has strong reservation about Nabataean influence in Damascus. See Lake's note in *Beginnings*, V, 193-194.

dream to allow a man named Ananias to lay hands on him so that he could be healed. Despite the protests of Ananias against visiting this famous persecutor of the church, the Lord insisted that he go to meet the man who would be a missionary to "the gentiles and kings and children of Israel." Ananias obeyed the command. He went and informed Saul that the Lord had sent him, the same Jesus who had appeared to Saul on the road, so that he might "recover [his] sight and be filled with the Holy Spirit. Immediately he recovered his sight and was baptized." Saul forthwith was associated with the Christians in Damascus among whom he proclaimed emphatically that Jesus was "the son of God," and the hearers were astonished at the fact that this man who had been a devastator of the Christians in Jerusalem and who had come to Damascus to arrest Christians was now forcefully preaching Jesus as the Messiah. After "some days," the Jews plotted to kill him; but when this plot became known to Paul,[78] he managed to escape. Although the gates were being watched night and day by his enemies, the disciples were able to let him down "in a basket through the wall." He then went to Jerusalem and made attempts to unite with the disciples there, but all were afraid of him until Barnabas sponsored him before the apostles and reported to them what had happened at Damascus. For some time Paul was in Jerusalem, "going in and going out," boldly speaking "in the name of the Lord" and disputing with "the Hellenists." These latter tried to kill him, but the brothers led him down to Caesarea and sent him from there to Tarsus (9:10-30).

A comparison of this account with Paul's reminiscences in Galatians produces such obvious discrepancies that they raise questions about the trustworthiness of Acts. Indeed, the Galatians account may almost be read as a refutation in advance of the Acts interpretation. In Galatians, Paul says that he did not receive his gospel "from men," nor did he obtain it "by means of men" but "by revelation." God indeed "had appointed [him] from [his] mother's womb" as evangelist among the gentiles. Immediately, he "consulted with no flesh and blood" and neither did he "go up to Jerusalem . . . but went away into Arabia and then returned to Damascus." Only "after three years" did he go up to Jerusalem "to confer with Cephas," and there he saw "no other apostle except James the brother of the Lord." While he was in Jerusalem he was utterly "unknown by face to the churches of Judaea." After fifteen days he went "into the regions of Syria and Cilicia" (Gal 1:11-22).

According to Acts, Ananias is the human agent through whom Paul receives his initial instructions in Damascus. It was Ananias who first learns

---

[78] For the sake of consistency, the name Paul is used throughout this introduction. For a summary of data regarding the change of the name from "Saul" to "Paul" at Acts 13:9, see *Beginnings*, IV, 145-146; Munck, AB, 119.

that Paul is to be a missionary to the gentiles. When he left Damascus, he went to Jerusalem. The escape "in a basket through the wall" is not recorded in Galatians; but, as already noted, it is alluded to in II Cor 11:32. In Acts Paul makes overtures to "the apostles"; and since this passage excludes Barnabas, the reference must be to the Twelve. After asserting the restriction of his contacts in Galatians, Paul adds emphatically, "God knows that I am not lying" (1:20). Neither Arabia nor Aretas are mentioned in the Acts account. Since Tarsus is the capital city of Cilicia, the final movement in this series in Acts and Galatians probably is not in contradiction.

Perhaps some of the inconsistencies of these records could be alleviated if we had more detailed information, particularly in the Pauline letters. In any case, such specific difficulties ought not to be taken as evidence against the general reliability of the documents.[79] Careful attention to possibilities can soften some of the contradictions. For example, the "some days" of Acts and the "three years" of Galatians may be somewhat reconciled by remembering that three years according to Jewish reckoning could be a period less than two years in duration since fractions of years were counted as full years. This would still be an awkward accommodation, but it does suggest caution in assessing difficulties. Paul's mention of the sojourn in Arabia is sketchy at best, and Luke either ignores it or does not know of it.

Luke knew that in Jerusalem Barnabas was well enough acquainted with Paul to introduce him to the apostles, but he does not state that Paul preached to the Judaean churches. "The Hellenists," with whom he debated, undoubtedly were Jews who had been opposed to Stephen and with whom at that time Paul had been allied. "The brothers" helped him to escape a plot of these Hellenists by sending him to Tarsus of Cilicia. Nothing in the nature of the case prevents all this from happening in fifteen days. It would not take long for Paul's arguments to stimulate the same lethal hatred that had caused Stephen to be stoned to death. While Paul says that he saw none of the other apostles except Cephas and James the brother of the Lord, he did not say anything about Hellenistic Jews with whom he may have been disputing. Therefore the only contradiction that seems irreconcilable is Luke's mention that Barnabas introduced Paul "to the apostles." At this time, Barnabas was probably not regarded as an apostle; and the term was being used to refer to the Twelve, to which number Barnabas did not, of course, belong. Paul's statement does exclude the possibility that he was introduced to any of the Twelve except Cephas; but since he adds James, and since James was not one of the Twelve, the matter is indeed confusing. Perhaps Luke has used here an introduction that

[79] So argues Cadbury in *The Making of Luke-Acts,* 366.

occurred elsewhere[80] or that he conjectured from Barnabas' later association with Paul (Gal 2:1).

After Barnabas brought Paul from Tarsus to Antioch, they spent a whole year teaching a crowd of people in that city, according to the Acts account. At this time, a world-wide famine was predicted by some prophets who came to Antioch from Jerusalem. As a result of the prediction, the disciples in Antioch stored up supplies according to the prosperity of each one in order to be able to send aid to the brothers who were living in Judaea at the time. This relief was brought to Jerusalem by Barnabas and Paul (11:27-30). This little account teems with thorny perplexities. One, why should prophets come to Antioch from Jerusalem to predict a famine instead of predicting it at Jerusalem? Two, how would it happen that a famine which would wither up the food crops of "the entire world" allowed the inhabitants of Antioch to have food enough to feed themselves and Jerusalem also? Three, when was this famine? Luke says that it happens "in the reign of Claudius"; but while numerous local famines occurred in the time of Claudius, no world-wide famine is known. Four, what disposed the people of Antioch to select the inhabitants of Jerusalem for their special concern since there were plenty of other neighboring cities and villages which presumably would be starving? Five, what did they send to Jerusalem? Food supplies? If so, what kind of caravan would go through wasted territory with food all the way from Antioch to Jerusalem? Six, if Barnabas and Paul were by themselves, they could not have carried food supplies. If, on the contrary, they were bringing money, that would not do any good when there was a scarcity of food. It might be possible to explain some of these puzzles by ingenuity, but the solutions would probably be artificial and forced.[81] Here again, perhaps the best solution is to assume that Luke has displaced the story of the collection which Paul actually gathered later on for the saints in Jerusalem. Acts does not refer to the collection at all when Paul went to Jerusalem for the last time (except for an incidental reference to alms) even though several of Paul's letters say that this is the reason for his trip to Jerusalem.[82] True, Paul makes no mention of a famine as the occasion of his benevolence, but neither does he indicate that he was prompted to raise the money because of a prediction of Agabus. It must be that there were some local famines that existed in the Jerusalem church, perhaps because Jerusalem was often overcrowded on feast days. Antioch, perhaps, felt close ties with Jerusalem as

[80] Antioch? Cf. Acts 11:22-26.

[81] One such suggestion, perhaps plausible, has to do with Paul's remark in Gal 2:2 that he went to Jerusalem "according to a revelation." If this may be referred to the prophecy of Agabus (Acts 11:28, "signified through the spirit"), a different chronological connection is involved. The precise identification of the Jerusalem visits in Acts and Galatians, however, will probably never be achieved. Cf. further *infra*.

[82] Acts 20:16; Rom 15:25-26; I Cor 16:1-4; II Cor 9:1-5.

the mother church. Hence, Luke has probably combined a tradition of relief coming from Antioch to Jerusalem with Paul's great relief expedition which he organized at the end of his ministry.

When, according to Acts, Paul and Barnabas returned from this trip to Jerusalem, they brought with them John Mark (called the cousin of Barnabas in Col 4:10). The church at Antioch was at this time ornamented by five prophets and teachers: Barnabas; Simeon, "called Niger" (the Black Man); Lucius of Cyrene; Manaen, the steward of Herod; and Paul. These officials were instructed by the Holy Spirit to "separate" (or choose) Barnabas and Paul for a task to which the Spirit was summoning them. They obeyed and sent them out after "fasting, praying, and laying their hands on them" (Acts 13:1-3). Does this anecdote contradict Paul's statement that he was an apostle to the gentiles by the instrument of no man; or could he have been appointed as an apostle by God and yet, at the same time, have hands laid on him by the prophets and teachers? Perhaps the particular circumstances in which the Galatian letter was written are responsible for Paul's describing his call with emphases and details that are only superficially at variance with the Acts report. Luke proceeds to describe a tour of Paul and Barnabas, accompanied by Mark, through the island of Cyprus. On this island, Paul silenced and blinded a Jewish magician named Elymas, a feat which so impressed the proconsul of the island, Sergius Paulus, that he professed the faith (13:4-12).

From Cyprus the three heralds crossed the sea to Pamphilia and proceeded to Antioch of Pisidia. On the way from Perga, John Mark departed and returned to Jerusalem. At Antioch Barnabas and Paul preached first in the synagogue as a result of an invitation extended by the rulers of the synagogue. Paul summarized the main outline of the history of Israel from the time of David, which gave him the cue to proclaim the coming of the descendant of David, the Savior prophesied by Old Testament seers. He described the mission of John the Baptist, the crucifixion of Jesus by Pilate, his burial in the tomb, and his resurrection from the dead, as a result of which, his followers were testifying about him among the people of Israel. The resurrection of Jesus was the fulfillment of the statement in Ps 16:10, "You will not allow your Holy One to see corruption." Since David saw corruption, this Holy One must be Jesus Christ who is alive and did not decay in the grave. By him forgiveness of sins is being proclaimed, justification is offered which could not be obtained from the law of Moses, and the hearers may witness the amazing wonders of God (13:13-41).

The author of the book undoubtedly means to display this speech as a typical evangelistic utterance of Paul to the Jews. There are some elements in common with the speeches of Peter in the first part of Acts. Both Peter and Paul allude to the crucifixion of Jesus, the resurrection from the dead, and the fact that Jesus Christ did not see corruption and David did. They both appeal to the prophets, though Peter refers to Joel and Paul refers to Habakkuk. Both likewise quote the sixteenth Psalm, and both refer to the fact that the original followers of Jesus are his witnesses. But Paul introduces his sermon by summarizing the history of Israel up to David's time whereas Peter in his two major sermons only alludes to the patriarchs of Israel. Peter in his second sermon asserts that Jesus is the prophet like Moses; Paul affirms that Jesus is the promised descendant of David. As a matter of fact, the title "Son of David" is not used by any of the early preachers in Acts—by neither Peter nor Stephen nor Philip.[83] Thus Acts avoids the title which Jesus in the Synoptic Gospels also seems to reject (Mark 12:35-37a//Matt 22:41-45; Luke 20:41-44.) The failure of Acts to mention the descent of Christ from David in the early speeches[84] seems to be a significant mark of Luke's acquaintance with the primitive Christology according to which Jesus was the prophet like Moses, predicted by Deut 18:15,18. Since Paul in Rom 1:3 calls Jesus the "seed" of David, Luke is also accurate in having Paul employ this term in Acts 13:23.

As a result of the eloquence of Paul in demonstrating that the prophets foretold the coming of the Messiah and that Jesus fulfilled these prophecies, the legalists of Antioch were filled with theological hatred and aroused some of the pious women of standing as well as the civic leaders and succeeded in driving Paul and Barnabas out of their province (13:42-52). The missionaries then proceeded through Iconium to the cities of Lystra and Derbe in the province Lycaonia (14:1-7). At Lystra, Paul was able to heal a man born lame, a feat which so excited the mobs of the city that they were ready to offer sacrifices to Paul and Barnabas as visiting deities, Barnabas as Zeus and Paul as Hermes.[85] "The apostles" were so upset at being considered heathen gods by the people that they tore their garments, cried out that they were only men, spoke about the life-giving God, and with difficulty arrested the people's attempts to offer sacrifice (14:8-18).

Following this, Antioch and Iconium legalists so stirred up the crowd against Paul and Barnabas that Paul now was stoned almost to death. He recovered, however; and the pair retraced their steps, strengthening and further organizing the churches along the way, including the ordaining of

---

[83] Classic discussions of these traditions are in Dodd, *The Apostolic Preaching and Its Developments* and *According to the Scriptures*.

[84] In the Pentecost sermon, 2:29-36 offers an apparent exception; but the focus is on the resurrection as contrasted with the permanent burial of David. Cf. Munck, AB, ad loc.

[85] An interesting sidelight on Paul's missionary function—Hermes was the messenger of the Olympian pantheon.

"elders." They then reported to the sponsoring church in Antioch of Syria (14:19-28).

In the catalog of sufferings recorded in II Cor 11:23-29 Paul says that he "was stoned once."[86] This provides one corroborative detail for the Acts record. If Luke were intending to manufacture a travel tale based upon random remarks in the epistles, it is curious that he did not try to provide more details from this catalog. Similarly, the failure to mention an Ephesian imprisonment—otherwise attested by extracanonical tradition—is a similar witness to Luke's general intention to be accurate to the extent of his knowledge.

At Antioch a disturbance shook the church when some visitors from Judaea were teaching the brothers that they could not be saved unless they were circumcised. Paul and Barnabas became the local focus of the dispute, and they were appointed "to go up to the apostles and elders in Jerusalem" (15:1-2).[87] The initial reaction of the ensuing meeting was acceptance of the report from Paul and Barnabas regarding "what things God did with them" (15:4). When a group of Pharisee converts insisted that gentile converts must be circumcised and required to keep the law of Moses, Peter espoused the cause of the missionaries by reminding the council that God had directed him to preach to the gentile Cornelius and to baptize him without circumcision. Then after a summary statement by Barnabas and Paul, James as moderator summed up the matter and delivered the judgment that the only instruction to be given to the gentiles was that they must "abstain from things offered to idols, from fornication, from anything strangled, and from blood" (15:6-20). This means that the gentiles were to forgo any compromise with idolatry or prostitution and were to eat meat properly slaughtered.

James's judgment was accepted officially by the church assembly, which formulated the famous "apostolic decree." This was incorporated into a letter to be taken by Paul and Barnabas along with a man named Silas to all the churches that Paul and Barnabas had established. When the churches received the letter and heard about the decision of the council, they were delighted; and peace prevailed in the communities that had been agitated by this question (15:21-35).

---

86 Cf. p. 26 *supra*.

87 There is a substantial problem concerning the identity of the visitors and whether it was they who arranged the Jerusalem consultation. They had a Jewish orientation but were evidently from within the Christian community. The seriousness of the matter was evident in several ways. Was the Christian group a form of sectarian Judaism? If so, where were its uniqueness and its independence? If not, how did it stand toward the venerable traditions? Variant textual readings attempt to clarify the ambiguities, one group making the rather obvious identification with the group of Pharisee converts mentioned in 15:5—who then also had authority to require the Jerusalem consultation.

This picture, which has so strongly impressed the history of Christian ecumenical decision-making, is marred by a historical question. According to Paul,[88] Barnabas and he went up to Jerusalem in accordance with "a revelation." This excludes the idea that they went by command either of emissaries from Judaea or of the Antioch church. Furthermore, Paul's account leaves no room for a public session with the apostles, elders, and church members since the message was presented in private. James, Peter, and John expressed their approval of Paul and Barnabas' mission and agreed to a division of fields of endeavor. No condition or requirement was set except that they were to be mindful of the poor, and Paul affirms that he was already committed to that. There is no room for a report by Peter about his previous work with Cornelius, no decision arrived at by the whole church, no apostolic letter committed to Paul, no insistence that the churches he had founded should obey any requirements laid down by the Jerusalem authorities. Paul apparently has full freedom to present the gospel to the gentiles and to guide "his" churches.

Not only does Paul not mention any such requirements as abstaining from idol offerings, fornication, blood, or unclean food, but his letters, which deal with some issues of idol offerings and food, show no knowledge of any decision made by the Jerusalem council for the gentile communities. In fact, he expressly denies that the leaders in Jerusalem imposed any requirements on him or on his Christian followers.

There must have been at some time a decision in the early church like this early decree because there are in the book of Revelation denunciations of those who justified eating food offered to idols and who authorized or tolerated fornication (2:14,20). Undoubtedly somewhere in the Jewish Christian sector of the church an agreement had been reached to the effect that gentiles would be accepted without circumcision but would have to avoid all forms of relationship with idolatry and the consumption of blood.

Hurd argues that this decision was reached after Paul's second missionary journey, during which he had evangelized Greece.[89] Some of the difficulties in the church at Corinth are attributable to the fact that Paul had to confront them with a decree from Jerusalem requiring absolute abstention from idol offerings even though, when he first preached to them, he had been relatively free from rigid demands on this point. But this suggestion, attractive and brilliant as it is, suffers from the weakness that Paul in his letters to the church at Corinth makes no mention of any decision arrived at in Jerusalem and argues the ethical question solely in terms of the spirit of love.

A new solution to the difficulty may be suggested. The account in Acts,

[88] Gal 2:1-10; cf. the discussion *supra*, pp. 8-12.
[89] Hurd, *The Origin of I Corinthians*, 261.

in a strange and mysterious manner, describes the meeting as if its conclusions were based upon the recollections of Peter and his decision to admit gentiles into the church.[90] As a matter of fact, the discussion centers around Peter and Cornelius rather than around Paul and the gentiles of Asia Minor. Acts 11:18 declares that the Jerusalem church accepted with joy Peter's report of the baptizing of Cornelius and his family. It seems that this occasion would be the proper one for the Jerusalem church to arrive at the kind of decision that is portrayed in Acts 15. The account has simply been associated by Luke not with its original setting but with one where it does not belong. Peter and his associates were instructed by the church to impose upon the gentiles these requirements, which undoubtedly they did on the eastern Mediterranean coast. But when Paul was sent forth, he was not informed about any such requirements laid down upon Peter and others; for according to his own report he had very little to do with the authorities in Jerusalem and had received from them no instructions. In fact, when he set out upon his first great invasion of the gentile world, he was dispatched not by the Jerusalem apostles but by prophets in Antioch. So he knew nothing about any laws demanding abstinence from blood or food offered to idols. Thus when he did go up to Jerusalem after having had a great success among the gentiles, the pillars of the church laid no proscriptions upon him and either intentionally or by oversight failed to mention the specifications of their original decision. Perhaps they felt that the universal success of Paul's gospel and the manifestation of the Spirit demonstrated that nothing more was needed than his guidance.

Thus it must be concluded that Luke knew that the church in Jerusalem had arrived at a decision about gentiles and that this decision included the above-mentioned requirements. He also knew that there was a considerable amount of unhappiness with Paul after he went out among the gentiles. So he concluded that this unhappiness was over the question of circumcision and that the apostles gave Paul instructions which would satisfy some of the scruples of the strict Jews. So far as we know, nobody ever suggested to Paul that he apply these demands to any of his churches.

Later Paul's rebuke of Peter in Antioch raised an issue of table fellowship with gentiles which would include the question of ceremonial uncleanness and of eating the wrong kind of food. Perhaps what happened was that after the three "pillars" had given permission to Paul to preach the gospel in his own way, and after Peter had gone from Jerusalem, James and others decided it would be best to revive some of the older decisions and have Paul live by them. So they sent emissaries to Antioch to inform Paul that the gentiles would have to accept the conditions that

[90] This fact is duly noted by Haenchen (*Acts*, 457-464, where Dibelius's interpretation is also cited); but quite different conclusions are drawn from the one proposed here.

Peter had accepted for them. Otherwise, Jewish Christians could not eat at the same table with unclean gentile Christians. Paul resisted this with all his might, and he rebuked Peter for having deserted the fundamental principles of the gospel by submitting to this kind of pressure.

The issue between Paul and the opposition of Antioch had nothing to do with circumcision. The two parties separated because of their difference on the question of unrestricted social fellowship between gentiles and Jews in the church. Nobody questioned the truth of justification by faith. Everyone agreed that the gospel is meant for all the peoples of the earth. No one demanded that the gentiles become imitations of Christian Jews. The agents from Jerusalem, however, were convinced along with the majority of the rabbis of all the ages that the gentiles should obey the rules of the so-called "Noachic covenant," which forbade murder and eating blood and required the worship of the true God. Since gentiles in the Pauline wing of the church had not been informed of any such requirements, the Jewish Christians felt that they were all still polluted and would infect them with the same pollution. Therefore they insisted on eating with persons who were clean.

The contradictions between Luke and Paul regarding the conference in Jerusalem has been a principal factor in the widely prevalent view, already noted, that the trustworthiness of Acts has been completely invalidated. It would seem rather that Luke, in accordance with a literary habit, has merely removed part of one incident from its original location to another and conflated it with another account. Thus the imposition of regulations upon gentiles by Jerusalem decree took place, but it is likewise true that Paul's missionary venture was independent of the Jerusalem church to begin with—so that his policy was guided by the Holy Spirit rather than by an ecclesiastical conference. Such regulations were not brought up when Paul visited Jerusalem; and when they were demanded at Antioch, Paul refused them completely.

The result of Paul's rebuke of Peter, as described in Galatians, is unknown. Haenchen and others conclude from the silence of Paul about the outcome that Peter did not accept Paul's rebuke and that a considerable number if not the majority of the Antioch church, along with Barnabas, sided with Peter.[91] Luke reports that Paul had a furious quarrel with Barnabas about taking Mark along with him as they were setting out to visit the churches of Asia Minor again (Acts 15:36-41). The ostensible cause of this quarrel was the fact that Mark had left Paul and Barnabas at Perga of Pamphilia (13:13). From Paul's report, as we have seen, the conflict was about eating with the gentiles and the fact that Barnabas joined with the hypocrisy of Peter and others. Haenchen insists that the two accounts cannot possibly be so reconciled that both could be giving

91 Haenchen, *Acts*, 476-477, and the references there cited.

different aspects of a true event. He argues that Luke's account is a presentation of a relatively insignificant quarrel about a personal matter, whereas Paul in Galatians describes a theological rupture which concerns the vitals of the gospel: the failure to apply the gospel of justification produced by the cross of Christ. It is hard to see how Luke, if he had been a companion of Paul, could have glossed over the kind of fundamental difference which separated Paul and Peter. Some attempts to alleviate this difficulty Haenchen rejects with amusement. A. Schlatter suggested that Peter of course accepted Paul's rebuke, and Paul refused to gloat over his surrender and thus covered it with silence. To this Haenchen replies that when Paul had charged Peter with hypocrisy, it would not be a very shameful thing to report that he repented of it. Haenchen rejects out of hand the suggestion that Luke reports the most painful quarrel (namely, about John Mark) as the cause of the conflict, and that it thus overshadows the other one (so O. Bauernfeind). Since Paul's report of the theological conflict with Peter reveals a passionate outburst and a life and death protest, this dispute in which Barnabas joined could not have been regarded as less painful than an argument about John Mark.[92]

Haenchen at the same time rejects the radical argument that Luke purposely concealed the truth in order to strengthen his apologetic case. He suggests that the author of Acts was not aware of the true nature of the conflict in Antioch because the Antioch church had allowed the events to slip from memory and had preserved no written account or oral tradition of it. Paul's description of the event to the Galatian church was unknown to the author of Acts.

There were, however, solidly based traditions to the effect that John Mark accompanied Paul and Barnabas on their first trip, that Barnabas was not along on the later tours of Paul, and that Mark had gone out with Barnabas. To Haenchen it seems clear that Barnabas separated from Paul because of the fierce dispute about eating with gentiles and that Mark simply went along with him. But since Luke was not aware of the big argument over the gentiles at Antioch, he conceived the idea that Barnabas separated from Paul because Paul did not want Mark along after he had prematurely departed from the first trip. Thus Haenchen saves the apologetical integrity of Luke by removing all reliable knowledge from his possession. The trouble is not that Luke falsified; he merely did the best he could with the poor information he had.[93] It is possible that this is the best we can do with our material.

If Haenchen, however, is not altogether justified by his use of the argument from silence in the conclusion that Peter, along with Barnabas, refused to be convinced by Paul, and if Paul's exposition of the implications

92 Haenchen, *Acts*, 476-477.
93 Ibid.

of the gospel actually convinced him, then we could find good reasons for Luke's manner of describing the events. Incidentally, in no other allusion to Peter or Barnabas in the other letters of Paul is there the slightest hint that a deep gulf divides them on the matter of table fellowship with gentiles. If they were reconciled, Schlatter's suggestion is not so far-fetched as Haenchen makes it out to be. The fact that Paul labels their conduct hypocrisy need not be taken as such a stinging insult as it might appear to some of us. Perfectly friendly rabbis in arguments could accuse each other of varying degrees of stupidity, obtuseness, and spiritual blindness without thereby fracturing their scholarly collaborations. "Hypocrisy," according to Albright, may have meant "overscrupulousness," and he presents considerable evidence to justify this position.[94] The popular interpretation of the word "playacting," is later; as used in Gal 2:13 it probably does not carry with it the poisonous sting that it has acquired in our day.

Luke's purpose is to show the progress of the gospel and the maintenance of the unity of the church in the face of this crisis but not to give a chronicle of every side eddy stirred up by the major whirlpools. He is not writing a long, detailed history. To his mind, the big crisis was met in Jerusalem, and the secondary effect of this in Antioch need not delay the progress of his story. His account deliberately avoids reference to any conflict caused by Paul's bypassing the decree. Barnabas, then, separated from Paul as a result of the conflict over table fellowship; but in the meantime, if a reconciliation had been effected, Paul, as Luke suggests, decided to try it again. This time, Barnabas wanted to take along Mark, who was a relative of his, and who indicated a sincere intention to remain faithful to the project. We have already suggested that Mark may have left in the first place because of theological objections to Paul's free approach to the gentiles; and perhaps because of this, Paul was skeptical about his genuineness and sincerity. Luke shows that he does not fear candor in reporting a furious dispute between Paul and Barnabas; so if it had suited his purpose to recount Paul's arguments with Peter, he would not have been afraid to do so. Since that matter had been settled, there seemed no reason to go into it.

In Acts 16:4 Paul and Silas take "the ordinances decided upon by the apostles and elders in Jerusalem" to the cities of southern Asia Minor. Luke has been accused of tendentious editorializing at this point (the Tübingen school), but Haenchen thinks he was rather "the victim of an unreliable tradition."[95] At first the pair retraced the road of Paul's first journey through the area. Here they are joined by a new travel companion, Timothy. Apparently in contradiction to the policy affirmed in Galatians,

---

[94] W. F. Albright and C. S. Mann, *Matthew*, AB, vol. 26, cxv-cxxiii.
[95] Haenchen, *Acts*, 478-482.

Paul circumcised Timothy, whose father was a Greek gentile, "on account of the Jews who were in those regions" (16:3). It is hard to see why it was necessary to circumcise Timothy on the basis of any principles that can be attributed to Paul. It is true that his mother was Jewish, and the Jews might have insisted that Paul agree that the son of a Jewish mother should follow Jewish law. That is not the reason given in the text, which implies that the circumcision was on account of the nationality of his father. There was strong Jewish objection to intermarriage between Jews and gentiles, and this may have aroused a scandal among the Christian Jews in connection with Timothy's parents. The failure of the parents to perform the Jewish rite could be viewed as a gross lapse into paganism. Paul, therefore, may have circumcised Timothy to counteract hostility and win for Timothy full standing as a good Jew. No attacks could be justified against Paul on the ground that he was showing callous disregard of the Jewish feelings about mixed marriages by taking an uncircumcised issue of one of these marriages along as a missionary colleague.

Paul and his retinue passed on through "Phrygia and the country of Galatia" (16:6). This little reference has probably caused more discussion than any similar number of words in the New Testament. According to the older view, Paul went through the eastern part of Phrygia northward into "Galatia," almost in the exact geographic center of Asia Minor, a territory which surrounded Ancyra (now Ankara). In this region he established the churches which are addressed by the epistle "to the Galatians." These Galatians were Gauls who had emigrated from France across eastern Europe and finally settled in the center of Asia Minor. Nothing is said in Acts about villages and cities in this region; in fact next to nothing is related about Paul's activities here. On his third journey he went again through the country of Galatia and Phrygia, "strengthening all the disciples" (18:23). From this it is clear that Paul had secured disciples in these regions, but we have no additional information.

Because of the lack of information about churches in "North Galatia" and for other reasons many scholars have concluded that the phrase "the Galatian country" refers to the territory around Derbe, Lystra, and Iconium, and that Galatians was written to the people of these cities. This "South Galatia" theory provides the advantage that the letter was written to churches and people of whom we have considerable information drawn from Acts. It draws the Galatian churches from an almost impenetrable mist of obscurity into the light of historic knowledge.[96]

---

[96] The North Galatia position was well stated by J. B. Lightfoot in *The Epistle of St. Paul to the Galatians* (London, 1865), 1-35. The South Galatia theory was given its definitive presentation by Sir William Ramsay (in numerous publications; cf. *A Historical Commentary of St. Paul's Epistle to the Galatians* [New York, 1900], 1-234, 314-321). A classic summary of arguments is in Burton's International Critical Commentary on Galatians, pp. 21-44.

Several difficulties, however, attend the South Galatia theory. Probably in the nature of the case the two chief problems are insoluble: (a) imprecision of geographical detail in the itinerary notes, and (b) lack of certainty regarding the chronology of Paul's epistles. Any attempt to decide the precise routes by which Paul traversed Asia Minor on his second journey fails simply because Luke gives too few loci to set a firm course. While it seems sure that Luke regularly uses the Roman political designations for geographical areas, that still does not settle the question of exactly how Paul made his way across central Asia Minor. Again, the fact that Luke gives some details from Paul's activities in the churches of South Galatia during his second journey is helpful only if it is certain at what point in these itinerations Paul wrote to the Galatians. This decision depends partly upon the identification of the visits to Jerusalem mentioned in Acts and in Galatians (to which allusion has already been made) and partly upon other details in the epistle and in Luke's report—matters best left to the detailed discussions in the commentaries. If tentative assent be given to the South Galatia theory, then at best some puzzles in the existing texts are resolved. If the North Galatia theory is adopted, some new puzzles are posed about churches otherwise not mentioned in the texts.

In any case, Paul and his company came down to Troas, on the northwestern coast, where Paul had his famous vision urging him to bring help to Macedonia. Accordingly, the missionaries crossed the corner of the Aegean Sea and reached Philippi, a military colony on the Egnatian Way in Macedonia (Acts 16:11-12).

Here a woman named Lydia, a seller of purple cloth, along with a few other women of Philippi were converted to Christianity as Paul preached to them outside the city. Then by curing a young woman who was infested with "a spirit of divination" Paul stirred up great antagonism because her owners had been able to make considerable profit by exploiting her gift. They incited a group to seize Paul and drag him into the marketplace where they informed the chief magistrates of the city, "These men—Jews —are agitating our city and are advocating practices which are not legal for us Romans to receive or practice." The magistrates cast Paul and Silas into prison after they had lashed them with rods. During the middle of the night Paul and Silas were freed by an earthquake which opened all the doors of the jail and broke their chains. Paul called out to the frightened jailer that all the prisoners were there. When the astonished man stumbled in, Paul preached the gospel to him. The jailer made a confession, took the prisoners into his own house, washed their wounds, and received baptism for himself and his whole house. The next day when the magistrates sent agents commanding the jailer to release the prisoners, Paul stood on his rights by informing them that they had beaten them in public even though they were Roman citizens and had thrown them into jail without charge and now wanted to let them go secretly. Paul insisted that they come and lead them to the center of the city and release them before the entire multitude (16:13-40).

The travelers forthwith moved on to Thessalonica. There they succeeded in the synagogue: Paul preached the suffering and resurrection of Jesus Christ, and some of the Jewish audience as well as a great number of pious Greeks were converted. Other Jews, however, whipped a city crowd into a rage against Paul. Although they did not catch Paul and Silas, an interesting charge against them is recorded: "These persons who upset the world . . . are violating the edicts of Caesar and saying that there is another king, Jesus" (17:6-7).

Paul and Silas left at night and went to Beroea, where they found a more receptive audience. Examination of the Scriptures brought many of them to belief. Troublemakers from Thessalonica, however, instigated such opposition that Paul was sent on to Athens, where his companions were to join him as quickly as possible (17:10-15).

PAUL AT ATHENS

A profusion of temples and altars dedicated to a variety of gods and goddesses crowded the streets of Athens. This aroused the ire of Paul, who detested idolatry both because of his heritage as a Jew and because of his convictions about the true God revealed by Jesus Christ.[97] In the Roman empire of this time neither Jews nor Christians enjoyed the luxury of speaking out against what to them were pagan abominations. They led a precarious civil existence, and treatment varied from place to place and official to official. Jews were legally permitted to worship their God and practice his law and the traditions of their fathers on the strict condition that they exhibit no contempt for the official religion and not publicly blaspheme the gods.[98] This meant that the Old Testament protest against idolatry was restricted to strenuous adherence to Torah and refusal to participate in idolatrous worship. The same restrictions affected the Christians, who were regarded, at least for a while, as a part of Judaism. Missionary zeal of Jew and Christian, therefore, had to be suppressed. God's messengers could only employ diplomatic and polite address to pagan hearers. They could use arguments derived from notable Greek philosophers, who in the interest of reason and the unity of all reality had either attacked

[97] For this and the following details, cf. Acts 17:15-34.

[98] Detailed information of a legal nature is difficult to identify for the first century A.D. Cf. Benko and O'Rourke, *The Catacombs and the Colosseum*, 255-258; they deny that there was a concept of *religio licita* at this time. Also, *Beginnings*, V, 277-297.

polytheism openly or had recognized the gods only as symbols of some parts of the physical or social world. Thus Paul confined his "paroxysm" to silent boiling of spirit and while he was waiting for Silas and Timothy, spent his time in the synagogue arguing "with the Jews and the pious people" and then "in the marketplace every day with the people who happened to come along." His conversations in the marketplace attracted the attention of people who belonged to the two great schools of ancient philosophy: the Epicureans and the Stoics.

The Epicureans were believers in atomism and the extinction of human personality at death. Though they believed in the existence of the pagan deities, they denied that they exercised any influence on men or the world. Thus there was no divine providence or plan for humanity. The only sensible life was to live for whatever happiness could be obtained from the pleasures of the senses and of the mind. These philosophers were not licentious gluttons or lustful indulgers in sex orgies but were rather refined tasters of beauty and intellectual systems as well as of the delights of food, movement, and love.

The Stoics believed that all reality was one, consisting of a universal mind or *logos*. The object of life was to live in accordance with the nature of universal reason or to follow the reason of nature. According to this point of view, the feature of man which is closest to universal reality is his own mind. With this mind he should control, according to universal principles, all his impulses and desires with the aim of being free from the power of anything external to his own will. Pleasure was not the Stoic's aim in life but self-control under the rule of reason. Often this rule could be discovered by observing the phenomena of nature which in their way expressed the rule of the universal mind. On the other hand, it could often be discovered by studying the logical rules of the intellect. Some of the Stoics felt that the movements of the heavenly bodies were directly guided by the principles of the *logos* and had a beneficent effect upon the minds of men if men understood them. Thus many of the most intellectual of the contemporary Greek philosophers were devotees of astrology. A popular sect of Stoics called Cynics endeavored to arouse the common people to a rational and austere mode of life. In the interest of their objective they invented short homilies which were probably the first examples of sermons in the Greek or Roman world; they harangued the multitudes with short, pithy speeches called diatribes. These Cynics were undoubtedly precursors of the Christian preachers, who borrowed their techniques and Christianized their diatribes. Many of the ethical teachings of the Cynics were identical with those of the Christian religion.

Paul therefore could openly discuss the new revelation in Christ with the general public of Athens because they had been accustomed to the sight of these dedicated philosophers who acted and looked very much like our modern street people or flower children. They had rejected the blandishments of the world and were appealing to the populace to accept a way of life based upon reason, self-control, and austerity. These virtues were by no means alien to the Christian movement. Sometimes it became difficult to tell the difference between the Christians and the Stoics. In fact, some early church fathers, like Clement of Alexandria, thought that some of the Greek philosophers were Christians before Christ and that the soul itself, when undefiled by superstition and corruption was *naturaliter Christiana*.[99] While Paul himself apparently did not go this far in irenical movement toward Greek thought, according to Acts he was willing to address the people of Athens on a common ground.

As a result of Paul's discussions some of the philosophers carried on conversations with him while some of them were contemptuous, probably regarding Paul as a borrower of ideas which he had not compacted together into a respectable system of thought. These were probably the representatives of the Epicureans, who often had the habit of expressing their feelings of superiority by deftly caricaturing people they did not like. But others, probably representative of the Stoics, were more interested in what Paul said and thought that he seemed to be a "messenger of strange divinities." In view of Paul's strenuous monotheism, Luke explains that this misconception was due to the fact that he was preaching Jesus and the resurrection as if both were new divinities.

Authorities took him to the Hill of Ares (Mars Hill, in Latin), the traditional site of an ancient Athenian court at which religious violations were tried and people were condemned for innovations and heresies against the piety of the state. It is possible that these authorities were putting Paul under arrest and bringing him to the place where he would be investigated as an instigator of worship of gods not recognized by the state. As many commentators have noted, ancient readers of Acts would think immediately of Socrates who had been tried before the demos of Athens on the charge of misleading the young and introducing unauthorized deities. The account here, however, seems to indicate genuine curiosity on the part of Paul's questioners: "Can we know what this new teaching is which is being proclaimed by you? For you are introducing strange things to our hearing; so we want to know what these things claim to be." Luke adds the comment that "all the Athenians as well as the tourists that visited there were accustomed to spending their time in nothing other than hearing or saying something new." Since Athens existed largely as the museum of ancient learning and as the center of contemporary schools of philosophy, people resorted to it from all parts of the world in order to imbibe the spirit of the old learning as well as to hear whatever brilliant new ideas were circu-

---

[99] Clement *Stromateis* I v, XIX; *Protreptikos* XI.

lating in the world. Because of this interest Paul was able to get an immediate hearing for his presentation of the gospel of Christ which struck their ears with the sound of something really new.

Paul proceeded to answer the inquirers by alluding first to the religious conditions revealed in Athens by their public structures, among which he had been struck with an altar on which was inscribed "To an unknown God." Archaeological discoveries have shown that such inscriptions existed at Athens and elsewhere at that time.[100] Very probably the original idea of this inscription was not to acknowledge the supreme and almighty god of the universe who was unknown to man, but rather to be a kind of safety device acknowledging their readiness to revere any god who may have been overlooked in all the temples and altars of the city. Paul very shrewdly refers to this inscription as a sign of the fact that there is indeed a God unknown to them but whom he is ready to announce. This God "made the world and all things in it." As "Lord of heaven and earth he does not occupy human temples." As one who embraces and possesses all things he needs nothing that human service can provide him. On the contrary, he is the benefactor who "gives life, breath, and all things to all" people. So far, Paul's hearers could thoroughly agree. On the ground of reason it is clear that the universe is a harmonious system which points to one source. "One source" was regarded by many of them as being the supreme mind.

At this particular time, many Greek intellectuals were ready to admit that the supreme god may have communicated special wisdom by revelation and ecstasy to chosen people on the earth. Some of them felt that esoteric wisdom had been treasured in Egypt and in various parts of the east, especially Syria and Babylon. Some Greek and Latin writers had discovered even the leading ideas of the Jewish religion and regarded the ancient Jews as having been divinely inspired philosophers.[101] So when Paul declared that he was ready to announce the nature and reality of the supreme God, he could at least count on an initial respect; for he came from the East and began to speak like a philosopher. He proceeded to declare that the entire human race had descended from one source which God had made. This doctrine, which, in Paul's mind, undoubtedly was rooted in the story of creation found in the book of Genesis, was at the same time the common opinion of many of the Stoics, who believed that the human race was a unity and that the truly educated man should regard himself as a citizen of the world, recognizing humanity as a whole as the family to which he belonged. Paul proceeded to insist that the race of men which God made was destined to occupy the entire surface of the earth,

---

[100] *Beginnings*, V, 240-242.
[101] Clement of Alexandria discusses this in *Stromateis* I IV, V, VI.

for which God had "determined by his decree seasons of the year and boundaries of suitable places for human inhabitation." This undoubtedly refers to the fact that according to Genesis, God divided the earth from the waters so that men could occupy the earth and fishes occupy the seas. He then affirms that the purpose of man's existence on the earth is "to seek God." This was the equivalent of the philosophical notion that man's nature was designed to discover the truth, and that since he is a rational being as Aristotle said, the main purpose of man's existence is to discover the ultimate reality by the use of his mind. Paul personifies the ultimate reality as God and not as some principle of being. This God is the object of man's groping which is like "feeling one's way" through the darkness in order to find him. The restless activity and relentless searching for new facts and features of our world, even though their immediate purpose may be selfish, materialistic, and economic, are still ultimately the expression of the fact that man, by nature, feels out and gropes for what he has not yet discovered, the true end of which is the supreme God. Thus he could sweepingly summarize the inner significance of all these temples and altars and all the schools of science and philosophy, the mystery of religions and the wondering features of rational life, as the ceaseless desire of man to find his creator. Unfortunately the competing variety of deities, cults, temples, and sacrifices displays the fact that the groping has not succeeded in the final discovery; for some hit on this aspect of reality and some on that and then deify the limited phase of being with which they have been impressed. But the paradoxical truth is that the supreme God, the maker of the vast universe, who has not been found, is still "not far from each one of us." He may be so close that people miss him in seeking someone far away. His closeness consists in the fact that "we live, move, and exist in him." It is as if he were the air we breathe or the environment in which we move. Of course Paul does not mean to identify God with any physical reality like air, water, or the embracing world; but he means that everything is continually supported and moved by the energy of God. Thus we cannot escape a close relation to him.

Paul then quotes a half-line from the Stoic poet Aratus:

We are also of his family.

This implies that the human race has in some way descended from God; perhaps Aratus had some metaphysical notion of the divine generation of the human race, so that men, and in particular their minds, were split-offs from the nature of God himself. Some of the ancient thinkers believed that from the ultimate being radiations went forth continually like rays of light which they called "emanations," and these solidified into realities in the world. The human race, therefore, could be understood as one of the emanations from God. Paul does not engage in criticism of the original meaning of the line; but, as he did to the inscription of the unknown God, he adapts it to his purpose. In biblical religion God is the father of men though his fatherhood is not understood as in any way analogous to procreation or the successive shedding of different layers of his own being. In biblical religion God creates all things by his word of power; but since he is the source of their being, he can be called by analogy the Father of what he has made. Jesus used the term "Father" as the characteristic title of God. In subsequent Christian theology the idea has been developed that Jesus Christ is the second person of the divinity whose individual personality is produced by eternal generation from the Father. Thus the Greek idea of emanation was apparently taken over and restricted to one person, namely the second person of the Trinity. Then by virtue of the fact that the Father and the Son sent forth the Spirit, which proceeds into human lives, spiritual people can, in a sense, partake realistically in the nature of God and thus in more than a figurative sense can be called the sons of God. But Paul is not employing here this later Christian theology. Merely on the basis of the creation, he can adopt the idea of a Stoic poet that we are the family or offspring of God.

Now Paul with something like the flick of a whip lashes them with the necessary conclusion that those who are either God's offspring or members of his family should not dream of likening God to any product of man's art made from silver, gold, or stone. One should not insult the Creator by thinking he is like anything man has made. Consequently, the truth acknowledged even by the perceptive minds of Greek thinkers should have led men to the conclusion that we do not reduce the divinity to something that can be copied or localized in an idol or man-made building. Thus Paul observed that though the gentile world was seeking to discover God and, in fact, had grasped some profound elements of the truth, they had been so blinded by their superstitions and traditions as not to be able to draw proper conclusions from what they knew. Part of the failure, of course, was undoubtedly due to fear, both of the rage of fanatical believers in the gods, and of possible mysterious punishment by the gods.

Paul does not accuse them of time-serving cowardice, but rather explains their failure to understand as a result of ignorance. He affirms that God has in the past "overlooked the times of ignorance" and therefore has allowed them to continue their blind wanderings and searchings and even their misguided religions. But he confronts them with the announcement that "God is now commanding all men everywhere to change their minds, to repent." The excuse of ignorance no longer will cover man's blind disobedience to the supreme God. "He has appointed a day in which he is about to judge the inhabited world by righteousness, namely by a man whom he has appointed." The proof of this man's appointment God provided by "raising him from the dead." Here Paul suddenly and abruptly leaves the realm of thought which was common to him and his philosophical auditors by referring to a historical person who had recently lived on the earth and had been killed and raised from the dead. It is on the basis of his life, teaching, and triumph over death that Paul can announce the true nature of the unknown God.

His hearers, however, immediately became startled, alarmed, or derisive; for now Paul had left the realm of rational thought and was pointing to a human person in history as someone who could reveal the inside meaning of life and existence. The claim to have inside knowledge of God or to be the recipient of special revelation is always a source of embarrassment to people who hear about it. The claim may be true, and then the person who makes it is uncanny. On the other hand, it may be false, and the person who makes it is a charlatan. Philosophical minds are initially weighted in the direction of dismissing such claims as delusion, fanaticism, or cheap exploitation of human credulity. Yet when a claim is presented by one who is obviously intelligent and whose word so far makes irrefutable good sense, the embarrassment is increased because what he says can hardly be shrugged off or dismissed. The hearers in Athens proceeded because of their embarrassment to divide into two groups, one of which endeavored by mockery to nullify the appearance of good sense, while the others, not being able to dismiss Paul by ridicule, said, "We will hear you again on the subject." (Perhaps the lapse of time will reveal what kind of reality you actually represent, and we may be able more sensibly to consider it.) The thing which drove them into this embarrassment and resistance to the gospel was Paul's statement that God had raised a man from the dead. The Stoics believed in some sort of vague survival of the human mind after death, but they did not believe it was possible for anyone who had been dead to be raised to life as Paul said this man had been. So Paul is either crazy, or perhaps something really new has occurred. They don't know. So they will wait and see. "Thus Paul went out of their midst."

This speech attributed to Paul by Luke has been regarded by recent critics, particularly of the form-critical school, as well as by Cadbury and Kirsopp Lake, as the product of Luke's composition.[102] Two lines of argument are employed to buttress this conclusion: first, the style of the speech is more like Luke than it is like Paul; second, the theological content of the speech reflects the somewhat universalizing trend of the early catholicism that emerged at the end of the first century. Therefore, the speech gives insight into the faith and theology of Luke but not into the thought of Paul. One may agree that the style of the speech is much smoother than paragraphs in the letters of Paul and that the vocabulary in it is not exactly close to the usage of Paul; yet one can also affirm that Luke knew what

[102] Haenchen, *Acts*, 82; Cadbury, *The Making of Luke-Acts*, 61; *Beginnings*, IV, 208, V, 5, 281, 402-427.

Paul basically preached when he entered new cities and that he also understood Paul's missionary approach to people of philosophical training. The report of the speech obviously intends to be a summary and not a verbatim account. The summary may retain the main points of the Pauline theology, though expressed in the language of the author or editor of the book. As far as the ideas of the speech are concerned, they are fairly closely paralleled by what Paul says in the first chapter of Romans and elsewhere, where he refers to the fact that God has made known the essentials of his being by the creation of the world, and yet man has not taken advantage of his opportunity to know God since he has been deluded by his own reason and has been so darkened in his mind as to exchange the truth of God for worshiping of images of corruptible humanity, birds, quadrupeds, and serpents.[103] In Romans Paul affirms that this delusion and darkness is a result of man's determination to be wise by worshiping the things he sees, while in Acts the reason for the mistaken notions about God is ignorance; but it is perfectly possible for the same mind on one hand to regard the paganism of the gentiles to be a result of ignorance and on the other hand to regard the ignorance as a result of refusal to worship the invisible because of preference for what is seen. Likewise in Romans Paul states that "the gentiles who do not have the law do by nature the things of the law," and thus have the law "written on their hearts" (2:14-15). This is parallel to the fact that God is "not far from each one of us."

In the letters of Paul there is no precise parallel to the statement that men belong to God's family as his offspring (*genos*). Throughout the letters people are sons of God by virtue of being adopted into the new humanity created by Christ. As such they belong to the divine family. In Rom 5:12-21, however, the doctrine of the divine creation of man is presupposed in the passage, which indicates that men have left the condition of creation and entered that of sin and death because of the sin of the first man. Since Adam was the creation of God and since all men are his descendants, it is to be concluded that all men, therefore, descend from the one who had his being from God. Likewise Paul asserts that "the first man Adam became a living soul" and was composed from the earth while the last man "became a life-giving spirit" (I Cor 15:45).[104] Here the emphasis upon the one who enables us to enter the kingdom of heaven is laid on the second man, but still the first man is regarded by Paul as the product of divine creation. The doctrine of the creation of man is likewise to be inferred from his statement that "a man . . . is the image and glory of God" (I Cor 11:7), an allusion to the creation story of Genesis. So while Paul does not in express words identify the creative act of God as setting

[103] Rom 1:19-23; cf. Eph 4:17-19.
[104] Paul quotes Gen 2:7.

up his family or his offspring, he does believe that all mankind belong to the same family as a result of descending from the first man whom God made. In his letters written to churches, Paul lays heavy emphasis upon the new creation in Christ, while undoubtedly in preaching the gospel to Greek intellectuals he would stress, as the speech in Acts does, the common nature of humanity which depends on God's original act of creation. This is a doctrine in which he and they could find common ground. He might not have used the words attributed to him by Luke in this speech, yet he undoubtedly expressed the ideas that the words represent.

Paul attacks idolatry in several places in his letters: Rom 1:23, "They exchanged the glory of the indestructible God for the likeness of the corruptible image of man and birds and quadrupeds and serpents"; I Cor 8:4, "We know that an idol is nothing in the world and that there is no God but one"; I Cor 10:7, "Do not become idolaters as some of them were." These citations reveal that Paul shared a common Jewish aversion to the worship of images or idols, and he could on occasion very well have uttered the words, "We ought not to think that the divine being is like gold or silver or stone carved by the art and plan of man." These specific words indeed are taken from various parts of the Old Testament, particularly Isa 40:18-20, 44:9-17.

Again there is no precise parallel in Paul's letters to the affirmation, "God overlooked the times of the ignorance but now is commanding all men everywhere to repent." It is stated, however, in Eph 4:18 that the gentiles are "alienated from the life of God because of the ignorance which is in them."[105] Paul, in addition, affirms in Rom 5:13 that "sin is not charged against people when there is no law." So the two statements may be combined: (1) that the gentiles were alienated from God because of ignorance, and (2) where there is no law there is no reckoning of guilt. The conclusion will be that God has failed to charge the sins of men against them because of their ignorance. This is only verbally different from the statement in the speech, "God has overlooked the times of the ignorance."

Certainly Paul insists in his letters that men are now being challenged by God to repent. In Rom 2:4 the moralists are sharply reminded that the kindness of God is meant to lead them into repentance but not into a practice of judging other men. In Rom 1:18 Paul states that "a wrath of God is being revealed from heaven upon the impiety and iniquity of men who suppress the truth by their unrighteousness." This present revelation of the wrath is exactly parallel in time to the revelation of the righteousness of God which is being revealed by Christ. This statement may be another way of affirming what is found in the Acts 17 speech, that God has "appointed a day in which he is about to judge the inhabited world by right-

---

[105] Begging the question of authorship. Cf. *supra*, 30-31.

eousness by a man whom he appointed." In Romans the fact that men have indulged in idolatry because of having their minds darkened and being self-deceived has led to a new revelation of the wrath of God, which is coincidental with the revelation of his righteousness. In Acts, while God has overlooked the times of ignorance up to now, he has appointed a day of reckoning. While the wording of the two sources is different, the underlying ideas again are quite the same. The Acts speech is broken off by the statement that he "provided proof of this to all men by raising [the man] from the dead." This statement is in thought and, to a degree, in wording similar to Rom 1:4, "Who was appointed son of God with power in accordance with the Holy Spirit by the resurrection from the dead." The word "appoint" (*horizein*) is found in both passages, and powerful demonstration is presented by the fact that Christ was raised from the dead.

Thus there are demonstrable similarities in the letters of Paul corresponding to every statement incorporated into the Acts speech except perhaps the excoriation of the belief that God would dwell in handmade temples or that he needs any service from men. Both of these statements express stark assertions of the Old Testament and certainly are not alien to the doctrine and practice of Paul though he may never have had occasion to express them in the letters which we now possess. Where Paul refers to the sanctuary of God as an entity of the present time, he identifies it with the Christian community. This implies that the temple in Jerusalem or temples constructed anywhere are obsolete. Thus, though he never in express words states that God does not dwell in temples made by man, he implies that God does dwell in the temple of the new society. So even in this particular Paul's statement (made repeatedly in I Corinthians) agrees with the idea that God does not dwell in temples made by hands.

The conclusion seems clear: the speech in Acts 17 is a reliable summary of the basic message of Paul to the thinking elements among the gentiles when he first approached them. It is undoubtedly a fact that Luke culled many of his statements from numerous recollections, either of his own or of other people, of speeches that Paul made on various occasions; and he put them together in this one speech, which he framed in his own style and organized according to his own plan. One cannot argue that we thus have the *obiter dicta* of Paul, but it can be affirmed that the speech conveys the essential elements of his original preaching (Cadbury, Haenchen, and Conzelmann notwithstanding).

The Athenian audience as a whole seems to have dismissed Paul's message, except that some men, among them Dionysius the Areopagite, a woman named Damaris, and a few others confessed and believed. If this was Paul's sole recorded venture into a quasi-philosophical approach to the gospel, at least it met with modest success. There is a chronological difficulty, however, raised by this enumeration of converts, for in I Cor

16:15 Paul calls the household of Stephanas "a first fruits of Achaea." (This problem is dealt with in the commentary.) Suffice it to say that Luke is often somewhat cavalier in his treatment of the chronological order of events even though nearly all his narratives seem to be based on some kind of historical information.

MISSION AT CORINTH

When he left Athens (Acts 18:1), Paul either sailed across the Saronic Gulf or went by land across the isthmus that joined Attica with the Peloponnesus. Corinth was located practically in the center of the narrow neck of this isthmus, which divided the Saronic Gulf from the Gulf of Corinth. The city was the site where goods were transferred from boats to overland vehicles to be carried across the isthmus on the way to all points in the western world. (In modern times a canal has obviated this process, but Corinth had been reduced to relative unimportance long before.)

The old Corinth had been destroyed by the Romans in the second century B.C. and rebuilt by Julius Caesar in the first century B.C. In the middle of the first century A.D. it was practically a Roman military location filled with people from all parts of the ancient world. In the description of Paul's activities in Corinth, Luke reports that a violent uproar compelled Paul to be brought before Gallio the proconsul (Acts 18:12-17). Gallio is named as proconsul of Achaea in an inscription from Delphi containing a greeting from Claudius Caesar.[106] The implication of the fragmentary data appears to be that Gallio was proconsul between January 25, A.D. 52 and January 24, 53; but it is uncertain whether Paul's mission in Corinth extended before or after this time.

Acts 18:2 states that a Jewish couple, Aquila and Priscilla, had arrived at Corinth shortly before Paul, "having come from Italy . . . because Claudius had ordered all the Jews to depart from Rome." Suetonius, the second-century Roman historian, writes that Claudius "expelled from Rome the Jews who were raising furious tumults because of the agitator Chrestus."[107] It has usually been supposed that "Chrestus" is simply a misspelling of "Christus." Apparently Suetonius, without precise knowledge of the internal relationships between Jews and Christians, assumed that Christ himself was alive and leading the agitation. Doubtless Christian preachers had secured adherents in Rome, and the Jewish community was

---

106 ". . . a report has been made by Lucius Junius Gallio, my friend, and proconsul of Achaea. . . ." *Beginnings*, V, 461; cf. 460-464.

107 *Judaeos impulsore Chresto assidue tumultuantes Roma expulit; Life of Claudius* xxv. Orosius, in the fifth century, identifies the year as the ninth of Claudius. This is probably A.D. 49, but the chronology is not absolutely certain. Cf. *Beginnings*, IV, 221; V, 459-460.

stirred by fierce conflict because of the Christian mission. For some reason Luke leaves out any reference to the cause of the expulsion, perhaps because he did not want to emphasize more than necessary the conflicts that had been stirred up in the Jewish community by Christian evangelism. If this interpretation is correct, it is a Roman attestation to the beginning of the Christian mission in the capital. This is not described anywhere else in the New Testament even though Paul implies in his letter to the Romans that the church there was a flourishing society by the time he wrote the epistle.[108]

Assuming that the expulsion of the Jews was occasioned by riots over the Christian activities of early anonymous missionaries, it is not difficult to conclude that Priscilla and Aquila were among the Christians in the Jewish community who had to leave Rome. In Corinth these newcomers became the hosts of Paul during the early portion of his stay. Paul apparently was self-supporting in this period, for Luke mentions that he joined in his hosts' craft (18:3).[109] He also prosecuted his mission energetically by discussing the Christian message every sabbath in the local synagogue, where he had opportunity to address both Jews and Greeks (18:4).

Some time after "Silas and Timothy arrived from Macedonia" a radical change in Paul's situation took place (Acts 18:5-17). His strenuous preaching—supporting the messiahship of Jesus, presumably from Old Testament scriptures—met with resistance and reproach, so strong that he "shook out his garments" and declared his intention to "go to the gentiles."[110] He seems then to have moved his headquarters to the house of a pious gentile named Titius Justus, next door to the synagogue. There followed a number of conversions; one was of a prominent synagogue leader Crispus, who is mentioned in I Cor 1:14 as among the very few people that Paul himself baptized. At this time Paul received divine approbation of his mission by a night vision, and his stay extended to a year and a half.

The reference to this stretch of time implies that Corinth is the first place where Paul remained so long. During a mission journey characterized so often by violent opposition to his message, Corinth afforded an important contrast by furnishing conditions for a stay of some duration. There is recorded, however, one violent incident from this period.

---

[108] Cf. Haenchen's summaries of the chronological data, *Acts,* 65-67. These data are crucial for establishing a chronology of the life of Paul.

[109] The exact nature of this occupation is uncertain. The traditional translation "tentmakers" is open to question and certainly needs some modification. Cf. *Beginnings,* IV, 223; the literature in AGB, 762b; and Michaelis's note in *TDNT,* VIII, 393-394 ("leather worker").

[110] Cf. Cadbury's note in *Beginnings,* V, 269-277. Paul's declaration that they are responsible for the results of their own intransigence recalls II Sam 1:16 and particularly Ezek 3:17-21.

Members of the Jewish community seized Paul and brought him before the bench of the court of the proconsul Gallio. Intent on discrediting the religious community which Paul was establishing as not being truly Jewish and consequently not protected by official toleration, they argued that he was teaching people to worship God contrary to the law—whether of the Romans or of the Jews is left indeterminate. Gallio declared the matter to be related to Jewish religious law and refused to make further judgment. This indifference to disputes among the Jews may be taken as an ignoble contempt for questions about most important matters, or it may be an example of judicial restraint according to which Gallio recognized that a government official had no business passing on theological questions so long as no damage to persons or property ensued and so long as the religious movement was not a cover for rebellion. There follows a cryptic statement that "all [the people] seized Sosthenes, the ruler of the synagogue, and set about beating him before the bench of the court." Confusion arises because it is not clear who is meant by "all." Were they Jews who seized Sosthenes and beat him because he had become a Christian convert? Or were they gentiles who in a spurt of anti-Semitism beat the Jewish ruler of the synagogue to express their antagonism to the Jews? Or might they have been violent numbers of the new Christian movement who attacked Sosthenes as the instigator of the agitation against Paul?[111] In I Cor 1:1 Paul mentions Sosthenes as the brother who joined with him in sending that letter; and while there could have been two men of that name, it seems more probable that the synagogue ruler and the Christian brother are identical. If this is so, the most likely reason for the attack would seem to be that Sosthenes was blamed by a Jewish mob for the successes of the Christian mission because he had provided Paul with a base of operation in the synagogue. A further reasonable guess would be that he became a Christian brother as a sequel to the treatment he received during this disturbance.

MISSION IN EPHESUS AND ASIA

Because of his special calling Paul was too restless to stay at one place for a long period of time. He was impelled by the command of God to

[111] The Western text and the Byzantine tradition identifies the "all" as "the Greeks." Several minuscules move the other way and add "the Jews." Metzger, *Textual Commentary*, 463, thinks this second form of variant "is much more unlikely to represent the real situation." The mob, however, was said in vs. 12 to have acted *homothumadon*, "with one impulse"; but there is no indication of identity for a Greek mob. Moreover, the conversion of Sosthenes makes better psychological sense if the mob was Jewish. "All," then, means the mob that was frustrated in its attempt to indict Paul.

preach the gospel in the main centers of the gentile world. So he bade good-bye to the Corinthian fellowship after his lengthy stay and went to Ephesus accompanied by Priscilla and Aquila. There he engaged in discussion with the Jews of the synagogue. Although they asked him to stay a longer time, he felt he had to return to Antioch (Acts 18:18-22).

While Paul was absent, Ephesus was visited by an Alexandrian Jew named Apollos (18:24-28).[112] He was "able" in the scriptures, an eloquent speaker, and "instructed in the way of the Lord." The pluperfect periphrastic construction implies that his instruction had preceded his arrival at Ephesus (which furnishes a slight probability that Christian propaganda had been disseminated in Alexandria by unknown emissaries). He was "fervent in spirit"—a characterization identical with that commended by Paul in Rom 12:11. For some reason Apollos was limited by the theological deficiency of "understanding only the baptism of John." The followers of John the Baptist seem to have persisted as a religious group until well into the fourth or fifth centuries.[113] For most of his followers, John himself was either the messiah or the final redeemer. Among the Mandaeans there is no evidence of honoring Jesus. Here, however, Luke supplies an instance of a man who combines fervency and loyalty to Jesus with adherence to the baptism of John. Whether he was an isolated instance or representative of a group (perhaps in Alexandria) that had synthesized the practices of the Baptist with the beliefs of Christianity is hard to say. Scholarly opinion about the significance of Apollos' position is diverse.[114] He may have been acquainted with some early gospel like Q which described Jesus as accepting the baptism of John but which did not indicate anywhere that Jesus authorized or especially commanded a different kind of baptism for his followers. There may have been a stage, or at least a group, in the earliest decades of the Christian church which emphasized the need for repentance as John did and employed baptism as the sacrament or sign of repentance. In view of the fact that John 20:22 attests that the Spirit was transferred from Jesus to his followers by breath, there may also have been a group which did not associate the reception of the Spirit with baptism or the laying on of hands. Apollos evidently combined his loyalty to the baptism of John with a spiritual life and accurate knowledge of traditions about Jesus.

It is conceivable that Apollos represents a group created by missionary

---

[112] The name is shortened from "Apollonius" (the reading of D). Sinaiticus and a supporting strain of tradition read "Apelles." Cf. Metzger, *Textual Commentary,* 465, 466, 469, for details and literature. The coincidence with the name of a Greek god would not have bothered Diaspora Jews, who often adopted Greek and Roman names.

[113] Attested by the Mandaean writings (studied and edited by M. Lidzbarski).

[114] Cf. Haenchen, *Acts,* 550, nn. 8 and 10.

activities of the followers of Stephen and the Seven (Acts 6-8). Luke indicates that members of this group were driven from Jerusalem and went through Phoenicia and then through Cyprus and Antioch and preached to the Greeks. It is no great distance from Cyprus to Alexandria so it is not too audacious to suppose that some of these men preached in Egypt. It is instructive to observe that when Philip, who was a member of the Seven, preached in Samaria, he succeeded in converting many people; but the apostles in Jerusalem sent Peter down to Samaria in order to investigate the group and see to it that they received the Spirit by the laying on of hands. These people had already been baptized by Philip and had witnessed signs and great miracles. So whatever may have been the original doctrine of the followers of the Seven, there seems to have been some sense of defect in their proclamation that had to be supplemented by the apostles in Jerusalem; and this defect referred to the reception of the Holy Spirit. Apollos may have had a point of view not very different from that of Stephen and Philip, and he must have been regarded in important circles as lacking in full ecclesiastical conformity. Priscilla and Aquila, as good authorities in "normative" Christianity, heard him speaking boldly in the synagogue, and they took him aside and "explained to him the way of God more accurately."

The use of the expression "the way of God" is instructive. The Christian mode of existence is referred to as "the way" several times in Acts: 9:2, 19:9,23, 22:4, 24:14,22; and perhaps 16:17. The same term (in Hebrew *hadderek*) is employed by the Essenes of the Dead Sea scrolls to describe their culture and mode of religious life. So Apollos, in order to be "instructed in the way," had to possess at least a minimal knowledge of the teachings of Jesus as well as of the way of life to be followed by those who believed in him as the Messiah. Luke draws a veil of silence over the question of the particulars which Priscilla and Aquila supplied to him "in a more accurate form." The only hint is supplied in 19:1-7 where Paul confronts people who had to be instructed about the Holy Spirit. It is possible that these persons had been converted by Apollos before he was instructed "more accurately" by Priscilla and Aquila.

Soon after this instruction Apollos decided to go on into Achaea, and the Ephesian brethren sent along a letter of recommendation to the Achaean disciples. Here the information in Acts supplements what we know from Paul. According to I Cor 2:4-6 there was an "Apollos party" in Corinth. This was undoubtedly formed as a result of Apollos' visit to Corinth which is described in Acts: "Apollos conferred extensively in a gracious manner with those who believed. He was continuously arguing with the Jews in public by demonstrating through the scriptures that Jesus was the Messiah" (18:27,28; cf. 19:1a).

It has occasionally been suggested that Apollos had been taught by

Philo, who was one of the most learned of first-century Jews, and who wrote volumes to prove by allegorical interpretation that all wisdom of Greek philosophy was contained in the books of the law and had been revealed to Moses. Philo was an expert in discovering "the spiritual meaning of the scriptures," which, in fact, turns out to be the complex of philosophical and ethical ideas current in the first century, with special Platonic and Stoic coloring. The description of Apollos gives no evidence of such philosophical leanings but it does suggest that he was distinguished and unique in the skill with which he could handle the scriptures especially with reference to discovering in them proof of the messiahship of Jesus.

The closest analogy to this kind of approach to the scriptures would seem to have been furnished by the commentators of the Qumran community, who were immensely skilled in discovering scripture predictions about their own "Teacher of Righteousness" and his mistreatment by contemporary authorities.[115] In the writings of Philo occurs one of the very few descriptions of the Essenes, with whom he had some very close acquaintance.[116] This seems to demonstrate that the Essenes had a group in Alexandria; so Apollos may very well have been an Alexandrian Essene before he became a Christian and may have learned to employ their methods of interpreting the scripture rather than those of Philo.[117] Undoubtedly this sort of ingenious interpretation fascinated many early Christians, and this would reveal the reason that led some of them to elevate Apollos to a position higher than Paul's, and it might explain to some degree Paul's denigration of eloquence and wisdom of speech in his discussion of the party conflicts in Corinth.

Paul returned to Ephesus while Apollos was in Corinth; and when he found some disciples there, he asked if they had received the Holy Spirit (Acts 19:1-7). The juxtaposition of this statement about the disciples and the previous description of Apollos' activity in Ephesus furnishes a fairly strong ground for inferring that these disciples had been recruited by Apollos. They replied, "We had not heard if there is a Holy Spirit." Then Paul demanded, "In what were you baptized then?" They said, "In the baptism of John." Here again is a link between this group and the previous statement about Apollos, who, when he was preaching in Ephesus, under-

---

115 Their method of applying scripture to contemporary events is referred to as *pešer*, a word meaning "interpretation," which introduced each application.

116 Philo *Quod omnis probus liber sit*, ch. 12.

117 As an interesting corollary of this suggestion, Luther's declaration that of all the men known in the New Testament the one who best fits the characteristics of the author of Hebrews was Apollos would seem to have great weight and probably to be correct. So in order to understand in what manner Apollos was eloquent and skilled in using the scriptures, one can study the book of Hebrews, which is remarkably subtle and eloquent in employing scripture passages (e.g. the description of Melchizedek, which, so far as is known, was applied to the future only by the Essene group).

stood only the baptism of John. Now Paul gives the correct doctrine, which is harmonious with the more accurate teaching that Priscilla and Aquila had previously bestowed upon Apollos. Paul said, "John baptized with the baptism of repentance as he told the people about one coming after him in whom they should believe, that is, in Jesus." It is puzzling that the correct doctrine here given says nothing about the Holy Spirit as would be expected but refers only to the fact that John the Baptist was looking forward to the coming of Jesus after himself. This should have been acknowledged by these disciples who had already believed. All that can be extracted from this statement is that since John looked forward to one coming after him, John's baptism belonged to a preliminary stage and not to the final form of true religion. Therefore they must be baptized in the name of the Lord Jesus instead of being baptized for repentance. "When Paul laid his hands on them, the Holy Spirit came upon them and they were speaking in tongues and prophesying." It is impossible to be certain about the meaning here since it may be saying that when Paul laid his hands upon them to baptize them, the Holy Spirit came upon them; or it may mean that after he baptized them, he laid his hands upon them and they received the Spirit. In either case, the result of this Spirit reception was the gift of speaking in tongues and prophesying.

A difficulty arises here, for in I Corinthians Paul enumerates speaking in tongues as a gift bestowed upon some members of the church alone, but not upon all; and he says the same of the gift of prophecy (I Cor 12:4-11). If Luke means to affirm that all the members of the church, when they believe and are baptized according to the orthodox way, receive the Spirit and thus receive the gift of tongues and prophecy, he is not in accord with the express teaching of Paul. A way out of the difficulty may be furnished by Acts 19:7, "All the men amounted to about twelve." The number twelve is significant in the New Testament. There were, of course, twelve apostles, who called to mind representatives of each of the twelve tribes of Israel. It is probable, therefore, that these twelve men were not the whole body of believers in Ephesus that had been recruited by Apollos, but that they constituted a sort of replica of the original twelve and therefore leaders in the church. These may have been the ones to receive the gift of prophecy and tongues, though this explanation is tentative.

After the contretemps with these Ephesian "baptists," Paul spent three months, according to his usual policy, in persistent, urgent argument with the Jewish community. Luke describes the subject matter as "the kingdom of God." As elsewhere, a considerable number resisted his arguments and attacked "the way" in public. So Paul separated from them and took some disciples with him to form a new independent community which met periodically "in the school of Tyrannus." Like Corinth, Ephesus furnished him with an opportunity for a semipermanent ministry, and he stayed two years. As a result "all the inhabitants of Asia heard the message of the Lord, both Jews and Greeks" (Acts 19:8-10). While the adjective "all" may be a kind of exaggeration, we learn from the letters that active churches existed in Paul's time at Colossae, Laodicea, and Troas. Revelation, which was written not long after Paul's time, addresses additional churches in Smyrna, Pergamum, Thyatira, Sardis, and Philadelphia. Undoubtedly these cities in the province of Asia had been affected by Paul's work and that of his followers during this two-year stay in Ephesus. Very likely other places not mentioned in the New Testament were also evangelized.

In Corinth Paul's preaching was accompanied by marvelous works of healing which developed to such an extent that people were healed by pieces of cloth taken from Paul.[118] So impressive was the healing activity of Paul that some Jewish exorcists began to use the same formulas that Paul had used even adjuring evil spirits by "the Jesus whom Paul preaches" (19:11-13). Lest this detail seem too improbable or bizarre to be credible, one may refer to discoveries of ancient papyri in which the name of Jesus is mixed in with the name of Yahweh and many other names in magic spells employed by Jewish and even gentile magicians.[119]

Luke candidly reports the wonders performed in Paul's meetings, and there is no doubt that events happened which justified his descriptions. Paul himself refers to signs and wonders which had taken place in the presence of the people to whom he is writing: "The signs of an apostle were wrought among you with all endurance, namely with signs and wonders and mighty acts" (II Cor 12:12). And he informs the Romans that "by speech and act, with the power of signs and wonders and with might of Spirit," he had spoken the gospel throughout the eastern Mediterranean from Jerusalem to Illyricum (Rom 15:18-19). This means that Luke is recording events to which Paul himself also alludes when writing to persons who had witnessed what he is describing. Now Paul does not refer to any such melodramatic details as the detachment of pieces of his clothes to heal the sick, but he furnishes ample confirmation of the fact that remarkable healings took place.[120]

As an illustration of the competitive spirit among the ancient healers,

[118] Cf. Haenchen's notes, *Acts*, 562-563.
[119] Deissmann, *Light from the Ancient East*, 254-265; also *Beginnings*, V, 121-140.
[120] Such phenomena have occurred from time to time throughout the history of the church to the present time. Their distribution and appearance seem to be without respect to race, creed, or culture. They have, indeed, occurred in many of the religions of the earth. The New Testament records seem to imply that miracles performed by Jesus, Paul, and other Christian figures were more marvelous or powerful than those of any rivals; and there are also hints that some of the healings by rivals may have been performed with satanic powers.

Luke selects an anecdote designed to ridicule some of the imitators of Paul. Seven sons of a Jewish high priest named Sceva were attempting to drive out evil spirits by using the name of Jesus.[121] When these exorcists said, "We adjure you by Jesus whom Paul preaches," the evil spirit answered, "I know Jesus and understand Paul, but who are you?" Then the afflicted man leaped on them and drove them from that house. This comedy strongly reinforced the Christian witness and brought about a spontaneous gathering of people who brought and burned their magic books worth "fifty thousand pieces of silver."[122] Haenchen notes that the people who burned the magic books were those who "had believed," the perfect participle indicating that they had become Christians before they began to confess and announce all their deeds.[123] This indicates that the first acceptance of Christianity was not accompanied by a clear-cut rejection of all previous magical and superstitious practices. From the beginning Christians were confronted by two points of view: one required a clean break with all of the magic and idolatry that pervaded the ancient world, while the other preserved as many of these practices as they could get by with. The exact wording of the passage indicates that not even here did all of the believers cast away and burn their magic books, but a great number of them did.

During the time these spectacular events were transpiring at Ephesus, Paul was formulating plans to initiate a new series of activities in the west (19:21,22). He decided to go through Macedonia and Achaea and then to go to Jerusalem, which is far to the east, on a projected trip to Rome. Of course, Paul's letters reveal that the reason for going to Jerusalem was to take an offering collected in Macedonia, Achaea, and possibly Galatia for the relief of the saints in Jerusalem. (In 24:17 Paul refers to a trip to Jerusalem to carry an offering there; so Luke apparently knows the reason for this trip in ch. 19 even though he does not mention it.) To prepare for his trip through Macedonia, Paul sends ahead Timothy and Erastus (19:22). In I Cor 16 one of the purposes of Paul's trip through Macedonia to Achaea is to receive the collection. He mentions in 16:10 that Timothy will probably visit Corinth before he himself arrives. Therefore it may be inferred that the purpose behind the dispatch of Timothy and Erastus mentioned in Acts 19:22 is the preparation of the offering.

---

[121] It is odd that Luke overlooked the record that when some disciples of Jesus rebuked a man who did not belong to them but was using the name of Jesus in driving out demons, Jesus, instead of approving their action, said, "Do not forbid them, because whoever is not against you is for you" (Luke 9:49-50). Since Luke had himself recorded this incident, he should at least have explained the difference between the non-disciple healers who used Jesus' name in his own lifetime and those who used it in Paul's time.

[122] In an economy where one piece of silver was approximately a day's wage for labor, Luke may have exaggerated with a large round number (19:18,19).

[123] *Acts*, 567.

In the meantime at Ephesus the fantastic success of Paul's preaching was accompanied by the desertion of idol worship and the burning of magic books, and this generated a tempestuous reaction. Demetrius, whose trade was producing miniature silver shrines of the goddess Artemis, led the members of his craft to form a plot against Paul, whom they regarded as subverting the foundations of the religion and temple upon which their whole economic prosperity depended. They stirred up a crowd, seized two Macedonian travel companions of Paul, rushed into the huge theater of the city, and demonstrated boisterously. A chant in praise of Artemis went on for some two hours, and the uproar might have resulted in a pogrom against the Christians in Ephesus and especially against Paul, but cool heads from the Christian community and the city authorities wisely prevailed upon Paul to stay away from the theater. The town clerk convinced the crowd that they had no real basis for the dangerous riot, and also that serious charges of blaspheming their goddess should be presented in an orderly manner before the courts. Thus the mob broke up and calm was restored in the city.

The question arises whether this riot may be the same as the trouble or persecution Paul refers to several times in his Corinthian letters. Allusions in I Cor 15:32 and II Cor 1:8 suggest that Paul had had a very dangerous experience in Ephesus that threatened his life. The Acts account of the riot does not describe Paul as encountering this danger publicly or doing anything like fighting with wild beasts. He is restrained by his Christian brothers from appearing in public during the riot, and there is no indication that he sustained actual harm. As the account stands, after the tumult Paul summoned the disciples, exhorted them in a farewell address, and left for Macedonia (20:1). Though there is no implication of a forced departure, it was likely hastened by the riot, which appeared more dangerous to Paul and his companions than the narrative suggests. If they did perceive the situation in Ephesus as containing a lethal threat to Paul's safety, this could account for Paul's strong language in II Corinthians about his incurring the risk of death. Since Luke does not describe all the major events of Paul's stay in Corinth, he may also have omitted another encounter with hostile forces at Ephesus which jeopardized his life and work. Paul's narrative in II Corinthians is really no more helpful; he gives no reason for leaving Ephesus. He had intended to visit Corinth both on the way to Macedonia and on his return, but his plans were changed by circumstances only hinted at (1:15-24, 2:12,13).[124] Neither in II Corin-

---

[124] The curious coincidence of details with Acts 16:9-12 probably offers a fruitless temptation. Was the "man of Macedonia" Titus or Timothy? Since the pronouns change from "they" to "we" at that point, it is also possible that the man was Luke. The materials for the resolution of the puzzle, however, are simply not available—and perhaps it is only coincidence.

thians nor in Acts is there a complete description of what happened. Paul's motivations are not clear nor is the logic of events, but there are no fundamental contradictions between the two records.

From Macedonia Paul went into Greece where he spent three months. Jewish enemies there formed a plot to kill him on his way to Syria, but Paul decided to go back through Macedonia and thus avoid ambush. Seven companions are named, including Timothy. These preceded Paul (and apparently Luke[125]) to Troas, where the party finally gathered for a week's stay (20:2-6).

One incident from this week is recorded, the story of a young man who, while Paul preached, went to sleep and fell from the window in which he had been sitting (20:7-12).[126] Paul reassured the group that the man was not seriously injured—there is no claim that Paul performed a miracle of healing or resuscitation.[127] Paul's discourse and conversation lasted all night before his departure for the east.

VISIT TO JERUSALEM AND SUBSEQUENT IMPRISONMENT

From Troas Paul and his party sailed among the Aegean islands to Miletus, near Ephesus. There he met elders from the Ephesian church since he was in a hurry to reach Jerusalem by Pentecost (Acts 20:13-17). No explanation is offered for this haste. Many Jews would be in the city for the feast, and perhaps he was hoping that he could get a favorable hearing because he was bringing an offering collected from gentiles for the Jerusalem poor.[128] He was concerned to reconcile Jewish and gentile Christians and also Christian and unbelieving Jews. Luke may have omitted reference to this purpose of Paul because it proved unsuccessful.

Acts 20:18-38 includes a speech which Paul delivered to the Ephesian elders at Miletus. It displays a sense of the future which was impending for the church at Ephesus and of the fate hanging over his own head, and based on this and other considerations it has been pointedly argued that the speech is Luke's idealized version of what he thought Paul should have said.[129] Paul is quoted as emphasizing the role of the Holy Spirit in impelling him to Jerusalem while warning him of the danger awaiting him

---

[125] An important "we" passage; cf. Munck, AB, XXIX-XXXII, XLII-XLIII.

[126] The passage contains one of the New Testament references to Christian gatherings "on the first day of the week," a practice which is explicitly regular by the early years of the second century.

[127] Could it be that in his deep sleep the young man was so relaxed that he was not injured, a common enough phenomenon?

[128] There is a possible hint of such a motivation in Rom 15:30-32.

[129] Cf. Haenchen, Acts, 590-598, and the literature cited there.

there; such interpretation of experience is similar to records surely from Paul's own hand. In Rom 15:30-32 he indicates that he knew before he made the trip to Jerusalem that it was an extremely dangerous venture. From a human point of view, as he went from place to place, he probably got more and more information which consolidated the assurance of the Spirit that in Jerusalem he would, in fact, be imprisoned. Thus what Luke quotes him as saying is by no means the kind of thing that requires knowledge after the fact, even ignoring the question as to whether Paul may really have been given insight into this fact by the Holy Spirit.[130] When Paul also states that the Ephesian elders will not see him again, this knowledge does not depend upon certainty after the fact; for Paul indicates in Rom 15:23-24,28 that he had decided that his work in the eastern Mediterranean area was completed and that he intended to go to Rome and thence to Spain. So, whether he would be killed because of his trip to Jerusalem or not, he would not, in fact, return to Ephesus. He was entering an entirely new area which would occupy him the rest of his life. This suggests that, whatever the recorded literary form of the speech at Miletus, Luke may very well be working from accurate reminiscence.[131]

From Miletus Paul sailed to Tyre, where the unloading of the ship gave him an opportunity to visit with local Christians for a week. "Through the Spirit" they warned Paul "not to go on to Jerusalem" (21:1-6). At Caesarea, where he disembarked, he stayed with Philip the evangelist; and the prophet Agabus provided another warning against the Jerusalem trip (21:7-14). These minatory prophecies, of course, are readily construed as *vaticinia ex eventu*.[132] An interesting question, however, arises in this connection. If Acts was written after the death of Paul—as most chronologies assume—it is hard to see why the author did not extend Agabus' prediction (or add a prophecy elsewhere) to include either the death of Paul at the hands of the gentiles or his release, whichever really happened. The failure to mention Paul's ultimate fate seems to suggest that Luke

[130] Jesus' anticipation of disaster in Jerusalem is in some respects analogous. While Luke lumps much material into his travel narrative (9:51 - 18:14), there is other evidence for Jesus' foreboding: cf. Mark 10:32-34 and John 11:7-10.

[131] Another example of assumed *ex post facto* knowledge is the reference in 20:29-30 to dire problems which were to beset the Ephesian church and which may be alleged to reflect a knowledge of early heresies and schisms at the end of the first century. It may be argued that Paul expected an early return of Jesus and makes no reference to a preceding corruption of the church by external enemies or internal deviations. There is, however, ample evidence in the Corinthian letters to show that Paul had already faced agitators from outside and schismatic divisions within; and since these letters were written before the time of the speech at Miletus, it is plausible that he might extrapolate from the Corinthian experiences to the future of another church. Again, this speaks not to the literary form of the speech but to the basic credibility and accuracy of its contents.

[132] Cf. Haenchen's discussion, *Acts*, 602-605.

wrote Acts before he himself knew what would happen to Paul. Indeed, Paul's response that he was "ready even to die in Jerusalem" supports this suggestion. Critical doubt about the reliability of the records of these prophecies must take account of more than their relationship to what did eventuate.[133]

When the travelers arrived at Jerusalem, Paul immediately reported to James and the elders the success of his ministry among the gentiles (21:15-26). In response Paul was apprised how many Jewish Christians had received the impression that he was teaching Diaspora Jews "to forsake Moses" and to ignore customs of the law including circumcision.[134] In order to avoid trouble Paul was advised to join four Christians who had undertaken a vow (apparently of a Nazirite sort[135]) and to provide for the expenses of this purification. This would demonstrate that Paul was neither by example or precept urging Jews to apostatize from the law. At this point the provisions of the decree described in 15:19-29 were related. Paul then agreed and the next day carried out the plan.[136]

While Paul was visiting the temple to fulfill his part of the vow agreement, Asian Jews who had witnessed his activities in Ephesus saw him in the temple and incited a mob against him (21:27-36). They charged that he had taught people to oppose the Jewish nation, the law of Moses, and the temple of Jerusalem, and that he had profaned the sacred precincts of the temple by taking some Greeks there—the latter charge because they had observed an Ephesian named Trophimus associating with Paul and had assumed that Paul had taken him into the temple in violation of the strict prohibition against non-Jews entering the temple area.[137] When the mob seized Paul with intent to kill him, the military tribune came quickly with soldiers from the nearby headquarters to quell the confusion. He arrested Paul; and since he could make no sense from the uproar, he had Paul carried to the barracks.

Paul engaged the tribune in conversation, convinced him that he was no common criminal, and received permission to address the crowd from the

---

[133] The possibility that Luke intended to write a third volume in which the last days of Paul's life and ministry would be treated is hardly a serious resolution of the matter. The differences that are exhibited within and between Luke's Gospel and Acts render such a projection precarious.

[134] Munck, AB, 209-210, emends the text to refer to non-Christian Jews in order to clarify the apparent contradiction between the welcome given to Paul and the anticipated trouble. There is no textual justification for the omission of the participle *pepisteukōton* in spite of the variants in the preceding phrase. Resolution of the difficulty may be sought either in differentiating the position of the leadership from that of the general membership or in assuming some confusion of details on the part of the author-editor.

[135] So Munck.

[136] Paul's relationship to the decree is discussed *supra,* pp. 63-66.

[137] For a discussion of possible grounds for the other charges, cf. *infra,* pp. 103-106.

barracks steps (21:37-22:30). Paul's bilingual ability is made explicit by mention of his speaking Greek to the tribune and Aramaic to the crowd.[138] The speech summarized Paul's background and recounted (for the second time in Acts) the story of his conversion. When he proceeded to tell of his commission to gentiles, violence broke out again; and the tribune took Paul into the barracks. There Paul was about to be scourged as a means intended to get the truth from him, but he pleaded exemption because of his Roman citizenship and was remanded to a meeting with Jewish authorities the next day. This was also inconclusive, for Paul took advantage of sectarian party animosity by claiming that he was on trial "concerning the hope and resurrection of the dead," a belief consistent with his Pharisaic training but rejected by the Sadducees (23:1-10).

A plot to kill Paul was uncovered by "the son of Paul's sister" and relayed to the tribune, Claudius Lysias. The case was now referred to the Roman governor Felix, and Paul was sent to Caesarea under heavy military escort. At a preliminary hearing Felix decided to hear the case and placed Paul under guard in the palace (23:12-35).

Five days later Paul's accusers appeared with a professional spokesman, Tertullus. After statements of the charges—agitation and profanation of the temple—Paul made his defense. He denied the charges; affirmed his Jewish loyalty, expressed, however, "according to the way"; and restated his hope in the resurrection. Felix put off final judgment until Lysias should come, and he ordered a measure of freedom for Paul (24:1-23). Two details are worthy of attention in this narrative. First, Tertullus does not accuse Paul of actually profaning the temple but of attempting to do so. Second, it is suggested that the authorities had arrested Paul for being a troublemaker among Jews everywhere and for attempting to profane the temple.[139] Thus the charges are, in the last analysis, inconclusive; and the weakness of the case and its consequent political involvement become believable.

---

[138] The substantial problems posed by this speech and its setting are set forth by Haenchen, *Acts,* 620-622. In any case, the apologetic value for Christianity is clear.

[139] The Western reading, which became vss. 6b-8a in the *Textus Receptus (TR),* makes explicit the role of Lysias in the arrest; and the resolution of the problem is difficult (cf. Metzger, *Textual Commentary,* 490). While the narrative elsewhere seems to make it clear that the Roman commander had rescued Paul and then had taken the initiative in the subsequent hearings, the shorter reading here may be supported by Paul's statement in 28:17, "I was handed over as a prisoner from Jerusalem into the hands of the Romans." There are thus two versions of the event, one which affirms that the Romans seized Paul to save him from death at the hands of the furious Jewish mob, and another which implies that Paul was turned over by Jewish authorities to the Romans for trial and punishment on semipolitical charges. A possible solution may be that Paul was arrested (at first for his own safety) during the mob riot; and then, when preliminary interrogation suggested his innocence, the Romans were importuned to keep Paul in custody for further examination. This process, then, dragged out and became clouded with political byplay.

Paul's indeterminate situation continued for some two years. The record (24:24-27) is a strange mixture of comment: if the author were fabricating without any knowledge of the details, he certainly would have been more specific.[140] In any case, Paul was still a prisoner when Felix was succeeded by Porcius Festus. One can only conjecture why Paul did not force the issue during the rule of Felix. He likely thought he was performing some worthwhile Christian mission or would ultimately make some particularly telling witness; for when he did precipitate an appeal, it seems as though he felt he had reached a clear impasse. Festus reopened the hearings but appeared to be playing into the hands of the Jerusalem authorities; so Paul appealed to Caesar (25:1-12).

Before Paul could be sent to Rome, another incident occurred which is given considerable space in Acts (25:13-26:32). Agrippa II and his sister Bernice[141] came to Caesarea; and after Festus had mentioned Paul's case, Agrippa expressed a desire to hear Paul. Paul's "defense" includes again a summary of his early career, the third account of his conversion, and a digest of the gospel Paul proclaims. The reactions to this presentation are interesting: Festus thinks Paul is mad, Agrippa (correctly) understands that Paul is trying to make a convert of him.[142] The conclusion of the interview is stated as a declaration of Paul's innocence, but his appeal to Caesar is allowed to stand.

Luke deftly demonstrates that Paul was innocent of any serious crime against either Jewish or Roman law. At the same time he interprets events to show a providential guidance of Paul's affairs toward a presentation of his case which would provide the widest testimony to the Christian gospel. Paul was not to be acquitted and released but to be put on trial before governors and kings and even the emperor so that he could give personal testimony to his own conversion and to the power of the gospel throughout the world. Thus, by being a prisoner, he had entrée to the highest officials (fulfilling what Jesus had told his disciples, according to Matt 10:17-20). So Paul's defenses are always concerned to show that Jesus had been raised from the dead, had appeared to him and authorized him to proclaim the gospel to the gentiles, and had established and verified the hope of the resurrection from the dead. Truth required that he maintain

---

[140] It is tempting to speculate what Luke was doing during this period. One possibility that has not received serious study is that he pursued the research which he claims in the introduction to his Gospel.

[141] For a concise note on the political situation, cf. Munck, AB, 237. Cadbury surveys "The Family Tree of the Herods" in *Beginnings,* V, 487-489.

[142] The exegetical difficulties in 26:28 do not affect this interpretation. At question is only Agrippa's attitude toward Paul's overture. Apparently it is condescending or cynical; perhaps he replied with a chuckle. (The textual variation is also of no substantive significance for this conclusion.)

his innocence, but the interests of the gospel did not require that he be set free. The only matter of importance was that he carry out the divine commission either as a prisoner or as a free preacher in the streets of the Roman cities.

TRIP TO ROME AND IMPRISONMENT THERE

The authorities delivered "Paul and some other prisoners" to Julius, a centurion of the imperial cohort; and the party embarked in a ship with a cargo of grain headed for ports on the coast of Asia Minor.[143] From Caesarea they proceeded to Sidon, where Paul was permitted to visit friends. At Myra in Lycia the centurion transferred the company to an Alexandrian ship sailing for Italy. They were held back at first by unfavorable winds which kept them hugging the coastline until they reached a point west of Cnidus. The wind forced them to head west instead of south, and they reached a harbor of Crete called Fair Havens. This slow progress and succession of roundabout courses caused considerable time to elapse so that it was already past the Day of Atonement (September-October).

The ship was anchored at an unsafe harbor; and the windy, rainy season was just ahead. Paul urged the centurion to remain at Fair Havens; for, as he said, he saw that a further journey at this time would cause great danger to the cargo and lives of the crew and passengers. The author does not state whether Paul's opinion was based on logical inference or upon divine inspiration. The centurion understandably gave more heed to the ship's officers than to the opinions of Paul. The harbor where they were located was unsuitable for a winter stay; and they consequently decided to head for a Cretan harbor called Phoenix, which apparently provided better protection from the fall and winter storms.

The capricious sea, however, confounded the judgment of the ship's officers. They set sail with a favorable breeze, but soon they were struck by a typhoon-like, northeast wind which drove them past an island called Cauda. Despite emergency measures they were afraid that they would be driven into the shallows of the Syrtis, west of Cyrene on the North African shore. When further precautions failed to better their plight, they despaired of survival. Finally, after passengers and crew had gone without food for a long time, Paul informed them he had been encouraged by a vision from God, which assured him that it was necessary for him to appear before Caesar, and that he and all aboard would be rescued. Paul could not re-

---

[143] This travel narrative, a "we" section, extends from Acts 27:1 to 28:16. Technical nautical information is readily available from the older commentaries.

frain from reminding them that he had anticipated this misfortune, but now he insisted that they take heart. On the fourteenth night of the voyage, as they were carried along the Adriatic Sea,[144] the sailors detected signs of land. Faced with the danger of running on the rocks, they dropped anchors and waited for daylight. Some of the sailors tried to escape in a small boat, but Paul warned the centurion that everyone had to remain on the ship if anyone was to be saved. This time the centurion believed Paul and cut the ropes of the lifeboat, casting it loose. (The ship itself was said to be carrying 276 persons.) Paul kept urging that all take some food. He himself took a loaf of bread, gave thanks to God, and began to eat; and the rest were encouraged and took food likewise. Then they lightened the ship by throwing the grain overboard.

At daybreak they did not recognize the land but thought it might be possible to run ashore. Then they cast off the anchors and under sail made for the beach. Running aground, however, the ship's stern was broken by the force of the wind and waves. The soldiers planned to kill the prisoners so they would not escape;[145] but the centurion, who wanted to save Paul's life, stopped them. He commanded all those who were able to swim to leap off first and make for land. The rest were told to seize planks or beams from the ship now floating in the water. The author records that eventually all managed to reach land safely.

The place where they landed was the island of Malta. The inhabitants received the victims of the shipwreck very kindly and kindled a fire to warm those who had been chilled by the rain and cold. Paul, by shaking off a viper concealed in wood he was collecting for the fire, was thought to be a god by the barbarian Maltese, who had at first assumed he was a murderer about to receive his just fate from the snake poison. The island chieftain was a man named Publius. Paul healed his father of fever and dysentery, and as a result other people were brought to Paul and healed.

The shipwrecked party remained for three months and then embarked on an Alexandrian ship which had been wintering at the island. They touched at Syracuse and Rhegium (Reggio) and finally landed at Puteoli (Pozzuoli) on the Bay of Naples. Here they found some Christians, who urged them to stay a week. Then they went on to Rome. The Christians at Rome heard of their coming in advance and went out to meet them at "the Forum of Appius and the Three Taverns." Paul thus finally arrived at his destination and gave thanks as he saw these Roman Christians. In Rome Paul was permitted to remain in a private dwelling with a soldier guard (under what might now be termed "house arrest").

---

[144] At that time this term was flexible and could cover a wide stretch of the central Mediterranean. Cf. references in *Beginnings*, IV, 335.

[145] Under Roman law the soldiers could forfeit their lives if prisoners escaped from their custody.

In Rome Paul summoned the leaders of the Jewish community and laid his case before them (28:17-22). His tone is conciliatory. He claims that his imprisonment is "because of the hope of Israel"—presumably referring to the Messiah and the resurrection. According to our records Paul's missionary strategy often involved an initial approach to the Jewish community when he came to a new city, and that seems to be one of his motives here. Not only would he hope to make fruitful evangelistic appeal to these people, but also amicable relationship with them would help secure for the Christian community the Roman tolerance afforded the Jews. The Roman Jews professed to have no information about Paul but set a time to hear him—adding that they knew nothing about his "sect."

The substance of Paul's daylong testimony is summarized as "the kingdom of God" and Old Testament witness about Jesus (28:23-28). The Old Testament witness is common enough in Pauline material, but the use of the phrase "kingdom of God" is less frequent.[146] Its use here would seem to indicate that Luke saw no divergence between Paul's preaching and the traditional theme of Jesus' message.[147] The response of the Jews was inconclusive, and Paul again declared his intention to go to the gentiles.

For two years Paul remained in his own rented quarters and was able to receive all visitors. He proclaimed "the kingdom of God" and taught with the utmost frankness and unhindered "the things concerning the Lord Jesus Christ" (28:30,31).

The ending of Acts has been a source of perplexity to its readers. This narrative which was perhaps as graphic as any from ancient times fades out with the pallid statement that Paul remained two years in a house under guard, but was able to evangelize unbelievers and instruct believers. It makes no mention of his relation to the Roman church to which earlier he had written his most famous and profound epistle. The readers' almost unendurable suspense over the question of what ultimately happened to Paul is left unsatisfied; the author never tells what Caesar did with the appeal.

Why such a lame ending? The question is pertinent here because it bears upon the ending of Paul's career and life.[148] The possibility that Luke intended to write a three-volume work has been argued on the basis of

---

146 Rom 14:17; I Cor 4:20, 6:9,10, 15:50; Gal 5:21; I Thess 2:12; II Thess 1:5; cf. Eph 5:5; Col 4:11.

147 Paul probably speaks of "the kingdom of God" infrequently because for him its nearness in Jesus has changed the focus to the continuing Spirit-experience of Christ. Cf. K. L. Schmidt, *TDNT*, I, 589; E. F. Scott, *The Kingdom and the Messiah* (Edinburgh, 1911), 104-105; Héring, *Le Royaume de Dieu et Sa Venue*, 147-245. Perhaps Paul's phrase "in Christ" is in some sense his way of speaking of the kingdom of God.

148 Kirsopp Lake's summary of the matter is given in *Beginnings*, V, 326-332.

prōton in Acts 1:1 with reference to Luke's Gospel, for the word usually refers to the first of a series of more than two. The argument, however, is inconclusive; for *prōtos* does occur meaning the first of two (e.g. Matt 21:18,31). It is strange, moreover, that the Gospel ends with an appropriate climax and then is followed by a sequel while Acts ends without such a climax.

Another possibility is that the ending is a kind of climax, one, indeed, that appropriately ends Luke's work. When Paul reached Rome and proclaimed the gospel there, he had succeeded in attaining a cherished goal. This overlooks the fact, however, that Luke has had a more detailed interest in Paul's career and had recorded a vision (27:24) which informed Paul that he would appear before Caesar.

The third possibility is that Acts was written before Paul's Roman trial occurred. This would require a date in the early sixties and would have far-reaching implications about authorship, traditions, and the relationship to the third Gospel. A corollary of this proposal might be that Theophilus was a high Roman official who could exert influence in Paul's case. This would help to explain details of the book in which Paul's dealing with Roman authority is cast in a positive light. Identification of the "we" passages with the author of Acts (assumed here to have been Luke) takes him to Rome with Paul; and this seems to add an element of likelihood to this explanation of the abrupt ending.

Another peculiarity of the last chapter of Acts is the failure to refer to any continuing communication between Paul and the leaders of the Roman church. The author was aware that there were Christians in Rome, for he stated in 28:15 that "the brothers came to meet us at the Forum of Appius and the Three Taverns." But these brothers slipped from sight in the remaining description of Paul's stay in Rome. Haenchen argues that this omission of reference to any official relationship between Paul and the Roman church is due to the author's intent to make Paul the responsible missionary at Rome in the same way that he had done in other principal cities of the empire.[149] In the light of Paul's remarks, however, in Rom 1:11 and possibly II Cor 10:15 and Philip 1:12-18, it seems clear that he did not think of himself as a pioneer missionary in Rome. His contacts with the Jews were explicitly unproductive and the results of his further mission singularly inconclusive. Such non-Christians as would visit him would likely be agents of government consulting him about details of his case, and proclamation to such people could be considered part of his witness before "governors and kings." Luke lays very little emphasis upon this preaching by omitting any stories of conversions and by confining remarks to the barest summary. The last chapters of Acts bring Paul to

[149] *Acts,* 729-731.

Rome for the sake of presenting his appeal to the emperor: it is difficult to see how Luke could have omitted the description of a favorable answer to the appeal if this had already been granted. It is equally difficult to see how he could have omitted the description of Paul's death if the appeal had been denied, for this would have been a remarkable instance of martyrdom comparable at least to that of Stephen. To construct a powerful story of a legal case and to end it with a brief reference to conversations with visitors in prison for two years is inexplicable procedure for such a writer as Luke. It seems probable, therefore, that the book was completed before the trial occurred; and lack of reference to the Roman church as such was due to Luke's concern with the legal position of Paul as a prisoner—a reasonable explanation if the book had as its purpose a defense of Paul the prisoner and the gospel he represented. Luke was not writing a comprehensive history of the formation of the Christian churches in the first century. He did not include a description of all the work that Paul accomplished in his missionary activity. He omits reference to Paul's preaching in Arabia. He gives no description of what happened when Paul preached in Tarsus and Cilicia. He mentions none of the churches established in the region around Ephesus (such as Laodicea, Colossae, Smyrna, Thyatira), and he gives no hint that Paul proceeded as far as Illyricum in the west. His account is very selective and is apparently designed to reveal (a) Paul's typical procedures in preaching first to the synagogue (in order to show that Paul was a Jewish believer), (b) his typical message to the Jews and then to different types of gentiles, and (c) the customary enlightenment of most officials in their dealings with Paul and Paul's uniform competence in presenting before these officials a persuasive statement of his own objectives. Luke shows that there is nothing in Paul's conduct or Christian propaganda that justifies his exclusion from the Jewish community or his prosecution by imperial officers.

All this makes good sense if Acts was actually composed to present the case of Paul to official Rome. This purpose explains both the omissions and the emphases of the book. The first part of the book that describes the church before Paul entered it serves to explain in brief what the Christian movement is; and it demonstrates that the church, in its early days, piously practiced the Jewish religion, while at the same time it was impelled by divine guidance to explode beyond the bounds of Judaism in a powerful movement to evangelize the world.

Acts should not be discredited as a sourcebook of historical information merely because it was written with a purpose akin to a legal argument for Paul and the whole Christian community. The author is not guilty of falsification if he emphasizes facts that support the cause of his hero and the movement he represents. When he thinks certain events and occurrences do not bear upon the case he is presenting, he is silent. The controversies between Paul and different parties inside the church have no real significance in discrediting Paul in the eyes of the law or of fair judges. Not only is Luke silent about some events that appear embarrassing, but he also leaves out any description of Paul's energetic effort to relieve the distress of the poor in Jerusalem with his great collection; and he fails to describe many of the hardships, dangers, and persecutions which Paul actually endured. For his purposes he did not have space to cover everything. The use of Acts, therefore, to gain information about details in Paul's life not referred to in his letters—and perhaps to construct an outline of events in his life from his conversion to his imprisonment—should not be rejected on a priori grounds.[150]

PAUL'S AUTHORITY AS AN APOSTLE

Although Paul deprecates confidence in one's own personality or achievement, he strenuously insists upon his authority to declare and interpret the gospel. He was "an apostle of Jesus Christ, not from the authorization of men nor appointed by man but by Jesus Christ and God the Father" (Gal 1:1). In the introductions to I and II Corinthians, Ephesians, Colossians, and II Timothy he is an "apostle of Jesus Christ by the will of God." He says, "God separated me from my mother's womb . . . to be the preacher to the gentiles," an appointment that occurred by God's decision "to reveal his Son in me" (Gal 1:15-16).[151]

Paul reiterates on different occasions that his first preaching in each place was empowered by the action of God to produce an effective result. Among the Thessalonians, at whose city he made his appearance after he had been insulted and injured at Philippi, he had boldly spoken the gospel so that his first introduction to them had not been in vain. Avoiding deception, misleading tact, or any arts designed to please men, he had passed the test as one entrusted with the gospel. His only motivation was to please God, and thus he eschewed flattery or covetous pretentions. Though he had the right to claim the dignity of an apostle of Christ, he abstained from any policy which would procure honor, security, or even support for his physical needs from his converts (I Thess 2:1-7). He followed the

---

150 The order of events in Paul's life as derived from his letters and from Acts is charted in the Appendix, pp. 124-131.

151 A common understanding of this verse takes it to refer to the revelation of Christ to Paul which occurred on the Damascus road, but the use of the preposition *en* to indicate an indirect object of a verb is extremely rare. The ordinary meaning of this preposition before non-spatial words is "by" or "by means of." Since this meaning makes sense in the context which affirms that God separated Paul and called him by his grace to reveal his Son in order that Paul might preach him among the gentiles, the interpretation of *en* as instrumental is to be preferred.

same course in Corinth where, without insisting upon apostolic prerogatives, he worked with his own hands to support himself and discarded the
use of any devices of rhetoric or wisdom in declaring the gospel to them (I
Cor 2:1-5, 4:9-13, 9:1-15). Such remarkable self-denial did not exclude
persistent and uncompromising claim to divine authority for his "gospel."
He commends the Thessalonians for the fact that they had received his
proclamation, not as a message from men, but as it really was, a message
of God (I Thess 2:13).

This sublime, even fanatical claim to divine authority for his message
does not carry with it the demand that all his opinions be accepted as revelations from God. He distinguishes between what the Lord says and what
he says in connection with the advisability of marriage for virgins, and
about the proper attitude for Christians who have been deserted by their
non-Christian spouses (I Corinthians 7). He likewise appeals to rational
inference from fundamental demands of love in his discussion of abstinence from idol offerings (I Corinthians 8, 10). Yet there are occasions in
which the authority of the gospel seems to flow over into his opinions about
details of church order and personal conduct. Even in a case where he has
acknowledged he has no word of Christ, he gives his opinion in the form
of command rather than advice (I Cor 7:12-16). When he expresses his
opinion that a widow will be happier to remain as such, he quickly adds,
"And I think I also have the Spirit of God" (7:40). He enjoins silence
upon women in the churches (undoubtedly in connection with the practice
of speaking in tongues and church discussions of policy) on the ground
that female silence is enforced upon women (perhaps wives) in the
churches as a religious custom (14:34). Such assertions of his own authority as Paul makes, though subordinate to Christ's authority, are made
in connection with dubious decisions about divorce and restrictions upon
women. Apparently Paul resorted to categorical imposition of his own
opinion only in matters pertaining to women, and there only in questions
that covered doubtful and unclear cases. When it is a matter on which the
gospel speaks directly and the issue is clearly defined, Paul made no claim
for the authority of his own opinions; he made such claim only where the
gospel was silent or the case perplexing. It seems that his assurance in the
gospel spilled over into some of his instructions in matters where the implications of the gospel are far from authenticated.

All of this raises sharply the question of what was the gospel. In Paul's
letters the term *evangelion* is specified as "the good news [gospel] of
God's Son," "the good news of Christ," "my good news," "the good news
which I have announced to you," "the good news which I am proclaiming," and "*the* good news." Each of these descriptive modifications
has a different meaning in the different instances. "The gospel of God"
may be "the gospel about God" or "the gospel from God." The same

holds for "the gospel of Christ." "My gospel" appears to be the gospel preached by Paul and especially revealed to him. This gospel of Paul which is identified with the gospel of Christ in Galatians 1 is contrasted with "another" gospel proclaimed by the Judaizers and is contrasted with the gospel authorized by the twelve disciples in Jerusalem (Gal 1:6-7; 2). In this case "gospel" (good news) emphasizes the acceptance of the gentiles into the kingdom of God on the basis of justification by the faith of Christ. This gospel was authorized by God and did not come from men; any who subvert it are under the ban of Christ (Gal 1:6-9). On the basis of his authorization to declare that the gentiles are equal to the Jews in receiving the privileges of God's children, Paul proceeds to insist upon total equality and openness of friendship between Jews and gentiles in the church.

Paul's gospel also includes judgment: God, according to Paul's gospel, judges "the secret things of men" (Rom 2:16). The fact that this action of God is disclosed by Paul's gospel, even though it is an action which might be expected by all Jews and Christians, suggests that Paul has concluded that the judgment was not simply upon the deeds of men, as implied in some of the teachings of the rabbis, but upon the instincts and motives which proceed from faith or the lack of faith. If this is so, Paul's gospel includes valid deductions from central principles.

PAUL, THE LAW, AND THE GENTILES

Paul's enemies frequently charged him with ignoring, breaking, or attempting to destroy the law of Moses; and they interpreted his mission among the gentiles as evidence of this. Such accusations had some basis in truth; but when Paul is allowed to speak for himself, they appear as distortions or misrepresentations. Paul indeed preached to gentiles that they were justified by the grace of God and saved by faith and that deeds done in obedience to the law were incapable of justifying anyone. He therefore invited gentiles to accept the faith he preached without undergoing the yoke of the law. He did not, however, preach against the law or against the Israelite people. In Rom 7:12 he writes, "The law is holy, and the commandment is holy and just, and good." Throughout his letters he treats the books of Moses as a divinely inspired source of truth and revelation.

It is necessary, however, to exercise care and to avoid generalization when considering Paul's treatment of the law.[152] His methods of inter-

---

[152] Cf. C. A. A. Scott, *Christianity According to St Paul*, 38-46; Bultmann, *Theology of the New Testament*, I, 259-269.

pretation of scripture are significantly strange to us today, but in his contemporary Jewish milieu they were respectable types of hermeneutic.[153] The most negative comment he made concerning the law was that, because it presents the occasion for sin, it cannot justify but becomes the way of condemnation to death (Rom 7:5-11). For those who rely upon it for life, the law becomes a "curse" (Gal 3:10-13). On the other hand, the law served as a preliminary arrangement made by God to lead people to the Messiah as a Greek "pedagogue" led a child to school (Gal 3:24-25). Paul is careful to say that it is sin and not the law which causes condemnation.

With reference to the Jewish people Paul's proclamation is complicated, even subtle, as may be seen in Romans 9-11. He contested the notion that Jews could be justified before God by careful observance of the law and by making their righteous acts more numerous than sinful ones. He was convinced that complete obedience to the law was in fact impossible. Obedience to the law rather required a kind of perfect life which proceeded from complete love for God and one's neighbor. Paul's Jewish contemporaries had failed to perceive that from the time of Abraham, Israel's favor with God rested on faith and not on deeds prescribed by the law. God's favor was expressed by the election of Israel to be his people. There had always been Israelites who recognized that their standing with God was based on his promise, and these were the true spiritual descendants of Abraham and Isaac. This "spiritual Israel" composed an enduring remnant which was now represented by Jews who perceived a consummation of the promise in the appearance of Jesus the Messiah, the "seed" of Abraham destined to bless the whole world. This blessing would increase as more Jews accepted the Messiah and united with gentiles in a common faith. Paul did not, however, draw the conclusion which his enemies foisted upon him, viz. that Jews who did not accept Jesus as the Messiah were condemned and irretrievably lost. Painstakingly, Paul reveals a "mystery": the Jewish rejection of the Messiah did not mean that they were rejected by God, but God had actually arranged this so that room could be made for the gentiles. God's purpose was mercy for the gentiles, and of course he had mercy in store for the Jews. The Jews who were enemies of God because of the gospel were at the same time beloved by God because of the patriarchs and divine election. "So all Israel will be saved" (Rom 11:26).

Probably the worst thing Paul wrote about the Jews is the statement in I Thess 2:14-16 that the Jews had killed the Lord Jesus and the prophets,

---

[153] In Galatians, for example, his comment on "seed/seeds" (3:16) resembles the pešer of the Dead Sea scrolls; and he explicitly uses allegory in 4:21-31.

persecuted Paul, displeased God, and opposed all people.[154] This is clarified, however, to mean a theological enmity: by prohibiting the preaching of the gospel to the gentiles they were denying to the gentiles the right to be saved. Paul's charge means that they have rejected the Messiah and have compounded the rejection by opposing the proclamation of the Messiah to the gentiles. So it is true that Paul considers the Jewish establishment to be out of accord with God's redeeming purpose, but this charge had often been leveled by the prophets, and it was certainly not a demonstrable manifestation of anti-Jewish feeling. (It is, indeed, a common human failing to oppose people who see a truth that the rest of mankind does not see.) Paul had a controversy with the Jews about the proper interpretation of the election of the Jews, but they were wrong to interpret this as speaking against them in a fundamentally hostile manner. On the contrary, Paul says that he would be willing himself to be banned from Christ if by so doing he could benefit the people of his own race.

There is no substantive record to support charges that Paul profaned the Holy City or the temple there. In his letters he refers to the Jerusalem temple explicitly only once, in I Cor 9:13, where he points out with approval that those who work in the temple eat from the temple offerings. Several times he uses "temple" (*naos*, "sanctuary"; in the previous reference alone, *to hieron*) as a figure for the body of Christians (I Cor 3:16-17, 6:19; II Cor 6:16; cf. also Eph 2:21); but this does not seem to figure in the charges of Paul's enemies. Once (II Thess 2:4) he writes of an eschatological event related to the temple, but again this is not related to the charges.

It is evident from the allegory in Gal 4:24-26 that Paul has an independent view of the meaning of contemporary Judaism. He associates Hagar, Mount Sinai, and Jerusalem as an allegory of religion that enslaves. True, he is saying that Jerusalem is the place where people are attempting to obey the law of God; but the rabbis of his time would probably have affirmed that obeying the law was a delight (so Pss 19:7-11 and 119 *passim*) and not a matter of slavery. Paul, however, is arguing theologically; moreover, he uses Jerusalem precisely for the figure of the heav-

---

[154] Because of the severity of these verses they have sometimes been regarded as a post-Pauline interpolation; indeed, vs. 16c has been taken as an *ex post facto* reference to the fall of Jerusalem (cf. B. A. Pearson, "1 Thessalonians 2:13-16: A Deutero-Pauline Interpolation," *HTR* 64 [1971], 79-94). R. Schippers, however, relates the passage to *paradosis* from primitive church traditions ("The pre-synoptic tradition in I Thessalonians ii:13-16," *NovT* 8 [1966], 223-234); and E. Bammel finds a setting in the lifetime of Paul ("Judenverfolgung und Naherwartung. Zur Eschatologie des Ersten Thessalonicherbriefs," *ZTK* 56 [1959], 294-315). Cf. also the balanced statement of J. T. Forestell in *The Jerome Biblical Commentary* (Englewood Cliffs, N.J., 1968), 230-231.

enly realm of freedom. Again, this can hardly be the basis for the profanation charges.

According to Luke's description of Paul's approach to philosophical
gentiles (Acts 17:24-29), Paul made a general denial that God dwells in
any building made by human hands; but this would have been offensive
only to Jews who held the quasi-pagan notion that Yahweh lived in the
Jerusalem shrine. Paul was applying the monotheism of his faith and was,
indeed, quite in accord with the tradition made explicit in Solomon's
prayer of dedication (I Kings 8:27). Many Jewish scholars contemporary
with Paul would have denied that God could be localized.[155]

In short it would seem that Paul was victimized by mob excitement
which was generated by a distortion of his teaching and a caricature of his
real position. His gospel of free forgiveness of sin and free life in the Spirit
as it expresses love and faith was threatening to those who regulated
goodness by rules and penalties. Finally Rome abetted Jerusalem in
repressing the man who carried the message of future hope for them both.

WHAT KIND OF MAN WAS PAUL?

Because Paul was the great apostolic missionary to the gentiles and became the authority in the Christian religion next to Jesus Christ, the characteristics of Paul as a person have often been overlooked. His letters
reveal an extremely complicated individual who balances opposite characteristics; so a clear delineation of his basic traits is an elusive task.
Paul was authoritative and pliant. He was strong-willed and unusually
amenable to suggestion. He was totally unconcerned about achieving any
kind of position in this world and was indifferent to praise or criticism, but
he almost nervously insisted upon his authority. He was severe in castigat-
ing those who rejected his gospel or tried to supplant him in the church.
His only aim was to spread the good news about Jesus Christ to as many
sinners of the human population as possible. In pursuing this end, he engaged in a bewildering number of activities: founding churches, refuting
Jewish and gentile opponents, formulating the main lines of Christian
theology, and buttressing these by detailed interpretation of the scriptures.
He managed the affairs of the churches, appeared on their behalf before
government officials, and used every device for conciliating the favor of
people who might be able either to harm or to aid the church in its in-
fancy. He traversed the entire axis of the eastern Roman empire and was
able to attract a core of followers in an incredible variety from a number

[155] Cf. Philo *De Monarchia* II 1.

of provinces and nationalities. The few letters of his that have been preserved constitute a major section of the New Testament.

He could earn his own living by plying a trade which required hard physical work. He was versatile enough to make productive contacts in any new town he entered. He directed a relief expedition for the benefit of the poor Christians in Jerusalem at a time when people were inclined neither to indulge in individual philanthropy nor to take the slightest interest in giving aid to people of another nationality. This kind of indifference was particularly evident in the relations between gentiles and Jews. Jews often were the object of mob hostility in the cities of the empire, and they were the butt of the polished scorn of literary geniuses such as Horace, Juvenal, and Lucian. Many gentiles were attracted to the monotheistic features of the Jewish religion and some were actually converted to the Jewish community, but most of these proselytes were not generous in meeting the needs of poverty-stricken Jews. Paul, however, was able to stir Christians, at least in Macedonia and Achaea, to take up a very sizable offering to be delivered for the relief of the poor saints in Jerusalem, no easy task as can be seen from his appeals incorporated in I and II Corinthians.

Another difficulty in trying to estimate or describe Paul as a human being arises from the fact that he was so unconcerned about the ordinary interests of common life and so completely absorbed in preaching the gospel that he reveals few of the hopes, disappointments, and ambitions that most people know. His letters reveal nothing of any personal love life, and they show total indifference to the acquisition of property or wealth. He was oblivious to honors, recognition, or favors of a political or financial nature from the powers in commerce or government. He revealed no personal dislikes of physical objects, nor any fascination with the fine points of speaking or writing. He seeks no credit for intellectual mastery of the subjects of human learning. There is no hint that particular kinds of persons grated on his nerves. His sole standard of evaluation of people was furnished by the revelation of God in Christ: anyone whose life exhibited loyalty to Christ, sincere effort to show Christian love, and participation in the new society of the Spirit was a beloved brother or sister to Paul regardless of human quirks or failings. He was devoid of gossipy interest in peculiarities and eccentricities of human behavior and in no way yielded to the temptation to sketch the profiles of people he knew so as to enliven his writings with human interest or to indulge in humor at their expense. He never describes a meal—the types of food that were offered, the kinds of people that were present, and sort of conversation that was indulged in. He likewise gives no inside information about the manner, style, or eccentricities of the governors and proconsuls before whose judicial benches he was often presented. He never names a Roman official, nor does he refer to the emperor by name. He never comments on the customs which prevail in the places he visited. We know nothing from his letters about the accommodations on the ships in which he sailed, the sort of overnight places where he stayed, nor the people with whom he carried on his business. Though he had intimate knowledge of many of the jails of the great cities in the ancient Mediterranean world, he tells nothing of the kinds of buildings utilized, the sort of diet furnished, or the treatment afforded prisoners. We learn nothing about how other prisoners regarded him—unless he refers to several of them as converts to the Christian religion.

Few men of his time had closer acquaintance with more people in more different places than did Paul. In the letters that may assuredly be ascribed to Paul, he mentions by name no fewer than forty-eight persons, a significant sum to be borne in mind over against his theological deliverances. These are mostly persons with whom he dealt and worked in the founding of churches, and a third of them are women. His interest is always focused upon contributions to the Christian cause or upon some defect in Christian service that needed to be corrected. In several instances he provides brief, personal, Christian profiles; but he relates next to nothing about personal, human characteristics.

One of the most significant facts about Paul's life is the absence of concern for popularity, personal amusement, or enjoyment of the society of others. He showed no interest in economics or in the goods produced and exchanged in the localities he visited. He all but ignored the poetry, art, drama, and science of his day. He had his mind fixed, not on the transitory events or currents of life in this world; but, as he himself says, he kept his eyes on "the things that are unseen" and consequently "eternal" (II Cor 4:18). It may be that the supreme characteristic of a great, creative personality is the ability to concentrate on one thing and to ignore or to subordinate everything else in the service of that thing. If this is true, then Paul was one of the world's truly creative persons.

In addition to the ability to concentrate wholly on one objective, the value of such a person to humanity depends upon the kind of objective he selects. He may pursue power as a conqueror or he may be drawn to the acquisition of knowledge as a scholar, or he may be devoted to establishing great institutions as a pioneer in human history. Paul selected none of these objectives but threw himself entirely into the effort to establish a transnational, interracial, nondiscriminatory society of men, women, slaves, freemen, saints, sinners, rich, poor, ignorant, learned—inhabitants of all the nations he could reach—in order to bring into being on this earth "the revelation of the sons of God" (Rom 8:19). The scope of this purpose is breathtaking when the difficulties and obstacles that obstruct it are considered. To produce a society like this requires a willingness to counter all the inherited social practices and prejudices of the ages, with a brazen audacity in defying past practice so as to bring people together who had been rigidly separated from the beginning of time. It likewise requires an infinite adaptability to the circumstances and complicated situations that exist in every different locality. It must help ordinary human beings to believe that such a chimerical society is possible, but this can only be achieved by stimulating the minds of astute and sophisticated persons and by attracting the sacrificial willpower of all peoples to commit themselves to such a venture. Paul had to awaken the feelings of hope, of love, and of religious devotion to something unprecedented and invisible in opposition to the magnificent displays of pageantry, ritual, inherited customs and beliefs, and religious and patriotic sentiments that all pagan religions had built up through the ages.

As if this were not enough, Paul had to face enraged mobs, stand unshaken when pelted with rocks and verbal abuse, endure lacerations of the flesh with whips and rods, and maintain presence of mind in countering charges directed against him in the courts by some of the cleverest legal minds of both gentiles and Jews. He had to prove that he was not an atheist when he denied the reality of all the gods of the nations. He had to demonstrate that his movement was not alien to Judaism (which had a legal status in the empire) even though he ignored the laws, dropped the venerable practices, and castigated the prevailing conservatism of his Jewish contemporaries. He had to demonstrate that his movement, which acknowledged only one Lord in this life or the world to come, was still not in violation of the fundamental laws of the Roman empire. He dealt with cosmic questions about the origin of the universe, the nature of man, the meaning of life and death, the being and nature of God, and the manifest operations of God under the form of the Spirit in human existence. He outlined the fundamental elements of a new morality which was not hidebound by old rules and regulations, no matter how ancient and sacred, and which gave a comprehensive set of principles by which people could make decisions and guide their lives in the confusing crosscurrents of the cosmopolitan Roman world. With all of this Paul was forced by circumstances to deal with the resentments, quarrels, petty egotisms, and licentious lusts of little people who brought with them to the churches much of what they had been before. He had to give guidance about how a man and wife should be related to one another, how masters and servants should conduct themselves in their households, how Christians should settle their disputes, how they should relate themselves to a world of enemies bent on their destruction, and how they should conduct themselves in the ordinary problems of making a living and gaining the respect of the non-Christian population.

Paul did not leave any systematic treatise on ethics, theology, or social deportment; but he analyzed and treated specific incidents that arose.

When the new Christians faced decisions about policy or conduct, they often disagreed among themselves; and their questions were submitted to Paul for some sort of answer. They were perplexed about how to distribute relief funds and to whom, whether to require Christians to separate from non-Christian marriage partners, what kind of daily social contacts they should enter with the pagan population around them, what sort of ethics should prevail in marriage and in the domestic business of their families, and how to conduct church worship and regulate the vivacious activity of newly created Christians with rapturous spiritual endowments. Their enthusiastic acceptance of the new religion caused friction among them on many matters that seem trivial from this distance; but Paul painstakingly treated each question by holding it up to the light of the Christian perspective from which he viewed all things. Some of the most impressive and moving words he ever uttered were put together in dealing with such problems. The great treatise on love in I Corinthians 13 was meant to guide them in the exercise of spiritual gifts, the most troublesome of which was "speaking in tongues." His profound discussion of the resurrection in I Corinthians 15 was occasioned by a dispute about whether those who had already died would be able to participate in the glories of the kingdom when Christ came back. His incisive discussion of the Lord's Supper, the kernel of which has been incorporated into the liturgies of Christendom, was stimulated by the thoughtless practice of some church members who ate their own food and drank their own wine without sharing it or waiting for the poor who had to come late. His treatment of the freedom of the Spirit and the new triumphant life in Romans 8 was composed to answer the question, Why not indulge in sin if we are freely forgiven by God as the result of his grace? Thus Paul did not compose a system of doctrine or an orderly treatment of all ethical problems or a sourcebook of fundamental moral axioms. In the hurry of a crowded life he had to take time to dictate letters to harassed church people so as to give them confidence when they were wavering in insecurity, hope when they were afflicted by fear, and light when they did not see how to conduct themselves in complicated conditions. All of his discussions are occasional. This makes some of his paragraphs very difficult to penetrate since they were written about incidents that the original readers fully understood but which later readers may find unintelligible. In spite of this, it is astounding to discover the intricate implications that careful study may draw from them. Who could believe that these short letters could have influenced mankind so seriously and so long? Such powerful stimulus to Christian life was furnished by the thoughts of a man long ago engaged in establishing new churches and dealing sympathetically with church questions from a totally committed Christian point of view, and the concrete nature of the events made his discussion fit human life exactly through the centuries.

Paul's discussion of these problems and perplexities reveals his absolute commitment to spread the gospel of Christ and win people to accept it. This commitment could not be diverted by any desire for rest, amusement, or intellectual activity. No pain or humiliation could induce him to seek ease or solace. No prospect of improving his status or enjoying self-satisfaction could entice him to depart from the course of life imposed upon him by divine "compulsion" (I Cor 9:16). The relentless goad spurred him to go from city to city and to provoke at every place an intense discussion of the ways of God, the needs of men, and the offer of Christ. Inhibitions of conventional courtesy never caused him to lose an opportunity to acquaint people with what had recently happened in Judaea and to insist on an immediate personal response to the news of these happenings. The spur that constantly prodded him was not an abstract ideal or purpose formulated by analytical thought but a vision of a divine man who, after an awful death, had appeared to him glorified and alive. This picture was etched on Paul's consciousness by God's revelation. Once Paul had seen God's Son, he could never forget. He could not be interested thereafter in any diversions, however appealing. No vision of comfort or position or power could entice him. The revelation which he had seen so engrossed his mind that he could never turn his thoughts to anything else. His experience had attached him to this divine person with the force of an irresistible magnet.

Words used to label psychopathic experience and hallucination fit Paul. He had a fixation, was obsessed, was driven, was alienated from ordinary existence, was rigid or inflexible, and was rapt by a vision unseen by other human eyes. He found no other interest or concern worth a moment's notice in comparison with the person to whom he was thus attached. Under the impulse of a drive that never relaxed, attracted by the splendor of a vision that never dulled, he pressed relentlessly toward the goal that was set before him (Philip 3:14). Like the proverbial stream that keeps flowing toward the sea, never stopping until it empties into the ocean, Paul kept on unswervingly preaching, teaching, urging, and helping people from Antioch to Rome, through mountain passes, in spite of shipwreck, in the face of screaming enemies, in and out of courts and prisons, and over the disdain, indifference, and ridicule of prominent antagonists. He seems never to have entered a town without gathering a group of people around him whom he then left as the core of a future church. Such concentration, hardly duplicated in history, does not mark Paul as unstable or neurotic. Fixated as he was toward his goal, he could still understand all the different types of people he met. He could placate those whose feelings had been ruffled and find a way to reconcile those who were bitterly hostile. He knew how to make use of the thoughts and whims of others to further his cause. He constantly distinguished between important and unimportant matters. He allowed absolute freedom for difference in things that did not affect the heart of the gospel. He lived effectively and efficiently under conditions of stress, persecution, or poverty, or under conditions where provision had been made for his comfort and ease. He remained a year and a half in Corinth when there was work to do there, though usually he felt impelled to go from place to place with more restless perseverance. If people differed from him in matters that did not affect vital interest of the faith, he did not allow that to disturb him: he welcomed their efforts even though they desired to interfere with his own progress or success (Philip 1:15-18). Yet he faced rivals in the church with anathemas if they perverted the gospel or threatened the unity of the church (e.g. Gal 1:8-9).

Paul expressed the intensity of his concentration on the goal of advancing the gospel by stating, "I live no longer, but Christ lives in me" (Gal 2:20). He also said, "I count all things as loss for the sake of Christ" (Philip 3:8). This means he had no regard for his existence as a personal self and laid no claim upon any possession or right, for he had surrendered it all to the cause of the gospel.

Besides this concentration Paul exhibited a remarkable attitude of thanksgiving. In Romans 1 he indicates that the source of human sin is the original failure of man to honor God and give thanks. The recognition that God is the source of all existence and at the same time has provided a free salvation filled Paul's eager mind with profound gratitude. This grateful glorification of God made it possible for him to endure all adversities with courage and predominantly with cheerfulness. He was subject to fits of almost uncontrollable anxiety about the conditions in the church—as in the case of a disturbance in Corinth when he could not refrain from going to Macedonia to find Titus in search of news (II Cor 2:13). When he was attacked by a "messenger of Satan," a "thorn in the flesh," he besought God many times for relief; but he had to learn to live affirmatively with weaknesses, insults, constraints, persecutions, and dire hardships, "because when I am weak, then I am strong" (II Cor 12:7-10). He had fears within and outside conflicts on various occasions (II Cor 7:5). Likewise he could be overcome with grief about an unfavorable turn in the course of the church's life (II Cor 2:1-4). This could cause him sleepless nights. But none of these cares or sufferings prevented him from persisting in thanksgiving. He begins every letter except Galatians with an outburst of thanksgiving or praise for the Christian graces and accomplishments of the people in his churches. To be sure, all ancient letter writers began by giving thanks to the gods for recent successes, healing, gifts of fortune, and rescue from danger; but Paul differs from them in expressing thanks for what had happened in the lives of other people. Never does he allude to anything which has accrued to himself. His mind is always flooded with gratitude for the faith, constancy, exercise of rich gifts, endurance of hardships and persecutions, and the abiding expectancy of his Christian friends as they are awaiting the triumphs of Christ's kingdom. Only on one occasion does he refer to anything they had done for him (Philip 1:3-7), and here he is more interested in the love and eagerness for gospel service revealed by the gift of the Philippians than he is in the benefit he himself received. His reaction of joy as he attributed all good things to God seemed to come naturally. Rabbinical prayers and teachings indicate that among pious Jews the habit of expressing thanks to God, especially for the good things of life, was universal. So Paul's constant expression of thanksgiving may be the result of his Jewish training, but his experience of life in the church contributed a special flavor to his adoration of God.

Paul showed an intense interest in everything that happened in all his churches. He described himself as the father of the church in Corinth (I Cor 4:15) and stated that he was like a mother enduring labor pains for the Galatians (Gal 4:19). He nourished the Thessalonians as a nursing parent nurses infants (I Thess 2:7).[156] The uncontrolled suspense which forced him to leave Troas to go to Macedonia (II Cor 2:12-13) is only one indication of how concerned he was for the outcome of his recent altercation with the Corinthian church. Of course, he zealously watched over all the churches to see that they were not led astray by perversion of the gospel in the direction either of undue legalistic severity (Galatians and Colossians) or of lax morals (I Corinthians). He expressed vividly his craving that they be united (I Corinthians), that they constantly help each other and show brotherly affection (Romans, Galatians, Philippians), that they manifest willingness to help sinners bear the burden of their guilt and to restore them with free forgiveness (Galatians); and he is concerned that the churches show consideration for the young leaders as well as the older members who should be honored and who in conditions of poverty should be supported (I Timothy). He involves himself in the life and needs of all these widely scattered people as energetically as any conscientious father in the affairs of his children. All of this displays a kind of nervous energy and emotional power that is never dulled or weakened by weariness or disasters.

Paul never relaxed in asserting his right to be the guide and leader of his churches. In a daring appeal he called upon them to imitate him (I Cor 4:16, 11:1). Such an appeal might seem presumptuous, but Paul was so sure that he had been completely taken captive by Jesus Christ that he could allow new Christians to use him as an example.[157] Paul meant for

---

[156] The difficult textual problem in the second clause of the Greek text does not materially affect this figure. If the more strongly attested *nēpioi* is read, one more illustrative item may be added to the above list. (Cf. Metzger, *Textual Commentary*, 629-630; and *The Text of the New Testament* [New York, 1968], 230-233.)

[157] Cf. the commentary.

the churches to look upon his policy and strategy in conducting his mission as a guide in their daily decisions. There was precedent for this in Paul's Jewish upbringing.[158] It is likewise implied in Paul's understanding of the presence of the Spirit of Christ. Certainly Paul had no hesitation in asserting that the essential meaning of Christ's life and death had been and was incorporated in his own personality. Hence on occasion he insisted upon acceptance of his authority in some basic matter affecting Christian life. He affirmed emphatically that the gospel he preached had come as a revelation from God and that any deviation from this must be anathematized (Gal 1:8). He affirmed that certain disturbers of the Corinthian church, even though appearing in the guise of apostles of Christ, were really angels of Satan (II Cor 11:12-15). All of these outbursts seem to have come as reactions against attempts to draw distinctions among people and to exclude certain ones from Christian fellowship. In Antioch representatives from James induced even Cephas and Barnabas to withdraw from table fellowship with the gentiles. In Galatia certain persons were insisting that Christian converts had to be circumcised. And in Corinth some seemed to be affirming that only those who spoke in tongues really had the gifts of the Spirit. Against all of these Paul inflexibly demands that the gospel must not be restricted, diluted, or enchained by human prejudice or snobbery. Thus Paul's demand that his apostolic authority be acknowledged had as its objective resistance to any narrow exclusivism. He affirms constantly the broad and universal boundaries of Christian fellowship.

His insistence on his apostolic authority was not based on personal egotism or selfish thirst for power. When a group in the Corinthian church claimed special loyalty to Paul, he rebuked them and insisted that he was nothing except a steward of the mysteries of God. He demands that their loyalty be attached to Christ, and not to himself or Apollos or Peter (I Cor 1:11-13, 4:1). Of similar intent was his attitude toward the partisan preachers in Philippi (Philip 1:15-18). When the Corinthians forgave a man who had in some manner injured Paul, he expressed his wholehearted concurrence—failure to do so would give Satan an advantage (II Cor 2:5-11). Thus Paul drew a clear distinction between loyalty to himself as an apostle and a living representative of the gospel of Christ and attachment to himself as a human individual. The first loyalty simply meant loyalty to the gospel, but attachment as an individual could mean perversion of the true gospel. A loving acceptance of human individuals is necessary, but partiality and preference of one person over another is a subtle contradiction of the equality of all people before God.

Surprisingly, this apostolic posture did not make Paul stiff, aloof, or arrogant. He remained sensitive to the feelings of the people with whom he

---

[158] Cf. Michaelis in *TDNT*, IV, 666-673; but also the reservations of W. D. Davies in *The Bible in Modern Scholarship* (Nashville, 1965), 178-183.

was dealing, he recognized the need for kindness even when rebuking them, and he adjusted his manner and style of presentation to the kinds of persons he confronted. He knew well the difference between Jews and gentiles, masters and slaves, learned and ignorant, and those who had strict, moral self-discipline and those who had lived a life of self-indulgence. To each and all he related in a manner suitable to their past experience. In fact, he says that he became "all things to all people" (I Cor 9:22). Whatever the historical trustworthiness of Luke's report of Paul's speeches in Acts, they accurately reflect the different kinds of approach Paul made to different types of audiences. To the Jews he stressed the teachings of the law and the prophets concerning the Messiah. To the Lycaonians he referred to the alternation of the seasons and the rich benevolence of nature as demonstrations of the goodness of God. To the Athenian philosophers he pointed out the absurdity of idol worship in the face of the creation of the natural universe and the unity of the human race. To Roman officials he described a harmony of the Christian message with good order and lawful existence in the empire.[159] He did not allow any particular framework of thought to restrict him as he spoke to different peoples. Through all his utterances there was a consistent loyalty to God and to his revelation, but there was also a clear modulation of approach to the diversity of human beings.

Another remarkable quality of Paul's life was his amazing endurance of hardships, both physical and spiritual. He gives a list of some of these in II Cor 11:23-29; and although it is specifically not intended to be exhaustive, it is more extensive than the recital in Acts.[160] This may suggest that Paul was a rather young man when he undertook his strenuous career, especially since he hints at poor health.[161] Nothing could deter or divert him from his main purpose. Yet when he referred to his troubles and obstacles, he felt some embarrassment; and he pointed to himself only when he was forced by attacks on his apostleship. It is hard to conceive of such tenacity of purpose and such resiliency of spirit which never became plaintive and never expressed self-pity. His heritage, his life experience, and the power of the gospel of Christ made him tough in holding out against all opposition or obstacles.

Paul took for granted the basic elements of a moral life even though he insisted that nobody was justified by righteous works. He shared the Jewish abhorrence of idolatry, but he was willing to be friendly to idolators. He kept himself above any suspicion of erotic interests in women, yet he maintained constant freedom of friendship and common life with them.

---

[159] Acts 9:22, 13:32-41, 14:15-17, 17:24-29, 24:10-21.

[160] Cf. also II Cor 4:8-12, 6:4-10. Héring has pertinent notes in his *Second Corinthians*, ad loc.

[161] Ogg, *Chronology*, 10. Cf. II Cor 12:7-10; Gal 4:13-15.

He renounced all avarice even while he worked for a living. He was constantly concerned with relieving the needs of widows, orphans, and the poor. While he was flexible in his approach toward various points of view, he was persistently truthful—he indignantly rejected the charge that he was using guile or flattery in presenting the gospel. He was temperate in the use of wine and food and insisted that all Christians should be sober and hardworking. Thus Paul would give place to no Puritan in his own self-discipline and virtuous mode of life. Yet he insisted over and over again that all of this, as a basis for human glory or pride, was utterly worthless: the basic reason for virtue was to commend the gospel.

Along with his intense commitment to the objective of spreading the news of Christ's death and resurrection in as many new places as possible, Paul acutely analyzed the principal intellectual doctrines involved in this message; and thus he laid the foundation for the systematic theology of the Christian religion. His mind was absorbed in creative theological activity which included doctrines of God, of human nature, of divine revelation, of justification and salvation for people, of the significance and destiny of the Jewish race; and he constantly exegeted the ancient scriptures. As he thought through all of this, he obtained a clear outlook upon reality from the point of view of Christian faith. The startling novelty of this outlook continually stirred up dangerous and hostile questions or criticisms thrust at him from acute Jewish and philosophical opponents, but his mind was agile enough to respond with apt and pithy answers to approaches from all quarters, and thus he supplied the foundation upon which all later Christian apologetics has been reared. Paul's fascination with creative theology tied him closely to human beings instead of isolating him from them. His theology was through and through personalistic and ethical. While it rose to the level of essentialist conceptualism, it remained practical and existential in all its parts. Romans 1 and Colossians 1, 2 do reveal by a few incidental remarks that Paul intimately manipulated the elements of a metaphysical view of the universe. He unquestionably possessed some sort of ontological theory in connection with problems concerning the reality of perishing things over against universal entities.[162] He resisted, however, the temptation to elaborate an ontological system; for important as this might be from a speculative standpoint to buttress his theology, he preferred to let each basic idea of his "salvation theology" blaze with a light that showed the pathway out of snake-infested jungles of sin and estrangement. Every discussion of a theological theme illuminated the life-situation of the ethical and religious underbrush. He never presented a thought for the mere purpose of describing abstract or subjective theories. Incisive and intellectual as Paul was, he may have been the world's foremost pragmatist.

---

162 Cf. II Cor 4:17-18, 5:1-5.

The actual death of Christ and his teachings provided the transcendent source of Paul's theological activity. His pragmatism was thus devoid of any self-seeking rationalization or accommodation of principles to private lust for wealth or power. Since he had filled his mind with the cosmic significance of the world's greatest person, Paul gained the ability to apply lofty spiritual ideas to human conditions with subtle flexibility.

Paul's faith inoculated him with an almost pathological aversion to glorying in or boasting of any personal religious or ethical achievement. The prime object of his aversion was the tendency of the moral man to feel self-satisfied or self-complacent with his own goodness. This all-pervasive moral assumption—that anyone who consistently keeps the moral law and who sacrificially aids his fellow beings has the right to enjoy the approval of his conscience and to anticipate the commendation of God—seems ineradicably fixed even in healthy human minds; and Paul explicates the powerful sway of this idea. He affirms (Romans 2) that anyone who obeys the law is justified by the deeds of the law. The crucifixion of Jesus Christ, however, destroyed for Paul the power of this truth, at least insofar as it might justify any human being under present conditions in preparing a statement of claims against God.

Over against God, no human being is justified—this for three reasons.

1) The infinite graciousness of God in providing for our existence in this world suggests that the only appropriate feeling toward God is gratitude. This must be continuous no matter how strenuously we may otherwise have been working to do God's will. The pains and difficulties of this life do not warrant complaint or bitterness, for ultimately the capacity to suffer pain becomes a means of defense against dangerous disease and weariness with life's struggles and is part of a system in which confronting obstacles develops and toughens moral character.[163] Thus the appropriate response to life situations overcast with trouble and pain may be thankfulness. Paul with remarkably clear vision, understood and felt the response of faith; for as an incidental feature of his pioneering work he lived through fearful dangers. Yet he never upbraided God for producing a world that endangered him with such destruction, or which constantly subjected him to agony and exhaustion. He likewise refused to take credit for bearing heroically all these troubles. Since these were simply incidents of life that had to be faced by anyone who had the privilege of living in this world and who had the special obligation of executing the divine mission, he was profuse in expressing thanks to God.

2) The sufferings he endured had the additional value of joining Paul with Christ in enduring hardship and pain which contributed to the salvation and comfort of other Christians, and sharing the agonies of Christ

---

163 Cf. Rom 5:3-5; II Cor 6:9-10, 12:10.

guaranteed a sharing of resurrection (II Cor 1:3-10). Since preaching the gospel aroused intense opposition, Paul and his fellow believers had to endure calumny, imprisonment, torture, and possibly death. But this was merely the price to be paid for offering a cure for the disease of the world, and the sufferings of any one person furnished an inspiring example for others to copy (I Thess 2:14-16).

3) Dominating all of Paul's thinking was the anticipation of glory to come. This he described as "the prize of the upward call of God in Christ Jesus" (Philip 3:14), "the glory which is about to be revealed" (Rom 8:18), "the freedom of the glory of the children of God" (8:21), inheriting "God's kingdom" (I Cor 6:9, 15:50), "an eternal dwelling in the heavens" (II Cor 5:1), resurrection in imperishability, glory, and power (I Cor 15:42-43) and "life eternal" (Rom 2:7 and *passim*). Paul refrains from any effort to delineate the characteristics of this immortal, transcendent glory. He makes no attempt to describe the state of paradise or the kinds of delights to be expected there. The only basis of his expectation was the resurrection of Jesus Christ and the present power of the Spirit of God. Since Christ had been raised from the dead and was manifesting the power of a conqueror against invisible enemies, Paul was convinced that a similar resurrection with comparable glory is in store for all those who are Christ's partners. This conviction assured him that the future glory will outweigh the oppression of present affliction beyond all comparison (II Cor 4:17).

PAUL FACING QUARRELS, SCANDALS, AND QUANDARIES IN CORINTH

The canonized collection of New Testament writings includes two letters addressed "to the church of God which is in Corinth." The place of these letters in the reconstruction of a life of Paul has already been treated.[164] Paul's mission in Corinth is important, not only for the strategic role it played in the spread of Christianity in the first century, but particularly for the literary deposit that it produced.

The geographical location of Corinth gave it great significance both commercially and politically. Julius Caesar made it a Roman colony in 4 B.C. Because of the immense traffic across the isthmus the city was a magnet for people of all sorts.[165] From the time of Homer the area had been characterized as "wealthy," a description reflecting the fertility of the

---

[164] *Supra,* pp. 14-28, 81-83.

[165] Not only was merchandise transshipped, but ships were dragged by wheeled machinery across a paved portage (*diolkos;* cf. Strabo *Geography* VII ii 1).

plain.[166] The citadel of Acrocorinth dominated the isthmus and made its defense quite feasible. The city Paul visited was just over a century old, but it maintained traditions that went back more than a millennium.[167]

First-century Corinth had a large agglomeration of Romans, Greeks, and Orientals including Jews. The cults of Ephesian Artemis and of Isis had places of worship.[168] Philo alludes to the presence of Jews in Corinth before A.D. 40.[169] A damaged stone found in Corinth near the end of the nineteenth century is apparently the lintel of the doorway of a Jewish synagogue, perhaps the very one in which Paul began to preach in Corinth.[170] The Graeco-Roman gods were also worshiped. Pausanias mentions statues and shrines of much of the pantheon in the city, at the harbors, along the roads, and throughout the isthmus.[171] The area was particularly devoted to Poseidon. There was a temple of Octavia, sister of Augustus; and the grave of the Cynic philosopher Diogenes was near the city gate. There was also the ornamented grave of a famous courtesan Lais. A statue and temple of Aphrodite might call to mind the story of Strabo that old Corinth had a temple of Aphrodite served by more than a thousand hierodules.[172]

The tremendous variety of religions and of peoples in Corinth furnished a wild environment, a chaos of customs, and all kinds of immorality. Paul notes the vast gap between the rich and the poor (I Cor 11:20-22) and uses an apt quotation regarding morals (15:33). It is likely, however, that Paul came to the city, not primarily because of the challenge presented by its particular wickedness, but because its importance in international commerce made it strategic for his program to evangelize the gentile world.[173] The Jews had learned to live in a kind of uneasy truce with paganism; indeed, here as elsewhere there may even have been accommodation on the part of some Jews to certain other religious beliefs.[174] The religious culture of the city acquainted people with theological and religious intercourse in which deep religious emotions were disciplined by dialogue. People entering the Christian church undoubtedly brought with them a habit of free discussion about gods, rites, and principles.

[166] *Iliad* 2.570; cf. Strabo viii vi 20.

[167] For details, see Robinson, *Corinth: A Brief History of the City and a Guide to the Excavations* and *The Urban Development of Ancient Corinth*.

[168] Pausanias *Description of Greece* ii ii 6 and iv 6.

[169] *Legatio ad Caium* xxxvi 281.

[170] Cf. Deissmann, *Light from the Ancient East*, 15, n. 7; also Finegan, *Light from the Ancient Past*, 281. G. Ernest Wright, *Biblical Archaeology* (Philadelphia, 1957), 261, thinks the synagogue was later than Paul's time.

[171] *Description of Greece* ii i-iv; so also for data following.

[172] *Geography* viii vi 20. Conzelmann's commentary, p. 12, sets this "fable" in historical perspective.

[173] So Robertson and Plummer, xiii.

[174] Schmithals, *Gnosticism in Corinth*, 118; Gunther, *St. Paul's Opponents and Their Background*, 10-12, 315.

It is difficult to date with precision Paul's first arrival at Corinth and the correspondence which he had with the church there. Putting together data about the presence of Aquila and Priscilla and the proconsulship of Gallio[175] it may be inferred that Paul came to Corinth about A.D. 52. Allowing for his stay of a year and a half, a trip to Syria and return to Ephesus, and the extended stay in Ephesus, the date of I Corinthians would be about 56. Although these dates cannot be established firmly, they are reliable approximations.

The correspondence of Paul with the Corinthian church is included in the two lengthy letters which are traditionally designated I and II Corinthians. Among New Testament critical scholars no one has questioned that Paul wrote these letters except, possibly, for several short interpolations.[176] The unity of the letters, however, particularly the second, has been in question throughout the modern period of study, and critics have proposed a wide variety of compilations of letters and fragments written to the church on different occasions and later assembled in their present form. Features of the letters justify this exercise, but there has so far been no substantial agreement either on the identification of original parts or on their arrangement in sequence.

Modern attempts to dissect the two letters into original letters and fragments generally follow the lead of J. Weiss; and they assume on the basis of internal evidence that Paul wrote at least four letters to Corinth.[177] In I Cor 5:9 Paul refers to a previous letter in which he had instructed his readers to have no dealings with immoral persons. In II Cor 2:9 he alludes to a letter which he had written about a recalcitrant member of the church, and in 7:12 he mentions a letter about a certain person who had done wrong. The simplest interpretation of these statements is that the first refers to a letter written before I Corinthians but now lost and the two in II Corinthians refer to I Corinthians. Some commentators, however, think that the "previous letter" is imbedded in II Cor 6:14 - 7:1 and that the references in II Corinthians point to II Cor 10-13, which was actually composed as a separate letter, the one which Paul was afraid had caused grief to the church. Still another reconstruction finds a narrative break at II Cor 2:13 with a shift to an entirely different series of topics, the earlier narrative being resumed at 7:13; therefore the material between 2:13 and 7:13 is assigned to another letter that was incorporated here by an editor.

---

[175] Cf. supra, pp. 81-82.

[176] Summary statements are in Feine-Behm-Kümmel, Introduction, 202-205, 211-215.

[177] Weiss (1910), xxxix-xliii; Earliest Christianity (Ger. 1917, after the commentary), 323-357. The various introductions set forth the variety of reconstructions of the correspondence. Cf. also Héring, First Corinthians, xii-xv; Conzelmann, 2-5; and Schmithals, Gnosticism in Corinth, 90-96.

Another question concerns Paul's attitude toward schisms in I Corinthians: in the first four chapters he assumes that schisms did exist in the church (1:10-11) while in 11:18 he says that he "in part" believed that there were schisms. This second reference seems to reveal an earlier stage in church division than that described in ch. 1. In addition, a break has been detected in the discussion of idol offerings: 10:23 resumes the discussion of ch. 8 smoothly, and the inserted material may have been part of an earlier letter which was not as subtle or well-balanced in its treatment of principles (in 10:20-21 eating food offered to idols is regarded as sharing somehow in the life of demons, whereas in the other discussion it is regarded as of importance only because of the conscience of weak brothers). There are also other schemes of editorial combination of part-letters.

Against these editorial theories there is responsible argument that I Corinthians as it now stands is a unity and that proposed dissections can be explained without difficulty.[178] Hurd furnishes an elaborate explanation[179]: on the basis of both I and II Corinthians he endeavors to infer certain stages in the relationship between Paul and the church in Corinth from the very beginning of his missionary activity there. He argues that the Council of Jerusalem (Acts 15) was not held at the conclusion of Paul's trip through Asia Minor but after his preaching at Corinth and Ephesus. Thus Paul had one set of ideas when he preached in Corinth the first time, and he revised these later as a result of the decisions of the council. The difference between what he said at first and later caused questions in the minds of the Corinthian church members, and the discontinuities in the canonical letters can mostly be explained as the results of Paul's attempts to respond to these problems.

It is not difficult to analyze I Corinthians as it now apppears. The first part of the book discusses disturbing reports which Paul had received concerning threatened schism among various parties in the church, concerning a mysterious and perplexing case of apparent incest, and concerning an alarming practice of fellow church members filing lawsuits against each other even in heathen courts. The second part of the book (beginning with ch. 7) discusses matters that had been raised in a communication from the church to Paul concerning marriage, eating food offered to idols, spiritual gifts, the resurrection of the body, and the collections for the poor in Jerusalem. Each of these matters is introduced by the phrase "Now concerning" (*peri de*). Interspersed in the discussion of these matters are lengthy treatments of the freedom of apostles to be married or to receive

---

178 E.g., Robertson and Plummer, xxi-xxvii; Kümmel, in *An Die Korinther I-II* [Lietzmann, *Handbuch*], 25 *et passim*.
179 Hurd, *Origin of I Corinthians*, 43-58; cf; *supra*, p. 64.

contributions (ch. 9), the danger of lapse into idolatry (ch. 10), advice about the headdress and conduct of women in the church (11:1-16), and disturbances in the celebration of the Lord's Supper (11:17-34). One has to decide whether these inserts are to be connected with the topics from the letters Paul is answering or are to be interpreted as independent items —and this in turn bears upon the editorial unity of the epistle. Since no critical reconstruction of I Corinthians has uniform support, it seems best to treat the epistle as a unity.

APPENDIX

ORDER OF EVENTS IN PAUL'S LIFE

FROM HIS LETTERS	FROM ACTS
Birth and childhood	
Born a Hebrew of the tribe of Benjamin (Rom 11:1; Philip 3:5)	A Jewish native of Tarsus (9:11, 21:39, 22:3)
Circumcised the eighth day (Philip 3:5)	Inherited Roman citizenship (16:37-38, 22:25-29, 23:27)
Education	
Instructed in the Hebrew and Aramaic languages (inferred from II Cor 11:22; Philip 3:5)	Instructed in Aramaic (21:40, 22:2, 26:14)
Instructed in the Greek language (inferred from his letters; cf. Gal 6:11; Philem 19)	Instructed in Greek (21:37)
Educated fully in the law (Philip 3:5-6) "Extremely zealous" in Jewish traditions (Gal 1:14)	Educated in Jerusalem under Gamaliel; prepared for the rabbinate; educated as a "zealot of God" (22:3)
A member of the Pharisaic party (Philip 3:5)	A member of the Pharisaic party (23:6, 26:5)
Early public career	
Engaged in persecuting the church (I Cor 15:9; Gal 1:13, 23; Philip 3:6)	Persecuted the church, even to death (8:1,3, 9:1-2,4-5, 13-14, 22:4,7-8, 26:9-12,14-15)
Perhaps a Zealot (Gal 1:14)	Zealot of God (22:3)

Christian career before the conference with the apostles

Revelation of the risen Christ to Paul (I Cor 9:1, 15:8; Gal 1:15-16)	Jesus revealed to Paul on the way to Damascus (9:3-6, 22:6-10, 26:12-19)
No conference with human authority (Gal 1:16-17)	Instructed and baptized by Ananias of Damascus (9:17-18)
	[No parallel]
Trip to Arabia (Gal 1:17)	Ministry in Damascus (9:19-22)
Return to Damascus (Gal 1:17)	
Escape from Damascus through the wall (II Cor 11:33)	Escape from Damascus through the wall (9:23-25)
Trip to Jerusalem "after three years"; saw only Cephas and James "the Lord's brother" (Gal 1:18-19)	Trip to Jerusalem; introduced to the apostles by Barnabas; short ministry in Jerusalem disputing with the Hellenists (9:26-29)
	Sent by "the brothers" to Tarsus (9:30)
Preached in the regions of Syria and Cilicia (Gal 1:21)	Brought from Tarsus to Antioch by Barnabas (11:25-26)
	Ministry of one year in Antioch (11:26)
(The chronology of Paul's trips to Jerusalem are *sub judice*; cf. *supra*, p. 60, fn. 81; also pp. 7-9.)	Trip to Jerusalem with Barnabas to bring famine relief (11:29-30)

First missionary journey (13:1 - 14:28)
  Commission at Antioch (13:1-3)
  Cyprus (4-12)
  At Antioch of Pisidia (14-50)
  At Iconium, Lystra, and Derbe (14:1-21)
  Return to Antioch of Syria (22-28)

The conference with the apostles at Jerusalem

Trip to Jerusalem "according to revelation" with Barnabas and Titus "fourteen years later" (Gal 2:1-10)	Trip to Jerusalem with Barnabas to settle question of circumcision of the gentiles before a conference of the apostles and elders (15:1-29)
Private conference with "the esteemed persons" (Gal 2:2)	Report to "the apostles and the elders" about the things that God had done among the gentiles (15:4,12)
No compulsion to have Paul's converts circumcised (Gal 3:3-5)	Insistence of the Pharisaic party that the gentiles should be circumcised (15:5)
Full recognition by James, Cephas, and John of Paul's right to go to the gentiles (Gal 2:7-9)	Peter's address: defense of the policy of admitting gentiles without circumcision (15:6-11)
	Decision delivered by James: gentiles admitted without circumcision; four moderate requirements added (15:13-21)
Paul's instructions to remember the poor (Gal 2:10)	Decision accepted and sent out by Paul, Barnabas, Silas, and Judas (15:22-30)

From the Jerusalem conference to the ministry in Greece

Confrontation with Peter at Antioch (Gal 2:11-21)

Back at Antioch (15:30-35)
Decision to revisit and strengthen the churches (15:36)

Separation of Barnabas and Paul over John Mark (15:37-39)

Second missionary journey (15:40 - 18:22)
Paul and Silas in Syria and Cilicia (15:40-41)
Return visit to Derbe and Lystra; Timothy recruited (16:1-5)
Through Phrygia and the Galatic country; vision at Troas (6-10)

Establishment of the church in Galatia (perhaps before the Jerusalem conference and in either north or south Galatia) (Gal 3:1-2, 4:13-15)

Mission from Macedonia through Achaea

Mistreatment and injury at Philippi (I Thess 2:2)	Establishment of the church at Philippi (16:11-40) Conversion of Lydia (14-15) Healing of possessed girl; imprisonment (16-24) Deliverance by earthquake (25-34) Vindication and departure (35-40)
Church established in Thessalonica (I Thess 2:1-14; Philip 4:16)	Church established in Thessalonica; Jewish reaction (17:1-9)
	Mission in Beroea (10-14)
Stay in Athens (I Thess 3:1)	Impromptu mission at Athens; address on Areopagus (15-34)
Church established in Corinth (I Cor 2:1-5, 3:6) Household of Stephanas the first converts (I Cor 1:16, 16:15) Baptism of Crispus and Gaius (I Cor 1:14)	Year and a half mission in Corinth (18:1-18) Work with Aquila and Priscilla (2-3) Jewish disputation before proconsul Gallio (12-17)

Mission in Asia Minor

First visit to Ephesus (18:19-21)

[Apollos at Ephesus (18:24-26)
         at Corinth (18:27 - 19:1)]

Third missionary journey (18:23 - 21:15)
Second visit to Ephesus; two-year stay (19:1 - 20:1)

Confrontation with exorcism and magic (19:11-20)
Riot provoked by silversmith (23-40)

Work in Ephesus (Rom 16:3-5; I Cor 15:32, 16:8-9; II Cor 1:8

Apollos' labor at Corinth (I Cor 3:5)

First letter to Corinth after Paul left (I Cor 5:9-11)

Arrangements to collect funds in Corinth as in Galatia (I Cor 16:1-3)

Timothy sent to Corinth (I Cor 16:10)

Visit of Stephanas, Fortunatus, and Achaicus from Corinth (I Cor 16:17-18)
A letter of inquiry received by Paul from Corinth (I Cor 7:1)

A sorrowful visit of Paul to Corinth (II Cor 2:1)
A letter written with tears to Corinth (II Cor 2:3-4)

Titus sent to Macedonia and Corinth (II Cor 8:6,16-18)

Titus' return from Corinth; Paul's anxiety relieved (II Cor 2:13; 7:6,13,14, 8:23)

New plan to expedite collection a year after the first effort (II Cor 9:2)

Post-Asian ministry

Continuation of ministry in Illyricum (Rom 15:10)

Offering made by the Macedonians and Achaeans completed and received by Paul for transmittal to Jerusalem (Rom 15:25-28)

[Intention to visit Spain via Rome (Rom 15:24,28)]

Writing of the letter to Rome (Rom 16:21-23)

[Plan to visit Rome (19:21)]

Trip to "Hellas" via Macedonia (20:1-5)

Return to Troas; voyage along coast (6-38)

Trip to Caesarea; warnings against going to Jerusalem (21:1-14)

Visit to Jerusalem and imprisonment there

Arrival at Jerusalem; report to James and elders (21:16-26)

Rescue from a mob in the temple; address to the mob; kept in protective custody (21:27 - 22:29)

Hearing before Jewish council; plot against Paul's life (22:30 - 23:22)

Imprisonment at Caesarea

Removal under guard to Caesarea (23:23-35)

Appearances before the procurator Felix (24:1-27)

Arraignment before Festus and Jewish authorities; appeal to Caesar (25:1-12)

Defense before Agrippa (25:13 - 26:32)

Trip to Rome and imprisonment there

Ill-fated voyage toward Rome; shipwreck (27:1-44)

Events on Malta (28:1-10)

Continuation to Rome (28:11-15)

Arrival at Rome; hearing before Jewish leaders; two-year ministry under house arrest (28:16-31)

Paul thrice shipwrecked (II Cor 11:25)

(Specifications of provenance of "prison epistles" are moot.)

SELECTED BIBLIOGRAPHY

Where books are translations, the language of the original is indicated with its date; thus (Ger. 1963) or (Fr. 1967) for German or French works.
Abbreviations used in this volume are placed in brackets after appropriate entries; thus [AB] refers to the Anchor Bible.

REFERENCE WORKS

Arndt, W. F., and F. W. Gingrich. *A Greek-English Lexicon of the New Testament and Other Early Christian Literature.* A translation and adaptation of Walter Bauer's *Griechisch-deutsches Wörterbuch.* University of Chicago Press, 1957. (Ger. 1952). [AGB]

Blass, F., and A. Debrunner. *A Greek Grammar of the New Testament and Other Early Christian Literature.* A translation and revision by R. W. Funk. University of Chicago Press, 1961. (Ger. 1954). [BDF]

Deissmann, A. G. *Light from the Ancient East.* Translated by L. R. M. Strachan. London: Hodder & Stoughton, 1927. (Ger. 1923).

Finegan, J. *Light from the Ancient Past: The Archaeological Background of the Hebrew-Christian Religion.* Princeton University Press, 1946.

Hennecke, E. *New Testament Apocrypha.* Vol. II: *Writings Related to the Apostles; apocalypses and related subjects.* Edited by W. Schneemelcher; translated by R. McL. Wilson. Philadelphia: Westminster Press, 1965. (Ger. 1964).

The Jerusalem Bible. Garden City, N.Y.: Doubleday & Co., 1966. (Fr. 1961). [*JB*]

Kittel, G., and G. Friedrich, eds. *Theological Dictionary of the New Testament.* Vols. I-IX. Translated by G. W. Bromiley. Grand Rapids: Eerdmans, 1964-1974. (Ger. 1933-1973). [*TDNT*]

Liddell, H. G., and R. Scott. *A Greek-English Lexicon.* Edited, revised, and augmented by H. S. Jones et al. Vol. I-II. Oxford: Clarendon Press, 1940.

The Mishnah. Translated with introduction and notes by H. Danby. London: Oxford University Press, 1933. [Mishnah]

Nunn, H. P. V. *A Short Syntax of New Testament Greek.* Cambridge: The University Press, 1938.

Richardson, C. C. *The Early Christian Fathers.* Library of Christian Classics, Vol. I. Translated and edited in collaboration with E. R. Fairweather, E. R. Hardy, M. H. Shepherd, Jr. Philadelphia: Westminster Press, 1953.

Robertson, A. T. *A Grammar of the Greek New Testament in the Light of Historical Research.* New York: Harper & Brothers, 1931. [Robertson, *Grammar*]

Zerwick, M. *Biblical Greek Illustrated by Examples.* Adapted from the Latin by J. Smith. Rome: Scripta Pontificii Biblici, 1963. (Lat. 1963). [Zerwick, *Biblical Greek*]

COMMENTARIES ON THE
CORINTHIAN LETTERS

Commentaries on I Corinthians are cited in the text by author's name only. Where page number is not given, understand "ad loc."

Allo, P. E.-B. *Première Épître aux Corinthiens.* Deuxième édition. Paris: Gabalda, 1956.

Barclay, W. *The Letters to the Corinthians.* Philadelphia: Westminster Press, 1956.

Barrett, C. K. *The First Epistle to the Corinthians.* Harper's New Testament Commentaries. New York: Harper & Row, 1968.

Baudraz, F. *Les Épîtres aux Corinthiens.* Geneva: Labor et Fides, 1965.

Calvin, John. *The First Epistle of Paul to the Corinthians.* Calvin's New Testament Commentaries, 9. Translated by J. W. Fraser. Grand Rapids: Eerdmans, 1960. (Lat. 1546).

Conzelmann, H. *A Commentary on the First Epistle to the Corinthians.* Translated by J. W. Leitch et al. Philadelphia: Fortress Press, 1975. (Ger. 1969).

Evans, E. *The Epistles of Paul the Apostle to the Corinthians.* The Clarendon Bible. Oxford: The Clarendon Press, 1930.

Grosheide, F. W. *Commentary on the First Epistle to the Corinthians.* Grand Rapids: Eerdmans, 1953.

Héring, J. *The First Epistle of Saint Paul to the Corinthians.* Translated by A. W. Heathcote and P. J. Allcock. London: Epworth Press, 1962. (Fr. 1959).

———— *The Second Epistle of Saint Paul to the Corinthians.* Translated by A. W. Heathcote and P. J. Allcock. London: Epworth Press, 1967. (Fr. 1958).

Lietzmann, H. *An die Korinther I-II.* Revised by W. G. Kümmel. Handbuch zum Neuen Testament, 9. Tübingen: J. C. B. Mohr (Paul Siebeck), 1949. [Lietzmann, *Handbuch*]

Meyer, H. A. W. *Critical and Exegetical Hand-Book to the Epistles to the Corinthians.* Translated, revised, and edited by D. D. Bannerman et al. New York: Funk & Wagnalls, 1884. (Ger. 1870). [Meyer, *Hand-Book*]

Plummer, A. *A Critical and Exegetical Commentary on the Second Epistle of St Paul to the Corinthians.* The International Critical Commentary. Edinburgh: T. & T. Clark, 1915.

Robertson, A., and A. Plummer. *A Critical and Exegetical Commentary on the First Epistle of St Paul to the Corinthians.* The International Critical Commentary. Edinburgh: T. & T. Clark, 1914.

Thrall, M. E. *I and II Corinthians.* The Cambridge Commentary on the New English Bible. Cambridge: The University Press, 1965.

Weiss, J. *Der erste Korintherbrief.* Kritisch-exegetischer Kommentar über das Neue Testament (Meyer[9]). Göttingen: Vandenhoeck & Ruprecht, 1910.

Wendland, H.-D. *Die Briefe an die Korinther.* Das Neue Testament Deutsch, 7. Göttingen: Vandenhoeck & Ruprecht, 1962.

OTHER COMMENTARIES

Beare, F. W. *The Earliest Records of Jesus.* Oxford: Basil Blackwell, 1962.

Burton, E. D. *A Critical and Exegetical Commentary on the Epistle to the Galatians.* The International Critical Commentary. New York: Charles Scribner's Sons, 1920.

Dibelius, M., and H. Conzelmann. *A Commentary on the Pastoral Epistles.* Translated by P. Buttolph et al. Philadelphia: Fortress Press, 1972. (Ger. 1966).

Foakes-Jackson, F. J., K. Lake, and H. J. Cadbury. *The Beginnings of Christianity.* Vols. IV-V. New York: Macmillan, 1933. [*Beginnings*]

Haenchen, E. *The Acts of the Apostles: A Commentary.* Philadelphia: Westminster Press, 1971. (Ger. 1965). [Haenchen, *Acts*]

Kelly, J. N. D. *The Pastoral Epistles.* London: A. & C. Black, 1963.

Knox, J. *Philemon Among the Letters of Paul.* New York: Abingdon Press, 1959.

Metzger, B. M. *A Textual Commentary on the Greek New Testament.* London: United Bible Societies, 1971. [Metzger, *Textual Commentary*]

Munck, J. *The Acts of the Apostles.* Anchor Bible, vol. 31. Revised by W. F. Albright and C. S. Mann. Garden City, N.Y.: Doubleday & Co., 1967. [Munck, AB]

Robertson, A. T. *Word Pictures in the New Testament.* Vol. IV. New York: Harper & Brothers, 1931.

Strack, H. L., and P. Billerbeck. *Kommentar zum Neuen Testament aus Talmud und Midrasch.* Vol. III. Munich: Beck, 1926. [StB]

WORKS RELATING TO I CORINTHIANS IN PARTICULAR DETAILS

von Allmen, J. J. *Pauline Teaching on Marriage.* Studies in Christian Faith and Practice, VI. London: Faith Press, 1963. (Fr. 1951).

Barrett, C. K. *From First Adam to Last.* New York: Charles Scribner's Sons, 1962.

Barth, Markus. *Das Abendmahl: Passamahl, Bundesmahl und Mesiasmahl.* Theologische Studien, 18. Zollikon-Zürich: Evangelischer Verlag, 1945.

Bouttier, M. *En Christ; étude d'exégèse et de théologie pauliniennes.* Études d'Histoire et de Philosophie Religieuse, 54. Paris: Presses Universitaires de France, 1962.

Caird, G. B. *Principalities and Powers.* Oxford: Clarendon Press, 1956.

———— et al. *The Christian Hope.* Society for Promoting Christian Knowledge Theological Collections, 13. London: SPCK, 1970.

Cullmann, O. *The Earliest Christian Confessions.* Translated by J. S. K. Reid. London: Lutterworth Press, 1949. (Fr., Ger. 1943).

Dahl, M. E. *The Resurrection of the Body.* Studies in Biblical Theology, 36. London: SCM Press, 1962.

Ford, J. M. *Baptism of the Spirit. Three Essays on the Pentacostal Experience.* Techny, Ill.: Divine Word Publications, 1971.

Furnish, V. P. *The Love Command in the New Testament.* Nashville: Abingdon Press, 1972.

Gunther, J. J. *St. Paul's Opponents and Their Background.* Novum Testamentum Supplements, 35. Leiden: Brill, 1973.

Hurd, J. C., Jr. *The Origin of I Corinthians.* New York: Seabury Press, 1965.

Isaksson, A. *Marriage and Ministry in the New Temple.* Translated by N. Tomkinson et al. Lund: C. W. K. Gleerup, 1965. (Swed. 1965).

Lengsfeld, P. *Adam und Christus. Die Adam-Christus Typologie im Neuen Testament und ihre dogmatische Verwendung bei M. J. Scheeben und K. Barth.* Essen: Ludgerus-Verlag Hubert Wingen KG, 1965.

Neufeld, V. H. *The Earliest Christian Confessions.* New Testament Tools and Studies, V. Grand Rapids: Eerdmans, 1963.

Pearson, B. A. *The Pneumatikos-Psychikos Terminology. A Study in the Theology of the Corinthian Opponents of Paul and Its Relation to Gnosticism.* Society of Biblical Literature Dissertation Series, 12. Missoula, Mont.: SBL, 1973.

Robinson, H. S. *Corinth: A Brief History of the City and a Guide to the Excavations.* Athens: American School of Classical Studies, 1964.

———— *The Urban Development of Ancient Corinth.* Athens: American School of Classical Studies, 1965.

Scharlemann, M. H. *Qumran and Corinth.* New York: Bookman Associates, 1962.

Schep, J. A. *The Nature of the Resurrection Body. A Study of the Biblical Data.* Grand Rapids: Eerdmans, 1964.

Schmithals, W. *Gnosticism in Corinth. An Investigation of the Letters to the Corinthians.* Translated by J. E. Steely. Nashville: Abingdon Press, 1971. (Ger. 1956).

Scroggs, R. *The Last Adam. A Study in Pauline Anthropology.* Philadelphia: Fortress Press, 1966.

GENERAL WORKS

Batey, R., ed. *New Testament Issues.* New York: Harper & Row, 1970.

Benko, S., and J. J. O'Rourke. *The Catacombs and the Colosseum. The Roman Empire as the Setting of Primitive Christianity.* Valley Forge, Pa.: Judson Press, 1971.

Bornkamm, G. *Paul.* Translated by D. M. G. Stalker. New York: Harper & Row, 1971. (Ger. 1970).

Bouttier, M. *Christianity According to Paul.* Studies in Biblical Theology, 49. London: SCM Press, 1966.

Bultmann, R. *Jesus and the Word.* Translated by L. P. Smith and E. Huntress. New York: Charles Scribner's Sons, 1934. (Ger. 1926).

———— *Theology of the New Testament.* Vol. I. Translated by K. Grobel. New York: Charles Scribner's Sons, 1951. (Ger. 1948).

Cadbury, J. H. *The Making of Luke-Acts.* New York: Macmillan, 1927.

Conzelmann, H. *An Outline of the Theology of the New Testament.* Translated by J. Bowden. London: SCM Press, 1969. (Ger. 1968²).

Daniel-Rops, H. *Daily Life in the Time of Jesus.* Translated by P. O'Brian. New York: Hawthorn Books, 1962. (Fr. 1961).

Davies, W. D., and D. Daube, eds. *The Background of the New Testament and Its Eschatology.* Studies in Honour of C. H. Dodd. Cambridge: The University Press, 1964.

Dibelius, M. *Paul.* Edited and completed by W. G. Kümmel. Translated by F. Clarke. Philadelphia: Westminster Press, 1953. (Ger. 1950).

Dodd, C. H. *According to the Scriptures. The Substructure of New Testament Theology.* London: Nisbet & Co., 1952.

———— *The Apostolic Preaching and Its Developments.* New York: Harper & Brothers, 1944².

Dungan, D. L. *The Sayings of Jesus in the Churches of Paul. The Use of the Synoptic Tradition in the Regulation of Early Church Life.* Philadelphia: Fortress Press, 1971.

Ellis, E. E. *Paul's Use of the Old Testament.* Edinburgh: Oliver & Boyd, 1957.

Feine, P., and J. Behm. *Introduction to the New Testament.* Completely re-edited by W. G. Kümmel. Translated by A. J. Mattill, Jr. Nashville: Abingdon Press, 1966. (Ger. 1965¹⁴). [Feine-Behm-Kümmel, *Introduction*]

Goodspeed, E. J. *Problems of New Testament Translation.* University of Chicago Press, 1945.

Hamilton, N. Q. *The Holy Spirit and Eschatology in Paul.* Scottish Journal of Theological Occasional Papers No. 6. Edinburgh: Oliver & Boyd, 1957.

Hatch, E. *Essays in Biblical Greek.* Oxford: Clarendon Press, 1889.

Hay, D. M. *Glory at the Right Hand: Psalm 110 in Early Christianity.* Society of Biblical Literature Monograph Series, 18. Nashville: Abingdon Press, 1973.

Héring, J. *Le Royaume de Dieu et Sa Venue. Étude sur l'espérance de Jésus et de l'apôtre Paul.* Nouvelle édition. Neuchâtel: Éditions Delachaux & Niestlé, 1959.

Ladd, G. E. *A Theology of the New Testament.* Grand Rapids: Eerdmans, 1974.

von Loewenich, W. *Paul: His Life and Work.* Translated by G. E. Harris. London: Oliver & Boyd, 1960. (Ger. 1949).

Longenecker, R. *Biblical Exegesis in the Apostolic Period.* Grand Rapids: Eerdmans, 1975.

Manson, T. W. *The Servant-Messiah: A Study of the Public Ministry of Jesus.* Cambridge: The University Press, 1953.

———— *Studies in the Gospels and Epistles.* Edited by M. Black. Manchester: The University Press, 1962.

Manson, T. W., H. D. A. Major, and C. J. Wright. *The Mission and Message of Jesus.* New York: E. P. Dutton and Co., 1938.

Moffatt, J. *An Introduction to the Literature of the New Testament.* International Theological Library. Edinburgh: T. & T. Clark, 1912².

Munck, J. *Paul and the Salvation of Mankind.* Translated by F. Clarke. Richmond: John Knox Press, 1959. (Ger. 1954).

Ogg, G. *The Chronology of the Life of Paul.* London: Epworth Press, 1968. [Ogg, *Chronology*]

Scott, C. A. A. *Christianity According to St Paul.* Cambridge: The University Press, 1939.

Weiss, J. *Earliest Christianity, A History of the Period A.D. 30-150.* Completed by R. Knopf. Translation edited by F. C. Grant. New York: Harper & Brothers, 1959. (Ger. 1917).

OTHER REFERENCES

Articles in periodical literature may be found by referring to the Index of Authors. Journals are cited by their JBL abbreviations:

Catholic Biblical Quarterly	[*CBQ*]
Evangelical Quarterly	[*EvQ*]
Evangelische Theologie	[*EvT*]
Expository Time	[*ExpT*]
Harvard Theological Review	[*HTR*]
Journal of the American Oriental Society	[*JAOS*]
Journal of Biblical Literature	[*JBL*]
Journal of Theological Studies	[*JTS*]
New Testament Studies	[*NTS*]
Novum Testamentum	[*NovT*]
Science et esprit	[*ScEs*]
Verbum domini	[*VD*]
Zeitschrift für die neutestamentliche Wissenschaft	[*ZNW*]
Zeitschrift für Theologie und Kirche	[*ZTK*]

TR indicates *Textus Receptus,* the Greek text of the New Testament most widely accepted in the sixteenth century. It is traced to Erasmus' text of 1516 and became accepted in the third edition of Stephanus' text, 1550. It is the Greek underlying the King James version [KJ] of the New Testament. WH refers to the 1881 edition of B. F. Westcott and F. J. A. Hort, *The New Testament in the Original Greek.* Other versions cited are *Today's English Version* (New York, 1966) [TEV] and the *New English Bible* (Oxford and Cambridge, 1970) [NEB]. *The Greek New Testament,* edited by K. Aland, M. Black, C. M. Martini, B. M. Metzger, and A. Wikgren and published by the United Bible Societies (1968²), sets forth the latest, commonly accepted text [UBS].

Other abbreviations used are those commonly recognized.

TRANSLATION
Notes and Comments

INTRODUCTORY
(1:1-9)

GREETINGS (1:1-3)

1 ¹I, Paul, called as an apostle of Christ Jesus by God's will, along with brother Sosthenes, ²to the church of God located in Corinth, to those sanctified in Christ Jesus, called as saints, together with all in every place who appeal to the name of our Lord Jesus Christ—both their Lord and ours: ³grace and peace to you from God our Father and the Lord Jesus Christ.

Notes

1:1. *apostle* is derived from the Greek *apostellō*, which means "I send (on a mission, or with a commission)." Its use in the New Testament usually represents the Hebrew *šālīaḥ*, a technical term employed in rabbinic Hebrew to designate a representative of a king or a private person sent on a particular mission, e.g. ambassadors or people with power of attorney. The term seems to have been selected early in the Christian church to refer to men who represented Jesus Christ. Cf. the extensive article by K. H. Rengstorf in *TDNT*, I, 398-447; to repeat details of that material or to cite again the literature listed there would be gratuitous. So also for the citations in AGB, 98-99.

2. *church.* *ekklēsia* is used in first-century Greek writing to refer to any kind of public meetings. It therefore has no religious coloring except what is given to it by its use in the Christian church. Its use to translate Old Testament Hebrew *qāhāl* may suggest that the people of the church are an equivalent of the people of Israel. Cf. K. L. Schmidt in *TDNT*, III, 501-536, and again the literature in AGB, 240-241.

3. *grace . . . peace.* The use of *TDNT* and AGB for study of the "great words" of Paul's theology is assumed from this point on. Cf. also the "Detached Notes on Important Terms of Paul's Vocabulary" in Burton, *Galatians*, 363-521.

For examples of ancient letters, cf. Deissmann, *Light from the Ancient East*, 149-227; Finegan, *Light from the Ancient Past*, 324-331.

COMMENT

Ancient letters began by naming the writer and by identifying him with a few phrases. All Paul's letters begin this way. Except for Philippians, I and II Thessalonians, and Philemon Paul calls himself an apostle of Jesus Christ. In Romans and Philippians he calls himself a slave and in Philemon a prisoner.

The connection between Paul's apostolic office and *God's will* is made also in II Cor 1:1; Gal 1:1; Eph 1:1; Col 1:1; and II Tim 1:1. Emphasis upon the divine will indicates Paul's sense that he had a commission from God to preach Jesus Christ to the gentiles throughout the world. He had authority to give an accurate summary of the gospel and to draw from it religious and ethical principles to be applied to the life of people in the churches. The authority of his statement of the gospel was so high that it would supersede even that of an angel from heaven (Gal 1:8). His inferences from the gospel had less authority than the teaching of Jesus but still were to be accepted as authorized by sound reason and spiritual insight (I Cor 7:10-12).

One *Sosthenes* is mentioned in Acts 18:17 as the ruler of the Corinth synagogue (cf. *supra,* p. 83). If he is the *brother Sosthenes* of this epistle, then Paul's preaching led to his conversion; and at least one member of the Corinthian church was a Jew—a factor which might have some bearing on the nature of the controversies in that church. In addition, Aquila and Prisca, Jews not natives of Corinth, are mentioned in I Cor 16:19.

The practice of designating particular churches by location, followed in Acts and most of Paul's letters, seems to have prevailed throughout the first century (cf. Revelation 1-3). The particular congregation is one along with others which together belong to the church of Jesus Christ, and the designation of its locale is simply a means of identification.

The people in the church are addressed as *those sanctified,* that is, made holy or consecrated by Christ Jesus. This does not mean primarily ethical goodness, though that is perhaps included, but that these people belong to the holy person who is God or Christ. Thus Christians were called "holy ones" or *saints* because they were the people of God. (Cf. Rom 1:7, 15:25,26,31; I Cor 6:1,2, 14:33, 16:1,16; II Cor 1:1, 13:12; Eph 1:1; etc.) Note that the people are *called as saints* just as Paul is *called as an apostle. Appeal to* seems to imply that people have accepted the name of Christian; and they appeal to Christ for aid, primarily for forgiveness of sin. To *appeal to the name* means that Christ is accepted as a living person, definitely known, ready to come to their aid and give them authority to be his representatives on earth. In the Old Testament the name of God is holy and specifies him as the God of Israel, but it is also applied to the people (Amos 9:12, "nations who are called by my name"). The idea was that a name characterizes a person and to some degree expresses or shares the quality of that person; the use of the name, therefore, can exercise power. On the wider reference of *both their Lord and ours,* see II Cor 1:1.

Letters in Paul's day very often ended greetings with a blessing. Paul appears to have modified the Greek greeting (*chairein*) and the Hebrew (*šālōm*) into a combination which is found in all his letters. It probably means to indicate that the Christian society is a new order composed of gentiles and Jews who have received the privileges and blessings of both cultures, and these come from *God our Father and the Lord Jesus Christ.* Christians relate to the authority and sovereign will of God through Jesus Christ. The title *Lord* is regularly assigned to *Jesus Christ* and not to *God* in Paul's writings as well as in the Gospels, and this probably has deliberate and double significance. First, *Lord* (*kyrios*) is the term employed by the Septuagint to translate the Hebrew Tetragrammaton (*Yahweh*); so the New Testament usage may be understood to mean that Jesus stands as Lord to the Christian church in the relationship in which Yahweh stood to Israel. In the New Testament the particular designation for *God* (Hebrew, *'elōhīm*) is *Father.* Accordingly, Christians relate to the Old Testament in the light of Jesus' interpretation. Secondly, *Kyrios* is a title of Caesar; and so the assignment of the title to Jesus has special meaning for the life of the church in the world. To have Jesus as Lord means to obey him above all worldly authorities. It is important to remember that there is often ambiguity in the New Testament use of the designation "Lord" because its connotation may be either sacred or secular.

THANKSGIVING (1:4-9)

1   4I am always thanking my God on account of you because of God's grace given to you in Christ Jesus, 5 because in him God enriched you in every way, in all speech and knowledge, 6 as God confirmed the testimony of Christ among you. 7 Therefore you lack no gift while you are waiting for the revelation of our Lord Jesus Christ, 8 who will also preserve you without blame until the end on the day of our Lord Jesus Christ. 9 God is faithful; he called you into partnership with his son Jesus Christ our Lord.

NOTES

1:4. *my.* The relatively unimportant textual problem in regard to this pronoun is adequately dealt with by Metzger, *Textual Commentary,* 543. Variations in pronominal usage are frequent in the MSS.

5. *God enriched you,* literally, "you were enriched" (*eploutisthēte*). Where it seems justified, passives have been rendered active with *God* as subject in accordance with the Aramaic usage to avoid the divine name; cf. BDF, §§130(1), 313, 342(1). Thus also *God confirmed* (vs. 6) and *he called* (vs. 9), where the usage is confirmed by the phrase *di' hou.*

8. *the day.* In II Cor 6:2 Paul employs "day" to mean the time of salvation, the present time which furnishes opportunity to respond to the first revelation of Christ; but more often "the day" is a coming time of judgment when the final victory of Christ over all enemies including sin and death will be manifested (Rom 2:16; Philip 1:6; I Thess 5:2). "This age" is still an ambiguous time with sin and righteousness mixed together and God's valuation of people quite unclear (Rom 12:2; Gal 1:4).

Lord Jesus Christ. For *Christou,* cf. Metzger, *Textual Commentary,* 543-544. (Hereafter consideration of textual problems will assume reference to Metzger's material.) There are many combinations of the names and titles applied to Jesus. Theological and stylistic considerations may occasionally be discerned, but it is doubtful that any prevailing patterns may be identified.

COMMENT

Among the papyri discoveries that have been so abundant in the last hundred years are many ancient letters. Many of the pagan letters follow the initial greeting by thanksgiving to the gods (frequently Apollo, Isis, or Serapis), usually for health recently restored, some good fortune received by writer or addressee, or delivery from danger or enemies. Paul expresses thanks to God after greetings in every letter except Galatians; but he is thankful for the faith of the church members, for the gifts they have received in the service of Christ, for the prayers they have offered, for their sharing of the gospel, for their love to the saints, etc. Christian dedication changed even his thanksgiving from personal and selfish happiness to joy for benefits and enrichment experienced by the church. It is significant that Paul's thanksgiving in I Corinthians is restricted to delight that the people of the church have been made rich *in all speech and knowledge* and in (spiritual) gifts. He does not mention their faith, love, or righteousness. From what he says later about the Corinthian church, it appears that his expression of thanksgiving is strictly adapted to the situation in the church.

Logos seems to mean *speech* in this passage. In accordance with a usage in I Corinthians and in other New Testament writings to refer to the message of the gospel (I Cor 1:18, 2:4, 15:2; Rom 15:18; Gal 6:6; Acts 8:4; etc.) if the Corinthians are *rich in all speech,* they are well equipped to proclaim the good news. *Knowledge* means awareness of the truth about God and Jesus Christ (cf. 8:1-7,10-11, 12:8) and is related to sound doctrine.

Endowment of the church with speech and knowledge was bestowed in accordance with confirmation of *the testimony of Christ* among them. This is either Christ's testimony about God, his kingdom, and the way of life for those who believe (subjective genitive) or the testimony about Christ delivered by the apostle himself (objective genitive). The second meaning is probably more prominent here, yet the ambiguity of the Greek may justify both ideas. The confirmation of the testimony had already occurred; so the result clause with the infinitive probably means that after Paul preached the gospel, the people were prepared to receive a unique plethora of spiritual gifts. In Corinth the mixture of occidental and oriental cultures produced a multiplex expression of Christian worship, theological argument, and community life as the result of the action of the Spirit of God among the extraordinary variety of people.

Two features of *the testimony of Christ* are prominent as Paul proclaimed it. The first is the revelation that has already occurred in the life, death, and resurrection of Christ. This revelation discloses God as the father of his people, his forgiveness of their sins, the nature of his rule, and his conquest over death. It also provides a foundation of the church. But this revelation was not regarded as final; for as they exercised their gifts, the Corinthian Christians were *waiting for the revelation of . . . Christ,* a revelation still to come *at the end on the day of . . . Christ.* The little community of Christian folk in Corinth were able to exercise marvelous gifts because they were looking forward to the final success of God's gospel and to the clear explanation of the meaning and value of their lives. The picturesque details which Paul records elsewhere about Christ coming in clouds and angels gathering people from life and grave as they fly up to meet him are entirely secondary to the hope of Christ's triumph and the resolution of the true meaning of life. The Corinthians faced extremely rigorous life conditions: most of them were poor, some were slaves, all had been victimized by the brutality of the evil society of the city; yet the Christian good news had given them a new vision and outlook toward the future. The epistle moves to a climax in a discussion of the resurrection; "the position of chap. 15 at the end of the epistle is no accident" (Conzelmann, p. 11).

Jesus Christ *will also preserve you without blame.* Two aspects are included in this statement: they will continue in their present state, justified by the free grace of God; and regardless of failure, backsliding, and corruption they will not be blamed *on the day of* the *Lord*. This is probably the most difficult of all the expressions of hope in this letter. Paul is writing to people who have already engaged in quarrels, nourished scandalous conduct, doubted some of the basic elements of the gospel, questioned the authority of the apostle, and threatened to go off into extravagant fanaticism. On occasion they have driven Paul to tears, yet here he states unconditionally that they will be blameless in the final evaluation. He is echoing the simple announcement of the gospel that those who believe in God's forgiveness will have nothing against them at *the end* (pointedly stated in Rom 8:1—but in Romans 2 the proviso of forgiving one another is introduced; cf. Matt 7:1-2).

The foregoing assurance is emphasized by the words, *God is faithful:* human faithlessness cannot cancel out the faithfulness of God (cf. II Tim 2:13). The evidence of this is the call *into partnership with his son*. This can mean sharing his friendship and love (Rom 15:27; Philip 2:1), or becoming sons of God as Jesus is (II Cor 13:13; Philip 3:10) or sharing the life of his redeemed society (I Cor 10:16; II Cor 8:4). It is a kind of pledge or guarantee of the faithfulness of God through all human vicissitudes.

THREAT OF SCHISM FROM PARTY QUARRELS AND CLASS RIVALRY (1:10-4:21)

PARTIES DERIVED FROM LEADERSHIP AUTHORITIES (1:10-17)

Absurdity of the claims

1 10 Please, brothers, by the name of our Lord Jesus Christ, all of you be in agreement when you speak; and let there be no divisions among you: be completely equipped with common mind and purpose. 11 For Chloe's people reported to me that there is squabbling among you, my brothers. 12 I am referring to this: that each of you is saying, "I belong to Paul"; "I belong to Apollos"; "I belong to Cephas"; "I belong to Christ." 13 Has Christ become divided? Paul was not crucified on your behalf, was he? Nor were you baptized into Paul's name.

Baptisms by Paul

14 I am thankful that I baptized none of you except Crispus and Gaius, 15 so none of you can say that you were baptized into my name. 16 (I did baptize also the household of Stephanas—besides that, I am not aware of having baptized anyone else.)

Paul's mission to evangelize

17 For Christ sent me, not to baptize, but to proclaim good news, not in wisdom of speech lest the cross of Christ be nullified.

Notes

1:10. *Please. parakaleō* connotes strong and urgent entreaty or plea. It is more than a request and at least formally, slightly less than a command. Exhortation is accompanied by intense feeling; "urgently appeal" is perhaps a good rendering. The translation here adopted, however, is derived from the usage of the verb in modern Greek with the intention of adding feeling by reducing formality.

by the name. The use of *dia* with the genitive of "name" occurs in Paul only here (but cf. Acts 4:30, 10:43). It designates agency instead of the more usual instrumental *en* (I Cor 5:4, 6:11).

Christ is a Greek translation of the Hebrew *māšîaḥ*, "anointed" or "smeared." The *māšîaḥ* has had oil poured on his head or smeared on his forehead to symbolize his reception of the spirit or the power of the spirit to perform a sacred office, either that of king, priest, or prophet. The term was widely used in pre-Christian Judaism as a technical term for the coming king who would restore the power of Davidic kingship, rule righteously over the peoples of the world, and establish a utopian society. The Dead Sea scrolls apply this term to the prophet who would come to acknowledge the royal messiah and also to the high priest who would offer perfect sacrifices in the messianic kingdom (1QS ix 11; 1QSa ii 11-22; 1QM ii 1-6). Since Jesus is called a descendant of David in Rom 1:3, the prophet like Moses in Acts 3:20-22, and a great high priest in Heb 4:14, it is impossible to be sure which of these designations is the primary intention unless "Christ" is defined in context. The messianic thought of the early church seems to have developed from prophet through priest so that finally Christ embodied all three functions at once. Possibly the combination of the three "offices" in the one person opened the way to regard him as more than human, and the association of "Christ" with "son of God" rendered the recognition of divinity inevitable.

This is the tenth reference to Christ so far in the epistle. Although half the occurrences are in this configuration (*our Lord Jesus Christ*), no special significance attaches to the order or inclusion of words in the titles. Cf. Burton, *Galatians,* 392-404.

be in agreement when you speak. A similar expression is in Aristotle's *Politics* III iii 3, "The Boeotians said the same thing as those of Megara and became quiet"—which means that they came to an agreement and settled the war.

12. *each of you.* Paul probably was exaggerating for effect. They were choosing up sides, and he personalized the divisions to draw attention to the absurdity.

Cephas=Peter. Cf. first NOTE on 15:5.

13. *was he?* The circumlocution is necessary to avoid ambiguity in translating the question; the Greek indicates it by *mē.* Cf. BDF, § 440.

into Paul's name. The literal translation seems best; cf. the extensive comments of Zerwick, *Biblical Greek,* §§ 99-111, esp. 106-109.

15. *none . . . can say that you were baptized.* The second verb is plural. Paul in this way is denying the use of his name in a party claim.

16. *I did baptize also.* The parenthetical correction adds a disarming, personal note of concern for direct and accurate communication.

17. *Christ sent me.* Although his apostleship is not in question here, Paul's incidental claim is worthy of note.

COMMENT

Absurdity of the claims

A disturbing report was brought to Paul by *Chloe's people* that the Corinthian church was being disrupted into rival groups. The seriousness of this break in Christian harmony from the apostle's point of view may be gauged by the immediate attention given the matter in the epistle. Who Paul's informants were is impossible to ascertain. Robertson and Plummer suggest that they may have been slaves of the freewoman Chloe, who could have been a resident of Ephesus. This is, of course, conjectural. If they had sufficient knowledge of the situation in Corinth to warrant Paul's sharp concern, they may well have been a part of the church there. Chloe was known to the Corinthians and so may also have been a member of the Christian community. To add conjecture, perhaps her house was one in which a part of the Corinthian Christian community met. Barrett's remark is more practical, that the reference demonstrates the "relative mobility" of people in that part of the world.

Paul addressed his readers as *brothers,* a term he uses to designate church members in every letter (a usage also common in Acts). The force the word may bear is brought out in Philemon 16, where Philemon is enjoined to receive Onesimus, his runaway slave, as a brother since he had been converted to Christ. The word was already in use in the Jewish community, sometimes to refer to national identity, sometimes more narrowly applied to members of the voluntary religious affiliations within Judaism (see the discussion in *TDNT*, I, 144-146). The Christians applied the term to each other, most often after the analogy of the voluntary brotherhoods of those united in a common religious profession, but with a wider frame of reference. (Note Paul's use in Rom 9:3.)

Paul's appeal *by the name of our Lord Jesus Christ* displays Paul's claim to be Christ's representative speaking with his authority. The appeal is not only personal: it intends to express the will of the Master.

The appeal to *be in agreement when you speak* obviously is not a demand that they use each other's words (the Greek reads, "say the same thing") but that the group be so united that they present a common front to the rest of the world and share a common outlook and value system. They must have such concern for each other that their loyalty is to the whole group; unity excludes the possibility of schism. Any divisive disposition in the New Testament church was considered equivalent to a denial of the faith. The disrupted condition of first-century society called for a true Christian brotherhood in a united church. The apostle implored the Corinthians to *be completely equipped with common mind and purpose*. For Paul "mind" (*nous*) means the higher capacity of the human personality to be aware of God's law, purpose, and truth (14:14-19; Rom 7:22-25, 14:5). Therefore for the community to have a *common mind* means that it is to be sensitized as a whole to the nature and will of God and to allow God's purpose to supersede petty motivations of human pride or prejudice. As he shortly showed, Paul was convinced that a fellowship of the children of God is possible by the living action of the Spirit which makes of the church a supernatural society. Failure to become this results from not being *completely equipped*.

The rivalries at Corinth seem at first glance to be somewhat innocent. The authorities to whom the people were attached were noble and worthy of admiration. As the text stands, the point of incongruity is in listing devotion to Christ alongside that to Paul, Apollos, or Cephas. Perhaps this ploy is deliberate; suggestions that the Christ-phrase is a later addition or alteration are without textual foundation. It is when lesser loyalties are weighed against loyalty to Christ that their potential danger becomes evident. Many of the quarrels and schisms in the church have originated from some noble enthusiasm or attachment to a true doctrine or a great Christian leader, in which circumstance it was difficult to see that such support might divide the Christian community and produce more evil than that which the loyalty was endeavoring to eliminate. Therefore, without hesitation Paul stigmatized divisive loyalty to himself, to Apollos, to Cephas, or to Christ among others as a desertion of the gospel.

The schismatic attachment to special persons in the church is absurd. *Christ* has not *become divided. merizō* means to split up into constituent parts, to divide into portions. Several commentators have suggested the interpretation here that Christ has been allotted to one group or another, that is, each group was claiming a monopoly of Christ's leadership and benefits. While this seems to fit the claim that each is making, it hardly adapts to Paul's argument: it is quite impossible that Christ has been split up so that part of him goes to one group and parts to others.

Paul emphasizes his concern for unity by choosing loyalty to himself as the illustration of the incipient, absurd evil. *Paul was not crucified* for them, and they were not *baptized into Paul's name*. Emphatically he demonstrates that no grounds for attachment to himself could possibly exist since he did not obtain their justification by being crucified nor was it his name by which they were known as the result of their baptism. He clearly implies the necessity of complete loyalty to Christ—without, of course, either rejecting his other followers or picking and choosing among them.

Baptisms by Paul

To reinforce his emphasis that in no way should the people show party preference for him, Paul expressed thanks that he had baptized so few of them. If he had baptized a significant number of the Corinthians, the possibility of divided leadership loyalty might have increased. He has no interest in gaining honor by the number and importance of people whom he has baptized.

Paul kept no record book on conversions and baptisms: that is evident from his somewhat haphazard recollection of persons he had baptized in Corinth. Later (16:15) he refers to *the household of Stephanas* as "the first fruits of Achaea"; so it is strange that their baptism is recorded almost as an afterthought here. There seems to be no reason, moreover, to doubt the record in Acts 17:34 that Paul's Athenian ministry produced converts. The most likely explanation of these apparent inconsistencies is that his relative indifference to baptisms in Corinth represents a genuine unconcern for church statistics. The scholars' desire to have all details fall into place in reconstructing the story of the New Testament churches is frustrated by failure of the literary sources to provide adequate information. This is partly due to the difference in the record-keeping customs of the times. It also indicates how Paul ordered his priorities.

Paul's mission to evangelize

Paul's commission from Christ was *not to baptize, but to proclaim good news*. This should not be pushed to mean that Paul felt that baptism was of secondary importance and more or less dispensable. Later (12:28-30) he distinguishes among various offices in the church and recognizes that different persons perform different offices. Perhaps other church officers customarily baptized those who were converted through Paul's evangelizing—a possible parallel is in the remark in John 4:2 about the baptismal activities of Jesus and his disciples (almost certainly an editorial reflection; see R. E. Brown, AB, vol. 29, NOTE ad loc.). It does seem that the risk of devotion to one whose preaching led to faith would be as great as to one who baptized; so the passage seems to suggest that baptizing is relatively less important than preaching, or perhaps that proclamation has a special importance by virtue of inevitably coming before baptism.

Even in preaching, to which Christ had called him, Paul recognized a danger that by virtue of his skill and eloquence people might glorify him instead of God. He was therefore not called to use *wisdom of speech,* by which he probably is indicating some combination of philosophical knowledge, religious and ethical insight, and comprehensive understanding of esoteric meaning in Old Testament scripture and Christian tradition, these presented by learned and artful methods. (This interpretation is contrary to the view that the Corinthians held a form of Gnosticism; so Schmithals, *Gnosticism in Corinth,* 137-144). Greek sophists had made a great art of public speech: various methods of influencing people's minds were studied and described; and devices for presenting persuasive argument—which had the appearance of rationality even when they consciously disguised the truth—were employed by public speakers, politicians, and legal advocates. Paul brusquely announced that in his presentation of the gospel none of these tricks would be employed, for they involve the danger that Christ's cross might be emptied of its meaning and power. He seems to say that to tell the story of the cross, what happened when Jesus was put to death, is sufficient. He was commissioned only to draw attention to that event without distracting, dramatic brilliance. He eschewed the temptation to compete with the speaking ability of other apostles or leaders. Besides the Greek elocutionary arts Paul must have been familiar with the unusual and refined methods of Old Testament interpretation that were current among first-century rabbis and scholars like Philo of Alexandria. The description of Apollos in Acts 18:24 suggests the possibility that he may have been expert in these methods. But for Paul all that counted was the clear portrayal of *the cross of Christ.*

THE MESSAGE OF THE CROSS VS. THE WISDOM OF THE WORLD (1:18-2:16)

Saving power and perishing folly

1   18 For the message of the cross is foolishness to those who are perishing, but to us who are being saved it is God's power. 19 For it has been written,

> I will destroy the wisdom of the wise,
> and the shrewdness of the intelligent I will set aside.

20 Where is a wise man? Where is a scripture expert? Where is a debater of this age? Did not God make the world's wisdom foolish? 21 For since, in the wisdom of God, the world did not come to know God through wisdom, God was pleased to save through the foolishness of the proclamation those who believed.

Jews, Greeks, and God

22 And since Jews ask for signs and Greeks seek for wisdom, 23 we keep preaching Christ as crucified, an offense to Jews and foolishness to gentiles; 24 but to the ones who are called, both Jews and Greeks, Christ is the power of God and the wisdom of God. 25 For God's foolishness is wiser than men, and God's weakness is stronger than men.

God's choice of the "nothings"

26 Note, indeed, brothers, that when you were called, not many were wise from a human standpoint, not many were powerful, not many were wellborn. 27 But God chose the foolish things of the world to shame the wise men; and God chose the feeble things of the world to shame the mighty; 28 and God chose the insignificant things of the world and the despised—the "nothings"—in order that he might nullify the existing things, 29 so that no human may glory before God. 30 From God's action you are in Christ Jesus, who became wisdom for us from God, as well as righteousness and holiness and redemption; 31 so that, as it has been written,

Let the one who glories glory in the Lord.

Paul's personal demonstration of God's paradoxical wisdom

2 1 And when I came to you, brothers, I came without any excellence of speech or wisdom as I was proclaiming the mystery of God. 2 For I decided to know nothing in your midst except Jesus Christ and him crucified. 3 And I appeared before you with weakness, fear, and much trembling. 4 My speech and proclamation were not expressed in persuasive words of wisdom but in a demonstration of spirit and power 5 in order that your faith may not be in human wisdom but in God's power.

6 Now we are speaking a wisdom among those who are mature, that is, a wisdom which does not belong to this age nor the rulers of this age who are about to pass away; 7 but we are speaking God's wisdom in a mystery, wisdom which has been hidden and which God predetermined before the ages to contribute to our glory. 8 None of this world's rulers knew this wisdom; for if they had known it, they would not have crucified the glorious Lord.

The Spirit as revealer of God's wisdom

9 But as it has been written,

> Things that no eye has seen and no ear heard
> and that have not occurred to human mind,
> things that God has prepared for those who love him—

10 God indeed revealed them to us through the Spirit; for the Spirit fathoms all things, including the depths of God's mind. 11 For what human being understands human affairs except the human spirit that is in him? Thus also no one has comprehended God's affairs except the Spirit of God. 12 Now we did not receive the spirit of the world but the Spirit which is from God in order that we might comprehend the things freely given us by God; 13 and we speak of them in words not instructed by human wisdom but instructed by the Spirit, for we interpret spiritual matters by spiritual words.

The spiritual person and the mind of Christ

14 Now the natural man has no capacity for the affairs of God's Spirit, for they are foolishness to him, and he is not able to comprehend them because they are investigated in a spiritual manner. 15 Yet the spiritual man investigates all things, but he himself is investigated by no one.

> 16 For who has comprehended the mind
> of the Lord so as to advise him?

Yet we have the mind of Christ.

NOTES

1:18. *being saved.* The participle (*sōzomenois*) is linear and is precisely parallel to *perishing* (*appollumenois*). Paul's doctrine of salvation is related not only to a fixed, past event (cf. *sōsai* in vs. 21), but also explicitly to present experience and to the future consummation. Cf. Nunn's illustration in *A Short Syntax of New Testament Greek*, 125.

19. The quotation from Isa 29:14 is identical with the LXX except for the second verb, *I will set aside.* The LXX reads, *I shall conceal* (*krupsō*), a rendering which follows the meaning of the Hebrew verb (*sātar*) but changes the third person singular passive force to first person singular active. Paul's render-

ing (*athetēsō*) follows the LXX first person but seems to abandon the meaning "conceal." Since the change of meaning is relatively minor, this is a useful passage for looking at the complex and moot question about the nature of Paul's Old Testament quotations. There are at least four possible explanations for the verb change here. (a) Paul is quoting a text of the Greek Old Testament that has not otherwise survived. Origen, so far as records exist, knew nothing of such a text here. The verb *atheteō* does occur in the LXX, some thirteen times in Isaiah; but it never renders *sātar*. There seems, therefore, to be no support for this option. (b) Paul is correcting the LXX from memory of the Hebrew text. Again, this appears to be unlikely; for both the meaning and the form of the Hebrew are abandoned in *athetēsō*. (c) Paul is quoting the LXX from memory. The single variation does not argue against this possibility; but it would be strange that the word he fails to remember accurately carries the approximate meaning of the Hebrew, with which he was also certainly familiar. Perhaps it is at least clear that he "remembers" the LXX, for he stays with the first person in his altered text. (d) Paul deliberately alters the LXX text, which he seems to remember well enough otherwise. This would be tenable if there were some reasonable explanation for the change. It is possible that Paul wishes to avoid the meaning "conceal" because it might suggest the possibility of an esoteric understanding of human wisdom; but as the verb is in chiastic parallel with *destroy*, this would be tortuous reasoning indeed. There is no metrical explanation for the change. Unless there is some other undiscovered reason for Paul's altered text, the third option seems to be the most tenable: Paul is quoting the LXX from faulty or careless memory. Lest Paul be faulted for this it must be borne in mind that reference to the text was not easy at that time, even under ideal conditions; he probably never had a "desk copy" of the Old Testament available.

21. *come to know God.* The verb is the aorist of *ginōskō*. At 2:11-16 it will be translated "comprehend." The meaning has much the same nuances as the Hebrew *yāda‘*.

the proclamation. The misleading translation of KJ, "preaching," has been superseded in almost all modern versions to indicate the content of the message (RSV, "what we preach").

23. *offense* renders *skandalon*. Cf. J. A. Walther, *Thesis Theological Cassette* (Pittsburgh, 1972), vol. 3, no. 1, side 2.

24. *the power of God.* For contrast, cf. Albright's note on Simon Magus, Appendix VII in Munck, AB.

the wisdom of God. On the relation of this epithet to Christ, cf. J. Wood, *Wisdom Literature* (London, 1967), 124-152.

26. *Note.* The verb *blepete* may be either indicative or imperative. There is no way to decide absolutely which is intended, but the location of the verb first in the sentence favors the imperative.

when you were called. The verbal noun *klēsin* is active in form, but it clearly refers to God's calling the Corinthians. In later Greek the formal meaning of the verbal suffixes had worn down so that the sharp distinction between active and passive forms was obliterated.

27. *the foolish things,* neuter plural (*tā mōra*), even though it characterizes

people. Since their opposites are *tous sophous,* masculine plural, there may be reflected a subtle disdain in which the more ignorant members of the society were regarded by the "intellectuals." On the other hand, *the foolish things of the world* might have included not only the persons but also the beliefs which they held. The reference would include, then, also the crucifixion and the proclamation of the cross.

28. *the "nothings,"* literally, "the things not being"; even with the Byzantine addition of *kai* this sums up what has gone before. Again a neuter, *agenē* ("things, including people, with no birth") is contrasted with *eugeneis* ("well-born") in the previous verse. Now, however, the contrast is completed; for *the "nothings"* are opposed to the *existing things,* a neuter plural, which must include the "somebodies."

30. *From God's action,* literally, "out of him," that is, God. He is the source of their becoming—*in Christ Jesus*—"somebodies."

31. *Let the one who glories glory in the Lord.* Again the quotation seems to be from the LXX, Jer 9:24. The context there is appropriate: "wise—wisdom," "strong—strength," "rich—riches" occur in pairs in vs. 23. (Note that the numbering of the LXX is 9:23.)

2:1. *And when I came.* The Greek emphasizes the transition to the personal illustration (*kagō elthōn*).

mystery. martyrion is also well-attested, but contextual fitness weighs in favor of *mystērion.* The spread of textual evidence and the existence of minor variants suggest that the variation arose early.

2. *to know nothing.* This use of *eidenai* is somewhat unusual in Paul (cf. also II Cor 5:16; Philip 4:12). He meant that this was to be the sole topic of his presentation.

crucified. Indicative forms of this verb are almost always aorist; so the perfect participle is probably significant. The grammatical force of the perfect is appropriate, and the form may have been a stereotype in the church (note Mark 16:6//Matt 28:5) to reflect a sense of the continuing theological force of the crucifixion.

4. *persuasive words of wisdom.* The textual situation is extremely confused: there are at least sixteen variations. The most difficult matter concerns the adjective *peithois,* which is unknown elsewhere in Greek literature. It is a reasonable enough formation, but it could be a mistake for the dative of *peithō.* This would explain the early absence of *logois* in some MSS and its variation in others; and the reading of uncial 35 (with some Old Latin support) would be original. *anthrōpinēs* appears to be a scribal addition perhaps influenced by vs. 13. In any case, the meaning of the sentence is not in doubt.

spirit and power. The two words are often associated; e.g. Luke 1:7, 4:14; Acts 1:8, 10:38; Rom 15:13,19; Eph 3:16; II Tim 1:7; Heb 2:4. By hendiadys (or Hebrew construct) the translation might read "spirit(ual) power" or even better "powerful Spirit."

7. *to contribute to our glory. eis* often has the force of "with (something) in view as an end."

8. On the identity of *this world's rulers,* out of an extensive literature cf. Origen *De Principiis* iii ii-iii; Lietzmann, *Handbuch,* 12-13; Gene Miller,

"*archontōn tou aiōnos toutou*—A New Look at 1 Corinthians 2:6-8," *JBL* 91 (1972), 522-528; and especially Caird, *Principalities and Powers, passim.*

9. The quotation from scripture cannot be precisely identified. Paul seems to have put together phrases (Isa 64:4, 52:15, 65:17; Jer 3:16; Sir 1:10), probably again from memory. The result certainly expresses a prophetic sentiment. It is curious, however, that if Paul was consciously "manufacturing" a quotation, he did not come out with one that fit his grammatical context better. The statement of Origen that the words come from an "Apocalypse of Elijah" (cf. the notes of Meyer and Héring) would provide a satisfactory alternative if it were better attested.

10. *the depths of God's mind,* literally, *the deep (things) of God.* It is possible that there is an allusion to a phrase which may have been current in Gnostic thought at that time. Hippolytus (fl. ca. A.D. 220) writes that the Naassene heretics later "called themselves Gnostics since they say they alone know 'the deep things'" (*Refutation of All Heresies* v 6.4). The phrase occurs at least as early as the LXX of Dan 2:22, and in Rev 2:24 its demonic counterpart is used.

11. *what human being.* The use of *anthrōpōn/anthrōpou* in this verse is difficult to bring into English. *the human spirit* is practically the equivalent of "the human consciousness." The idea is that no being can understand the inner situation of a human being unless that being shares the form of human experience, and this is used to demonstrate that no human being *has comprehended God's affairs* ("the [things] of God") without possessing the Spirit of God.

It is also quite possible to take *anthrōpōn/anthrōpou* in a more particular sense: it is the spirit of each individual which alone understands his own purposes and desires, and *anthrōpou* with the article would refer to any individual taken as an illustration. The relation of the Spirit of God to God's affairs, then, would be juxtaposed to an individual person's unique consciousness of his own affairs. The singular arthrous form *tou anthrōpou,* however, is somewhat unusual in Paul's letters; and it seems better to stress a general context by rendering the noun on the analogy with the common usage in the plural to mean "humanity" (as in 1:25). Thus "spirit" here refers to the human power of knowledge, consciousness, feeling, and social purposes.

The human spirit in Paul's writings appears to be the place of connection between man and God (cf. Rom 1:9, 8:10; I Cor 5:5, 14:14; II Cor 4:13; Gal 6:1). It is capable of being present where the body is absent in the deliberations of the church; it is contrasted to the body on one side and the mind on the other and thus is different from abstract reason in the moral or intellectual sphere; but it is open to the seizure of the divine Spirit and is subject to feelings produced by the responsibilities and burdens of the church.

Whether Paul had a thoroughly thought out and consistent doctrine of the human spirit cannot be demonstrated. Here (and indeed in all his psychological terminology) he seems to have had a fluid conception which was capable of different meanings in different contexts.

anthrōpos is technically a "species" word, and it therefore readily relates to the generality "humanity." It is also adaptable to translation which avoids sex specificity, but it is doubtful whether Paul considered such a distinction outside the particular passages where the matter is moot (chs. 7, 11, 14).

12. *we did not receive the spirit.* The verb is aorist, which implies that at one point Paul and his readers did or did not receive the spirit/Spirit. Presumably they possessed the spirit of the world all along, but like the Galatian Christians they "received the Spirit when they heard the gospel by faith" (Gal 3:2).

13. *words not instructed by human wisdom* (*en didaktois anthrōpinēs sophias logois*). An alternative translation is, "not in learned words of human wisdom." The difference between the alternatives is somewhat refined but perhaps important. The translation accepted here means that human wisdom is an instructor teaching words to be used in our speech, while the alternative means that the words themselves either arise from human wisdom or are about human wisdom. The genitive *sophias* may be subjective, objective, or of kind if it is construed with *logois* (the alternative choice); if it is taken with *didaktois* (the translation adopted), it is an unusual genitive of instrument or agency (cf. John 6:45 and Matt 25:34). Héring adopts a conjecture rather diffidently made by Blass (BDF, § 183) that would delete *logois*. Then *didaktois* is treated substantively, *en* becomes locative ("among") rather than instrumental, and the phrase is directly parallel with *en didaktois pneumatos*. It is alluring to tidy the passage in this way and in so doing make it parallel to vs. 6. The elimination of a word attested by all the MSS, however, is a drastic procedure; and since the other grammatical difficulties balance out, it seems prudent not to adopt unnecessary conjecture.

by spiritual words (*pneumatikois*). The decisions reached concerning the first part of the verse determine the rendering of the last phrase, which by itself is certainly ambiguous. (This accords with the alternative translation of RSV margin.)

14. *natural man* (*psychikos anthrōpos*); the translation has been traditional since Tyndale. It means a person with a human psyche, a being with human life and experience.

investigated in a spiritual manner. No simple translation seems to be entirely satisfactory. *anakrinō* can mean (a) to question or interrogate for the sake of information (I Sam 20:12, LXX), (b) to subject to cross questioning or persistent inquiry, to elicit the truth from an unwilling source (Acts 12:19), and (c) to conduct systematic research into a subject (Acts 17:11). The difficulty here is compounded by the personal reference of the word in the second clause of vs. 15. Paul may have had in mind that the things of the Spirit of God are information to be obtained by questioning; or they may be like the teachings of scripture, which must be systematically studied, analyzed, and compared. It is also possible that he regarded the Spirit as a witness to be subjected to cross examination (as prophets in the Old Testament called upon the people to put God to the test and even engaged in legal contest with him). The nuances of *anakrinō* might be consolidated in the translation "judicially examine"; but that is clumsy, especially when repeated three times here and again in 4:3-4. "Investigate" seems to be a good contemporary compromise, bearing as it does today both proper and pejorative overtones.

16. The quotation is from Isa 40:13, following the LXX. It is interesting to note that of the three clauses in the original Paul quotes the first and third here, while in Rom 11:34 he quotes the first two. In the last clause Paul reads an Attic future (BDF, § 74[1]), which is a secondary reading of the LXX text.

COMMENT

Saving power and perishing folly

The contrast of wisdom of speech and the cross of Christ leads Paul to a series of related ideas. First, *the message of the cross is foolishness to those who are perishing*—"the *logos* of the cross" being a pregnant phrase combining at least three possibilities: the message proclaimed about the cross, the message which the cross implies, and the suggestiveness of the very word "cross." The message is the story of the self-sacrifice of a man worshiped by believers as the Son of God. Minds that believed in a god outside the Judaeo-Christian tradition stressed his power and freedom from pain, suffering, and death. Elaborate philosophical arguments had been developed among the Greeks to demonstrate the god must be free from distress and even from influence from any source outside himself. It was impossible for the divinity to be overcome by weak and fallible men. A divine being could not suffer as men do, and therefore it was unthinkable that a son of God, a being with divine characteristics, could endure death like a criminal. Consequently, the cross was declared to be foolishness to those who, by rejecting its saving power, were perishing; *but to us who are being saved it is God's power*—Paul includes himself by the personal pronoun. This carries Paul's conviction that the message of the cross has the ability to speak to the human heart, to affect conscience, to make plain the nature of sin, and to give a basis for hope and life. Thus when the story was told, God's power was set in motion. But this is foolishness to some, for the process cannot be proved in an ordinary sense; the role of faith in effecting this process is introduced in vs. 21.

An Old Testament quotation extends this idea to note that, under human conditions, wisdom and shrewdness come to nothing. It is precisely *the proclamation* about the cross, foolish as it seems, that reveals the bankruptcy of human wisdom. When those who are being saved understand the action of God in Christ, they realize that no wise man could ever have discovered that God would do this. God's action is the kind of surprise that makes startlingly clear the ultimate inanity of the deepest human intelligence and its irrelevance to destiny.

Paul implies that the deepest human need is the knowledge of God: *the world did not come to know God through wisdom*. Great minds had been searching for knowledge to fill the void which left life without meaning, groping for reality and sense of destiny. These researches had been fruitless, had not proved that there is or is not an ultimate reality, that there is or is not an ultimate divine concern for humanity. Paul declares that this has been *in the wisdom of God:* the inability of the human mind to discover God has been part of God's wise plan. Paul does not develop this idea here; in the sequel he suggests that it depends upon the qualitative difference between God and men.

Jews, Greeks, and God

Throughout his writing Paul differentiates between Jews and gentiles in their relationship to God. Here the gentiles are Greeks: *Jews ask for signs and Greeks seek for wisdom.* The Jews were looking for a saving action of God that would occur through the sending of his messiah (Christ). The identity of the messiah would be made known by signs, perhaps in the sky, perhaps on the earth. He would inaugurate a glorious kingdom and would sweep to power over the forces opposing God. Now to proclaim that God's messiah had come and had been crucified without an identifying portent was *an offense to Jews.* Jesus could not have been God's promised agent since he was maltreated, scorned, and put to death as a lawbreaker by the will of men.

The ones who are called includes *both Jews and Greeks.* The Greeks represent those Paul had been writing about who consider God's wisdom to be foolishness. To affect them the message must overcome the obstacles created by cultivated human knowledge. But *God's foolishness is wiser than men, and God's weakness is stronger than men.* The foolishness of divine love is wiser than the wisdom of human pride; it is the unadorned, stark display of willingness to enter the worst condition that ever faced a human being. This is wiser than the security sought by the skill of intelligent persons because it accomplishes what no human wisdom can achieve: the reclamation and remaking of the victims of sin and death. The weakness of God is the weakness of the death of Christ. In human experience death is the ultimate weakness, but the death of Christ is more powerful than all human strength. Paul's acquaintance with Christ caused him to change all his previous ways of thinking. Here was indeed the supreme metamorphosis. Now he understood that wisdom and strength were to be found in weakness, life in death.

God's choice of the "nothings"

Paul applies this insight to the Corinthians. Their Christian calling was not on the basis of their standing in society. *Wise from a human viewpoint* would include people with education, learning skill, or philosophical knowledge—some branch of human learning; one might say "intellectuals." *Powerful* would refer to people in high positions in government or in the pagan religious establishment, perhaps also slave owners and military officers. *Wellborn* would be free persons, usually with Roman citizenship and perhaps descendants of ancient, noble families. People who could be characterized in these three ways were represented very sparsely in the Corinthian church. This ran counter to the wisdom of the world; for from a human viewpoint the new movement should get people of influence, wealth, and power to lend it prestige and to attract other persons. From God's viewpoint, however, the church found its strength among the powerless and positionless members of society. This caused *shame* to the *wise* and *mighty;* that is, the despised, feeble, and foolish (ignorant) people of the earth have received from God a wisdom and power that shows up as worthless the qualities in which the wise and powerful of the earth take pride. Although they had no part in the power structures of society, the Corinthian Christians were performing works of the Spirit that the might of the world could not accomplish.

The insignificant things of the world is Paul's vivid description of these people: these are "baseborn," and so he goes on to call them *"nothings."* By the deliberate act of God these people were called to become the core of the world's greatest redemptive revolution. *The existing things,* including people "of substance," were nullified precisely by these despised *"nothings."*

God's purpose in this is *that no human may glory before God*. This rejection of pride and boasting is a principal motif in Paul's Christian life view. A primary mark of the non-Christian is his incurable desire for personal glory. So closely is this attached to the center of his motivation that it is almost impossible for him to eliminate it. This is why God chose people who were so insignificant that they could have no natural cause for boasting, and Paul wants those people never to forget.

This is the result of *God's action:* whatever status or wisdom the Corinthians had was *in Christ Jesus*. Christ became not only *wisdom* but also *righteousness and holiness and redemption*. He became the basis of acceptance with God, the source of consecration which gives deep importance to life, and the means of release from sin, guilt, alienation, and hostility. Thus, Paul declared, Christians live on charity, but their status *in the Lord* is ground for a glory higher than that of the greatest person in the world.

Paul's personal demonstration of God's paradoxical wisdom

Additional illustration of the difference between divine and human wisdom is furnished by the example of Paul himself. The Corinthians were not persons of wisdom and status; and when Paul appeared in Corinth, his presentation of the gospel was not with *excellence of speech or wisdom*. He declined to take credit as a fine speaker or a master of style. (One cannot help wondering, of course, after reading I Corinthians 13 whether Paul is being overmodest.) He had no desire to enter into competition with the master orators of the ancient world. Something far more important engrossed his mind, *proclaiming the mystery of God*—the secret of God which had not been made known to the world until Christ appeared, the revelation of the justification of people by the crucifixion of Christ and the conquest of death by his resurrection. For Paul it was of prime importance that people discover what God had done; so he made a deliberate decision *to know nothing in* their *midst except Jesus Christ and him crucified*. The aorist verb indicates that this occurred at one time, and *in your midst* suggests that the decision was made when he first came to Corinth. What caused this statement of policy is not clear; there is little evidence that Paul's message ever had any other focus. It has been proposed (see e.g. Grosheide, 59) that he came to this decision after his speech in Athens (Acts 17), which used what seem like philosophical phrases and arguments and which could be considered a failure because of the supercilious response of the Athenian philosophers. The notion that Paul's enthusiasm for eloquent speech was dampened by Athenian indifference, however, is hardly tenable not only because of the general evidence that Paul's proclamation was always Christ-centered but also because of the evidence in Acts that the Athenian speech did in fact win Christian followers, several of whom are identified by name (17:34; and see Munck's remark, AB, 174). In any case, the emphasis upon the story of Jesus Christ and his crucifixion was intended either to apply to Paul's initial presentation to the Corinthians or more likely to be a general statement of his theme. Certainly his letters often say "we know" or "you know" when referring to details other than this central one.

Jesus Christ and him crucified was undoubtedly the most scandalous feature of the Christian message. Crucifixion was so abhorred in the Roman world that modern man can hardly feel its full significance. That a crucified person had been selected for worship and was emphasized in Paul's preaching was a startling and vivid matter. The proclamation was simple but devastating. Jesus had died by crucifixion, and the time it happened was definite and in the past. Yet, as the perfect participle suggests, he defied the transition of time; for unlike all other men, his death is perpetual. It acts on behalf of people of all time. So Paul felt that to tell this with any exhibition of oratorical genius would be a contradiction: it would be totally inappropriate to tell about the crucifixion of the Son of God in dazzling words and phrases which would draw attention to the speaker. Indeed, Paul was so overwhelmed by the paradoxical nature of the details of the gospel that he presented it *with weakness, fear, and much trembling*.

Conzelmann rightly suggests (p. 71) that Paul's physical condition was God's way of making his preaching conform externally and internally to the cross. This was no superficial part of the orator's art: it was part of the apostle's experience of the awesomeness of the crucifixion. He did not want the attention of his hearers to be distracted from what he said to how he said it. Nothing in the phraseology, diction, or rhetoric of his speeches was designed to do anything but show the man on the cross—as a telescope brings into view an object and fails in its purpose if one becomes aware of anything on the lens.

Paul's message itself did not move his hearers but it was an action of God's Spirit, which has the power to produce the effects of Christ's miraculous energy among the congregation, to win people to belief, trust, and obedience. *Human wisdom* is no proper object of faith; Paul was soliciting a decision that they put their confidence *in God's power*.

Now we are speaking a wisdom among those who are mature. This may be understood in two ways. (a) Paul may mean that at the outset of his ministry in Corinth he preached only the crucifixion of Christ, but among the mature Christians he was able later to speak a message on a deeper level. (b) He may mean that the preaching of Christ crucified is God's wisdom among the mature, real wisdom over against sophistical, spurious human wisdom. The former interpretation seems at first look to be supported by the text, and this understanding is accepted by Héring and Conzelmann, among others. The Greek particle *de* may indicate a shift to a new subject or a contrast to what has just been said. Thus whereas he *decided to know nothing except Christ crucified* at first, now he referred to a deeper message that is to be shared with those who can understand it, a message expressed in learned, philosophical language. This may be interpreted as an anticipation of 3:1-2, where two stages of speaking are compared to milk and solid food.

On the other hand, there is substantial reason to doubt that Paul regarded any teaching as containing wisdom deeper than that of the Christ crucified. He has already (1:17) marked this as his mission in distinction even from such a basic church function as baptism. No detail of a new wisdom is offered here. It *does not belong to this age* but is revealed in a *mystery;* it *has been hidden* and was *predetermined* by God. In vss. 9-13 Paul will show that God's wisdom is revealed only by God's Spirit. In view of what he has already said in ch. 1 about wisdom and foolishness it does not seem necessary to assume that he is speaking about additional wisdom here. Twice he says *we are speaking,* and the present linear verb suggests that he is speaking this wisdom all along. Comparison with Rom 8:29, Eph 1:5, and Col 1:26 suggests that God's hidden mystery is the choice of his children to be accepted because of Jesus Christ; and this does not suggest a higher, esoteric wisdom. The entire wisdom of God is contained in the message of the cross; and even though occasions may reveal implications of that message, there is no indication that such are intended here. The mature people, then, are not Christians belonging to an inner circle but are all those who have embraced the message of the cross.

This world's rulers . . . crucified the glorious Lord. The identification of these rulers is a difficult problem. As long ago as the third century they were identified with spirit powers; and they have been variously treated as demons, as angels, or as Gnostic aeons. In this connection, they are often associated with "the ruler of this world" (John 12:31, 14:30, 16:11). It is true that Gnostic ideas early attached to statements such as this. Ignatius says (*Ephesians* 19:1) that the "ruler of this world (age)" did not notice the Lord's death; and this was open to appropriation by Gnostics who interposed the aeons between the earthly Christ and his heavenly identity. Origen's idea (*De Principiis* III iii) that the rulers had a wisdom of their own is beside the point here. There seems to be no convincing reason to interpret "this world's rulers" as being any other than those who actually took part in the condemnation and crucifixion of Jesus, and the wisdom they did not know was that their action would have a result exactly opposite to their intention: the ignominy of the cross was turned into the glory of redeeming lordship.

There is evidence that Paul saw supernatural powers working in and through earthly powers (Rom 8:38; I Cor 15:24; Col 2:15), but his use of terminology is not conclusive, and Rom 13:1 should be evidence enough that he thought of earthly rulers as directly responsible to God. Moreover, throughout the Gospels demons and angels know very well who Jesus is; and no statement in the New Testament implies directly that supernatural beings effected the crucifixion. The nearest to exceptions would be in John's Gospel, where Satan enters Judas (13:27) and where Jesus speaks of the judgment of "the ruler of this world" (16:11); but these have to be placed over against the statements about the crucifixion (John 19:23 or even Acts 2:36), which tell of a very human act.

There is no uniform meaning attached to *mystery* in the New Testament: see Mark 4:11; Rom 11:25, 16:25; I Cor 15:51; Col 1:26; II Thess 2:7; Rev 1:20, 10:7, 17:5,7. There is, however, a common element: secret information is made known by some special action of God. In I Cor 2:7-8 it is quite reasonable to understand that Paul is saying that just as people to whom he preached took the message about the cross as a "scandal" or "foolishness," so those who had been responsible for the crucifixion in the first place did not know what they were doing. Perhaps Paul deliberately uses terminology current in Corinth under the influence of mystery religions or Gnostic philosophy. It is quite another thing to maintain that his thinking was shaped or even seriously influenced by these pagan ideas, and it seems just as remote a possibility that the Corinthian church people he had just described were deeply or extensively involved in them.

The Spirit as revealer of God's wisdom

From the consideration of the nature of God's wisdom Paul turns to the way by which it becomes known. The transition is made by a summary scriptural quotation, and then he says that God *revealed them to us through the Spirit.* Again it seems to be straining the text to infer that these things are secret mysteries reserved for an inner circle of Christians with special endowment of the Spirit. In Rom 1:16-17 and Gal 3:2 it is the gospel message itself which is revealed, and with the preaching of the gospel comes the gift of the Spirit. There seems to be no basis for supposing that the revelation made *to us* here is anything other than the significance of Jesus Christ, his death on the cross, and the results of this for those who believe the good news. *The depths of God's mind* (literally, "the deep things of God") is another way of saying the same thing: this is God's eternal plan, the details of which could be known to human beings only through revelation. Thus the Spirit is a bridge between humanity and God whereby people find out what before only God knew.

This is a daring thought: that some of the thought-process of God actually enters our being so that we can comprehend at least some of God's purpose. To a first-century Greek mind this might not have seemed surprising since the gods of the Greek pantheon, though great and immortal, were conceived as engaging in activities close to those of human beings and commonly entering human beings to use them for their purposes. The God of first-century Judaism, however—Paul's God—was the infinite creator of the universe, greater than all things taken together, far above and beyond mankind; and for this God to take habitation in human beings was a great paradox. The very sublimity and transcendence of God made it impossible for a human being to understand God (Isa 55:8-9); yet Paul's Christian faith led him to declare confidently that God revealed himself. An analogy supports the point: that quality in a person which distinguishes him as human is the only basis upon which he can identify with and understand humanity. So only one who has received the Spirit of God can understand and believe his revelation.

The activity of the Spirit can be interpreted in two ways: (a) that the Spirit gives life to the message about Jesus Christ crucified so that hearers are enabled to receive and trust in this action of God; (b) that the Spirit makes known to the human mind further truths and actions of God. Specific mention of *the things freely given* suggests that Paul had in mind perhaps both activities but primarily the first: that is, the essential good news about the saving action of Christ. Mere human hearing of the words of the message as human language would not enable a person to believe in them or to perceive that through them God freely gives his unique "things"; but the Spirit enables one to base life on this message with assurance. Thus Paul rejected excellence of speech and persuasive words of wisdom; and the words by which he presented the message were either suggested by the Spirit or closely and fitly accommodated to the nature of the things revealed. He interpreted *spiritual matters by spiritual words* (and "spiritual" means "belonging to the Spirit of God").

The spiritual person and the mind of Christ

Paul now makes a summary of the points he has introduced. He reiterates the contrast he has already established between persons with and without God's Spirit. One who is simply human *has no capacity for the affairs of God's Spirit.* He is the epitome of the Greek, the gentile, the wise man of the world: God's intentions for humanity are outside the range of his understanding; *they are foolishness to him.* (This is a biblical buttress to Karl Barth's insistence that natural reason cannot discover or prove the truth of God. It may also illuminate the twentieth-century rejection of Christian revelation which exists along with a conviction that human reason, hopes, and values are absurd, that existence is nonsense.) *The affairs of God's Spirit* include the insights about the meaning of the gospel and, as the sequel seems to indicate, the application of the spirit of the gospel to all problematic areas of life. These things *are investigated in a spiritual manner.* Only by the agency of the Spirit can one carry out the kind of research, systematic examination, or questioning that enables one to discover or understand these things. The use of the first person plural throughout this section suggests that the *locus operandi* of the Spirit is the fellowship of the Christian community. The examination which produces spiritual comprehension is not properly conducted by one person in isolation but in the common life of the church (a point which will be considered again and again in the epistle).

One who participates in the life of the Spirit in the Christian fellowship examines all things, is free to *investigate all things* pertaining to God. Paul proposed that there should be no censorship nor obstruction to the systematic search for truth. This implies that the spiritual person is capable of evaluating properly the good and evil he confronts, of estimating what things are worth while and what things are not. For Paul this included: matters not covered by clear Christian precedent (I Cor 7:40); virtues and attitudes of life in relation to one another that do not conform to the prudence or customs of the world and that do not arise spontaneously from natural human impulses and desires (Gal 5:18,22-25); wisdom to make judgment by virtue of divine reconciliation (I Cor 6:3-6); and the new mode of exercising powers and gifts for the benefit and progress of the whole Christian community (I Corinthians 12).

On the other hand, the spiritual man *is investigated by no one*. Since he knows the wisdom of God and is being saved by the power of God in Christ, no human being can bring a valid charge against him. (Paul applies this to his own case in 4:3-4.) The person who received God's Spirit is free from fear of any judgment except that of God himself. This is reinforced by a quotation from Isa 40:13. In Rom 11:34 Paul used the same reference to illustrate that the ways and judgments of the Lord are unsearchable. Here, however, it seems to be reassurance against any human attack. The purpose of God to save human beings and to instruct their lives is contradictory to human wisdom, but it is assuredly the determined *mind of the Lord*.

The passage ends with a startling declaration that *we have the mind of Christ*. The thread of thought is clear enough: the natural man thinks the affairs of God's Spirit are foolishness; the spiritual man comprehends these affairs; because this relates him to the self-determining mind of God, the spiritual man is not subject to other judgment; the common denominator in all this is *the mind of Christ*. The sublime and almost unbelievable claims that Paul has made all become comprehensible and humanly accessible because of the revelation in Christ. The mystery, wisdom, and power of God—*the mind of the Lord*—these *affairs of God's Spirit,* which are foolishness to the natural man because *he is not able to comprehend* the cross, all this is the permanent possession of the Christian community, in *the mind of Christ* revealed through God's Spirit.

LEADERSHIP AND NURTURE IN THE CHURCH
(3:1-23)

Strife and immaturity

3 1 Yet I could not address you, brothers, as spiritual persons but as physical ones, as infants in Christ. 2 I supplied you with milk to drink —not solid food, for you were not yet able to take it. Indeed, you are not able to take it even now; 3 for you are still physically oriented. Whereas jealousy and contention are among you, are you not physically oriented, and are you not conducting yourselves according to a human standard? 4 For whenever anyone says "I belong to Paul," and another says, "I belong to Apollos," are you not on human standards?

Cooperative roles of leadership

5 What, then, is Apollos? And what is Paul? They are servants by whose efforts you came to faith, and they serve as the Lord has given ability to each one. 6 I planted, Apollos irrigated, but God caused the plant to grow. 7 So neither the one who plants nor the one who irrigates amounts to anything; but the important one is God, who gives growth. 8 The one who plants and the one who irrigates serve one function, though each will receive his own wage according to his own labor. 9 You see, we are partners in God's work; you are God's farm, God's building.

The church as God's building

10 In cooperation with the kindly favor of God, which was given to me, I laid a foundation like an experienced master builder; and another person is building the superstructure. But let each person take care how he does his building; 11 for no one can lay a foundation other than the one which is laid, that is, Jesus Christ. 12 If anyone builds on the foundation a structure of gold, silver, precious stones, wood, grass, or thatch, 13 each person's work will become exposed; for the day will clearly show it because it is being revealed by fire; and the very fire puts to the test what sort of work each person has done. 14 If anyone's work which he built on the foundation remains standing, he will receive his wage; 15 if anyone's work burns down, he will sustain a loss though he himself will be saved, being rescued, as it were, through fire. 16 Do you not know that you people are God's temple and that the Spirit of God dwells among you? 17 If anyone destroys God's temple, God will destroy this person; for God's temple is holy—and you are it.

Belonging to God

18 Let no one delude himself: if anyone thinks that he has superior worldly wisdom in your company, let him become foolish in order that he may become wise. 19 For the wisdom of this world is foolishness from God's viewpoint; indeed, it has been written,

He is the one who catches the wise by their craftiness;
20 and again,

The Lord knows that the dialectics of the wise are nonsense.
21 Therefore let no one glory on human grounds; for all things are yours — 22 whether Paul or Apollos or Cephas, whether the world or life or death, whether things present or things to be — 23 all things are yours; and you belong to Christ, and Christ belongs to God.

Notes

3:1. *Yet I.* The transition is the same as at 2:1 (*kagō*), but the context requires slightly different treatment.

2. *milk to drink—not solid food.* Zeugma, with the verb (*epotisa*) strictly applicable only to the first object. Paul's style often admits closely clipped forms of expression. Thus the completion of *you were not yet able* must be supplied.

3. *physically oriented* (*sarkikoi*) in distinction from *physical* (*sarkinois*) in vs. 1. While the original differentiation between these two adjectives was not strictly observed in first-century Greek, it is possible to make it here: in vs. 1 the very being of the brothers was physical (i.e. "fleshly"; "carnal" from the Latin derivation); in this verse physicality is their characteristic.

contention. The addition of "dissension" (*kai dichostasia*), not only in TR but also in some early witnesses, seems to be a gloss, perhaps based on Gal 5:20.

according to a human standard (*kata anthrōpon*). Paul uses several expressions as approximate synonyms: "human," "physical," "of this world," "in this age." Some attempt has been made to preserve the distinctions in translation, a task made doubly difficult by language change and sex specification.

5. *What, then, is Apollos?* Early alteration of the interrogative to "who?" is certainly secondary; the more difficult neuter, however, anticipates *anything* in vs. 7. Moreover, the name of Paul was placed first in a later textual tradition, either because of Paul's preeminence or because of the order in the preceding verse.

you came to faith (*episteusate*). The past aorist is frequently used in the New Testament for that uniquely Christian experience of passing from the status of "not faith" to the status of "faith."

13. *the day will clearly show it because.* The ambiguity in *hoti* (or *ho ti*) makes possible two other translations: "will show that it is being revealed" or "will show what is being revealed." "The day" hardly refers merely to daylight, for then the sequence of statements would make little sense no matter which reading were accepted. Then if "the day" is a time of judgment, the causal *hoti* seems most acceptable.

15. *he will sustain a loss.* On the shades of meaning of *zēmioō,* cf. A. Stumpff, *TDNT,* II, 889-890.

16. *you people are God's temple.* Cf. 6:19 and especially II Cor 6:16.

17. *If anyone destroys.* A simple condition, assuming its factualness.

18. *delude.* A Pauline word in the New Testament; cf. Rom 7:11, 16:18; II

Cor 11:3; II Thess 2:3; I Tim 2:14. This is the only instance where it is reflexive.

in your company. The word order suggests that Paul means, not "someone in your company," but someone presuming wisdom in reference to the Christian society.

19. *He is the one. . . .* The quotation is from Job 5:13, but hardly according to the LXX (cf. M. H. Pope, *Job*, AB, vol. 15, NOTE on 5:13a). Paul may have known another translation, or he may have translated freely from the Hebrew. The participial form (*ho drassomenos;* LXX, *ho katalambanōn*) reflects the Hebrew (*lōkēd*).

20. *The Lord knows.* Ps 94:11; exactly as the LXX (93:11) except for *the wise* in place of *humankind.* The reason for Paul's inconsistency in quotation is uncertain but is likely influenced by the context of the quotation.

23. *you belong to Christ.* The construction appears to be the same as that in 1:12 and 3:4.

COMMENT

Strife and immaturity

At first the immaturity of his hearers hindered Paul from communicating the full message of the gospel. This immaturity was the result of lack not of wisdom but of submission to the Spirit. He described these people as *physical,* literally, "composed of flesh." They were merely human beings under the power of human impulses, thoughts, and ideals. In relation to Christ they were *infants,* born into the Christian family but not matured in its ways or spirit. This is why Paul fed them on *milk . . . not solid food;* the limitations imposed by their degree of development prevented him from communicating the full meaning of his message. Presumably he means that he had announced to them that Jesus Christ, the Son of God, had delivered them from their sins on the cross and had given them a new life, free from fear, free to approach God with confidence as the objects of his love. He would have exhorted them to love God and their fellow creatures, unhampered by taboos and ritual rules, regulations, and customs. This, as the bare minimum of the gospel, was insufficient to guide them in the complicated and perplexing entanglements in which their relationships to each other and to the outside world involved them. In order to grow into maturity in these relationships they needed food, but Paul doubts that they were yet able to digest it.

The evidence of this immaturity is that the Corinthians are *still physically oriented.* Since they are "in Christ," they have made "a spiritual beginning" (Gal 3:3); but although they are not, strictly speaking, "composed of flesh," they are still dominated by "fleshly" considerations rather than by the Spirit. Paul has written at some length about the fleshly life (Rom 8:1-17; Gal 5:13-26; II Cor 10:1-6); he treats it as the life which simply accepts psychophysical existence as regulative for conduct. In ordinary existence the individual feels or senses the world existing all around, but the individual is at the center. Reason indicates that the individual is not the center of all existence, but the actual sensation of centrality seems impossible to eliminate—the egocentric delusion. If this delusion dominates life, one is living according to the flesh, "physically oriented." This principle, which Paul treats succinctly, has elaborate implications which seem to be reflected in the problems of the Corinthian church. They were living for themselves, seeking their own pleasures, regarding others as means of satisfying their own desires. As overt evidence Paul put forward again the *jealousy and contention* that exist in their congregation. Even in the Christian fellowship he saw evidence that the people were divided against each other trying to gain some kind of superiority. This arose from submission to the flesh and caused conduct that was within the range of mere human behavior rather than that inspired by the Spirit.

Cooperative roles of leadership

These impulses to preferential favoritism indicated that the Corinthians were guided by the way leaders impressed them, appealed to their feelings, excited their interests, or confirmed their prejudices. Paul implied that the people were assuming a wisdom which could decide which of their leaders were better qualified or were truer to Christ. This, he insisted, was domination by *human standards* (vs. 4), not by the Spirit. Actually, Apollos and Paul were *servants*. The early meaning of the word, waiters at table, had carried over into the Christian church; and dominical sanction had given a humble word a holy nobility (Mark 9:35, 10:43; Acts 6:1-6; Rom 15:8). The particular service of the leaders was to supply the effort by which the Corinthians *came to faith,* and the ramifications of this task utilized the *God-given ability* of each one.

Paul illustrates this servant role with a figure from the land: he had been assigned the task of planting whereas *Apollos irrigated* the plant. Paul felt a special commission to go to new places where the gospel had not been preached and there to proclaim it for the first time, winning converts and establishing churches (Rom 15:20; II Cor 10:14-16). Others, like Apollos, then directed the work of the established church, instructing it and guiding its growth—which Paul compares to irrigation. Though each leader has an appropriate function, the important thing is that *God gives growth.* When this is remembered, no one can assign much importance to what Paul or Apollos does (and certainly the Corinthians are wrong to set one over against the other). The effort of human beings in any sphere ultimately consists in merely moving things around. The farmer puts the seed in the prepared ground, he covers it with soil, upon occasion (regularly in the Near East) he waters the sprouting plant, and he removes weeds; but no human being can create a seed, and one can only adjust somewhat the conditions for growth. The Christian apostle or leader went to the people and spoke the gospel message to them, but it was God operating through his Spirit who brought the people to faith and established them in a fellowship. Proper faith perceives that the human servants—whether they plant or irrigate, whether they found churches or guide their growth—*serve one function:* they are all one, performing the work of God, whose activity uses their service for life and growth.

Viewed the other way around, there is an importance to what God's servants do in that God does not found and nurture churches without using servants: *we are partners in God's work.* Paul, however, always lays stress on the other view: the people are *God's farm,* however much effort Paul or Apollos may have expended. The servants will, of course, be paid; *each will receive his own wage.* And although the people are not to make relative judgments, God will reward each servant *according to his own labor,* the kind and quality of work he has performed. The wage may be understood in two ways. Paul may have in mind the successful and harmonious operation of the church as a society united in redemptive work. If the servant of God worked well, the society would work well; and that would be the wage. On the other hand, Paul may have had in mind the eschatological dimension of the wage—and the two aspects are not mutually exclusive. In the further development of this section of the epistle this second dimension seems to be present (vs. 14); and Paul elsewhere expresses both aspects (Rom 6:23 [with a different word for wage]; I Cor 9:17-18). The figure has been agricultural, but there is a quick change of figure. The stream of thought is as follows: labor of servants; God's role; wage, cooperative relationship of servants and God; status of the church as the farm belonging to God; status of the church as a building belonging to God.

The church as God's building

In the construction of this building Paul laid the foundation *in cooperation with the kindly favor of God* (literally, "according to the grace of God"; "grace" indicates the disposition of God, which is favorable without any particular merit on the part of the recipient, and may include the favorable gift given by God as a result of his disposition; hence, "favor," which may bear both implications). God was kindly disposed toward Paul and gave him a special gift to enable him to begin the formation of churches in pagan cities. The work is compared to that of *an experienced master builder* (*sophos architektōn*), whose first responsibility in directing construction was to provide an adequate foundation. Every phase of the construction requires care, but the foundation is crucial. Paul evidently was comparing this to his primary proclamation of the gospel. Since he at once identified the essential foundation as *Jesus Christ,* he must mean that by his preaching he spread Jesus Christ underneath the forming church so that it could be regarded as built on Jesus Christ. This is a bold figure, but it is in keeping with the idea in the church that Christ is present as the basis for the Christian society. (The idea appears with some variations in Matt 7:24-25; Rom 15:20; I Cor 10:4; Eph 2:20; Heb 11:10; I Peter 2:4-6; the figure was useful but not rigid in the early church.)

Apparently Paul was thinking of the specific situation; *another person* was *building the superstructure.* This could refer to organizational development, elaboration of scriptural and doctrinal understanding, leadership of worship and witness, and/or congregational social service. Since the rest of the letter is concerned with problems that had risen in worship and ethical relationships in the Corinthian church, Paul may have been referring to the local leadership in these matters when he wrote about "building the superstructure." His remark about "taking care" may be a hint that all was not well with the building. This is developed by the statement about the Christ-foundation: what was being built in Corinth rested upon the foundation Paul laid. This implies that there could be no fundamental division. Since there could be no other basis for the church, rivalry among congregational groups was evidence of a difference in quality of construction material. The materials Paul listed were all in use in first-century building. While the first three, *gold, silver, precious stones,* are properly decorative, they appear to be listed here in a kind of value scale. The apostle treats his figures in this section rather loosely.

The value of the work of each builder will be *revealed by fire.* When the building burns, what survives will expose *what sort of work each person has done.* Again the figure is not to be pushed, for in the first-century world stone was the only building material that survived conflagration. Indeed, the meaning of the figure is not entirely clear. The church as a building must be able to survive the fire. *The day* is probably not a simple reference to sun time but the eschatological judgment which regularly was thought to entail a fiery ordeal. (The sequence of tenses and the grammatical uncertainty suggest caution in interpretation.) Presumably Paul had in mind an ultimate testing to be imposed upon the church, but he offers no specific information. Once the work is tested, wages will be assigned. Again this must be an eschatological reference; otherwise the idea that payment is to be postponed until the building has stood the test of fire is quaint indeed. And again the wage could be both the satisfaction of observing the permanence of the church and the eschatological felicity mentioned elsewhere by Paul. On the other hand, if the builder's *work burns down, he will sustain a loss.* Here the loss apparently consists in witnessing the destruction of the church by the fire. This might be a this-worldly event; but since *he himself will be saved, being rescued, as it were, through fire,* the eschatological dimension seems clear enough. In any case, the salvation of the church builder does not rest upon the success of the church he has built; so his reward seems to have a double dimension: his delight in the effective existence of the church, and the happy destiny of his life in the coming age.

To carry the point to a personal, practical application for his readers Paul specified that they were *God's temple and that the Spirit of God* was dwelling among them. The fact that "you" in English may be singular or plural should not be allowed to obscure the more precise meaning of the Greek text: Paul did not mean to say that each person is God's temple and that the Spirit of God dwells inside each person. He had been writing about the church as a building, and it is clear that here he meant the congregation of persons who composed the Corinthian church. Now he was writing about a special, holy building, a temple. The Jerusalem temple played no significant role in the life of the gentile Christian churches; so he could freely make a figurative contrast: God's sanctuary was no longer a material building but was rather the collection of people among whom God's Spirit dwells. Unlike the Jerusalem temple, in which the invisible God dwelt with his people in a numinous holy of holies, the Christian society was now God's habitation. This has a dreadful consequence which was precisely applicable to the Corinthian church: the destruction of God's temple is an evil which brings destruction upon the one who causes it, and in the context this must mean that people who acted to divide the church by contentious acrimony were liable to God's destroying power. In chapters 11 and 12 Paul will use another figure, the body, and make much the same point. God's temple—the church that Paul and other Christian leaders have built with materials which can withstand a fiery ordeal from outside—*is holy,* it partakes of the numen of God himself; and so Christians are responsible for every effort to maintain the unity of the church. In Corinth this required maintaining a disposition of kindness and concern among the differing groups, recognizing that they were all the holy abode of God's Spirit.

Belonging to God

Having worked through these ideas about the place of leaders in the development of the church, Paul drew them together in a kind of summary. Let there be no misunderstanding: he was not writing about *superior worldly wisdom.* That might have value in some contexts, but in relation to the Christian society such wisdom would surely lead into error the mind of one who prided himself in it. Again he emphasized God's *foolishness.* True wisdom comes from accepting this, for God ultimately determines what is worth while and what is not. This eternal principle Paul supported by two scriptural quotations.

The reference from Job suggests that human craftiness is some kind of handhold by which God *catches the wise.* The wise think that by their complicated and clever schemes they can elude God, but it turns out that this shrewdness is precisely what involves them in failure. God then seizes the wise, ostensibly for punishment, but possibly for salvation if the wise are willing to *become foolish.* In Edward Hall's *Chronicle** there is a story (probably embroidered in the telling) which offers a pointed illustration of Paul's thought. When the English Bishop Tonstall was intent upon preventing the dissemination of William Tyndale's first translation of the New Testament, a merchant friend of Tyndale's sold the bishop all available copies of the book although it was certain they would be burned. In this way Tyndale's debts were paid, new imprints were made possible in increased number, the burning of the books advertised Tyndale's work, and thus the bishop became a helper of the cause he sought to destroy. The bishop thought, Hall wrote, "that he had God by the toe, when indeed he had (as after he thought) the devil by the fist." Paul's quotation from a Psalm is to the same intent: human reasoning in no way outwits God.

The conclusion of the matter is that though mankind because of his knowledge appears to be the crown of the visible universe, unique within its systems, Paul had no doubt about the superlative glory of the Creator, whose wisdom infinitely excels that of mankind. Therefore there is no ground for *glory on human grounds;* the most amazing human achievements are futile. But the Christian has no need for this glory, for he already has *all things.* Paul's illustrative enumeration, presumably identifying all things, is somewhat cryptic; but he seems to mean that there is no room in the life of faith for setting one man over against another in the church, for envying those with much property, for being afraid of death, or for clinging to the fragile joys of this life. Christians have everything worth while because they *belong to Christ;* and (allowing Paul's way of stating the intimate relationship) *Christ belongs to God.* Perhaps there is no better commentary on these verses than Rom 8:38-39: "I have become persuaded that neither death nor life, neither angels nor authorities, neither the present nor the future, not powers, not height nor depth, not any other created thing will be able to separate us from God's love in Christ Jesus our Lord."

---

* *The Union of the Noble and Illustre Famelies of Lancastre and York* (1542), banned later by Queen Mary.

STEWARDSHIP OF APOSTOLIC MINISTRY
(4:1-21)

The Lord as judge

4 ¹ Given such conditions a person should consider us as assistants of Christ and managers of God's mysteries. ² In this connection, moreover, it is demanded of managers that each one turn out to be dependable. ³ Now as far as I am concerned, it is a matter of very little importance for me to be investigated by you or by any human judiciary. Why, I do not even investigate myself, ⁴ for I am conscious of nothing against myself. Yet I have not been justified by this fact; the one who investigates me is the Lord. ⁵ Consequently, do not make any judgment before the proper time—until the Lord comes. Then he will bring to light the dark secrets and will disclose the innermost purposes. And then God will praise each one.

Standards of Christian living

⁶ These things, brothers, I transferred to myself and Apollos for your enlightenment in order that by reference to us you may learn the meaning of the saying, "Go not beyond the things that have been written"—in order that none of you may be puffed with pride on behalf of one against another. ⁷ Who, indeed, is singling you out for distinction? What do you have that you did not receive? And if you received it, why do you glory as though you did not receive it? ⁸ Have you already been stuffed full? Have you already become rich? Have you become kings without us? Well, I wish you had become kings so we also might reign with you. ⁹ For God, I think, appointed us apostles as the least of men, doomed to death, since we became a spectacle for the world and angels and men. ¹⁰ We are fools for the sake of Christ, you are wise in Christ. We are feeble, you are mighty. You are eminent, we are without honor. ¹¹ Until the present hour we have been going hungry and thirsty and poorly clothed; we have endured a rough and homeless life. ¹² We have become weary working with our own hands. When we are insulted, we return blessing; when we are persecuted, we put up with it; ¹³ when we are slandered, we try to conciliate. We have become, as it were, until now the dirt scoured from the world, that which cleanses all.

Paul's authority in Corinth

14 I am writing these things to you not to put you to shame but to admonish you as my beloved children. 15 For if you have thousands of guardians in Christ, yet you do not have many fathers, for it was I who begot you in Christ Jesus by means of the gospel. 16 Thus I urge you to go on imitating me. 17 For this reason I sent to you Timothy, who is my child, beloved and faithful in the Lord. He will remind you about my ways that are in Christ Jesus, just as I am teaching everywhere in every church. 18 As though I am not coming to you, some have become puffed with pride; 19 but I will come to you quickly, if the Lord wills; and I will find out, not the talk of the ones who have been puffed with pride, but their power. 20 For the kingdom of God is not in talk but in power. 21 What do you want? Should I come to you with a rod, or with love and a gentle spirit?

NOTES

4:1. *Given such conditions.* The transition is smooth enough in Greek but not easy to translate. The *houtōs* not only anticipates *hōs* but also ties to what has just been written. Paul's subservient position is stressed as a further development of the role of persons in relationship to God's supremacy in the church.

assistants. The origin of the word in galley slavery was, by the first century, no longer in focus. By then, the term had developed from "under-rowers" to refer to assistants of physicians and of the courts and so came to mean those in secondary service to persons of official position.

managers; alternate translation, "stewards." *Oikonomos* means literally "a divider for the household." The term goes back to the practice of assigning to one servant the responsibility for distributing supplies, tools, and food to the workers on ancient Greek estates. Note Jesus' parable in Luke 16:1-8.

mysteries. Cf. the earlier discussion, pp. 162, 164-165.

3. *a matter of very little importance.* On the elative force of the superlative, cf. BDF, § 60.

investigated. Cf. the discussion in second NOTE on 2:14.

5. *the innermost purposes,* literally, "the counsels of the hearts."

6. *I transferred.* Cf. AGB, *metaschēmatizō.* The idea is that Paul has discussed the situation regarding Apollos and himself to make a point that is of much more general application.

the saying, "Go not beyond the things that have been written." "Go" has been supplied by conjecture; TR supplies *phronein* (KJ, "to think"). The admittedly problematic Greek text has been subject to much discussion. The most ingenious explanation, proposed by Baljon in 1884, shows the clause to be a scribal gloss; and both Schmithals (*Gnosticism in Corinth,* 122) and Héring have accepted this, the latter omitting the words in his translation. Weiss considered the explanation too clever. Robertson and Plummer thought the words may have been a rabbinic maxim. Conzelmann decides that the clause is *unverständlich* as it is, but suggests a possible similarity to the sentiment of Rev 22:19. If "the things that have been written" are to be identified at all, they should refer to Old Testament scripture from which the readers are to discover what is included in the following *hina* clause, which would then be epexegetical. Cf. also J. M. Ross in *ExpT* 82 (1971), 215-217; and M. D. Hooker in *NTS* 10 (1963/64), 127-132.

8. *Have you . . . ?* Nestle[26], UBS, and most modern editors and translators regard these clauses as declaratory statements. The punctuation as questions, accepted here, is that of Westcott and Hort. There is no infallible characteristic in the Greek here to tell which decision is correct, and ancient tradition is certainly not a finality in this instance. As questions, the clauses continue the series of jabs directed by Paul at the consciences of the church members. In effect he asks them to ponder a few absurdities: could anyone claim satiety with spiritual gifts or riches? could new Christian believers have achieved a degree of spiritual rule superior to and independent of the apostolic leaders? These questions lead smoothly into Paul's ironical wish that if, by chance, the neophytes had become rich, spiritual rulers, this might confer some power by association upon the leaders who had converted them and founded their church. If, per contra, the clauses are taken as statements, they are immediately canceled out by the final wish; and the irony seems to be somewhat heavy-handed. The technical decision does not, after all, finally change the apostle's meaning.

9. *the least of men.* The adjective *eschatous* can refer either to temporal sequence (translate "last") or to relative position of honor. Both ideas are used by Paul (15:8 and 9), but the context suggests the second interpretation. Cf. Mark 9:35, 10:31. The derogatory implication further suggests that while Paul uses the first person plural throughout the passage, probably intending *pro forma* inclusion of other leaders—Apollos, at least—he has in mind primarily himself. He can argue, if occasion requires (9:1-6; Gal 2:6), that he is not inferior to the other apostles; but the catalog of dismal experiences here suggests reference to his own life.

10. *without honor.* Cf. Mark 6:4.

12. *working with our own hands.* Cf. Introduction, p. 82; and Acts 18:3, 34.

13. *that which cleanses.* On this difficult term and *dirt scoured,* cf. O. Stählin's discussion in *TDNT,* VI, 90-91.

all. Since the form *pantōn* can be masculine or neuter, Paul could mean either "all people" or "all things"; perhaps he means both.

14. *these things. tauta* usually refers back to things that have previously been mentioned, but no hard and fast usage occurs in Paul's writings. The reference backward would point to what he has just said contrasting the complacency and security of the church with the dangerous poverty of the apostolic leaders. If the reference is forward, it may point to the strong rebukes he is about to

deliver in the face of scandals that have been reported to him. In either case he is assuring them that his admonition is intended to enable them to correct their conduct. In 6:5 he does speak to shame them, but perhaps he may find a subtle difference in the situations.

15. *guardians.* The commentaries on Gal 3:24-25 deal amply with *paidagōgos,* a family functionary of Greek society.

I who begot you. Paul uses the figure again specifically in Philem 10.

16. *imitating me.* Cf. W. Michaelis' discussion in *TDNT,* IV, 666-673.

17. *I sent to you Timothy.* In 16:10-11 Paul urges them to receive Timothy well. The double reference may offer some slight argument for the unity of the epistle unless, of course, one views the personal references as editorial apparatus.

my ways that are in Christ Jesus. hodos was commonly used to refer to the pattern of life adopted by a religious group (e.g. by the Essenes and in Acts). Here the plural seems to point to the range of Paul's practices: his policies as a missionary, his attitudes toward people, and his concern for the moral and spiritual welfare of his congregations.

in every church. en pasē ekklēsia may mean "in the whole church," but in either case he was referring to the congregations with which he had personal contact.

19. *talk. logos* seems to require this somewhat unusual translation in this context.

power. Since this is often associated with the activity of the Spirit (2:4; I Thess 1:5), Paul probably had in mind the idea set forth in 3:16.

20. *the kingdom of God.* The familiar translation has been retained though "kingship" or "sovereignty" would be preferable. The literature on the phrase is immense.

COMMENT

The Lord as judge

Paul concludes this part of his letter by pointing out the function and significance of the apostolic leaders: this consists exclusively in rendering assistance to Jesus Christ. The leader has no independent position, nor is he to be honored apart from Christ. The *managers of God's mysteries* are official representatives of God. To them the divine secrets have been entrusted, and they are responsible for making them known at the appropriate time to the proper people.

At 2:1 Paul has mentioned "the mystery of God," a secret now made known by revelation, specifically salvation in Christ. The use of the plural here in 4:1 seems to broaden that primary concept, and this more general reference occurs also in 13:2 and 14:2. In 15:51 the singular occurs in reference to a detail of the resurrection. In Rom 16:25-26 the mystery is the gospel as a whole, now revealed by prophetic scriptures to all mankind. This is mentioned also in Col 1:26; and the converse (regarding Israel) is set forth in Rom 11:25-33. The letter to the Ephesians uses "mystery" in several ways: 1:9-10, 3:1-12, 5:32, 6:19. It is applied to another eschatological detail in II Thess 2:7-10. Paul's role as "manager" of God's mysteries seems to pick up his thought from 2:1. In his mind the mysteries include preeminently the gospel of justification by faith, the inclusion of all gentiles in God's family, the presence of Christ among the gentiles, the sure salvation of all Israel, the transcendent significance of certain human relationships (marriage, for example, which he will develop later in the epistle), and events still to come in the final consummation. These remarkable items have been entrusted by God through the Spirit to the apostolic leaders, who are to make them known when and as the Spirit guides. The contextual significance of all this is that the leaders have no personal preeminence and should in no way be compared invidiously or favorably with each other.

Those who engage in comparing the leaders overlook the divine operation by means of the leaders. The human abilities and personal qualities of the apostles are irrelevant. The only requirement of these persons is that they perform their duties faithfully and be utterly loyal to their master (see Jesus' parable, Luke 12:42-47). Just as a secular steward is to distribute supplies to the persons for whom they were intended and to do so in a completely honest manner, apostolic leaders are to make known the mysteries at the right time to the right people and to be strictly loyal to Jesus Christ. For this reason Paul was not concerned whether he was the object of human investigation. No church members or other human court might question whether he was efficient, attractive, skillful, successful in gaining the confidence of people, or loyal to civil authorities. Nor did Paul ask these questions of himself. His own clear conscience, however, did not place him in a favorable status before the Lord. He understood clearly that the only one who might "investigate" him was the Lord himself since only the Lord knew whether he had been dependable.

Judgment, indeed, cannot be properly assessed in the present time. This is an eschatological matter. The proper time for judgment will be when *the Lord comes*. Before that no one can correctly evaluate the meaning and worth of a person's life. No one communicates more than a small fraction of his life and being to another person, even in the most intimate of relationships. (This is illustrated by the high percentage of marital troubles that arise out of misunderstanding and mistaken judgments.) *The dark secrets* and *the innermost purposes* of people's lives will be made known completely only in the Lord's final revelation. The disclosure of the truth about persons, however, is an occasion for God's praise. Paul's readers might learn with relief that the time of ultimate judgment is not necessarily a dreadful day of wrath. At last everyone will be fully understood, and God will disclose the basis for true praise.

Standards of Christian living

In the context this means that the praise of Apollos, Cephas, and Paul must be reserved until God praises them accurately. This is the last in a series of points which Paul has made in regard to himself and the other apostolic leaders, which he now declares he had *transferred* in order to elucidate principles that are applicable to all Christians. This is a common practice with Paul: the quarrels, entanglements, and dilemmas that confront people in daily life are dealt with in relationship to the deep principles of the gospel. An incipient split in the church was to be resolved with reference to the foundation principles of the gospel itself. Favoritism in following one leader against another was evidence of being *puffed with pride,* and this is *beyond the things that have been written.* What seems a matter of passing concern is seen to be contrary to the divine revealed will, so it must be avoided at all costs.

A series of sharp questions is aimed at bringing the Corinthians to a sober realization of the true state of affairs. At first they seem to be directed at divisive leadership: vs. 7 is second person singular, but vs. 8 shifts to the plural, and it is evident that Paul is addressing the followers who had declared loyalty to a leader even when he was not willing to head a movement. The questions imply that the people addressed felt unduly important and were trying to exercise functions reserved for God: they were substituting a human leader in place of exclusive loyalty to Christ and were assuming the right to evaluate the worth of God's servants. They affected exemption from the ordinary limitations of human ability and forgot that whatever powers of insight they possessed were granted by the gift of the Spirit.

The wish—impossible of fulfillment—that the apostles might have the royal prerogatives assumed by some Corinthian Christians leads to a description of the actual condition of the apostles, calculated to make the readers realize all the more the vanity of their schismatic ebullience. The apostles had walked the way the Master marked for them: they had been in the humblest of circumstances and had lived on the brink of death. Instead of being rich and powerful, they were bedraggled, insulted, and harassed victims of such universal malice that they were an astonishing sight for the great and small of the world and for the angels who populate the invisible regions. Repeatedly Paul has mentioned the foolishness of the gospel. Here he declares that those who proclaimed it were *fools for the sake of Christ*—and this in contrast to the relatively favored situation of the Corinthian Christians. There is no record of any persistent harassment of the Corinthian church at this time; the social position of the members was one of comparative calm and safety. By contrast Paul had lived from one danger to another; he had aroused antagonism, calumny, and abuse; and he had suffered physically and mentally. The degree of prestige that an oriental religion might enjoy in a settled community did not often attach to the apostolic mission as it moved from one new field to another.

The vagabond nature of the apostle's work meant that he had to establish himself in every new locality, usually with only a few traveling companions and no other support. Therefore he knew what physical deprivation meant. Even in the new Christian communities he attempted to support himself by labor. His reward was often insult, persecution, and slander; but Paul responded according to the irenic admonition of Jesus. The end result of all this was that *the dirt scoured from the world* was poured upon him and his apostolic co-laborers. Then they acted as cleansing agents, taking to themselves hate, malice, and bitterness; and by absorbing this without violent or vengeful response, they took away those evils. Thus in a particular way they were carrying on the work of Christ.

Paul's authority in Corinth

Paul was seldom if ever bland. His final note in this section, therefore, is an attempt to put into proper perspective his relationships with the church. He had already made sharp comments in this letter and he was about to take up reports of scandal. So although he was delivering serious admonitions, he addressed the Corinthians as *beloved children.* This he justified by claiming to be their father *who begot* them in *Christ Jesus by means of the gospel.* By establishing the new church in a pagan city the apostle became the father of the believers; he was the only one who could actually claim that relation to them. This fatherly authority gave him the right to instruct them, and it also laid on them an obligation to heed what he said, wrote, and did. Paul was so completely dedicated to the gospel that he did not hesitate to offer himself as an example for imitation. In perplexing difficulties they should recall how he acted. This was not naive egotism but the assurance of a tried and tested faith, the confidence of his experience in Christ.

The section concludes with a not very subtle threat. Lest there be any doubt about their duties in filial imitation of Paul, he *sent Timothy* with a commendation which seems to designate him elder brother *in loco parentis.* Apparently Paul had expected to visit the church himself, but for some reason he had not carried out his plan. When he failed to arrive, some people in the church seem to have made undue pretension of their importance in the church. Perhaps they made captious criticism of the apostle for not coming, or they may have been claiming that they could conduct the affairs of the church with their own wisdom without regard for his instructions. (This self-assertive activity seems to have been responsible for many of the troubles in the Corinthian church.) Paul was very specific: when in God's providence he did arrive, he would match talk with power. The divine rule of God is exercised through the activity of the Spirit, not by wordy boasting. So Paul offered a blunt alternative: he would come and settle the situation by his own harsh authority; or if affairs were put in order in response to the admonition of the epistle, they might expect a pleasant, pastoral visit.

SCANDALS REPORTED
IN THE CHURCH
(5:1-6:20)

A CASE OF INCEST (5:1-8)

Toleration of one having his "father's wife"

5 ¹ Actually it is being reported that there is sexual immorality in your midst—and such sexual immorality as is reported not even among the heathen—of such a kind that a man has his father's wife. ² And you have been puffed with pride! But should you not rather have mourned so that the one who did this deed might be removed from your midst?

Judgment pronounced by Paul

³ Indeed for my part, though absent in body but present in spirit, I have already come to a decision in the name of the Lord Jesus (as though I were present) about the one who acted thus, ⁴ that, when you and my spirit have come together with the power of our Lord Jesus, ⁵ we hand over such a person to Satan for destruction of the flesh in order that his spirit may be saved in the day of the Lord.

Analogue: leaven and the Christ-passover

⁶ Your arrogant pride is not good. Do you not know that a little leaven leavens the entire batch of dough? ⁷ Clean out the old leaven in order that you may be fresh dough, inasmuch as you are unleavened. For Christ our passover lamb has already been slaughtered; ⁸ therefore let us keep celebrating the festival, not with old leaven or with leaven of evil and wickedness, but with leavened bread of purity and truth.

NOTES

5:1. *Actually.* The first word in this section *holōs* can have a local meaning, "everywhere"; and Héring so takes it. When Paul moves to a new topic, his style generally calls for a transitional word; so after the admonition about overbearing conceit (4:18-21) he specifies here an extreme instance of their error.

immorality. porneia literally means "prostitution" or "harlotry," from a root meaning "to sell." In classical Greek the word usually refers to the practice of selling sexual favors. Among the ancient Jews *zānāh* was extended to cover any kind of sexual relationships practiced when a marriage did not correspond in some manner to rabbinical requirements (cf. the extended discussion in StB, III, 342-358). *znūth* could refer to the sexual practice of a woman who was involved in extramarital or wrong marriage relationships with a man whether done for hire or not. It was applied to marriage within a forbidden degree of consanguinity. The term is even applied to intercourse consummated between a man and the woman to whom he is engaged. In the New Testament it is always a question whether the term should be understood in some extended sense. It seems clear in this context that such a sense is indicated.

among the heathen. ethnesin could also be translated "nations" or "gentiles"; but since the term here seems to exclude the Corinthian Christians, it is best to use the term that appears to differentiate them. For Jewish data, cf. StB, III, 358. On Roman practice, cf. Conzelmann, esp. p. 116, n. 29.

father's wife. The very phrase, *ēsheth āb* (translated by LXX as *gynē patros*), occurs in the prohibition in Lev. 18:8. StB point out that almost without exception this phrase in Hebrew usage refers to the father's wife who is not the mother of the man in question. It would therefore be another wife in a polygamous situation or a stepmother in case the man's mother has died. Instances where the term refers to the man's actual mother are uncommon.

2. *mourned.* The word is used in both the Old and New Testaments to refer not only to lamentations over the dead but also to sorrow for people who had sinned and not repented (Neh 8:9; Isa 24:4; Dan 10:2; Amos 8:8; II Cor 12:21; James 4:9). The *hina* clause is explicative; that is, it explains the nature of the mourning. Since this includes the decision that the man be removed from membership in the community, some sense of excommunication may be involved. Cf. NOTES on vss. 5 and 7.

3. The order and relationship of the phrases in this sentence (through vs. 5) is complex, and the arrangement arrived at here is by no means definitive. Conzelmann lists six possibilities. The critical phrase is *in the name of the Lord Jesus.* The present translation construes it with the principal verb *kekrina.* This attributes strong authority to Paul's decision, but he assumes this in other places (7:40; II Thess 3:6). Paul is an "apostle," a person commissioned in the tradition of the Hebrew *shaliah,* who had full power to act for the person he represented (cf. *TDNT,* I, 415). Dominical authority for such decisions could rest on Matt 18:18 or John 20:23. Another interesting possibility is to take the phrase with its immediate antecedent *the one who acted thus*. It would then represent the reason why the Corinthians were *puffed with pride:* this man had sinned boldly, probably presuming upon his "freedom in Christ"—perhaps a conscious antinomian, or more likely a bad theologian. *kekrina* has two objects: (a) *the one who acted thus* is given first as the object of Paul's decision; (b) but the decision is presented again in vs. 5, "to hand over," and the object of *paradounai* is *such a person*, which repeats the first object.

5. *for destruction of the flesh.* The smoother translation *physical death* is rejected in favor of the more literal because of the nature of the context. Jewish punishment by "extirpation" is treated in the Mishnah, *Kerithoth* (cf. Danby's note on p. 562 of his edition).

The peculiarity of the situation described by Paul raises the question whether "Satan" may not refer here to the public prosecutor. (There is a wide variety of usage in Hebrew; cf. I Sam 29:4; II Sam 19:22; I Kings 5:4, 11:14,23,25; Job 1, 2; Zech 3:1.) If it is possible to extend this idea far enough, Paul's decision may have been to turn the offender over to Roman officials so that they could punish him for violation of Roman law, which prohibited incest and, according to the second-century *Institutes of Gaius* (i 63), prohibited marriage with a stepmother even when widowed. Then it might be concluded that the man in suffering civil punishment could be brought to repentance and thus be saved from the final judgment. Unfortunately for this suggestion there is no evidence that the Jews ever referred to Roman officials as "the Satan." Also there was widespread feeling against turning over fellow religionists to heathen authorities (cf. Paul's argument in 6:1-8); but this would account for the solemn invocation of spiritual unanimity which Paul recorded. (Cf. also fourth and fifth NOTES on 7:5.)

6. *arrogant pride.* The same root word translated *glory* in 1:29,31, 3:21, 4:7.

leaven. Modern usage suggests "yeast," but the traditional translation has been retained because of the passover context. In Exod 12:15, 13:7 the original participants in the Egyptian passover were instructed to remove all leaven from their homes. In subsequent practice a meticulous ritual developed whereby the entire house was systematically searched to ensure that no leaven or leavened product remained during the festival of unleavened bread. In some way, from this practice leaven became a symbol for false teaching or bad conduct. This is reflected in Matt 16:6,12//Mark 8:15. (The other Gospel example, Matt 13:33//Luke 13:20-21, appears to treat leaven as good; but the parable may be an instance of Jesus' use of ironic comparison for emphasis.)

7. *you* is plural throughout the sentence.

unleavened. The exhortation seems to ask them to be in practice what they are in principle by virtue of their inclusion in the Christian society.

our passover lamb . . . slaughtered. Paul apparently knows the tradition that Jesus died at the afternoon hour when the passover lambs were being slaughtered (cf. J. A. Walther, "The Chronology of Passion Week," *JBL* 77 [1958], 116-122).

8. *let us keep celebrating the festival.* There is a twofold point to the linear

exhortation: (a) as the rest of the sentence shows, Paul emphasizes the ethical dimension of Christian life, which is here marked by sacrament observance; (b) he anticipates his discussion in chapter 11 dealing with a Corinthian problem related to sacrament observance.

COMMENT

Toleration of one having his "father's wife"

Having treated the general problem of threatening schism in the Corinthian church, Paul then turned to specific problems which had come to his attention. The spiritual analyses and principles which he developed in his first main section (1:10-4:21) were used as he moved into the complex difficulties besetting his congregation. The first of these is an instance of *immorality,* reprehensible in itself, but intolerable on a wider scale because of the apparent attitude of the church members toward the situation. The general nature of the problem seems clear enough, but a series of interrelated difficulties makes the details uncertain.

A man has his father's wife, that is, a male member of the Corinthian church was cohabiting with a woman who had been or was still married to the man's father. From Hebrew usage it is probable that the woman was the man's stepmother or another wife of his father in polygamous relationship. There is nothing in the text to indicate whether the father was dead, though this has often been assumed. It is also possible that the father and the woman had been divorced. At best, the woman was the man's widowed stepmother.

The degree of immorality is further complicated by uncertainty as to whether the man and woman married. The verb in this context means to possess a woman physically, either inside or outside of marriage. Since the church seemed to accept the situation *puffed with pride,* it might be supposed that the couple was considered married. Otherwise Paul might have been expected to treat in this context the matter he in fact delayed until 6:9-20.

Another complication is the statement that *such immorality* was *reported not even among the heathen.* In contemporary Judaism there seems to have been no particular objection to admitting a proselyte who was married to his stepmother. The premise was that such a relationship was permitted in gentile society, and Judaism therefore would not invalidate a relationship authorized in the society from which the proselyte came. The only hindrance the older rabbis raised was violation of common morality. On the other hand there is evidence that the Romans rejected marriage between stepparents and stepchildren. Thus Paul's statement would appear to be supported by Roman but not by rabbinic tradition. Since Paul would not likely have been more rigid in his attitude in this matter than the rabbis were, the probability is increased that either the man was living with his stepmother while the father was still alive or they were living together without marriage.

The scandal was not a simple case of sexual immorality, however: the attitude of the church was involved, and Paul chided the church for indulgent pride. The implication is that they were proud in the assumption that their Christian freedom was enhanced by their sympathetic understanding of this unusual sexual relationship. Paul, on the other hand, proposed they should *rather have mourned,* in accordance with a Jewish custom that would have treated a rejected person as one who was dead. Indeed, he proposed that, mourning or not, the man must be removed from membership in the community.

Judgment pronounced by Paul

Paul realized his precarious position in acting as judge when he was not present for a trial. He therefore belabored a kind of principle of "pneumatic ubiquity" as an apostolic prerogative. He then passed judgment on the man and anticipated that it would be carried out when the Corinthians and his spiritual communication became the united channel for *the power of our Lord Jesus.* This was a daring proposition on the part of the apostle, but he seems boldly assured that divine action would occur in this way.

The final difficulty with this passage concerns the judgment itself: the man was to be handed over *to Satan for destruction of the flesh.* (The only New Testament parallel is in I Tim 1:20, where the sin was some sort of religious transgression and the deliverance to Satan seems to have been a religious penalty.) Satan is most naturally taken to refer to the devil, the plenipotentiary of evil. It is peculiar, however, that the purpose of handing over the man was that his flesh might be destroyed so that *his spirit may be saved in the day of the Lord.* It might be presumed that one turned over to Satan would be lost eternally. The best explanation of the situation is that among the Jews certain sins, especially those against the laws of marriage, were punished by "extirpation," which means that they were cut off from human life by the hand of God. When the Jewish community imposed this ban, it was believed that the offending party would die a premature death. Since the sin of the Corinthian man was certainly a violation of Old Testament marriage law and, according to Paul, of gentile practice, Paul could well have been consigning him to extirpation, which would be executed by Satan as the agent of divine punishment (on the analogy of the Job story; usually the hand of God was the executor in Judaism). *De-*

struction of the flesh, then, would refer to premature death. Under such circumstances the man would have some time to come to repentance, and so his spirit would finally be saved.

Analogue: leaven and the Christ-passover

Paul moved with almost inevitable reciprocation from the general to the particular and back again. Although the scandal must be dealt with by action in the individual case, the involvement of the whole congregation was by no means to be ignored: their *arrogant pride*—their unwarranted, tolerant freedom in accepting the immorality—was *not good.* Unlimited confidence in discarding established, honored institutions in the name of Christian freedom, especially when the substituted conduct is actually evil, is at least inadvisable. To indulge one person in conduct that violates moral standards invites the spread of such conduct throughout the entire society with the danger that it may all become corrupt. Paul used a homely maxim: *a little leaven leavens the entire batch of dough* (he used exactly the same words in Gal 5:9). This apt reference suggested passover practice, and Paul exhorts the people of the church to make an ethical application of the cleaning out of *the old leaven.* His metaphors are not to be pushed at this point. The old leaven seems to refer to the life followed by the people before they entered the new, Christian fellowship. The *fresh dough,* then, would be the life of the church as a collection with its own organic life. This may be carried further. Leavened bread soon gets stale while unleavened bread retains its freshness longer. But Paul was in a further dilemma: the Christians of Corinth had been baptized and so were fit for passover—they were *unleavened.* He did not, however, back away from his exhortation; for he was convinced that remedial action was necessary. He wanted them to be in church practice what they already were in theological faith. He wanted individual spirituality to issue in church ethics.

The thought of cleansing the church from leaven-evil led by direct association to the thought of the slaughter of the passover lamb, and Paul affirmed the role of Christ as the slaughtered lamb of God's passover by which Christians gain their freedom. The idea was hardly new with Paul, but his development here is particularly vivid. Christians must make a practice of *celebrating the festival,* not merely in the literal sense, but spiritually by living continuously without *evil* and in an atmosphere of *purity and truth.* The complicated tangle of allusions in this passage ought to be unraveled with patient care and without any detailed attempt at sacramental application. It is important to bear in mind the context: Paul addressed a case of scandalous immorality and broadened its resolution into a theological lesson for the church.

CLARIFICATION OF PAUL'S INSTRUCTION
REGARDING ASSOCIATION WITH IMMORAL
PERSONS (5:9-13)

5 9 I wrote you in my letter not to mix with sexually immoral people
—10 not at all meaning the sexually immoral people of this world, or
the greedy and swindlers, or idolaters, since then you would need to
depart out of the world. 11 But now I write you not to mix with any
so-called brother who is sexually immoral or greedy or is an idolater,
reviler, drunkard, or swindler. Do not even eat with such a person.
12 For why is it my business to pass judgment on the outsiders? Is it
not your business to pass judgment on the insiders? 13 But God will
pass judgment on the outsiders.

Clean out the evil one from your own people.

Notes

5:9. I wrote you in my letter. The verb (*egrapsa*) is the same as that in vs.
11. It is possible in vs. 9 and likely in vs. 11 that the epistolary use of the aorist
is intended, the courteous acceptance of the time situation of the reader on the
part of the writer. In this verse the context seems to make it clear that Paul
refers to a former letter; in vs. 11 the emphasis on *But now* suggests the present letter. This conclusion that vs. 9 refers to a letter written before "First Corinthians" is supported by *in my letter* (literally, "in the letter"), a phrase
hardly appropriate in connection with the epistolary aorist. It is likewise evident that in the present letter there has been no general statement about
avoiding association with sexually immoral people. Implications of this decision for the over-all structure of Paul's Corinthian correspondence have been
noted in the Introduction, pp. 18-24, 120-122.

It is possible to argue that vs. 9 refers to the case presented in the previous
section, vss. 1-8. It enjoined breaking off relationships with the man who was
living with his father's wife, which Paul could have regarded as implying a general injunction. Verse 11, then, would give the case more precise detail. Thus
both aorists would be epistolary. This appears, however, to force the details;
and difficult as it is, most commentators agree that in vs. 9 Paul refers to a previous letter, whether now lost or included as a part of the two canonical epistles. (Although Conzelmann thinks "now" in vs. 11 is not temporal but logical,
meaning "as a result" or "in short" or "I mean to say," he takes vs. 9 as referring to an earlier letter.)

not to mix. The verb occurs in the New Testament only in this context and in

II Thess 3:14. It refers to any kind of conversation, eating together, or meeting with people.

sexually immoral people, pornois, the masculine cognate with *porneia,* discussed at vs. 1 *supra.* It has an extended sense, meaning male persons who are involved publicly or notoriously in sexual irregularity. The translation adopted here is repeatedly specific to distinguish from other forms of immoral conduct introduced in the succeeding verses.

10. *of this world . . . out of the world.* The relationship to John 17:15 seems inescapable.

the greedy. Traditional translation, "covetous"; a person whose acquisitiveness is publicly obvious.

swindlers. Literally, "snatchers." The derivative meaning seems to be more generally applicable in the social situation.

idolaters. Paul will treat this category in detail beginning in ch. 8.

11. *so-called brother.* Two words are used for "naming": *kaleō* and *onomazō* (the latter here); usually the tone is neutral. In this instance it is clear that Paul is fencing the nominal inclusion of such persons in the Christian fellowship.

reviler, drunkard. The extension of the list from the previous verse indicates how Paul broadened a specific complaint about the Corinthian congregation to cover their general lack of moral sensitivity.

12, 13. The translation here adopts the punctuation of the UBS text. It is also defensible to place a comma after *insiders* (vs. 12) and a question mark after *outsiders* (vs. 13). NEB places periods with both these clauses but paraphrases to maintain the same meaning which the other punctuations suggest. The verb of the clause in vs. 13 may be present or future, depending upon the accent of the verb *krinei.* A decision for the future may be based upon the putative eschatological expectation of the primitive church (Metzger, *Textual Commentary*), but it is possible to make too much of an issue of a verb tense.

13. *Clean out the evil one. . . .* The adjective-plus-article is masculine singular. The clause is a refrain (with singular verb) recurring in Deut 17:7, 19:19, 22:21,24, 24:7. In this context Paul surely means to apply the quotation to the proscribed members of the Corinthian congregation. It is possible, though unlikely here, that *the evil one* refers to Satan. Indeed, in the Pauline literature there are only two other places where such a reference is possible: in II Thess 3:3 one can read either "evil" or "the evil one"; in Eph 6:16 it is clearly "the evil one."

COMMENT

It was somehow brought to Paul's attention that the Christians in Corinth had inferred that he was advising them not to associate with sexually immoral, swindling, or idolatrous persons at all. He informed them that if this had been his meaning, they would have to leave the world altogether—either by becoming recluses or by dying, probably the latter. His rejection of this alternative is implied by the restriction of the command to such people as have entered the Christian society and have been recognized (superficially, it would seem) by the Christian designation "brother." This means he required that the members of the church banish from their society those guilty of the vices already mentioned, and to this list are added those who heap verbal abuse on others and those who are drunkards.

The listing of vices was common in antiquity (cf. Deissmann, *Light from the Ancient East,* 315-318) and occurs often in the New Testament (cf. 6:9-10). The inclusion of drunkenness here points up the necessity of considering Paul's positions in the light of first-century scientific and sociological information. (Certainly modern knowledge of alcoholism modifies the applicability of this injunction in the church today.) It is even more important, however, to consider the implication of the pagan vice lists. Paul's point is a generalization of the stricture against the vice considered in 5:1: *reported not even among the heathen.* If pagan society proscribed certain actions, it behooved the Corinthian church to eliminate from its fellowship any persons who were guilty of the same actions.

The dissociation is drastic: there is to be no table fellowship. Many social systems have recognized eating together as an associating bond. In the Christian church there was from the start an even deeper stratum of significance because of the Passover-Lord's Supper background. Moreover, Paul probably saw in this another threat to the very survival of the church. The stricture is not as severe, it may be noted, as that in II John 10, where a doctrinally errant person is not even to be greeted!

Paul's pronouncement is justified by his distinction regarding fields of responsibility. It is not the function of a Christian to impose a ban or curse upon unbelievers. Indeed, it is clear that Paul's program includes precisely outreach to sinful unbelievers. To cut off relationships with unbelievers would make impossible the offering of the gospel to them. Christians need not be bothered that they may seem thus to be condoning the sins of non-Christians; *God will pass judgment on the outsiders.* Moral reaction to the lives of sinners can be left strictly up to God. In order to make the church an effective and redeeming evangelistic society, however, it must be preserved from the kinds of sinful members who bring contempt upon the church from unbelievers (cf. also Rom 2:23-24).

The church must evaluate the public reputation of all its members so that they do not commit such sins as to bring the progress of the gospel into jeopardy. In this the church was the inheritor of the radical moral judgment that was meant to keep Israel pure. The Old Testament is replete with incidents in which members of the Jewish community were condemned for their unfaithfulness to divine commandments enforced in the community (sometimes to the point of death). There also the survival of the separated people in a pagan environment seems to be a motivating element.

LAWSUITS AMONG CHURCH MEMBERS (6:1-9a)

Scandal of appearing before heathen judges

6 ¹ How dare any of you, when he has a case against another, go to law before the unrighteous judges rather than before the saints! ² Or do you not know that the saints are going to judge the world? And if the world is judged by you, are you unworthy of hearing the most trivial cases? ³ Do you not know that we are going to judge angels—not to mention everyday matters? ⁴ But then if you do hold court for everyday matters, do you seat as judges people of no repute in the church? ⁵ I say to you, "For shame!" Is there no one among you wise enough to be able to render a decision between one of his brothers and another? ⁶ As it is, brother goes to law with brother, and this before unbelievers!

Incongruity of injustice among brothers

⁷ But then it is actually already a defeat for you that you have lawsuits with one another. Why do you not rather suffer injustice? Why do you not rather let yourselves be defrauded? ⁸ But you yourselves are committing injustice and fraud—and this against brothers! ⁹ᵃ Or do you not know that unrighteous people will not inherit God's kingdom?

NOTES

6:1. *How dare any of you.* This passage displays several literary affinities with the "diatribe" form, a kind of public address popular among moral preachers in the Hellenistic age. Here the device is a "put-down" of one who would practice what is being opposed in the context. (The literary form is more extensive in the epistle of James; cf. J. H. Ropes, *A Critical and Exegetical Commentary on the Epistle of St. James* (New York, 1916), 10-16.

a case. pragma can be used to refer to a business transaction, a decision of society, any kind of particular act or affair, or a dispute. This is the only case in the New Testament where it clearly means a dispute which leads to litigation.

before the unrighteous judges. "Judges" is a reasonably certain inference from the context. "Unrighteous" as a translation for *adikōn* is intended to point the contrast with *the saints.* The more usual translation "unjust" (contrary to equity or to the requirements of fair and equal treatment) would certainly be out of place here. Paul means pagan judges in a restricted, religious sense, those who have not accepted divine justification. Cf. I Peter 3:18, where *adikōn* refers to the whole human race in contrast to Christ.

2. *Or do you not know.* Another expression characteristic of diatribe; note the parallel questions in vss. 3 and 9.

the saints are going to judge the world. Although *krinō* may be understood to mean "rule," the idea here seems to be apocalyptic, perhaps derived from Dan 7:22 (cf. also Wisdom of Solomon 3:8; Jubilees 24:29; Enoch 38:5, 95:3).

is judged. The shift of tense to the present may be explained in two ways. (a) The present may simply be used with a futuristic meaning, thus parallel with the previous verb, this due to the instability of usage of the future (cf. Zerwick, *Biblical Greek,* §§ 277, 278; also BDF, § 323). (b) Since the point is in the present (*are you*) and the condition is simple (i.e. of the first class), the verb of the protasis is made present to emphasize the point of the argument: "Since you are, in effect, judges, are you unworthy?"

by you. The instrumental connotation is derived from a locative force and is parallel to the *epi* phrases in vs. 1 (BDF, § 219[1]).

the most trivial cases. Conzelmann suggests that these matters are minor by comparison with the final judgment of the world. The sequel, however, seems to indicate that civil suits (in which no crime is involved) are intended here. Paul's disposition of the case of the man guilty of sexual immorality (5:1-5) shows that it was unquestioned that the church should act against the criminally guilty.

3. *judge angels.* The background for this idea is the Jewish apocalyptic notion that some angels rebelled against God and were cast out of heaven along with Satan. There is no suggestion in the Old Testament that human beings will judge these angels. Jude 6 refers to the angels, but God seems to be their judge. Paul elevates the saints to a position that is of almost the same dignity as that of Christ, undoubtedly because the church is the habitation of the Spirit. The community of believers is therefore no mere human society.

4. *do you seat . . . ?* The verb can be construed three ways: as a question, as a statement, or as a command. Since the condition is general, it seems least likely that the main verb is a statement; for it would not contribute much to Paul's argument. Calvin held strongly for the imperative; his point was that the most insignificant person in the church was to be preferred to a civil magistrate in the settlement of internal church affairs. Most modern editors take the clause as a question, which seems best to fit the tenor and style of the passage. Paul has been directing diatribe-like questions at his readers earlier in the passage, and the question in the next verse suggests that there has been fault not only from the failure of Christian litigants to submit to church adjudication but also from the relative indifference of the church to the provision of the most able judges from among the membership.

of no repute in the church. It is possible to understand these phrases to refer to the *unrighteous judges* of vs. 1 (then perhaps *exouthenēmenous* should receive its more pejorative translation, "despised"). The translation adopted here, however, follows upon the understanding of *kritēria echēte* in the protasis to refer to the consideration of legal matters by the Christian community. Unfortunately, it is impossible to demonstrate unequivocal support for either interpretation.

5. *Is there no one . . . ?* 2:15 makes it clear that Paul's answer to his own question would be negative.

6. *before unbelievers.* This is evidence for the correctness of the interpretation of unrighteous judges.

7. *suffer injustice.* Plato, in *Gorgias* 509C, says, "Then of these two, doing and suffering wrong (*adikeisthai*), we declare doing wrong to be the greater evil, and suffering it the less."

8. *committing . . . fraud.* Curiously, in Mark 10:19 a command against fraud is included in the commandments enumerated by Jesus to the rich man. The word occurs in the New Testament elsewhere only in I Cor 7:5 and I Tim 6:5.

9a. The break seems proper in the middle of this verse. The first part is another *do you not know* question and concerns *unrighteous people.* The second part is another diatribe-form exhortation: *do not be deceived;* and the emphasis reverts to sexual immorality and other evils.

inherit God's kingdom. "The kingdom of God" has already been mentioned, 4:20, in the arthrous form (i.e. with the article). The omission of the article here probably has no significance and appears to be stylistic with Paul. The recurrence of the phrase at the end of vs. 10 provides a tie between the two passages. The structure of the whole is quite clever.

The use of this phrase is an evidence of correspondence with the teaching of Jesus. Proclamation about the kingdom of God was certainly a principal theme in Jesus' message. The term "inherit" came from Old Testament usage, for example, reference to gaining the land of Canaan. Jesus' vocabulary was flexible; he utilized the variety of expressions available in contemporary Jewish theology to make his unique formulations. (Cf. the word sequences in Mark 10:17-27.) Thus it is not strange that Paul uses "kingdom of God" relatively infrequently (besides the two occurrences here and 4:20, cf. 15:50; Rom 14:17; Gal 5:21; Eph 5:5; Col 4:11; I Thess 2:12; II Thess 1:5; also Acts 28:31). Perhaps the political rule in the Roman empire, where Paul's churches were located, suggested to him the advisability of using other more or less interchangeable terminology.

COMMENT

Scandal of appearing before heathen judges

It is a brazen act, Paul declares, for one Christian to enter a lawsuit against another Christian before a pagan court. This implies that such a practice was occurring among the Corinthian church members, and it is further proof of their indifference to the requirements of unity and brotherhood in the Christian society.

The exterior aspect of this action was that the judges were *unrighteous.*

Paul did not mean to imply that the pagan judges were "unjust"; certainly the Corinthian Christians would not be interested in having such arbiters preside over their cases. The subsequent course of Paul's argument makes it clear that he wanted Christians to resolve their differences among themselves. He again calls them *saints* (as in 1:2), a startling designation in light of what he has already written to them; but it is pertinent to the point of this passage.

The Corinthians should have known what appears to have been a common Jewish expectation that the faithful people of Israel will be given victory over their enemies on earth and will pass judgment upon their sins. Paul transferred this idea to the Christian community and suggested that Christian believers will *judge the world*. Since they had inherited this privilege from Israel, they were acting in a peculiarly incongruous manner when they pleaded their own cases before pagan judges. By the common Jewish argument from the greater to the lesser, Paul reasons that people with a cosmic destiny ought to be able to decide disputes about very minor matters.

The human tendencies to friction and competition, however, had prevailed over the spiritual gifts that should have ruled in the church. Thus even when the Corinthians did sit to decide *everyday matters,* there must have been a tendency to entrust the hearing to members who were least qualified for the task.

It hardly seems necessary to point out that Paul's feeling against submitting cases of legal dispute to outsiders had its precedent in the Jewish tradition. It is rooted in the belief that Yahweh himself was the judge of his people (cf. I Sam 25:15; Isa 33:22; Ps 50:6). The Exodus tradition dealt extensively with the function among the people (Exod 18:13-26, 21-23). Cf. also Deut 16:18-20. Perhaps more to the point is the post-exilic situation; cf. Ezra 7:25.

It is notoriously difficult to assess Jewish practice contemporary with the developing Christian church, for the records are later. In this present matter such records may probably be used. A rabbi from the end of the first century was quoted: "In general where you find co-judges among the non-Israelites even if their judgments correspond to those of the Israelites, you are not justified in uniting in a common judgment with them. . . . Whoever leaves a judge of Israel and goes before a foreigner has first denied God and then has denied the law. . . ." (StB, III, 362). Jewish law distinguished between criminal and civil cases. Criminal cases had to be decided by judges authorized by the patriarchs or by the high court; but property cases could be decided by three laymen (men untrained in the law) or by one authorized judge. Usually in a property case the disputants could choose judges that were acceptable to both parties. Both parties would also agree beforehand to yield to whatever judgment was issued (ibid., p. 364). Paul probably had in mind that the people in the church should follow a similar practice and should choose mediators or judges acceptable to both disputing parties, but he wanted to ensure that the judges would be those who had standing in the church on the basis of proper spiritual qualification. The Christian mediator should have in view the reconciliation of the parties that they might get rightly related to the forgiving and loving God by forgiving one another.

In 4:14 Paul was careful to specify that he did not intend to shame them for their preferences among leaders. Here, however, their unbrotherly conduct is shameful. In James 2:1-7, where discrimination on the basis of wealth is in focus, the rich people "who drag you into court" are indirectly denounced. Evidently it was not unusual for Christians to be involved in legal cases, but the practice was a particular failing in the Corinthian community.

Incongruity of injustice among brothers

The real defeat of a Christian is not to lose a case in court: it is to get involved in a lawsuit with a fellow Christian. The short-sighted view is that one is defeated by not gaining what one wants. Paul's long view is that a conflict with a brother is in itself a spiritual defeat; it shows that one has failed to overcome oneself. For those who understand Christian faith and fellowship such a defeat is worse than suffering injustice or being defrauded.

This ethical resolve was far from a new idea, for the Greeks were familiar with it. What would seem to be new in Christian teaching is the scope of application. For Plato it was the sensible thing to do. Jesus (Matt 5:39-42) makes it a principle of life in God's kingdom. It became understood that Jesus had lived out this principle to the end (I Peter 2:23). So Paul writes the verbs in the present linear (continuous aspect): this is not to be a token action but a way of living.

The Corinthians were doing precisely the reverse: they were repeatedly inflicting injustice and fraud upon others, and in particular, Christian brothers. Paul declares that the ultimate issue of such practice is failure to *inherit God's kingdom*. Here is the other side of the commonly emphasized Pauline doctrine of justification by faith. It is not correct to conclude that justification by faith eliminates the basic need for a righteous life; it rather provides a true basis for it. Those who inflict injustice upon each other exhibit that they do not believe in forgiveness or in reconciling love. Thus they really have not accepted the love of God for themselves, and thus they have rejected the justification offered by God. Paul's stress on the spiritual nature of the gospel does not keep him from a tremendous concern about its application to all the personal and social relationships of life. Paul moves surely from a particular scandal in the Corinthian church to a general pronouncement for the whole church.

PROSTITUTION, A PARTICULAR INSTANCE OF IMMORALITY (6:9b-20)

The kingdom of God and immorality

6   9b Stop deceiving yourselves. Neither sexually immoral persons, idolaters, adulterers, effeminate men, male homosexuals, 10 thieves, greedy people, drunkards, revilers, nor swindlers will inherit God's kingdom. 11 And some of you were these things. But you washed yourselves; yes, you were sanctified; yes, you were justified by the name of the Lord Jesus and by the Spirit of our God.

God and the limitations of legality

12 All things are permissible to me, but not all things are advantageous. All things are permissible to me, but I will not be overpowered by any of them. 13 Food is for the stomach, and the stomach is for food, but God will nullify both of these. The body is not for sexual immorality but for the Lord, and the Lord is for the body, 14 but God both raised the Lord and will raise us by his power.

The Christian body
a. Not to be joined to a prostitute

15 Do you not know that your bodies are parts of the body of Christ? Shall I take the parts of the body of Christ, then, and make them parts of the body of a prostitute? Certainly not! 16 Or do you not know that the one who joins himself to a prostitute is one body with her?—for it says, "The two will become one flesh." 17 But the one who joins himself to the Lord is one spirit with him. 18 Shun sexual immorality. Every sin which a person commits is outside the body, but the one who commits sexual immorality is sinning within his own body.

b. *To glorify God as a temple of the Spirit*

19 Or do you not know that the body of you people is a temple of the Holy Spirit among you, which you have from God? And you are not your own, 20 for you were bought for a price. Praise God, therefore, in your body.

Notes

6:9b. *Stop deceiving yourselves.* Another diatribe expression. So also is the listing of vices (or virtues); cf. 5:10-11.

effeminate men. For an early use of this word in this sense, cf. Deissmann, *Light from the Ancient East,* 164, n. 4.

11. *you washed yourselves.* The reference is to baptism, and the two verbs following are to be read in a series with this verb (cf. COMMENT). The middle voice governs the meaning, *pace* Conzelmann. The use of the reflexive, which is not, of course, to be taken as implying self-baptism, could be avoided by paraphrase: "You presented yourselves for baptism."

by the name. The Greek has the preposition *en.* This is an instance, not uncommon in the New Testament, where locative and instrumental meanings shade into each other. The baptismal process introduces the individual into the sphere that is denominated by the name and Spirit, and at the same time these are the means by which the effects of baptism take place.

the Lord Jesus. Accepting Metzger's preference for the Byzantine reading. The likelihood of a scribal addition (*Christ*) seems to outweigh the stronger MS witness for the fuller text.

12. *advantageous. sympherei* carries the sense of "bring together" what is appropriate or helpful. Paul may be referring to a saying current among some of the Corinthian Christians.

The structure of the passage is stylized. Héring suggests a structure like Hebrew poetry with vs. 12 as a strophe and 13-14 as another. *Food is for the stomach,* . . . *food,* in vs. 13, sounds like a popular saying.

13. *for the Lord.* The use of *Kyrios* for Christ was well established in the early church. Cf. W. Foerster in *TDNT,* III, 1086-1094; Neufeld, *The Earliest Christian Confessions, passim.*

15. *parts of the body of Christ,* literally "members of Christ." Paul treats this at some length in 12:12-30, where his use of *mele* makes it necessary to employ a more inclusive meaning than "limbs" or "organs."

Shall I take . . . and make. Héring finds philological difficulty here, and he changes the participle *aras* to the particle *ara* (or *āra?*) and the verb to first person plural. The MS evidence for this is scanty, and the alteration is really unnecessary. It is not unusual for Paul to use himself as an example in his exhortation of the church; there are instances in chs. 2, 3, and 4; and note especially 6:12.

Certainly not! The interjection is common in Epictetus. Paul's use of Hellenistic rhetorical devices and expressions is not to be understood as evidence that he was unduly influenced by Hellenistic thought. The accusation of the Athenians that Paul was a *spermologos* (a "seed picker," Acts 17:18) had an element of truth in it: he ranged through the cultures he had studied and utilized them to produce what must have been arresting and interesting communication to his contemporaries.

16. *with her.* The addition is necessary to give the intent of the somewhat cryptic Greek *hen sōma estin.*

"The two will become one flesh." An exact quotation of the LXX of Gen 2:24. Paul holds a kind of literalistic understanding of the primitive story. The same sense appears in Matt 19:5-6.

17. *with him.* The addition is for the same purpose of clarification as in vs. 16.

18. *sin.* The unusual word *hamartēma* bears no unusual significance here.

outside . . . within. Paul's view of intercourse with a prostitute leads him to this somewhat difficult distinction. *eis* could be translated "against" or "in," but it seems necessary to find a specific contrast to *ektos.*

19. *the body of you people.* It is requisite to indicate somehow that the second personal pronouns in this and the following verse are plural. The idea is an extension of that in 3:16-17.

among you. As often, it is a question whether to employ the alternative translation "in you." The force of the plural pronouns has determined the choice here.

20. *bought for a price.* Héring finds a problem in the anarthrous form *timēs* (without an article). He and Conzelmann both conclude that the figure of ransom is implied. It would seem more natural in the context to understand the "price" as the antithesis of the amount paid for the favor of a prostitute. (The question to whom the price was paid is no more relevant than in the clear-cut ransom context of 7:23.)

COMMENT

The kingdom of God and immorality

From his statement that *unrighteous people will not inherit God's kingdom* (vs. 9a) Paul moves to warn against specific kinds of immorality which eliminate persons from kingdom heritage. In this there must be no self-deception, either from a fallacious misapplication of the doctrines of the Christian religion to ethical matters, or from an extension of the idea of freedom to the level of license, or by being more conscious of the evils of others than of themselves. With clear lapidary categories Paul lists sex sins, property sins, sins that destroy the efficient functioning of the mind, and sins against human beings.

With specificity but some delicacy Paul reminds the Corinthians that they had been guilty of these sins. This means that the Christians had been recruited not only from the lower social orders (as is plain in ch. 1) but also from the ranks of the most scandalous sinners. The glory of the church is the willingness of its God to receive just such persons. The line of distinction is also clearly drawn between the faith of the church and Gnostic-type contemporary thought. The disdain of the latter for the human body, since it was the inferior dwelling of the human spirit, allowed gross immorality since it did not at all affect the spirit.

Paul describes the process by which the Corinthians were changed in three verbs. The first has to do with baptism, the other two with its effects. The first is middle voice, the other two passive; and the distinction seems to carry theological significance: the washing of baptism is accomplished upon our own initiative while the passive forms indicate that the action was performed by another. It is within the power of human freedom to take the initial step to clean one's life from such vices and sins as Paul enumerates. The deliberate choice of the verb forms here suggests that care is necessary in attempting to state a radical Pauline theology. Yet justification and sanctification are explicitly the action of God *by the name of the Lord Jesus and by the Spirit of our God.* To be sanctified means to be consecrated in God's service and enrolled in his family. To be justified means to be forgiven of sins and accepted as righteous. (It is interesting, perhaps important, to notice the order of these two divine actions vis-à-vis the ordering insisted upon in some traditional theological systems.)

God and the limitations of legality

This leads Paul to consider what was, in his thinking, a scandalous problem in the church. According to the gospel which he preached, Christians are free from guilt by the unearned favor of God, and as a result of the love of God they are emancipated from slavery to the literal requirements of the law. Under the guidance of the Spirit Christians are supposed to have the will of the Lord so united with their wills that they freely want to do his will. In this situation no rules and regulations are necessary; threats and rewards of the law are out of place. This ideal condition the apostle expected to see fully operative. The residual influence of paganism, however, the surrounding pressure of Gnosticizing ideas, the down-drag of human laziness, and the effect of habitual indulgence checked the emergence of the pure, new condition of responsible freedom.

What is to be done when recipients of the gospel, upon realizing that they have been invited into God's home with full privileges, as it were, start wrecking the furniture, befouling the floors, and even tearing the building apart? One set of alternatives is to cast these people out or to subject them to rigid police discipline. But then the whole question of the validity of the gospel would be raised and/or the expedient adopted of going back to the way of law. Paul was not ready to surrender the glory of the gospel to the demands of the tragic revelations of what had happened at Corinth; neither was he ready to allow the corruptions to continue without correction. He enters, then, into a painstaking discussion of what the gospel means in relation to some of the kinds of conduct that had become notorious in the Corinthian Christian community.

Under the gospel no law based on threat of eternal annihilation or punishment requires or prohibits any particular kind of conduct. Christ on the cross has satisfied the requirements of the law. (Note that Paul is dealing with the theological matter in a very practical setting. In Romans, where the practical pressure seems to be quite secondary, he approaches the problem somewhat more systematically.) The immediate inference from this is that the gates are thrown open for entry into a free territory. This situation, however, has a concealed hook in it; for it presupposes that people entering this freedom have accepted the love of God by loving him (Augustine's *obiter dictum,* "Love God and do as you please"). When one loves God, *all things are permissible;* but when one loves God, one loves what he loves. This means love for all others, for they are loved by God; and conduct will be regulated by this love. Although questions of conduct are no longer under apodictic command, they must be faced with the decision as to what is *advantageous*—how do these actions affect the persons who will be involved? Paul also *will not be overpowered by any of them,* that is, he felt under the perpetual necessity of responsibly maintaining that freedom which he found under the gospel. The maintenance of personal freedom involves the voluntary acceptance of self-discipline.

Paul's apothegm about food and the stomach might be taken as a truism, but it seems more likely to have reflected an Epicurean (possibly Gnostic) justification for prandial excess. The limitation which the apostle adds carries the immediate meaning that physical satisfactions are only temporary and that concern for such things ought therefore to be limited. But Paul returns again to the focal concern in this discussion of immorality: sex. Whether or not those who are the object of his concern had drawn the analogy, he insists that no analogy exists. The sexual capacity of the body does not imply that this is to be exercised with abandon, and he will insist in the next section that this particularly interdicts prostitution. Although the body is designed by nature for sexual gratification, it is also designed *for the Lord.* (Sex in marriage will be treated in ch. 7 and the corporate nature of the Christian body in ch. 12.) In contrast to the perishing nature of that which is exclusively physical, the total human personality will not be brought to an end. The resurrection of the Lord is evidence that God *will raise us by his power*. This is in clear contrast to the Gnostic denial of resurrection based upon rejection of any spiritual value in the physical body.

The Christian body
a. *Not to be joined to a prostitute*

Since human bodies are *parts of the body of Christ,* Paul declares it unthinkable that they participate in prostitution. Based on his understanding of the nature of creation, he believed that sex union makes the two participants one body. To become one flesh is the proper destiny of those who incorporate their sex desires into a total relation of love and loyalty so that they can become one joint personality and in their relationship express faith in God and love for the other. This cannot be done in the isolated, commercialized action of prostitution. The mysterious unity of the flesh where there is no concern, loyalty, or love is sharply rejected by Paul.

He may very well have in mind also that the prostitute in Corinth, as well as in many other ancient cities, was dedicated to the service of pagan gods. To resort to such a person was to effect union with the god she served. The Christian has dedicated his body to be a part of Christ's body, and he is therefore dedicated to the God of Christ. Joining the Lord makes a person *one spirit with him,* that is, Christians unite with other Christians to constitute the body of Christ, which is guided by the Spirit, which inhabits the whole body. Paul's view of sexual immorality, therefore, as a particularly inner sin is precisely applicable to his doctrine of the body of Christ.

b. *To glorify God as a temple of the Spirit*

Paul develops somewhat a concept which he suggested in 3:16-17, that the Christian society is the particular sphere in which the Holy Spirit operates. His introduction of *the body* is significant; it will be developed in startling dimensions in chs. 11 and 12. At this point he is trying to impress his readers that they collectively are Christ's body, his physical presence in the world, the locus of God's personal activity designated as his Holy Spirit.

This places a boundary to their freedom. They are not free to do as they please because of the relationship between them and God. Whether Paul's argument is that they have been ransomed into a higher slavery by the price Christ paid with his life (as most commentators seem to understand) or that they have been bought by that same price into a new love relationship with God, his point is plain: they are no longer owners of their destiny. They have been given a display of love at the cost of the life of their Lord, and this lays a claim on them to unite with him in individual and corporate living which will praise God.

FIRST QUANDARY FROM CORINTH: CONCERNING MARRIAGE (7:1-40)

SEXUAL INTERCOURSE (7:1-7)

The mutuality of marriage

7 ¹ With reference to the matters about which you wrote: is it good for a man not to have sexual relations with a woman? ² Now because of sexual immorality let each man have his own wife and each woman her own husband. ³ Let the husband pay the debt he owes to his wife, and likewise the wife to her husband. ⁴ The wife does not have jurisdiction over her own body, but the husband has; likewise also the husband does not have jurisdiction over his own body, but the wife has.

Special instances of abstention

⁵ Do not deprive each other, except by agreement for a limited period to have time for prayer and then to resume the same marriage relations in order that Satan may not put you to the test on account of your lack of self-control. ⁶ Now this I am saying by way of concession, not command. ⁷ I rather wish all people to be even as myself; but each has an individual gift from God, the one this way, the other that way.

NOTES

7:1. *is it good* . . . ? The Greek has no copula; and, of course, the earliest MSS had no punctuation. It is not certain whether *estin* or *einai* should be inserted. There is nothing in the wording itself to indicate whether the clause is a statement of Paul or a citation from the letter of the Corinthians. Similar expressions in 7:8 and 26 are not exactly parallel; and the phrases introduced by *peri de* scattered throughout the remainder of the book (7:25, 8:1, 12:1, 16:1,12) are not used with verb forms which may be followed by an indirect statement. The matter is probably to be settled only contextually. If the clause is the apostle's stated opinion *with reference to the matters about which* the church had written, then the succeeding argument in the passage is a loose sequel indeed. If *einai* is supplied, then it would appear that the Corinthians have proposed an ascetic option which is singularly out of keeping with the problems just discussed. It seems best to understand that the Corinthians have raised the question of the ascetic life. Probably, then, *estin* and a question mark are to be supplied; but this is for the comfort of the modern reader. Whatever is supplied, the Greek must have been clear enough to Paul and the Corinthian addressees.

for a man. anthrōpō can carry a variety of connotations, and so it is not exegetically definitive here. Since *anēr*, however, is usually used for "husband" (cf. the following verses), the inquiry probably intends "man/woman" in this clause. (Paul wrote ages before it became necessary to be sensitive about sex-specific terminology.)

to have sexual relations. The verb *haptesthai* means "to touch"; but the sexual reference is well established in Greek usage. StB take the word to mean "marry," but the LXX use of the verb refers to physical intercourse without reference to marriage (Gen 20:4,6; Prov 6:29).

2. *have.* The verb *echein* in many instances in the LXX means physical cohabitation when it refers to the relation between the sexes; cf. Exod 2:1-2; Deut 28:30; Isa 13:16. There is no instance of this verb referring to the act of marriage distinct from its sexual consummation.

his own . . . her own. The use of the possessive reflexive pronoun *heautou* and the adjective *idion* imply monogamy, one of the few biblical passages supporting this condition, which has been generally assumed by the church.

4. *have jurisdiction over.* exousiazei literally means "have power over," but such a translation seems too crass in a context where volition is to the fore. Perhaps the nearest approach to such a statement of equality of rights and obligations is found in the writings of the stoic teacher of Epictetus, Musonius Rufus; cf. Weiss, 172, n. 2.

5. *Do not deprive each other.* The verb *aposterein* occurred in 6:7, where the meaning "defraud" was used. Here there appears to be no legal implication or subterfuge. An interesting precedent for this recommendation is in the Testament of Naphtali VIII 8,

> For there is a season for a man to embrace his wife,
> And a season to abstain therefrom for his prayer.

except. On the unusual connective *ei meti an* cf. BDF, § 376.

to have time . . . and then to resume. The first verb in the purpose clause follows loosely upon all of the previous sentence. The second verb serves to explain *for a limited period.* The meaning is clearer than the sentence structure. Cf. I Peter 3:7.

in order that Satan. Again it is not exactly certain what the antecedent of this purpose clause is. It makes good sense to refer it back to the main imperative; it also follows reasonably the second part of the previous purpose clause. Cf. COMMENT.

Satan. It is unnecessary to translate the definite article, which is here used with the proper noun employed as the name of evil personified. (Only once in ten Pauline uses is the name anarthrous: II Cor 12:7.) "The devil" occurs only in Ephesians and the Pastorals. Early in the developing Christian vocabulary there was a fluidity of terminology for the putative leader of cosmic evil forces (in Rev 12:9-10 six titles are equated). Paul's choice may presumably be attributed to his Jewish background.

6. *this.* It is not certain what Paul means by *touto.* Classical Greek generally refers *houtos* back to something already mentioned. Paul, however, does not always follow this usage; cf. 1:12, 7:26, and possibly 11:17. Here, then, *this* may refer to the discussion beginning in vs. 8. If it refers backward, there is some difficulty in identifying its reference; but most editors have allowed it to stand thus in spite of the uncertainty.

7. *rather.* There is little doubt that the connective should be *de,* not *gar.* Paul really felt moderately negative about the concession. Although "for" really somewhat beclouds the intended connection of the clauses, it is probably secondary; the stronger conjunction is likely to have replaced the weaker particle. In seven verses (6-12) *de* occurs six times, and it is precarious to base exegetical decisions upon them.

gift from God, the one this way, the other that way. Paul speaks often of God's gift(s). He will discuss "diverse gifts" in ch. 12. Here the unusual correlative phrases at the end of the sentence indicate that he has in mind both continence and normal marriage relations as falling under God's blessing.

On this and subsequent sections, cf. von Allmen, *Pauline Teaching on Marriage.* He insists that the morality of marriage is not under consideration but its appositeness in the eschatological situation (so p. 15). On the question of Paul's marital status cf. W. E. Phipps, "Did Jesus or Paul Marry?" *Journal of Ecumenical Studies* 5 (1968), 741-744.

COMMENT

The mutuality of marriage

Paul now takes up the first of a series of points which the church at Corinth, or perhaps a group from the church, had mentioned in a letter in which they were seeking information from the apostle about right policy in connection with certain problems. The first matter they raised was that of relations between the sexes, perhaps occasioned by Paul's strictures on sexually immoral persons in a previous letter mentioned in 5:9. It is reasonable to assume that Paul picks up the items he deals with here in the same order in which the Corinthians had raised them in their letter. (This helps to explain what some may feel to be a rather illogical arrangement of material in this chapter.)

The first question is about physical relationship between the sexes, whether men and women should abstain from sexual cohabitation. The query is worded, *is it good?* Usually in the New Testament "good" in such an expression means something more than merely "fitting" or "advisable." It is a kind of understatement for "right" or "necessary." The lack of specificity in the use of "man/woman" leaves it quite open whether the Corinthians were concerned about continence within or outside marriage. Since Paul treats both in the sequel, the unrestrictive terminology is apparently deliberate. It is moreover impossible to discover from what source this problem had arisen. It would be difficult to derive the question from Gnostic beliefs, but it could represent reaction to such beliefs. The idea relates well to Essenian doctrine, but there is no evidence to connect this with Corinth.

Paul's reply begins with a recommendation about husbands and wives. This is in an imperative form, and there is no reason to reduce the command to permission or concession. Neither is the intention a universal proposal that every person should marry a spouse. The verbs are "present" (linear) jussives; so the intention of the command is to continue a condition, evidence that Paul is treating a marriage relationship in this passage. The sexual implication of the verb *have* leads, then, to the conclusion that the apostle is affirming that within marriage cohabitation between husband and wife should not be broken off. One reason given in this verse and elaborated in the next paragraph is that this will tend to obviate sexual immorality.

The requirement of continuing sexual relations in marriage is emphasized in terms of a mutual payment of *debt*. There is some evidence from rabbinic sources supporting the idea of such a marriage debt (cf. StB *ad locum*). Paul seems to be insisting that the continuation of intercourse in marriage is not a free option so much as it is an obligation that cannot be cancelled by religious or ascetic scruple. The obligation is equally binding on the husband and the wife, a remarkable statement of conjugal parity, which has exegetical relevance for several later considerations in this epistle and certainly to the Christian understanding of marriage according to New Testament teaching.

This principle is enforced by an enunciation of mutual *jurisdiction* on the part of husbands and wives. It is precisely the same balance of rights and the assertion of an absolute equality between marriage partners as stated in vs. 3. It involves the surrender in marriage of one's right to control one's own body. Paul declares that it is not optional but an obligation: the partner has a mutual and equal right to the other person's body. Each one is to meet the needs of the other. A clear promulgation of such an idea is found nowhere else in the Bible.

Special instances of abstention

Paul emphasizes the principle of the interchange of conjugal authority by discussing one exception, a mutually agreeable abstention for a period of prayer. This particular concession is somewhat enigmatic: it is hard to see why regular practice of sex in marriage would interfere with regular prayer. Paul seems to recognize, however, that there might be occasions in which one or both parties would concentrate *for a limited period* upon prayer to the exclusion of normal life concerns. He does not specify how long such a period should be, but he does specify that the time must be terminated by the resumption of ordinary relationship. Thus Satan's power to *put to the test* may be thwarted. It is possible that it is the special *time for prayer* that defeats the satanic testing. It is more probable in the context that Paul understands the normal exercise of conjugal relationships to be the means whereby husband and wife may escape temptation to infidelity either with respect to the marriage bed or possibly in reference to the prayer devotion. Satan as the figure who accuses and stirs up strife will have no opportunity for testing the married Christians who do not venture undue periods of sex abstention.

Since Paul has made his previous statements with imperative force, the *concession* directed back would be either a general one which depends for its clarification upon his implication when he says *even as myself* or a specific reference to the exception he has described with relation to sex abstention. If the concession anticipates what he is about to say in the next passage, the thought progression and literary pattern is somewhat loose.

His *wish* for *all people to be even as* himself will become clearer in the sequel. The question of Paul's marital status has been much debated with inconclusive results. Aside from what may be implied in this letter, there are two important facts to note: (a) Jewish leaders holding the position attributed to Paul in the New Testament ordinarily were married; but (b) Paul certainly had no spouse during the period of his Christian activity described in the New Testament. One obvious way to mediate these data would be to assume that Paul was a widower. When Paul recommends his present estate as an option, then, he would be referring simply to the fact that he is not married when he is writing. There are other possibilities. He could have been divorced before his conversion. It is even possible that his wife (if she was also a Roman citizen) separated from him after his conversion. The last half of vs. 7 may provide help in resolving the problem: it appears that Paul makes a rather simple distinction between those who are able to live godly lives without the sex relationship and those who serve God better with that relationship in marriage. Whichever is one's way of life, he notes, it is a manifestation of dependence upon God.

REMARRIAGE OF WIDOWS AND
WIDOWERS (7:8-9)

7 8 Now I say to the widowers and the widows, that it is good for them if they remain even as I am. 9 But if they do not have self-control, let them get married; for it is better to marry than to be inflamed with passion.

NOTES

7:8. *widowers. agamois* means etymologically "unmarried"; the word may indicate either one who has not been married or one who has been but is no longer married. The masculine noun *chēros,* counterpart to *chēra,* "widow," is used in some Greek literature but never in the LXX or the New Testament. It is possible, then, to take *agamois* here to mean "widowers"; and it provides, in fact, a balance of expression and a particular point to this passage. Verses 25-35 treat of those who have not been married. In vs. 11, moreover, the adjective form of this word is applied to a woman who has been married but is separated from her husband; and in vs. 35 the *agamos* woman is distinguished from the virgin. *Agamoi,* therefore, are those who are "de-married," in this case "widowers."

9. *to be inflamed with passion.* This is a middle (possibly passive) infinitive of a verb which means "to burn," either literally or figuratively (cf. KJ, "to burn"). M. L. Barré has argued (*CBQ* 36 [1974], 193-202) that the meaning is "to be burned in the fires of judgment"; but the biblical evidence for this (LXX and New Testament) is not convincing. The figurative meaning relating to physical passion seems as well supported and preferable in the context.

COMMENT

Having dealt with the sex relationship within marriage, Paul addresses the situation of those who have lost their marriage partners. He reiterates what he has introduced in the previous verse: he recommends his own marital status. This has been understood to be evidence that Paul was indeed a widower (and the implication of Acts that he was a member of the Sanhedrin and therefore necessarily married is satisfied). This resolves the problem which would arise if Paul should be understood to recommend the unmarried state to those who were married—or even to recommend widowerhood to them.

Paul apparently recognized the particular problem of widowers and widows, that because they had been abruptly deprived of the enjoyment of the physical relationships of marriage, they encounter serious emotional distress. He affirms that remarriage is preferable to the consuming *passion* that they may experience if they are unable to exercise such *self-control* as makes possible his own estate.

DIVORCE (7:10-16)

The Lord's charge against ultimate separation

7 10 Now I command (not I, but the Lord) those who have been married that a wife is not to be separated from her husband 11 —but even if she is separated, let her remain unmarried or let her be reconciled to her husband—and that a husband is not to divorce his wife.

Paul's recommendation that believers not divorce unbelievers

12 Now to the rest I say (not the Lord): if any brother has an unbelieving wife, and she consents to keep on living with him, let him not divorce her; 13 and if a wife has an unbelieving husband and he consents to keep on living with her, let her not divorce her husband. 14 For the unbelieving husband has been made holy by the wife, and the unbelieving wife has been made holy by the brother—otherwise, then, your children would be unclean; but now they are holy.

Believers not bound by broken marriages with unbelievers

15 If the unbeliever separates, let him separate. The brother or the sister has not been bound in such cases. God has called you in peace. 16 For how do you know, wife, whether you will save your husband; and how do you know, husband, whether you will save your wife?

NOTES

7:10. *I command*. The verb is commonly used in the Synoptics with respect to Jesus' instructions (Mark 6:8, 8:6, and //s; Luke 5:14, 8:29,56, 9:21; cf. also Acts 1:4).

the Lord. Cf. D. L. Dungan, *The Sayings of Jesus in the Churches of Paul*, 83-101.

11. *but even.* The intrusion into Paul's main point has been allowed to stand in the translation.

12. *to the rest.* The assumption is that vss. 10-11 refer to cases where both parties are Christian.

brother. Again the male orientation of the society as it has affected the Christian community is evident. Paul is careful to delineate equality in the rights of the marriage partners, but he does not attempt to change the social mores—or vocabulary—of the church.

unbelieving. apistos can, of course, mean "unfaithful"; but the reference here is certainly the same as in 6:6.

13. *and if a.* The textual evidence is fairly evenly divided between *ei tis* and *hētis.* The meaning is not really affected. The UBS reading, adopted here, is chosen partly because of the frequency of structural parallelisms in I Corinthians and partly because of some textual preferences (cf. Metzger's note).

14. *has been made holy.* The Greek perfect is significant: the presently existing condition stems from an event in the past (i.e. the marriage).

by the wife. The shading of locative into instrumental is again almost imperceptible. *en* has a meaning here something like "in the person of." Agency gives the smoother English translation though it is not the main notion in the Greek.

otherwise. The same unusual connective as in 5:10.

would be. The verb (*estin*) is present indicative, but the implied contrary-to-fact condition requires the conditional translation.

15. *let him.* The masculine article with *unbeliever* justifies the use of the masculine pronoun here. Again, in the second part of the verse, Paul equalizes the intention of the instruction.

in peace. A locative interpretation does not seem to supply an intelligible idea in the context. It more likely is associative-instrumental, "in a peaceful manner." The peace inherent in the Christian calling is to govern relationships in the crises of life. The meaning would be that the separation is to take place without recrimination and anger.

16. *how do you know . . . whether. ti* in this rhetorical question has the force of a negative. *ei* functions like Hebrew *'im;* the indirect question implies the meaning "that." Conzelmann's notes summarize the fruitless discussion whether *ei* can stand for *ei mē.*

COMMENT

The Lord's charge against ultimate separation

Paul affirms flatly that for couples who are both Christian divorce is forbidden. This is not by his word but by the word of *the Lord,* evidently the teaching of Jesus. It is not Paul's practice to quote dominical sayings, but he evidently takes Jesus' instruction (Matt 5:31-32 and 19:9 [without the exceptive phrases] Mark 10:11-12; Luke 16:18) as absolutely binding on the church.

This is reinforced by the extension to the effect that separated Christians are to *remain unmarried* or *be reconciled*. The wording which seems to single out the wife for these charges is offset by Paul's other statements which clearly establish a mutuality of requirements.

Paul's recommendation that believers not divorce unbelievers

When a Christian is married to a non-Christian, it is the apostle's opinion (not based on the teaching of *the Lord*) that the situation is different. In the first place, the continuance of the marriage depends upon the will of the non-Christian, who does not accept the authority of Christ. If this is a Jewish husband, rabbinical law permitted him to divorce his wife. If the couple is Greek or Roman, Roman law permitted either partner to divorce the other. Such legal prerogatives might be exercised no matter what the opinion of the Christian partner might be. Therefore Paul gives advice to the Christian member of such a marriage, and he makes no distinction between the husband and wife—either may be the believer.

If the unbeliever *consents to keep on living with* the Christian, the believer shall never divorce the unbeliever. To dispel in advance fears that contact of this close and intimate kind with an unbeliever should somehow pollute, pervert, or mislead the believer, Paul offers the assurance that the unbelieving spouse is *made holy* by the Christian—a kind of "uxorial sanctification." No condition is laid down for this to take place other than consent to live together. Apparently Paul recognizes that the attitude of aggressive evangelism does not befit a marriage partner. If evangelism leads one to harass, cajole, or harangue the other partner, that partner is driven further from Christian belief, and the marriage peace is jeopardized. The object of the believer is to make the marriage happy for the unbeliever. The close contact produces a corporal unity between the two so that the unbelieving member actually is made holy by the faith of the believer. This is an astounding doctrine!

Paul reinforces this statement with a further startling argument. If one of the marriage partners were unholy, the children of their union would be *unclean*—this is the gist of the matter. *But now they are holy!* Because they are the children of a sanctified partnership, both parents having been made holy by the faith of one partner, all are united by the holy kinship in the family. In the Jewish community the family came under the covenant because of the father; the instance of David's ancestors Boaz and Ruth is evidence enough. It is remarkable that the Christian community could accept the sanctifying influence of the mother (cf. the relevance of II Tim 1:5 in this connection). Jewish teaching, moreover, had proliferated the rules governing uncleanness (note Hag 2:11-14 as typical of what continued to develop into Mishnaic times). Here the usual process is reversed: the clean (*holy*) makes holy what has been *unclean*.

The relationship of this declaration to New Testament statements about the universality of human sin is complex (e.g. Eph 2:3). Calvin notes this problem and suggests that Rom 11:16 supports what Paul teaches here. He intimates that this is a reason for the baptism of children. (The full argument, he adds, comes properly in consideration of Romans 10-11.)

Believers not bound by broken marriages with unbelievers

A different condition prevails when the unbeliever refuses to live with the believer and exercises the legal prerogative of divorce, whether because of disaffection from the Christian partner or from contempt for the Christian religion. In this case Paul counsels the believer to permit the unbeliever to *separate* without controversy or attempt to hold the marriage together. The deserted partner, then, is free to marry again, whether it be *the brother or the sister*.

The reason for this permissive decision appears to be the evident uncertainty about the survival of the marriage if the separation is opposed. *Whether you will save* could refer to a "healing" so that the manner in which the partner is permitted to leave might have an influence on recovery of the relationship, or it could mean that there is no assurance that the marriage situation would be salvaged even if the spouse were kept from leaving.

The alternative possibility that vs. 16 refers to Christian salvation has been suggested or assumed by various commentators (e.g. Robertson and Plummer, Grosheide, Héring, Baudraz, Barrett). If that is the meaning, then there seems to be a contradiction to vs. 14.

EXCURSUS: CHRISTIANS TO REMAIN IN
THEIR PRECONVERSION STATUS
(7:17-24)

7   17 But let each one conduct his life as the Lord has assigned it to him and as God has called him. This is the direction I am giving to all the churches. 18 Was anyone called when he had been circumcised? Let him not attempt to disguise his circumcision. Has anyone been called when he was uncircumcised? Let him not be circumcised. 19 Circumcision is nothing, and uncircumcision is nothing, but observance of God's commandments is what matters. 20 Let each one re-

main in the calling in which he was called. 21 Were you called as a slave? Do not let it bother you. But even if you are able to become free, rather make use of it. 22 For the one who was called in the Lord as a slave is a freedman of the Lord; likewise the one who was called as a free man is Christ's slave. 23 You were bought for a price. Do not become slaves of men. 24 Let each one, brothers, remain with God in the state in which he was called.

NOTES

7:17. *But*. The force of the connective and the relation of this passage to the foregoing are not entirely clear. *ei mē* is to be read as the equivalent of *alla;* cf. BDF, §§ 376, 448(8); Zerwick, *Biblical Greek,* § 470.

conduct his life. The use of *peripatein* with this meaning is particularly Pauline; there are some thirty-two occurrences in the epistles.

the Lord . . . God. Perhaps no distinction of function is intended. Paul does usually associate "calling" with God, and it may be that the assignment of conduct is implied to be the result of the teaching of Jesus.

18. *Was anyone called*. The passive might be active with "God" as the subject (cf. NOTE on 1:9). Since God has already been named as the caller, the periphrasis would be gratuitous here.

attempt to disguise his circumcision; a *hapax legomenon* in the New Testament. It indicated an attempt to draw up a foreskin. The practice of the Hellenists in I Macc 1:15 is to the same intent though the word is not used.

19. *is what matters*. This paraphrase seems warranted and necessary as the counterpart of *nothing*.

21. *rather make use of it* The meaning is moot. Is "slavery" or "freedom" to be supplied: If "freedom" is to be taken advantage of, then *mallon* must refer back to *do not let it bother you*. Since there is already an adversative transition in *all' ei kai*, it seems slightly more appropriate to supply "slavery." Cf. the extensive bibliography in AGB, 892; also I Tim 6:2; and COMMENT.

22. *freedman . . . free man*. The distinction is made in the Greek: the first has become free after slavery; the second has been free before slavery.

23. *for a price*. Cf. the NOTE on 6:20.

Do not become. The present linear imperative indicates a command to cease what is already in progress. In this context it seems to mean, "Do not go any deeper into your slavery." The translation is not to be understood, "Do not become what you now are not—slaves."

24. *with God. para theo*. The idiomatic use of *para* with the locative is subtle. In 3:19 it was translated "from God's viewpoint," and the phrase has that force in other instances in Paul (Rom 2:11,13; Gal 3:11; II Thess 1:6). In the present verse such an interpretation might be shown by translating "as far as God is concerned." A clearer possibility is to take the phrase as the antithesis of *anthrōpōn*, as is done in the COMMENT.

COMMENT

This passage appears to be a digression. Perhaps the material is meant as a commentary upon *in peace* (vs. 15). Reflections on circumcision and slavery are added to show that the *conduct* of *life* for the Christian is not determined by his physical or social situation but rather by divine "assignment" and "call." The change of social status or physical condition, therefore, are not to *bother* the Christian brothers (again, in a milieu where male domination was assumed—circumcision being evidential). And Paul assured the Corinthians that his instruction in this matter was not *ad hoc* because of the particular scandals in their church: it was part of his *direction . . . to all the churches.*

The matter of circumcision was of more consequence in at least two other churches (in Galatia and Rome). Friction between Jewish Christians and gentile converts had arisen (early and from deep roots; cf. Acts 6); and it was natural that circumcision should become a matter of dispute (cf. Introduction, pp. 10-12, 68-69). Those who felt the force of the Jewish background of the new faith would appreciate the covenant significance of circumcision, while those who understood the freedom from legal requirements which is given by the gospel might wish they bore no evidence of relationship to the old covenant.

Paul's emphasis upon *observance of God's commandments* seems to be a contradiction to his deemphasis of circumcision. His new faith must cause him to consider as valid commandments of God only what is specifically applicable to Christians in their new situation. This bridges from his first example with its religio-historical aspect to the second, which is socio-ethical.

The calling in which he was called bears a double significance of the term "call." *The calling* in which one is to *remain* must refer to what one was doing occupationally at the time of conversion. Whatever it was, Paul dignifies it by designating it a *calling*. The second "call," the passive form, refers evidently to the call of the gospel through which one became a Christian. The first calling is not to be negated or necessarily changed by the second.

Slavery was an omnipresent fact in the early church. The first congregations held many members from the lower social strata (as will be explicit in ch. 11). Paul did not confront overtly the obvious problem raised by slavery. He did have at least three ways to deal with it. First, he insisted that the slave *not let it bother* him. The remainder of the pericope implies that this is feasible because the Christian is *a freedman of the Lord* and ultimately answerable to God, not men. Second, the slave could *make use* of his status, undoubtedly for Christian witness. This would be a particular application of injunctions in the teaching of Jesus (e.g. Matt 5:39,41, 43-45; notice that these verses are in the same collection that counsels against divorce, 5:31-32). Third, Paul worked within the fellowship of the churches to eliminate the relationships which were incompatible with Christian brotherhood. The epistle to Philemon is the documentation of this approach.

The interweaving of principle and practice (which can be the despair of the literary analyst) is a clue to the effectiveness of Paul's influence in the church. Every Christian is, after all, *Christ's slave, bought for a price*. This relationship supersedes all human relationships. It deals specifically with the dilemma of the slave-convert in the Corinthian church; it is applicable to the personal situation of every Christian.

PAUL'S OPINION REGARDING
THE UNMARRIED (7:25-35)

*Marriage permissible but inadvisable because
of "the form of this world"*

7   25 Now with respect to the virgins, I do not have a command of the Lord; but I am giving an opinion as one who has been granted mercy by the Lord to be trustworthy. 26 So I deem this to be good because of the present pressure, that it is good for a person to be as follows: 27 Have you been bound to a wife? Do not seek release. Have you been released from a wife? Do not seek a wife. 28 Yet even if you get married, you do not commit a sin. And if a virgin gets married, she does not commit a sin. Such persons will have physical distress, but I am trying to spare you. 29 Brothers, I say this: the season has become short; from now on those who have wives are to be as though not having them; 30 those who weep as though not weeping, and those who rejoice as though not rejoicing; those who purchase as though not possessing, 31 and those who make use of the world as though not using it up. For the form of this world is passing away.

*Marriage as a potential distraction from
devotion to the Lord*

32 Now I wish you to be free from concern. The unmarried man is concerned about the affairs of the Lord, how he may please the Lord; 33 but the one who is married is concerned about the affairs of the world, how he may please his wife; 34 and he has become distracted. Both the unmarried woman and the virgin are concerned about the affairs of the Lord, to be holy both in body and in spirit; but the married woman is concerned about the affairs of the world, how she may please her husband. 35 I am saying this for your particular benefit, not to put a noose on you, but that you may be in good order and devoted to the Lord without distraction.

NOTES

7:25. *I do not have a command . . . but . . . an opinion.* It is clear that Paul does not think that the Spirit had bestowed upon the church the creative power to produce ad hoc sayings of Jesus to fit the situation in the life of the church —as is sometimes assumed in modern scholarship (cf. Bultmann, *Jesus and the Word,* 12). If any early Christian prophet or enthusiast would have been so empowered, certainly Paul should have been.

Manson has discussed Jesus' teaching on marriage and divorce (in *The Mission and Message of Jesus,* 428-430) and concluded that "the new principle . . . that husband and wife in marriage meet on a footing of real equality" (in *Studies in the Gospels and Epistles,* p. 199). It is such *a command of the Lord* that helps drive Paul to his conclusions elsewhere in this chapter, but it is the absence of such that prompts him to *an opinion* here. Cf. also Dungan, *The Sayings of Jesus in the Churches of Paul,* 83-101.

trustworthy. Rather than "faithful." On *pistos* cf. the substantial note in AGB, 670. On the distinction between the passive and active signification of the root, cf. Burton, *Galatians,* 475-485.

26. *the present pressure.* Both *enestōsan* and *anagkē* are liable to different translations. The suggested renderings in AGB are not consistent. With *kairos* and *aiōn* the participle can clearly be used to mean "present" (Heb 9:9; Gal 1:4). The alternate meaning "impending" would be fitting if the understanding of the eschatological attitude of the apostle were appropriately changed. "Pressure" is an attempt to find a way between the usual but uninstructive "necessity" and "distress," which seems more appropriate for *thlipsin,* in vs. 28.

that it is good. Best taken as a clause explaining *touto;* cf. the NOTE on *touto* in vs. 6.

27. *release . . . released.* Paul's use of the general verb *lyō* in this context is probably deliberate. He has already treated divorce (vss. 10-16); so while that

is surely included in *lysin,* Paul is making a somewhat different point here. *lelysai* is not to be understood as, "are you free now from marriage by not ever having been married"; but the force of the perfect aspect means, "Have you been released from a wife"—presumably by her death. The consideration is therefore proper here rather than in vss. 10-16.

28. The syntax of the conditions in this verse is difficult. The general (second class) conditions have two forms of the aorist subjunctive, probably with no subtlety of meaning intended. But the apodoses would normally contain either present or future indicatives; here there are past aorists. Robertson allows for the timeless force of the aorist here, but he rather prefers to explain the usage as a quick change in the standpoint of the writer, the condition looking forward, the main clause backward (*Grammar,* 1019-1020, 1022; cf. also Zerwick's explanation, *Biblical Greek,* § 257).

a virgin. Robertson and Plummer note that it is unlikely an instance at Corinth is in view. The definite article, then, has not been translated because the subject is almost certainly generic. (Vaticanus and several other MSS omit the article. It is tempting to adopt this reading, for then "virgin" could be construed as either feminine or masculine. The UBS Committee, however, think that the omission was because of contextual inappropriateness [Metzger, *Textual Commentary*]).

physical distress. Literally, "oppression in the flesh."

I am trying. The conative force is evident (so Barrett).

29. *season.* The common distinction between *kairos* and *chronos* is patent here: the emphasis is upon "time" with reference to its content and import, not its duration.

from now on. The language is cryptic. *to loipon* followed by a final clause must be paraphrased.

those who have . . . as though not having. The use of the participle *echontes* with and without the article indicates a distinction, not between two groups of persons, but between the actual situation of the persons and the way they are to treat their situation.

30. *weep . . . rejoice.* In Rom 12:15 Paul uses the same verbs in making a somewhat different point.

31. *form.* The intention is that of the idiom "the shape the world is in." Conzelmann says, "the essence, that is, the world itself."

32. *concern . . . concerned.* The words imply more than "attention" and less than "anxiety." "Distraction" is etymologically appropriate.

34. *distracted. Both. . . .* There are at least nine variant readings here. The choice of the UBS Committee (cf. Metzger, *Textual Commentary*) coincides with the judgment of the Nestle text; and it has been followed here. One supposes that the "very high degree of doubt" ("D" evaluation; ibid., xi) is in deference to the multiplicity of textual alternatives. Only the reading of Papyrus 46 has sufficient external support to rival the chosen text: it adds "unmarried" to "virgin," which Metzger describes as "a typical scribal conflation." This interpretation is probably preferable to retention of the adjective as *lectio difficilior.*

the unmarried woman. Cf. the NOTE on vs. 8. The distinction drawn to *the virgin* supports the view that Paul has in mind women whose marriage has been terminated by a separation other than divorce.

35. *put a noose on.* The unusual metaphor (*hapax legomenon* in the New Testament) is important only to demonstrate Paul's remarkable ability to illustrate his communication in striking language.

COMMENT

Marriage permissible but inadvisable because of "the form of this world"

Paul resumes the discussion about marriage, using the connective *peri de,* with which he began this section of his letter. He has considered what is proper for married people, those whose marriages have been or will be dissolved, those who are thinking about divorce, and those who are involved in marriages of mixed religions. Now he turns to those who have not been married, persons whom he calls *virgins.* This term is feminine in the overwhelming majority of cases both in Greek and in English, but it can be applied to men, and in Rev 14:4 there is an explicit instance of the masculine use. So in this passage Paul may mean both men and women who have never been married; indeed, where the discussion broadens to consider the advisability of marriage, both men and women are included; and in vs. 27 men become the subjects.

Again the equality of men and women is implied. Paul's discussion is by way of opinion, not the imposition of divine command. If Manson is correct about Jesus' views of this equality, then Paul falls back upon his own advice here because he found nothing applicable in the dominical traditions available to him. This suggests that he had knowledge of a collection of words of the Lord (the extent of which we, of course, do not know), that these words had binding authority in the church, and that Paul recalled them when a situation arose to which any of these words applied (though he did not on any occasion quote the words literally). Paul authenticates his opinion by asserting that his trustworthiness is divinely given. This is in keeping with his claim elsewhere (especially in Gal 1:11-12) that he proclaimed the gospel by divine, not human, sanction. Paul was fully confident that he could make reliable applications of the good news he had received.

The gist of what follows is that Christians do not have time available to devote to change of marital status; and, in fact, they need to adjust their existing status to imminence of the end of *this world.* Since this is counsel and not command, it is not a sin to do otherwise. The difficulties of those who disregard the advice, however, will be considerable though Paul does not specify what the difficulties will be.

It is hard to see why special difficulty attaches to married people more than to single persons in a prospective eschatological season unless the certain suffering of women and children is in the apostle's mind. He insists that people should live in their life condition as if they did not live in it— almost a prophetic threnody. It is not immediately evident why such statements are not equally valid in view of the universal imminence of death and why the particular generation preceding the end of days should live by different principles from all other generations, which presumably all face their end and the divine judgment. Elsewhere Paul does allude to the exigencies imparted by the imminence of death (e.g. 15:58). It does not seem to be evident, as some modern writers imply, that New Testament ethics is determined by eschatological pressure (cf. A. N. Wilder in *The Background of the New Testament and Its Eschatology,* 524-527).

The whole question of Paul's eschatology elicits no agreement among New Testament scholars (nor, for that matter, is there any consensus for the rest of the New Testament). The matter is better treated in other contexts, here in I Corinthians in ch. 15. Here at 7:31 Paul offers as substantiation for his opinions only his conviction that *the form of this world is passing away,* by which he means that the life situation of the Christian community is transitory since it exists in the final season of the last age— and that season is nearly over.

Marriage as a potential distraction
from devotion to the Lord

The pressure of the near end of opportunity to carry on *the affairs of the Lord* suggests that it is imperative to avoid distracting concerns. Already in vs. 5 Paul has intimated his notion that marital matters may be a negative influence upon the conduct of spiritual activity. Now he elaborates by maintaining that married people are concerned to please each other rather than the Lord. It seems unlikely that Paul could have meant this as a simple generalization, for unmarried persons would seem to become as perplexed *about the affairs of the world* as married people do. He more probably is referring to dedication of the whole life in a career, which is appropriate for Christians. An unmarried person could concentrate all his or her leisure time on special service of God, whereas the married person must concentrate a good part of his or her time on family needs.

In view of the idea that it was the last generation, Paul may have had in mind that there was no need of having children. If the world was coming to an end, procreation in marriage was futile. Nowhere, however, does the apostle suggest this specifically; so it is a dubious suggestion here.

This section concludes with another affirmation of the nonbinding character of this opinion. Men and women have a right to marry in the face of the eschatological situation. Nevertheless, Paul is convinced that his advice is for the *particular benefit* of the addressees; it will help them live a more orderly, devoted, undistracted life in the church.

THE MARRIAGE OF "VIRGINS" (7:36-38)

7 36 Now if anyone thinks he is not acting in good order toward his virgin, if he be of strong passion, and if he ought to become so, let him proceed to do what he wishes: he is not committing a sin; let them get married. 37 But he who stands firm in his heart without pressure and with control over his own will, and who has decided in his own heart to keep his virgin himself, he will do well. 38 So both the one who marries off his own virgin does well and the one who does not marry her off will do better.

NOTES

7:36. *not acting in good order.* The transition from the previous verse is facilitated by the juxtaposition of *euschēmon* and *aschēmonein.* Paul's opinion and the optional freedom are now applied to a peculiar situation.

his virgin. There is no question that the *virgin* indicated here is female. The relation to the possessive pronoun is the crux; cf. COMMENT.

if he be. General condition with the subjunctive; this condition is dependent upon the preceding first class (simple) condition.

of strong passion. Again the interpretation governs the translation. The compound adjective can be either masculine or feminine and so can refer to the indefinite subject or the virgin. If it refers to the virgin, the translation would be "of mature years" or perhaps "past her prime." Barrett, who takes it to be masculine, translates "over-sexed."

and if he. Although *opheilei* may be impersonal, it draws this somewhat diffuse sentence together better to take it as a continuation of the first condition with the same subject.

let him proceed to do. The linear form of the jussive imperative could be construed "let him continue to do," but that makes nonsense of the sentence. This rendering adds some linearity to the aoristic sense.

37. *and with control over.* The indicative form ("and he has") seems to con-

tinue the initial relative clause and at the same time offer an opposite alternative to *without pressure* (literally, "not having"). *Control* (*exousian*) is the foil of *pressure* (*anagkēn*).

38. *So.* An actual result (*hōste*).

marries off. This translation is an attempt to avoid the usual "gives in marriage," which is a part of the interpretative problem. Cf. also COMMENT. The verb *gamizein* regularly means "give in marriage" and not "marry" in the New Testament, and it does not occur in Greek literature prior to the New Testament literature. Lietzmann (*Handbuch*, 35-36) gives a number of examples of verbs in *-izō* that have shifted from the causative force; but it would be tendentious to settle the matter on this evidence. AGB, 150, has an extensive bibliography dealing with this verb and its context here.

COMMENT

Few passages of scripture of such length bristle with more difficulties than does this. Lietzmann states that if any one reads without prejudice vss. 36-37, there will be no doubt that Paul is writing (though with somewhat clumsy phraseology) about a young man with his fiancée, but that if one reads vs. 38 without reading the foregoing verses and again without prejudice, there will be no doubt that the subject is the father of a virgin daughter. The first of these alternatives was known to Chrysostom. Héring enumerates six objections to this interpretation and opts for a third understanding: that Paul is describing a kind of "spiritual marriage" in which a couple lives together without sex relations (so also Manson, *Studies in the Gospels and Epistles,* 199-200). J. M. Ford has argued for a fourth possibility (*NTS* 10 [1963/64], 361-365; and cf. Barrett, ad loc.) that a levirate marriage is under consideration. (For representative support of the fiancée interpretation, cf. Kümmel, Wendland, and Barrett.)

Besides the problems regarding meaning of words (cf. NOTES) there are severe difficulties about subjects of clauses. It is not clear who is the subject of *if* (he) *be of strong passion* (or "of mature age") nor of *let* (him) *proceed to do what* (he) *wishes.* Four combinations of "he" and "she" are possible, and there is really nothing in the verse itself to indicate which alternative is correct. Nor does the plural subject of the jussive clarify the matter, for it can be shown to be possible with any of the four interpretations of the passage: it takes two to make a marriage.

There is considerable ambiguity in the phrase *his virgin.* Again, no line of argument offers incontrovertible evidence; the explanation given will usually support the over-all interpretation adopted (so Barrett finds "a close analogy" to "the colloquial English 'his girl'"). There is evidence in Greek literature for the use of *parthenos* as both "fiancée" and "daughter." This passage must finally be understood without a sure decision about this phrase.

What kind of freedom from *pressure* ("necessity") was it that made it possible to postpone marriage indefinitely? There is no likelihood that pregnancy is what Paul had in mind in this context. If he meant emotional pressure, then the love of a fiancé would be tepid and warrant release from the betrothal. The emotional pressure of a "spiritual" partner makes sense in the context if it indicates a reluctance to continue the relationship without sex relations. It is perhaps easiest to consider this verse as referring to a father who has tried to determine the marriage destiny of his daughter. If, under the spell of Christian enthusiasm, he has committed himself and his family to absolute service of God in view of eschatological expectation and has then found his daughter developing an interest in a young man, he may stand *firm in his heart* by believing that she should be kept single; and he may have the kind of relationship with her by which his will has authority in her mind. Thus he is *without pressure* because she as yet has no commitment of love toward marriage. In this case *he will do well* to keep her as his *virgin* daughter and continue to support her.

By interpreting the person in question as a father, vs. 38 readily makes sense. The meaning of the New Testament word *gamizō* is clearly "to give in marriage" in the only other occurrences: Matt 22:30, 24:38, and parallels. Paul's final judgment is that acquiescing to pressure is *well,* for his rabbinic background prevents him from disparaging marriage. But his sense of the urgency of Christian commitment in the eschatological season causes him to add a declaration of *better for the one who does not* give *his virgin* in marriage.

The objections of Héring to this more or less traditional interpretation are substantive. Several of them have already been addressed; but the real answer is that the same or similar objections can be directed, *mutatis mutandis,* to each of the interpretations. Hurd presents a careful argument for "spiritual marriages" (*The Origin of I Corinthians,* 169-182), but his decision is set forth with some caution. Paul's acceptance of an ascetic trend in the Corinthian church seems unavoidable, whichever direction one goes in this passage. A final decision, then, will relate to the kind of asceticism that is in view; and it is impossible to adduce any decisive evidence from the middle of the first century to support any of the alternatives. (For example, Miss Ford cites the Mishnah; but the validity of that evidence—apart from other objections to the argument—raises the notorious problem of the relation of that source to first-century practices.)

The problem of the bearing of eschatology upon the decisions recommended in this passage is also moot, but this is not the proper context for the discussion. It is well to enter a caveat, however, against circular reasoning in this matter: this passage indicates Paul's expectation of an imminent end of the age; Paul expected an imminent end of the age; this passage should be interpreted in the light of Paul's expectation of the imminent end of the age.

REMARRIAGE OF WIDOWS (7:39-40)

7 ³⁹A wife has been bound for as long a time as her husband lives; but if the husband dies, she is free to be married to whomever she wishes—except that it should be in the Lord. ⁴⁰But she is happier if she remains as she is, according to my opinion; and I think I also have the Spirit of God.

NOTES

7:39. *dies*. The use of *koiman* ("to sleep") as a euphemism for "die" is common. In the LXX it occurs regularly in the formula applied to the death of kings (e.g. I Kings 2:10). The idea has persisted: thus the English derivative cemetery, a "sleeping place."

40. *happier*. AGB proposes that this occurrence of *makarios* is "without religious coloring" and cites Luke 23:29 as a related usage. In light of the preceding passages, however, it is probable that religious overtones are not lacking.

as she is. Greek *houtōs;* i.e. unmarried.

COMMENT

Paul's summary statement seems rather obvious. He has indicated several parameters of the permanence of the marriage relation in vss. 10, 11, 13, and 24. Two observations may be added. One, that while the first clause appears to reflect Paul's male-dominated thinking, the second specifies for her the same freedom that a man enjoyed in the event of his wife's prior decease. Two, that while Paul speaks a word again in vs. 40 for the value of the unmarried state, he carefully guards the regularity of marriage and implies that the woman should be an equal partner in its arrangement (*whomever she wishes*).

The addendum, that remarriage should be with a Christian, is a sequel to his comments on marriage relations with unbelievers (vss. 12-16).

The observation that a widow will be *happier* if she remains unmarried is a logical concomitant of his comments in vss. 32-35. Again, the pressure of time may be assumed. And again, Paul offers this observation as *my opinion.* Here, however, he suggests that his opinion is validated because he has *the Spirit of God.* It seems overingenious to associate this with his later discussions of the Spirit in relation to the Corinthian church. Conzelmann is correct to connect this claim to the general affirmation of authority in vs. 25.

SECOND QUANDARY:
CONCERNING IDOL-OFFERINGS
(8:1-11:1)

LOVE, NOT KNOWLEDGE, THE
GUIDING PRINCIPLE (8:1-3)

8 ¹ Now with reference to meats offered to idols: we know that we all have knowledge! Knowledge puffs with pride, but love builds up. ² If anyone thinks he has known anything, he has not yet come to know as he ought to; ³ but if anyone loves God, this one has been known by him.

NOTES

8:1. *With reference to.* The transitional phrase *peri de* identifies the move to a different item of inquiry from Corinth.

meats offered to idols. The Greek has simply "the idol-offerings"; the UBS section heading has "foods"; but "meats" is clearly intended; cf. COMMENT.

we know . . . knowledge. Weiss long ago pointed out that the absence of the article with *gnōsin* generalizes this usage: it is not simply knowledge about idol-offerings that is in view (p. 214). Schmithals (*Gnosticism in Corinth,* 143) goes further to infer that this is a *terminus technicus* in Corinth, and the Corinthians employed it in their letter to which Paul is responding. (Indeed, this sentence may be a verbatim quotation from that letter—as illustrated in 7:1.) How specific the content of this *gnōsis* was is certainly moot. Paul's reply will deal with the ethical responsibility imposed by knowledge of the gospel.

2. *anything.* Papyrus 46 omits (with some patristic support) the indefinite pronoun. This renders the force of *has known* stark, and an anti-Gnostic overtone would be heightened. The scribal addition of *ti* would be natural enough; if Paul wrote it, it certainly adds to his belittling of *gnōsis.* A decision is likely tied to the P 46 omissions in the next verse.

has not yet come to know. The past aorist defies the translator. The protasis of the condition and the adverb *oupō* combine to suggest the solution adopted here.

3. *loves God.* P 46 omits *God;* and if the reading is followed here and in vs. 2, a general contrast is presented, parallel to the second half of vs. 1. Later in

the chapter Paul will emphasize the love of fellow Christians, particularly the weak. In other passages of Paul's letters there are only ambiguous references to love directed from persons to God; for example, in Rom 5:5, 8:35, 15:30, and II Cor 5:14 the phrase can be interpreted with subjective or objective genitives. In no instance is it clear that people's love for God is meant; probably divine love is indicated in each case. Nor does the omission of *by him* help to solve the problem. This latter P 46 omission is supported by Sinaiticus and 33, and it is certainly a *lectio difficilior*, especially since God is clearly the intended subject of the passive verb. It is not necessary, however, to conclude that the object of *loves* must therefore be *God* since this reading then becomes all the more difficult. The decision against P 46 to accept the longer readings will finally be because the MS tradition is too limited to carry the omission. The similarities of this passage to I John 2-4 *passim* are striking. An original relationship is doubtful, but there may be a connection in the MS tradition.

COMMENT

Paul now turns to the second of the topics which had been mentioned in the church's letter. This is the question: should Christians totally refrain from eating anything which was offered in the temples to the pagan gods? —an everyday practice that would be hard to eschew.

Faithful Jews were absolutely prohibited from any participation in idolatry (epitomized in Exod. 20:4-6). Included under this prohibition was eating meat that had been offered to idols or making a profit from the sale of such meat. (Rabbi Aqiba defined a qualification of the profit restriction: "Meat that is about to be brought in for the idols is permitted for profitable sale, but what is brought out is forbidden for this purpose, because it is like an offering for the dead" [StB, III, 377]; that is, it is permissible as an article of merchandise before it goes to the temple but not after.) The formulation of the Jewish proscription of idol-offerings in general is found in Tractate *Chullin:* "When one slaughters an animal in honor of the sun, the moon, the stars, the signs of the zodiac, the great archangel Michael, or even for a tiny worm, lo, it is thus meat of an offering for the dead" (2.18, in StB, III, 377; cf. Danby, *The Mishnah,* 516-517). (Comment about selling of meat follows in 2.20: "Meat that is in the possession of a pagan is available for merchandising, but that which is in the possession of a heretic is forbidden even for profitable sale. Meat that comes out of an idol-temple is meat offered to idols.") It is clear that the prevailing Jewish regulations laid an absolute interdict upon the consumption or use of food that had been slaughtered in the name of any pagan deity or that had been brought from the temple of the deities. The reason that meat which has been in possession of heathen may not be eaten by Jews but may be sold is that the risk of its having been offered to an idol is great enough to prevent a Jew from becoming unclean by eating it, while the uncertainty of its having been offered allows him to sell it (presumably to a pagan) without scruple. The principle is that the Jew must not knowingly participate in food that has been slaughtered in the name of the nature gods or offered on pagan altars; in cases in doubt he must not eat food obtained from pagans though he may sell it.

The form of Paul's reply to the Corinthians implies that they had affirmed that their possession of Christian knowledge justified uninhibited consumption of idol-offered meat. After laying down the general guideline, Paul will address specifically this application of knowledge, beginning in vs. 4. There was a sense in which the Corinthians' understanding of their knowledge was valid. Paul insists, however, that the value of such knowledge is limited in that those who possess it have an almost irresistible tendency to become *puffed with pride,* to get a feeling of distended theological importance. Those who are confident in their own knowledge may become arrogant and contemptuous of other people, and thus a good thing can be corrupted into a very dangerous thing. The feeling that the knowledge of God is accurate and comprehensive may bring to some persons a sense of superiority that is disruptive of community.

By contrast, *love builds up* the whole community. Here Paul introduces love as the guiding principle for the church (the reference in 4:21 was personal). In Rom 13:10 he affirms that "love is the fulfillment of the law." In ch. 13 he will present love as the indispensable virtue of Christians, superior to all others. It is the primary fruit of the Spirit (Gal 5:22), and it is the fundamental motivation of God in Jesus Christ (Rom 5:8; II Cor 5:14). The "building" metaphor is a favorite with Paul: he has already introduced it at 3:9, and he will pursue it at 10:23 and 14:3-5,12. Applying the metaphor to the church, he has in mind that some things destroy the church and some things build it up or supply strength or permanence to a weak structure. Human qualities that are commendable when considered solely in relation to the individual may have to be tempered or modified when people live in relation to one another. Pride puffed by knowledge readily overlooks the concerns of other people. It must be turned outward into love; love takes into account the nature and purposes of other people. Love is the primary social virtue.

Paul argues that the very confidence that one has some item of knowledge demonstrates that one has not made a proper adjustment to knowledge, for one has failed to realize that human knowledge is only partial. Furthermore, this puts an emphasis on one's own, subjective, intellectual ability. (A modern example is C. von Tischendorf, who gave preference to the readings of Codex Sinaiticus, undoubtedly because of his emotional attachment to it, which was rooted in his discovery of the MS under fantastic circumstances.) This amiable human weakness can lead to serious error, for knowledge corrupted by pride can do damage at the highest level of human perception. Superficial overconfidence in religious knowledge, since it closely affects the emotions and the will, damages life relationships.

Love is therefore far more important than knowledge. Love for God is more vital than knowledge about him. For Paul, with his deep background in the Torah, knowledge of God would include acceptance of an obedience to God as supreme sovereign (cf. Exod 6:7, 10:2, etc., 18:11; Deut 29:6). Perhaps Paul had in mind that the knowledge of God can really occur only when we love God; thus knowledge without love would be knowledge of something but not real knowledge of God.

Paul's argument leads him, however, to a more striking conclusion: love of God (which, as he will show, means love of one's fellows) leads to the realization that *one has been known by him!* This beautiful perception (systematized by Protestant reformers as "prevenient grace") was a part of Paul's heritage (Deut 13:3; Isa 65:24; Ps 139:1-18). This knowledge on God's part certainly includes acceptance (cf. Matt 7:23). So then the basis of Christian community is the interaction of love for God and his acceptance of his people.

THE QUESTION OF EATING FOOD OFFERED TO IDOLS (8:4-13)

Idols nothing; God in Christ everything

8 4 With reference, then, to the eating of meats offered to idols: we know that an idol is nothing in the world, and that there is no God but one. 5 For even if there are so-called gods, whether in heaven or on earth—as indeed there are many gods and many lords — 6 yet to us there is one God the Father, from whom all things exist and we are for him; and there is one Lord Jesus Christ, through whom all things exist, and we exist through him.

Obligation of deference to the conscience of a weak brother

7 Nevertheless all do not share this knowledge; but some, by being accustomed to the idol until now, are eating meat as an idol-offering; and their conscience is being defiled because it is weak. 8 Now food will not affect our standing with God: we neither lack anything if we do not eat, nor do we have an abundance if we do eat. 9 But see to it

that this liberty of yours does not somehow become a stumbling block to those who are weak. 10 For if anyone sees you, who have knowledge, dining in an idol-temple, will not his conscience, if it is weak, be built up to the point of eating the meats offered to idols? 11 Then because of your knowledge the one who is weak is perishing, the brother for whose sake Christ died. 12 In this way, when you are sinning against the brothers and wounding their conscience which is weak, you are sinning against Christ. 13 Therefore if food is causing my brother to fall, I will never eat meat lest I cause my brother to fall.

NOTES

8:4. *With reference, then,* repeats with more specificity the phrase from vs. 1. Paul turns from the general principle to particular argument. Thus *we know* is repeated but with a different object. Whereas *knowledge* in vs. 1 seems to have overtones of reference to the influence of outside ideas upon the Corinthians, here the Judaeo-Christian heritage is clearly in focus.

The knowledge of God mentioned in commenting on the last passage is now Paul's topic. It may be significant that he uses *oidamen* rather than *ginōskomen* to introduce the knowledge statements in both vss. 1 and 4. Both verbs translate *yāda'* in the Old Testament, and the use of both roots here may be stylistic. If, however, Paul is trying to divert his readers from a preoccupation with some sort of Gnostic ideas to the knowledge of God in the Old Testament, his usage is judicious. In Exod 8:18 and 9:14 (LXX) *eidenai* is used of the knowledge of Yahweh's unique power. In many places in the Old Testament *ginōskein* refers to God's knowledge and human knowledge that comes from God as well as knowledge of the right way of life that accompanies wisdom (e.g. Josh 22:31; Ps 138 *passim;* Isa 5:19; Hosea 6:3). Paul is aware of other dimensions of knowledge (note 13:2,8,9), but here his emphasis is on this special kind of religious knowledge.

5. *many gods and many lords.* It is possible that this is an allusion to a popular saying though there is no other evidence for it. Otherwise, it is a felicitous (though difficult; cf. COMMENT) expression of the apostle.

6. *one Lord Jesus Christ.* On the confessional significance of this, cf. Neufeld, *The Earliest Christian Confessions,* 42-68.

through whom all things exist, and we exist through him. The Greek has no verb (as similarly in the first half of the verse). On the role of Jesus Christ in creation, cf. H. Langkammer, *"Christus mediator creationis,"* in *VD* 45 (1967), 201-208 (also a later article in *NTS* 17[1970], 193-197). He finds the source of the belief in the implication of Ps 110 as interpreted in Acts 2:34-36, in the extension of the title *kyrios,* and in retrointerpretation of the "new" creation.

7. *this knowledge.* It is precisely statements of this kind that the epistle of James calls "faith" (e.g. 2:19). This sheds light on the popular assumption that

there is a profound antithesis between James and Paul. But it seems from this passage that James labels "faith" what Paul calls "knowledge." This means that when James says one "cannot be justified by faith alone" (2:24), he means that one cannot be justified only by believing true propositions about God. Paul would not call these propositions "faith" since for him they are "knowledge." Therefore Paul and James agree that belief in true propositions must be accompanied by something else: James says "works" (2:26), Paul says "love." Since for James the works are really deeds of love, the logomachy is resolved.

by being accustomed. There seems little doubt that the TR reading "conscience" is taken from the latter part of the verse.

8. *food.* Paul deals with the particular by general principle. There is somewhat of a parallel in Mark 7:15-20 // Matt 15:11,17-18.

10. *dining in an idol-temple.* Oxyrhynchus Papyrus 110 includes an invitation to dinner at the temple of Serapis. Participation seems to be an ordinary social possibility for inhabitants of such a city as Corinth.

11. *because of your knowledge.* This can be construed with the verb or the participle (*ho asthenōn*); but since vs. 7 assumes that there are already weak persons in the community, it is probable that the phrase is associated with *apollutai.*

is perishing. Note the present linear; cf. 1:18. Paul evidently does not consider the process irreversible. Perhaps we should render, "is on the point of perishing."

12. *wounding,* literally "striking" (*typtontes*). This can happen either (a) by inducing the brother to commit an act which his conscience disapproves and which produces a guilt feeling or (b) by causing him to accept as right an act which his conscience has disapproved and so to weaken the regulative power of his conscience.

13. *I will never.* The negative is very intense. To *ou mē* and the subjunctive Paul adds *eis ton aiōna*—"certainly not, forever."

to fall. Cf. the NOTE on *skandalon* at 1:23.

COMMENT

Idols nothing; God in Christ everything

Paul applies his statements about knowledge and love directly to the question of eating idol-offerings. The problem arose in Corinth, it would seem, because of two facts, which Paul could agree are acknowledged: the actual nonexistence of idols and the existence of only one God. The former fact had come to be recognized by Hebrew writers long before: Ps 115:3-8 is an explicit statement. The latter fact was a central affirmation of Judaism, summarized in the *Shema;* cf. Deut 4:35,39, 6:4; also Mark 12:29.

This is in the face of popular reference to "gods," the evidence for which was in every gentile city Paul visited; and Luke relates how Paul confronted this in Athens (cf. Introduction, pp. 71-81). There were imagined divinities both this-worldly and other-worldly. Not only were they referred to as "gods"; they were known as "lords" (*kyrioi*), the term used by Christians to refer to Jesus Christ—and one of the epithets of Caesar. Paul's wording, *as indeed there are,* is not to be taken to affirm that the gods and lords of the pagan religions have some sort of existence (a reality conferred by the belief of people, as Hermann von Soden is quoted by Weiss to have maintained). In Gal 4:8 Paul clearly contrasts the pagan gods, which *are no gods,* with the God the Christian knows. In 10:14, 19-20 Paul will identify the gods of the heathen as demons; but neither there nor anywhere else in the New Testament are demons described as gods. In 4:9 and 6:3 he has mentioned "angels" as a special kind of being, but they are not divinities. The parenthetical clause here seems to be equivalent in reference to the main clause: all these gods are *so-called.* Paul is merely acknowledging the existence of numerous sacral societies who believe in and worship deities that exist only in the worship and thought of their believers. He is not affirming that these gods have any actual reality, for this would be directly contrary to the Jewish-Christian faith that *there is no God but one.*

This God is identified as the one who originated the entire universe and who is the aim (Paul Tillich, "ground") of our existence (*eis auton*). He is denominated *father,* a direct legacy from the teaching of Jesus. This father God has focused his revelation to us in the unique Lord, Jesus Christ. (Thus the *many gods and many lords* have their antithesis in the oneness of the God and Lord Paul worships.) By virtue of a deep relation to God this Lord existed before human life and indeed was the agent by whom God brought all things and beings into existence.

How Paul arrived at the conclusion that Jesus Christ participated in the creation is never clearly explained. In Rom 1:4 he declares that Jesus was "defined as God's son in power from the resurrection" (cf. also Acts 17:31), and in Philip 2:6 he speaks of Jesus existing in the form of God and cites his self-emptying as a voluntary retreat from equality with God. Col 1:15-20 is the most elaborate statement of the Pauline belief in the "preexistence" of Christ. Evidently the resurrection and the theological implications which Paul considered to be revelation convinced him that Jesus was more than human. It may be further inferred that the authority of Jesus' teaching and the loving quality of his life led Paul to believe that the character Jesus lived was identical with the loving character of God. So he must have concluded that one with this revealed character had come into the world from an origin higher than that of ordinary humanity. From this he could infer that Jesus' prehuman character was the same as that of God the Father and that Jesus was in an essential unity of activity with

God from the beginning of the universe. There is no specific evidence that Paul carried his thoughts further; later theological formulations were grown from these germs. The essence of this belief, however, appears in other strands of the literature of the early church (John 1:3,10, 8:58; Heb 1:2); and it is unlikely that Paul was responsible by himself for the idea and its development.

When he affirms that *we exist through him,* Paul probably is not referring to our existence as human beings; for that would be included in *all things.* Here he means that he and his fellow Christians exist as a divine and redemptive society by means of Jesus. By the lordship of Jesus Christ the church of believers exists (he will develop this under the figure of "the body of Christ" in chs. 11 and 12).

Obligation of deference to the conscience of a weak brother

From these statements which Christians *know* (vs. 4), it could be concluded that the dedication of anything to an idol confers upon the offering no power or sanctity and that such dedicated objects may be used precisely as any other objects are used. In vs. 7, however, Paul proposes a ramification of the statement in vs. 1 that *we all have knowledge. All do not share* an inner certainty about some of the conclusions that follow from the propositions all accept, in particular that food dedicated to an idol has no different quality from other food. For some, their long-practiced pagan custom has produced a built-in reaction to sacred objects that they are not strong enough in faith to eradicate. Then if they eat food offered to idols, it still has an aura of taboo. So on the positive side it may give the participant a false sense of power or good fortune, and on the negative side it may produce a guilt feeling for one who assumed that willingness to eat offered food implied belief in the sacred reality of the idol. Paul is clear that this is the effect of a weak conscience, but the danger is nonetheless real. Eating idol-offerings may be the same for some people as bowing down before an image. They are either acting out of residual belief in the idol or contradicting the requirement to worship God alone.

The orientation of this is in the person, not in God. The association of *lack* with not eating and *abundance* with eating could logically be reversed: that we do not lose anything if we eat, and we gain nothing if we do not eat. Apparently Paul is arguing that for those who are consciously and freely eating food offered to idols their eating does not give them any spiritual advantage, while for those who are not eating no loss is incurred. The point is that neither practice will *affect our standing with God.*

The people who understand this truth, however, are pointed to an additional factor in the situation: free use of legitimate *liberty* may *somehow become a stumbling block* for someone who draws precisely the wrong inferences from the actions he sees. Paul insists that this person is not solely responsible for his mistake: the Christian who acts from courageous knowledge of the truth must beware of causing a brother to misunderstand. A knowledgeable Christian may even join in a banquet in an idol-temple precinct, and such participation may be a way of asserting that idol-offered food means nothing whatever. But if there is a brother who perceived what the other is doing as a participation in the favor of the idol, a brother for whom the food has numinous power, he may be led to a new venture in idolatry or a belief that somehow he can accommodate his Christian faith to idol-worship.

For Paul worship is a desperately serious matter, and worshiping a false god produces disastrous consequences (cf. Rom 1:18-23). To believe in the one God means that one must worship only one God and must avoid any participation in anything which includes or implies even marginal worship of anything else. Such worship causes one to perish, and one must not contribute to this end for another member of the community. That weak brother is also an object of Christ's total concern. To be the cause of another's downfall, then, is a sin *against Christ* inasmuch as Christ's purpose toward that person is love. (The principle is remarkably like the idea set forth in Matt 25:45.)

Paul's conclusion is a strong assertion of his sense of responsibility for his *brother*. His own sense of liberty in Christ is everlastingly circumscribed by the weakness of others. Christ's life-and-death concern for these persons binds Paul, and this condition he is trying to lay upon the Corinthian church.

EXCURSUS: PAUL'S EXERCISE
OF HIS RIGHTS (9:1-27)

His apostolic freedom

9 ¹Am I not free? Am I not an apostle? Have I not seen Jesus our Lord? Are you not my work in the Lord? ²If I am not an apostle to others, at least I am to you; for you are the seal of my apostleship in the Lord. ³To those who are investigating me this is my defense. ⁴Do we not have the right to eat and to drink? ⁵Do we not have the right to take around a sister as a wife as do the rest of the apostles and the brothers of the Lord and Cephas? ⁶Or do only Barnabas and I not have the right of freedom from physical work?

Traditional guarantee of support to God's workers

7 Who ever serves as a soldier and pays his own wages? Who plants a vineyard and does not eat its fruit? Who shepherds a flock and does not partake of the milk of the flock? 8 I am not saying these things according to a human standard, am I? Does not the law also say these things? 9 For in the law of Moses it has been written: "You shall not muzzle an ox as it is threshing grain." God is not concerned for the oxen, is he? 10 Rather he certainly is speaking for our sake. It was indeed written for our sake because the one who is plowing should plow in hope, and the one who threshes, in hope of sharing. 11 If we sowed spiritual seed for you, is it a great thing if we reap your physical harvest? 12 If others are sharing the right of being supported by you, should not we all the more? We did not, however, use this right; but we are enduring all things in order that we may not cause any hindrance to the gospel of Christ. 13 Do you not know that those who perform the temple-rites eat the temple-offerings, and those who serve at the altar share in the altar-sacrifices? 14 So also the Lord directed those who are proclaiming the gospel to live from the gospel.

Paul's waiver of his rights
a. His compulsion to preach free

15 Now I have used none of these rights. I have not written these things in order that they may turn out so in my case; for it is better for me to die than—no one is going to nullify my basis for boasting. 16 For if I am preaching the gospel, it is not a basis for me to boast; indeed, I am under compulsion: for woe is me if I do not preach the gospel! 17 If I am doing this voluntarily, you see, I have a wage; but if involuntarily, I have been entrusted with a stewardship. 18 What, then, is my wage? That while I am preaching the gospel, I may deliver it free of charge so that I may not use up the right I have in the gospel.

b. His adaptability for the gospel

19 Though I am free from all people, I have enslaved myself to all in order that I may win more of them: 20 I have become as a Jew to the Jews in order to win Jews. I have become as one under the law to

those who are under it (although I myself am not under the law) in order to win those under the law. 21 To those not under the law I have become as one not under the law (although I am not free from the law of God but am subject to the law of Christ) in order to win those not under the law. 22 I have become weak to those who are weak in order to win the weak. I have become all things to all people in order that I may by all means save some. 23 I keep doing all these things for the sake of the gospel in order that I may become a partner with the gospel.

An athletic analogue

24 Do you not know that all who run races in the stadium compete, but only one receives the prize? Run so that you may win! 25 Now everyone engaging in a contest submits to self-discipline in all respects. They do it to receive a perishable winner's wreath, but we do it to receive an imperishable one. 26 So I am running, not on a zigzag course; and I am boxing, not as though punching the air; 27 but I am beating my body black and blue and bringing it into subjection lest somehow I preach to others and myself become disqualified.

NOTES

9:1. *apostle.* Cf. NOTES on 1:1 and 4:9. Paul's insistence on the authenticity of his apostleship is a recurring theme in his epistles; it is argued particularly in Galatians. The following question, with its expectation of an affirmative reply, is epexegetical to this one; and the last question is also related.

Have I not seen. The change to the strong form of the negative (*ouchi*) may be only stylistic; Paul uses it frequently (1:20, 3:3, 5:12, etc.). Since the Damascus-road appearance, however, seems to be so important to Paul, the alternation of the particles here may be deliberate for emphasis.

Jesus our Lord. This relatively uncommon designation probably is to be associated with Paul's stress on the activity of the risen Lord. The wording of his claim here is unique. Cf. Robertson and Plummer's note.

3. *To those who are investigating me.* On the rendering of *anakrinō* cf. second NOTE on 2:14.

this is my defense. Schmithals, *Gnosticism in Corinth,* 383, takes this with vss. 1 and 2, and elucidates the structural relationships of the charges against which Paul is defending himself.

4. *Do we not . . . ?* The subtlety of the double negative (*mē ouk*) is scarcely possible in English.

the right. This is to be understood in relation to authority granted to the

Christian community through the power of Christ. W. Foerster (*TDNT*, II, 569-571) points out that "this is the subject of Paul's quarrel with the Corinthians." The "freedom of choice" implied in *exousia* is genuine but must be exercised within the framework of Christ's revelation to and in his church.

5. *sister . . . brothers*. Some difficulty may be imagined in construing the first term as a Christian woman and the second as siblings of Jesus. Statistics of Pauline usage are really not determinative. Allo discusses the matter at some length (pp. 211-214); Héring dismisses it with a cursory note (p. 77).

6. *Barnabas*. This sounds like a friendly reference to Paul's former travel companion and supports the view that the rift at the beginning of the second missionary journey was not a lasting division (cf. Introducton, pp. 66-68).

freedom from physical work (literally, *not to work*). This is transitional to the consideration of the support of *those who are proclaiming the gospel* (vs. 14). The statement is indirect confirmation of the tradition in Acts 18:3 that Paul had a trade, which he plied upon occasion. There is no other evidence of Barnabas working for a living. Acts 4:36-37 does assert that he had property.

7. *wages. opsōnion* originally referred to the provisions that were the main substance of wages. C. C. Caragounis (*NovT* 16 [1969/70], 35-37) argues that this meaning should be preserved; but there is satisfactory evidence for the developed meaning (cf. Robertson, *Word Pictures in the New Testament*, IV, 143).

Who plants . . . ? The principle was established in Torah: Gen 9:20-21; Deut 20:6.

8. *according to a human standard*. The phrase has already occurred in 3:3.

Does not. It seems better to separate the two questions (as is done in most of the modern versions). The distinguishing force of *ē* is like that at the beginning of vs. 10, but here its translation is awkward.

9. *"You shall not muzzle. . . ."* Deut 25:4. The curious substitution of *kēmōseis* for *phimōseis* of LXX is undoubtedly genuine, but the reason must remain conjectural. Neither word is common. Where the same verse is quoted in I Tim 5:18, the verb of the LXX is employed, but the word order is altered (the LXX follows the Hebrew word order). Perhaps one can only say that there was no concern to be meticulous in quoting from the Old Testament.

God is not concerned for the oxen, is he? The answer of the Deuteronomist would be, "Yes, he is." Paul's exegetical procedure in his use of Old Testament citation is much less precise than modern hermeneutical standards allow. Cf. also COMMENT. Also R. N. Longenecker, *Biblical Exegesis in the Apostolic Period*, 104-132.

10. *Rather. . . .* The textual editors agree that the question introduced by *mē* in vs. 9 is continued by *ē* (cf. BDF, § 452[2]). The force of *mē*, however, surely does not carry over; for it would destroy the sense. The question would seem to require *ou* expecting an answer opposite to that of the preceding one. Weiss says, *"legei* does not express a question but a declaration" (p. 237), and this offers a better understanding of the series of clauses.

plow in hope. Cf. Deut 24:15.

11. *physical*. Cf. 3:3; the translation used there has been adapted here. An alternative would be "material."

12. *sharing the right of being supported by you.* The text has "sharing your right." Conzelmann, Barrett, and others (AGB) take the pronoun as objective genitive; but the subjective use, with Robertson and Plummer and Héring, seems to suit the sense of *metechein* better. In the former case Paul would be sharing with the *alloi,* but the emphasis in this context is upon the Corinthians and hence what they have to share.

UBS editors make a break in the middle of vs. 12; Nestle[26] places one after the verse. Paul's structure is somewhat interlocking: in the midst of his illustrations of "traditional guarantee" he inserts remarks about his own relationship to the principle he is developing. Since vs. 13 contains another illustration, and vs. 14 a kind of summary, it seems best to make the break before vs. 15, which begins with the strong transition *egō de.*

13. The rights of the Levites are set forth in Deut 18:1-4; cf. Num 18:20-24.

14. Paul must have in mind the tradition recorded in Luke 10:7-8. Cf. Dungan, *The Sayings of Jesus,* 3-80.

15. *for (gar)* occurs five times in vss. 15-17. There is evidence that Paul indulges in "streaks" of word use, including conjunctions and particles (cf. *de* in 4:2-10, 7:25-40).

The break in sentence structure in which Paul does not complete his comparison is not unusual in the apostle's letters; cf. 15:1-2; Rom 5:12, 9:22-24; II Cor 12:6-7; Gal 2:3-6. Robertson, *Grammar,* 435-443, 1203-1204, draws fine lines among the various sorts of grammatical inconsistencies; the present example might be classified under anacoluthon or aposiopesis or even *oratio variata.* However it is described, it is the result or expression of intensity of feeling: Paul's mind moves more quickly than the pen can accommodate.

no one is going to nullify. The variant readings appear to be attempts to correct the grammatical incongruity. The difficulty of the Byzantine reading is not sufficient ground for accepting it over the very substantial MS support of our text.

boasting. A distinctively Pauline word (only four examples in the New Testament outside the Pauline literature).

16. *if I am preaching.* A present general (third class) condition: "any time I am" or "given the condition that I am."

18. *That . . . I may deliver.* The *hina* clause may be loosely epexegetical, but it surely retains something of its final force.

19. *all people.* Although the previous context could admit the neuter, the sequel makes it clear that Paul has moved to specific relationships with persons.

I have enslaved. The verb is past aorist as is *I have become* in the following verses. The Greek emphasizes the change that took place, but the *Aktionsart* requires the perfect in English.

win. Verses 22b-23 show that Paul is here concerned to relate people to the gospel in a saving way.

20. *although I.* The particle phrases here and in the next verse are parenthetical, according to the structure pattern of the sentences. Paul wants there to be no mistake about his true status even in his strategic accommodations.

21. *free from . . . subject to.* "Paul has created the bold phrase . . . where the gen[itive] seems to depend on *nomos*" (BDF, § 182[3]).

22. *I have become weak.* The absence of *hōs* is probably deliberate. This move on Paul's part is of a different sort than those in the preceding verses. Comparison with II Cor 10:10 is intriguing.

by all means. Robertson, *Word Pictures,* IV, 148, notes a wordplay. This helps determine the precise meaning of *pantōs* here.

25. *submits to self-discipline.* The only other example of the verb in the New Testament is in 7:9. In Gal 5:23 the noun is listed as one of "the fruits of the Spirit."

26. *not on a zigzag course.* Greek, "uncertainly."

27. *beating my body black and blue.* Greek, "strike under the eye." Paul's mixed figure would be "give my body a black eye."

COMMENT

His apostolic freedom

Paul defends his position about the need to temper freedom by the concern of love as he brings forward his own case in illustration. Chapter 9 is an excursus in which his own life and example confirm the main points of his previous argument. By a series of rhetorical questions he establishes his own right to privileges others have assumed, yet he has declined to make use of any of these rights for weighty reasons concerned with the effectiveness of the gospel and his own self-respect in his gospel ministry. Concomitantly he defends himself against criticism that has apparently been directed against him and his policies. He is confident of his credentials, and his conduct has been determined by the desire to serve the gospel in the church. He has lived by the same principles he is urging his readers to follow. His self-defense becomes a plea for them to exhibit greater maturity in their life.

In the Galatian churches Paul had to defend his apostleship, and he seems to be aware that it is in question at Corinth. He argues that the power he has to win converts and form new churches is a guarantee of apostleship, and this is specific in Corinth: they are believers because they heard the good news of Jesus Christ through his preaching. He insists (as he did to the Galatians) that he has seen *Jesus our Lord,* presumably in the Damascus-road experience. According to Acts 1:22 this was a qualification of an apostle. So Paul's apostolic authority in Corinth is not only proprietary but essential. There is evidence in II Corinthians that rebellion against Paul's authority developed there (e.g. 1:23 - 2:11); and the defense here may be directed to the first stages of such insurgence.

Another series of questions in vss. 4-6 introduces other implied questions about authority. The first has to do with food and drink, probably that which may not meet the requirements of Jewish dietary laws. This is directly connected with ch. 8. The freedom which has been misused in Corinth is not per se a problem; Paul has that same freedom.

The next question implies that a traveling apostle has the authority to have a wife and *to take* her *around* with him in the work of founding and regulating the churches. There is some reference back to ch. 7. The principal matter, however, is a blunt comparison with other apostolic figures: other leaders have exercised this right. *The rest of the apostles* could refer to the Twelve but rather seems here to be a more general term. "Apostle" is, of course, not always equivalent to "the Twelve." The mention of *Cephas* as a special case does not settle the matter. It is hardly an indication of special rank, but he did enjoy a practical primacy in the early church, and Paul's ministry was sometimes in confrontation with Peter's. Particular mention is made probably because Cephas was the patron of one of the parties at Corinth (1:12, q.v.) and therefore had some specific rating in the minds of the membership there. *The brothers of the Lord* is a separate category referring here to the blood brothers of Jesus. Although four are named in Mark 6:3, there is other testimony only about James (cf. Gal 1:19). Cf. also NOTES.

Traditional guarantee of support to God's workers

The third question, about *freedom from physical work* (vs. 6), leads into a lengthy illustrative passage to demonstrate that apostolic persons should be supported by the churches. A first series of rhetorical questions taken from the experiences of everyday life indicate that all classes of people get paid for their work. There may be some personal appropriateness in the references to soldier, planter, and shepherd; for Paul can think of himself in each function: cf. Eph 6:12-17; I Cor 3:6; Acts 20:28-29.

The analogies, however, need not be pressed. The same point can be made by actual commandment of the law, by the practice of the temple, and by the commandment of Jesus Christ himself. Paul takes a point of the Deuteronomic code (25:4) and interprets it by the rabbinic principle of argument from the lesser to the greater (*qal wa homer*): if God decreed that the oxen must be allowed to eat from the grain which they are threshing, a man must be allowed to eat from the work he is doing—and in particular, this applies to an apostle. *Those who are proclaiming the gospel* are supplying spiritual blessings, services, and gifts, which are greater in value than material things of the world; so they should receive material things to support this essential work.

Paul claims a superior *right* to this *support,* probably because he has run much bigger risks than *others* and has endured greater hardships as the embattled defender of offering the gospel to the gentiles. Perhaps because of this very hostility he has not used his right of support; or perhaps he refrained because he has persecuted the church to begin with (cf. 15:9); or perhaps he felt that people might try to discredit his preaching on the ground that it was motivated by a desire for worldly gain. Paul is at pains to establish both principles as he proceeds: he has the right to physical support, but he has not presumed upon that right. His function is analogous to that of the Levitical temple servants so far as support is concerned. *The Lord* Jesus validated the application of this to servants of the gospel.

Paul's waiver of his rights
a. *His compulsion to preach free*

Now Paul makes it explicit that the purpose of his argument is not to convince his readers that they should support him. His present policy is the basis of a kind of *boasting,* which he does not want anyone to make void. For the most part Paul is opposed to self-glorification, but here he prides himself on a course of life that affords some ground for precisely that. Just to *preach the gospel* brings no *basis for boasting,* for God has drafted him—he has no other option. His life would be bankrupt if he rejected this necessity. His reasons for feeling this compulsion are probably the same as those which led him to disclaim his right of support.

But if Paul supports himself while preaching the gospel, he has *a wage* because he is going beyond the requirement. The only thing required of him is to preach the gospel. For this he could receive pay, but then he would have no further reward because the pay would have compensated him for what he had to do. If he received pay, he would simply have been doing his duty as an official employed in the management of the gospel— *entrusted with a stewardship.*

Paul is not, of course, slipping into his letter a teaching of "merit by works." He puts a kind of value on the satisfaction which comes from knowing that he has done all he could and has tried to do a little bit more. This is not the same as salvation; it is a kind of balance established in life over against sins committed and over against the tremendous benefits received from God and from people. Persons who assert their rights, he implies, may be overly zealous and lack a certain readiness to practice the injunctions of love. They have a dim perception of what is required to keep a society of people of various personalities working harmoniously and developing together in knowledge and love of God and humanity.

b. *His adaptability for the gospel*

Paul's positive procedure is voluntarily to submit to slavery in serving others for the sake of winning to Christ as many of them as possible. This consists in accommodating his practice to that of the people to whom he is preaching. It is a breathtaking relativizing of national and legal values to the absolute value of the gospel. Paul was ready to renounce citizenship, legal attachments, customs. This did not take the form of flaunting his independence, however, by obstreperous nonconformity; but it took the opposite form of changing his conformity according to the people with whom he was dealing. Paul is no ordinary turncoat who adjusts his habits for the sake of his own gain: Paul's policy is determined by the fact that he is under the compulsion of God and has a message that must be directed to people of all nationalities, customs, and characteristics. A believer in this gospel does not belong particularly to any group but can belong to all; so that he is at home wherever he is and at the same time is a stranger even when he is at home. Paul's overriding allegiance is as *a partner with the gospel*.

An athletic analogue

The strenuous effort of gospel labor and its single-minded purpose leads Paul to a comparison with athletic competition. The Graeco-Roman world put great stress on athletic endeavor, especially what we classify as track and field events. The Olympic races, celebrated every four years, were highly valued throughout the Mediterranean world; and the victors were acclaimed everywhere. This points to the obvious fact that only one contestant wins; so he must exert great effort toward that end. The effort is not only in the race but in training for it, when rigid *self-discipline* is a requisite. Paul applies this to Christian life by *ad maius* argument: contestants in games compete for a *winner's wreath* and other perquisites of honor which are perishable; but *the prize* for which the Christian strives is *imperishable*. Paul seems to be thinking of heavenly honor (cf. Philip 3:14); and he may have in mind something in addition to being saved, something to be granted to those who perform service beyond the requirements. So he emphasizes his own super efforts: he does not waste time on futile pursuit and combat on any and every occasion, but he directs his struggle to worthy contests. Indeed his blows are directed more against himself; for this is worthwhile discipline. If he becomes concerned with selfish purposes (his rights?), he may not win (others and/or a heavenly wreath) but *become disqualified*.

A WARNING FROM THE EXODUS
HISTORY (10:1-15)

Advantages of the Israelite fathers

10 ¹ I do not want you to be ignorant, brothers, that all our forefathers were under the cloud and all passed through the sea, ² and they all underwent baptism into Moses in the cloud and in the sea. ³ They all ate the same spiritual food, ⁴ and all drank the same spiritual drink, for they were drinking from the spiritual rock that was following; and the rock was Christ.

Their idolatry in the desert; its monitory function

⁵ Yet God was not pleased with most of them, for they were laid low in the desert. ⁶ Now these things happened as examples for us so that we might not be desirous of evil things even as they desired. ⁷ Do not become idolaters as some of them were—as it has been written, "The people sat down to eat and drink, and they got up to play around." ⁸ And let us not commit sexual immorality as some of them committed, and so twenty-three thousand fell on one day. ⁹ Neither let us keep putting Christ to the test as some of them tested him, and they perished by the serpents. ¹⁰ And do not keep grumbling as some of them did, and so they perished by the destroyer.

The warning afforded and God's escape provided

¹¹ Now these things happened to them as an example; and they were written as admonition for us, to whom the end of the age has drawn near. ¹² Therefore let the one who thinks he stands firmly look out lest he fall. ¹³ No temptation except that of a common, human kind has overtaken you. And God is faithful: he will not permit you to be tempted beyond what you are able to resist; but with the temptation he will also provide the way out for you to be able to endure it. ¹⁴ Wherefore, my beloved ones, shun idolatry. ¹⁵ I am speaking to you as intelligent people: judge for yourselves what I am saying.

NOTES

10:1. *I do not want you to be ignorant.* This formula occurs also at 12:1; Rom 11:25; II Cor 1:8; I Thess 4:13; and in positive form at I Cor 11:3 and Col 2:1. It usually prefaces an interpretation of some critical item of Christian faith or experience.

our forefathers. Gentile readers are included because Paul assumes that the Old Testament traditions are the common background for the faith of all Christians. He can, of course, develop this idea theologically into a doctrine of the church as the new Israel; cf. Romans 9-11.

under the cloud. Cf. Exod 13:21-22, 14:19-20, 33:9-10; Num 14:14.

through the sea. Cf. Exod 14:21-29.

2. *underwent baptism.* The third edition of the UBS text changes to the aorist passive from the aorist middle reading of the earlier editions. Metzger and Wikgren dissent, arguing plausibly that copyists would more likely replace the middle with the passive, which would correspond to Christian practice. In Jewish practice "the convert baptized himself" (Metzger, *Textual Commentary,* 559).

into Moses. Probably an analogy to Christian phraseology; cf. 1:13,15, also 12:13; Gal 3:27.

in the cloud and in the sea. Presumably the cloud moved from in front of the Israelites through their camp to rest behind them so that they were in or under (vs. 1) it as it passed. The passage through the sea explicitly did not wet the people. Paul is not concerned with the technicalities of the typology; in each case the Israelites could be regarded as having undergone baptism.

3. *spiritual food.* "Spiritual" probably has two aspects: food supplied by God's special action, and food which has a spiritual or typological significance. Paul undoubtedly has in mind particularly the manna (cf. Exod 16:4,35; Ps 78:23-28; also John 6:31,49).

4. *spiritual drink.* Again the double significance. Cf. Exod 17:5-6; Num 20:7-11; Ps 78:15-16.

spiritual rock. Paul was not the first to allegorize the rock. Philo wrote: "The Akrotomos Rock is the wisdom of God, which he separated as the highest and the first from his powers, out of which he gave a drink to the souls who love God" (*Legum Allegoriae* 2:21). A midrash on Exod 17:6 indicates a rabbinic belief that God was the rock from which the water came and that the rock was always present to their need because God went wherever Israel went (StB, III, 408).

Christ, rather than "the Messiah," since the interpretation is clearly a Christian one. If Paul knew the interpretation suggested by Philo, he could be making the transfer through the "wisdom" idea; see second NOTE on 1:24.

5. *were laid low;* also vs. 6. Cf. Ps 78:30-31. The records in Exodus and Numbers indicate a series of rebellious actions as the basis for God's anger with

Israel. It was reaction to the report of the twelve spies that is said to have kept the people from their goal in the promised land (Numbers 14).

6. *examples* (*typoi*). In the recounting, Paul seems to be pointing to a typological understanding (and cf. COMMENT). He moves almost at once, however, into paraenesis; and the place of this passage in the outline of the epistle is certainly paraenetic, not paraenetic typology but typological paraenesis.

7. *as it has been written.* The story in Exodus 32 is apropos of the whole context of this section of the epistle. The quotation is from vs. 6. *leṣaḥēq* may indicate simple amusement, but sexual implications are possible (Gen 26:8, 39:17), and this is the way Paul understands it—not surprising in view of the Corinthian situation.

8. *twenty-three thousand.* Paul may have in mind the story from Num 25:1-9, in which many Israelites were guilty of sexual immorality with Moabite women, who also invited them to their altars. The result of this combined sin of sexual immorality and idolatry was the death of twenty-four thousand men. At the time of the golden calf incident the Levites slew three thousand men (Exod 32:28). Perhaps Paul confused the two numbers since he would be writing from memory.

9. *Christ.* The third edition of the UBS text accepts *Christon* instead of *kurion* as "the reading that best explains the origin of the others" (Metzger, *Textual Commentary,* 560). The interpretative move is analogous to that of vs. 4.

perished by the serpents. Cf. Num 21:4-9; also John 3:14-15. The verb is past linear (imperfect), but in the next verse it is past aorist. In this case the destruction was arrested, and this may be behind Paul's usage here. In vs. 10 the general effect of the grumbling is in view.

10. *keep grumbling.* A summary statement. The root *gonguz-* occurs some sixteen times in the Pentateuch. (The imperative was accommodated in some MSS to the hortatory of the previous verse.)

destroyer. A *hapax legomenon* in the New Testament; but the verb occurs at Heb 11:38, and the cognate *olethros* at I Cor 5:5 (q.v.); I Thess 5:3; II Thess 1:9; I Tim 6:9. Paul may have in mind I Chron 21:11-16, where the compound *exolethreuon* occurs (in the New Testament only at Acts 3:23). Cf. also Exod 12:23 and Wisdom of Solomon 18:20-25. The uncertain identity of this figure is discussed by J. Schneider (including the StB material) in *TDNT,* V, 167-171.

11. *as an example* (*typikos*). Cf. vs. 6.

the end of the age. Both words are plural in the Greek text. At least three interpretations are possible. (a) Paul may be generally summarizing all previous ages: the time in which he is writing is the eschatological inheritor of all that has preceded. (b) The wilderness generation was the generation of the beginning and was in its own way messianic since Christ was with them and they had the foresigns of baptism, the Lord's Supper (cf. COMMENT), and guidance of the Holy Spirit. Paul's generation is the final messianic generation. What happened in the old age of Israel is now being brought to an end at the conclusion of the final age. (c) "The plural *telē* is to be understood in a singular sense of the end of a unity" (Conzelmann, 168). This differs from (a) in that there is no assumption of an epochal pattern. This third interpretation is assumed in the translation (cf. also AGB, s.v. *aiōn*, 2b).

13. *temptation*. It is almost always a question whether to translate *peirasmos* as "testing" or "temptation" in the New Testament. The translation here differs from that of the verb in vs. 9 because here the context implies the possibility of sin.

14. *Wherefore*. This and the following verse provide a transition to an analogy with the Lord's Supper; but they really summarize the diverse preceding material as it relates to idolatry.

shun idolatry. In 6:18 Paul used *pheugete* to summarize his argument regarding sexual scandal. Although he has been writing about idol-offerings and idolaters, this the first and only explicit mention of *idolatry*. The word refers to the worship of an image or divinity which seems to exist but does not exist—a presupposition of his appeal in the next verse. (The root word *eidos* means an image or likeness that may represent something real [cf. Luke 3:22; note John 5:37] or unreal. The compound had certainly come to have a pejorative meaning.)

COMMENT

Advantages of the Israelite fathers

Despite confidence in their own knowledge and in the implied right to indulge in idol-offerings, the people of Corinth are reminded that complacent self-confidence is no certain guarantee of constant loyalty to God. They are reminded of instances in the past where people who had perhaps greater spiritual endowments and who experienced special and miraculous actions of God yet failed to withstand the temptation to depart from faithful adherence to God.

Paul makes spiritual applications of several incidents from the Pentateuch. By somewhat curious reasoning, which he does not delineate, he uses the stories of the pillar of cloud at the Israelite encampment and the passage through the sea at the exodus to declare that in these experiences the people had undergone *baptism* with Moses as the intermediary figure. Then he alludes to the manna (and the quails?) as *spiritual food* and the water from the rock as *spiritual drink,* which suggest the eating and drinking of the Lord's Supper (as becomes evident from 10:16-22). Thus the Israelites had supernatural experiences which prefigured the sacramental experiences of the Christian community.

This is confirmed by an allegorical association of the water-giving (*spiritual*) rock with *Christ*. In order to prepare for a monitory application to his readers, Paul uses a reverse application to the Old Testament stories.

So interpreted, the ancient events will warn the Corinthians that they are not the first to have received the benefits of Christ; and therefore the experiences of the earlier time should speak to the New Testament situation.

Their idolatry in the desert; its monitory function

God's remarkable actions for his people in the exodus time did not prevent them from falling into disaster. Instead of the experiences ensuring their obedience and faithfulness to God, the people shortly fell away, God became displeased, and *most of them* died in the desert.

Paul maintains that these events had a deeper meaning than lies on the surface. The apostasies and fatal plagues which struck these people are significant only for their instructive value. They are types which *happened as examples*. Their evil desires led some of them to *become idolaters*. The focus is on the incident of the golden calf.

Idolatry in Israel almost invariably entailed sexual immorality, for the religious practices of Israel's neighbors lacked the ethical sensitivity of Yahwism. Paul appears to connect this with the worship of the golden calf, and this provides another bridge to the Corinthian experiences and ties his discussion of idolatry again to his earlier strictures about sexual immorality. He reminds the confident believers in Corinth of the self-assurance of the old Israelites, and he sounds a warning by recounting their end.

To rivet this connection he extends the allegory of Christ in the Sinai wanderings by putting Christ into the bronze serpent incident—as also occurs in the Fourth Gospel. Paul practically develops a pattern of desert experience here, for the stories seem to overlap in this passage. The point, however, is uniform: departure from God's way and will brought and brings destruction.

The warning afforded and God's escape provided

The generation in which the Corinthians had received the gospel was one which confronted *the end of the age,* Paul affirms. As the messianic generation to whom Christ has appeared, it is the point of reference for all the Old Testament scriptures; *they were written as admonition for us.* Thus Paul thought it proper to take them from their original, historical setting and apply them to the decisions being made in the first century A.D. The transfer required reading meanings different from what they had at first, but the analogies were so close that the scriptures were not perverted or destroyed. Paul's people must at least learn that, if the Israelites who were so highly favored with evidences of God's power had stumbled into sins which led to their destruction, they dare not be overweening about their spiritual status; for then their fall is sure.

One reassurance they have: no supernatural testing will confront them; their temptations are of the sort which beset all humanity. But beyond this, their reassurance rests upon the faithfulness of God. The ancient problem of the power of evil is given a confident, if indirect, answer by Paul: though God does not keep his people from temptation, he guarantees a delivering resource.

Thus strengthened, the Christian may confront the danger to which Paul has been addressing himself: they are to *shun idolatry*. In common with Jewish belief Paul is sure that idolatry is impossible for a gospel believer. No amount of knowledge of the nonreality of an idol-god justifies participation in idol-worship in any form. Sophisticated understanding of the nature of idols and of the anthropomorphic jealousy attributed to God does not go far enough. Paul challenges the Corinthians to a discriminating consideration of his arguments. He has entered the caveat about the conscience of a weak brother, and he has warned about the immorality that may entrap idolaters. He will now consider the incongruity of idol-association and participation in the Lord's Supper.

THE LORD'S SUPPER AND FOOD OFFERED TO IDOLS (10:16-22)

An analogy provided

10 16 As for the cup of the blessing that we bless, is it not a partnership of the blood of Christ? As for the loaf that we break, is it not a partnership of the body of Christ? 17 Since there is one loaf, we, the many, are one body; for we all share from the one loaf. 18 Consider the people of Israel from a human standpoint: are not those who eat the sacrifices partners of the altar? 19 What, then, am I saying? that an idol-offering is anything? or that an idol is anything? 20a Rather that what [the gentiles] sacrifice, they sacrifice to demons and not to a god.

Restriction against partaking of both

20b I do not want you to become partners with the demons. 21 You are not able to drink the cup of the Lord and the cup of demons; you are not able to share in the table of the Lord and the table of demons. 22 Or are we trying to provoke the Lord to jealousy? We are not stronger than he, are we?

NOTES

10:16. *the cup of the blessing.* The phrase has a clear Semitic ring; it apparently represents *kōs šel brākāh* (or Aramaic *kāsā' dbirktā'*). The relative clause following is an alternate rendering of the idea; but the style here seems to reflect liturgic solemnity; so all elements are retained in the translation. The cup in mind is probably the third cup of the Passover meal (cf. StB, III, 419; also Daniel-Rops, *Daily Life in the Time of Jesus,* 400).

[For the antiquity of the idea in Semitic culture, cf. J. J. Jackson and H. H. P. Dressler, "El and the Cup of Blessing," *JAOS* 95 (1975), 99-101. Professor Jackson also notes Ps 116:13,17; and cf. 468, where Ps 23:5 is related.]

a partnership. Any rendering of *koinōnia* is exegetical; so the COMMENT is determinative here. The translation used at 1:9 is retained (q.v.).

loaf. artos means not only the substance "bread" but the shape or form in which it is baked (the plural almost always is "loaves"). The particular shape here is like a flat, round, thick pancake (cf. Daniel-Rops, *Daily Life,* 229-230).

17. *one loaf.* Didache 9:4 says that the "broken piece [of bread] scattered over the hills and brought together became one." This may be a reference to a legend about the fragments at the feeding of the multitude, but it certainly reflects Paul's understanding of the function of the sacramental loaf.

one body. This will be elaborated in chs. 11 and 12. Cf. also Rom 12:5; Eph 4:16; Col 3:15.

18. *from a human standpoint.* Construe with *the people of Israel.* Cf. 1:26.

the altar. Probably a pious circumlocution for God, to whom the altar belongs (but cf. S. Aalen, "Das Abendmahl als Opfermahl im Neuen Testament," *NovT* 6 (1963), 128-152).

20. *demons.* Paul has just insisted in the previous section that other gods are nothing. He may, then, speak of demons here as a concession for the sake of his argument. More likely he makes a distinction between gods worshiped by means of idols and evil forces at work in paganism that may even have a relationship to the gods that, as such, are nonexistent. The *ad rem* nature of most of his arguments never brought him to deal with the perplexing subtlety of this distinction. (Cf. W. Foerster, *TDNT,* II, 1-20.)

not to a god. In this letter Paul usually employs the article with *theos* when there are no other words to identify "the" God (e.g. vss. 5 and 13; cf. 9:9 and 21, where in the latter instance *theou* is contrasted with *christou*). Demons, then, are here distinguished from deities.

21. *you are not able,* i.e. it is not a viable option for you.

22. *trying to provoke.* On conative present, cf. BDF, § 319. Cf. also Deut 32:21 and Rom 10:19.

COMMENT

An analogy provided

The Lord's Supper is a meal in which the participants drink from a cup over which a blessing (or "benediction") is pronounced. At the beginning of the meal the people receive fragments broken from a loaf of bread. From earliest times throughout the Middle East eating food with another person established a fellowship, and the persons who ate together became bound by mutual obligations (e.g. Gen 18:1-15). It was not uncommon for people to band together to eat the Passover (cf. *Pesahim* 8:3,4,7). Paul's discussion of the Lord's Supper must be considered against the backdrop of Passover (and only secondarily against contemporary pagan practices except as he is specific in this regard—*pace* Schmithals).

The cup and its contents are identified in some way with the blood of Christ. This has been understood in several ways. It has been regarded as a real and metaphysical identification in which some kind of change takes place in the matter or substance of the wine; it becomes the blood of Christ by an invisible change apparent only to the believer. Again, the identity is defined as symbolical and analogical; the wine is like the blood of Christ, the beneficial properties of which are granted to those who drink in faith. The emphasis in this passage, however, is not on the contents of the cup but on *the blessing*. The "benediction" (which figures prominently in Jewish worship—*bārūk 'attāh 'ᵃdōnāy*) is offered to God for his benefits including the wine; and so the cup is accepted from God (in 11:25 it will be related to the new covenant). Following this idea it may be suggested that the blessing makes the cup the Lord's cup and the partakers drink as his guests. Since in the Old Testament the blood is equivalent to the life (Lev 17:11) and can be used to refer to the death of an individual (Lev 20:9), Paul can mean that by drinking the cup of the Lord, one receives the benefit of his death. This is not because of the color, taste, smell, or viscosity of the contents of the cup but because the cup has been dedicated to the Lord, who gives it to us.

At a Jewish feast the host broke the loaf of bread and passed pieces to all the guests to indicate that the meal had begun. Paul says that in the Christian observance this is *a partnership of the body of Christ*. As in the case of the wine, this has been understood to mean some identity with the flesh of Christ, whether actually or symbolically; and so the participant would gain his divine characteristics by a kind of hallowed "Christophagy." But again this passes by Paul's point: it is the breaking of the bread, which begins the supper, that constitutes the partnership of Christ's body.

The explanation of how this happens is offered in the remarks about the *one loaf,* which when shared constitutes the *one body* out of *the many* persons. The body of Christ is the people who are united in table fellowship with him. Since it is Christ's loaf, when people receive it, they are united into one body. (This "Christosomatosis" is developed in 12:12-27.)

When the Jewish festival meal, particularly Passover, is properly understood, it provides a perception of the way in which it closely united people into an organic unity where they felt each was a part of the others. To participate in the Lord's Supper, then, is to be guests of Christ and have table fellowship with him, and thus to accept the benefits of his death and to become one body which actualizes his presence.

This transaction is illustrated by the eating of the temple-sacrifices by the Israelites. Those who eat the sacrifices become "partners" of the altar. This does not mean, of course, that when the Jews partook of the sacrifices, those sacrifices were changed into the substance of the altar or of the God of the altar. The idea of the sacrifices seems to be that they were gifts of the people to God, who was pleased with the action and (by his command in the Torah) gave portions to the priests and the worshipers. Thus table fellowship was established with God; the participants were established as his people.

Interesting as this is for understanding the liturgical practice and theology of the early church, the point in Paul's argument has to do with food offered to idols. He clarifies his point that *an idol-offering* is not a sacrifice to a god. *An idol,* indeed, is nothing. The sacrifices to idols are offered to beings which he calls *demons.*

Restriction against partaking of both

Because of the nature of the demons and their relation to pagan idols Paul's view differs from that of the "intelligent people" of Corinth, who thought that idol-offerings made no difference. His understanding of these demons is complex. They seem to be beings more powerful than men, less powerful than God. This outlook is difficult for a generation which, for the first time in human history, has discarded belief in evil spirits. No one, however, can prove by reason and experience together the existence or nonexistence of some kind of extra-human, evil power; so no one can be absolutely sure about demon-worship, and hence Paul's views must be given open-minded consideration. He took the matter seriously and believed that the pervasive practice of people who express belief in demons by worship corresponds to the existence of super-terrestrial entities that do evil. This does not mean that the food offered to the demons changed into a demonic substance or represented demons. He is arguing that sacrifices to demons is evidence of yielding allegiance to them and entering into an unholy partnership with them. This partnership Christians must renounce and be partners only of God in Christ.

Drinking a cup dedicated to the Lord and at the same time (i.e. in the same temporal context) drinking a cup dedicated to demons must be unthinkable for Christians. *To share in the table* (i.e. by metonymy to share a meal) with the Lord and with demons is impossible for one who is aware of being united with Christ. The two unions are absolutely incompatible (the import of the dominical saying in Matt 6:24).

To venture into this complete incongruity is an affront to God. Paul uses language that recalls the allusions in vss. 1-10. The God who demanded exclusive worship from his ancient followers now requires the same of those who become constituted as Christ's body. The warning in vss. 11-12 is repeated in the final rhetorical question of this section.

CONSCIENCE AND FOOD OFFERED TO IDOLS (10:23-29)

When no question is raised

10 23 All things are permissible but not all things are advantageous. All things are permissible, but not all things build up. 24 Let no one seek his own interest but rather that of the other person. 25 Go on eating everything that is sold in the meat market, and ask no questions because of conscience — 26 for "the earth and that which fills it are the Lord's." 27 If anyone of the unbelievers invites you and you wish to accept, eat everything that is set before you and ask no questions because of conscience.

When another's conscience is concerned

28 But if anyone says to you, "This food is a temple-offering," stop eating because of that person who informed you and because of conscience — 29 I am not saying your own conscience but the other person's; for why is my freedom being judged by another conscience?

NOTES

10:23. The problems of the unity of this section (8:1 - 11:1) have been over-emphaszed; cf. Introduction, pp. 120-121. It seems that scholars frequently forget that Paul's letters are expressly not theological treatises. The structure of this section is fairly well knit together, and the chief problem of the exegete is really the perennial one of gaps in understanding caused by the author's assumptions of what his readers know. Hurd, *The Origin of 1 Corinthians*, 128-131, shows how this present passage (10:23 - 11:1) carefully summarizes the content of chs. 8 and 9.

This verse reproduces 6:12 with the omission of the first personal pronoun and the change of the final verb to one Paul has introduced at 8:1. Again, he may be citing a Corinthian slogan.

24. *the other person. heteros* in this sense occurs at 4:6 and 6:1.

25. *meat market.* There is an interesting literature on *makellon.* H. J. Cadbury identified an inscription that verifies the existence of such a market in first-century Corinth (cf. *JBL* 53 [1934], 134-141).

26. The quotation is from Ps 24:1[23:1, LXX].

27. *eat everything.* There were elaborate regulations restricting Jews in their social relationships with gentiles (cf. *Abodah Zarah, passim*).

Paul's openness regarding dietary restrictions raises again the question of the connection with the decrees of the council at Jerusalem (Acts 15:29; Introduction, pp. 63-65). There is no hint here of an apostolic decree involving food laws. This supports the idea that the instruction was issued for the direction of Peter and other Jerusalem leaders and was never given to Paul. The decree, of course, concerned not only idol-offerings but also kosher meat.

28. *temple-offering.* It is interesting that Paul does not use the term "idol-offering"; the gentile would certainly use the term that Paul uses here.

29. *judged by another conscience.* Paul's encounter with Cephas at Antioch (Gal 2:11-14) provides an instructive illustration. It might be argued that Paul did not have regard for Cephas' conscience in that encounter, but Paul evidently did not think the point involved danger to the weak conscience of another but rather his own freedom. The distinction was a nice one.

COMMENT

When no question is raised

Having discussed in some detail matters relevant to the quandary about idol-offerings, Paul now offers a summary and sets forth a practical plan for a Christian living in a pluralistic society. Everyday life could provide complicated situations for members of the Corinthian church. He recapitulates his earlier insistence that there is no divine prohibition against social practices per se (he probably has in mind certain areas of action; one may doubt that he means *all things* quite literally). Some things, however, are constructive and some are injurious; and since he immediately focuses upon the *interest of the other person,* he must have in mind the *build*ing *up* of a good Christian society. The rule is that one is to be completely unself-centered.

Paul counsels his readers not to be constantly raising scruples about food. His implication is clear that it is all right to eat idol-offerings if they are not identified as such. The food in itself has not been changed. It has received no property of the idol or demon, and eating it does not set up partnership with the demons it may represent. This partnership is set up when the food is eaten at a meal where the dedication to the idol is identified. The Psalmist has declared the proprietary control of the Lord over *the earth and that which fills it;* therefore all food belongs to God, and the right to eat it cannot be refused when it is sold merely as food. Thus there is no conflict between permission to eat food purchased *in the meat market* and the prohibition against eating food at a table which belongs by dedication to an idol or demon.

The same question may arise when a Christian is invited to eat at the home of an *unbeliever.* Paul extends the principle he has stated by affirming that it is quite permissible for a Christian to have table fellowship with non-Christian acquaintances (in 5:10 he has indicated how utterly impractical it is to try to avoid all association with the nonbelieving world around). In such a social situation he is to *ask no questions* about the food that is served.

When another's conscience is concerned

The situation is changed, however, if in this social situation information is volunteered that the meat has indeed been offered in the temple. Now the Christian must not eat. This abstention is to give witness to the informant that the Christian does not share belief in the god represented by the temple. This witness is directed to the conscience of the unbeliever, for the conscience of the Christian should not oppose eating this meat even if it was offered to an idol since it is here being presented in a private house. This seems to be an extension of the principle regarding the "weak brother" in ch. 8. Not only is the Christian to be concerned about the effect of his actions upon fellow believers who are not so theologically settled, but he is to consider how his actions will be understood by nonbelievers. If other persons' consciences will be offended, his way is clearly determined (cf. 8:13).

Paul is careful to make clear that the principle of Christian *freedom* is not to be jeopardized. A free Christian is not to be judged by the conscience of another person; he must not allow his own conscience to think that he is doing something evil by the mere act of eating the food. In order not to damage the other person's conscience, he will refrain from eating; but in his own mind he knows he has a right to eat this food as food—nothing has happened to it, it has not been changed, it has no particular power. He must not, however, let anyone think that he believes in idols; nor must he do anything to establish table fellowship with demons—nothing to him, but everlastingly fatal to the other person.

PAUL'S CHRISTIAN EXAMPLE (10:30-11:1)

10   30 If I share in grace, why am I being slandered because of that for which I give thanks? 31 So whether you are eating or drinking or doing anything, do all for God's glory. 32 Be inoffensive, both to Jews and Greeks and the church of God — 33 just as I also am trying to please all people in all ways as I seek not my own advantage but that of the many in order that they may be saved. 11   1 Be imitators of me as I also am of Christ.

NOTES

10:30 *If I share.* First-class condition, assumed to be true. Paul's position before God is not in question.

32. *Be inoffensive.* The verb *ginesthe* is linear imperative, which is difficult to translate; "continue to become" is awkward. The point is that Paul is diplomatic; he does not imply that they are now offensive but that they should develop a stance already taken. The adjective does not suggest a colorless character. The implication of not putting a stumbling block in another's way summarizes directions already set forth: 8:7-13, 9:19-22, 10:24,28-29a.

the church of God. The Corinthian church is so addressed (1:2; II Cor 1:1), but Paul uses the term flexibly. In 11:16, I Thess 2:14, and II Thess 4:1 the plural occurs; and in 15:9 and Gal 1:13 the whole Palestinian church is meant (cf. also 11:22).

33. *trying to please.* The conative overtone is inherent in the verb.

that they may be saved. Cf. 9:22.

11:1. The verse is clearly transitional but reflects primarily what has been discussed in the preceding section of the letter. 11:2 is also transitional but leads into the new section that occupies the rest of the chapter.

Be imitators. Cf. *supra*, 10:32. Paul's exhortation here is more modestly expressed than in 4:16 (the verbs are the same).

COMMENT

Paul's declaration of his *share in grace* is the clue to the understanding of how he is consistent through this whole discussion. "Grace" may mean the particular gift of God that makes all food suitable for mankind; or it may refer to the life with God that is based on his grace, the result of which is that one is not legitimately subject to the indictment of others for anything which one does out of thankfulness to God. The apostle's view of freedom had been attacked in Corinth, but his summary defense is in his relation to God. When he eats food, even though it may have been offered to demons, when he *gives thanks* to God for it, then the food is no basis for blame. No one has ground for condemnation, and there is nothing in his own conscience against eating the food that, whatever its past, is now offered with thanksgiving to God. Circumstances make the difference, and the key to circumstance for a Christian is *God's glory*. Indeed, this is a touchstone for all Christian action.

Paul summarizes his teaching also on the basis of human interaction. One is to consider other people's feelings, sensibilities, and beliefs so as not to cause them to stumble or to offend them unnecessarily. For the Christian church this had three dimensions, which are easily generalized for all churches: (a) *Jews,* those who have godly beliefs which are substantially different from those of the Christian church; (b) *Greeks,* pagans of whatever moral character and religious belief; (c) *the church of God,* where Paul found the instruction most difficult to realize.

He insists (rightly, as the foregoing chapters have shown) that his own life direction is oriented to the *advantage of the many*. He delineated his principle of adaptability in 9:22—*all things to all people*—which has as its ultimate goal that God may save his people. This is an *imitation of Christ*. Insofar as his readers find Paul true to this purpose, they are enjoined to use him as a pattern.

SCANDALS IN CHURCH SERVICES
(11:2-34)

HEADDRESS OF WOMEN AND ITS
SIGNIFICANCE (11:2-16)

11   2 I praise you because you remember me in all ways and hold fast the traditions as I delivered them to you. 3 But I want you to know that Christ is the head of every man, and the man is the head of the woman, and God is the head of Christ. 4 Whenever any man prays or prophesies with something on his head, he disgraces his head; 5 but whenever any woman prays or prophesies with an unveiled head, she disgraces her head; for this is one and the same as being shaved. 6 If a woman is not veiled, then let her be sheared; and if it is disgraceful for a woman to let herself be sheared or shaved, let her be veiled. 7 For a man ought not to have his head veiled since he is the image and glory of God; but the woman is the glory of the man. 8 Man, you see, is not from woman but woman from man; 9 for indeed man was not created for the sake of the woman but woman for the sake of the man. 10 Because of this, the woman ought to have authority over her head for the sake of the angels. 11 In any case, neither is woman without man nor man without woman in the Lord; 12 for just as the woman is from the man, so also the man is through the woman; but all things are from God. 13 Judge for yourselves: is it proper for a woman to pray to God unveiled? 14 Does not nature itself teach you that if a man wears long hair, it is a dishonor to him; 15 but if a woman wears long hair, it is a glory to her?—because her hair has been given for a covering. 16 Now if anyone seems to be contentious, we do not have such a custom, nor do the churches of God.

NOTES

This passage really interweaves two discussions, one general, one particular. In vss. 3, 8-9, 11-12 Paul clarifies the tradition about man and woman. In vss. 4-7, 10, 13-15 he applies this to worship by discussing head coverings when praying or prophesying. Verses 2 and 16 provide inclusive brackets with an apostolic imprimatur on *the traditions*. W. O. Walker, Jr., in *JBL* 94 (1975), 94-110, divides the passage into three pericopes; but he concludes that they are non-Pauline and have been woven together by a later editor. His arguments make too easy assumptions about the editorial process.

11:2. *I praise you*. Transitional. Certainly Paul has not praised them in the foregoing passage. Beginning with vs. 17 he advances a matter in which he finds no ground for praise. His transitions, however, bear only a formal relationship to the contexts; for the matter now introduced would hardly be presented unless there were irregularities at Corinth. Perhaps again it was a factional affair, and the word of praise will reassure those who have been conforming to apostolic *traditions* and put in a receptive frame of mind those whose practices are irregular.

you remember me. On the present or "durative" force of the perfect, cf. Robertson, *Grammar*, 895, and BDF, § 341.

traditions. The noun in this sense occurs in Pauline writing only here and at II Thess 2:15 and 3:6. The corresponding verb (*delivered*) occurs also at vs. 23 and at 15:3.

3. *I want you to know*. The relation of this to *the traditions* is tenuous at best. Paul is certainly adding to those traditions, but whether he implies that the addition is traditional is open to question, and what its actual relation to traditions may be is also moot.

the man . . . the woman. Throughout this passage it is difficult to decide whether *anēr* should be translated "man" or "husband" and even more particularly whether *gynē* should be translated "woman" or "wife." Certainly in the case of *anēr* some instances must be rendered "man." The whole passage, however, could be referring to conduct of a man and his wife; and "woman" would be "wife" in the critical occurrences and possibly in all instances. Cf. COMMENT. In order not to beg the question, which is in any case not provable, the translation here uses "man" and "woman" throughout.

4. *with something on his head*. The phrase is cryptic (literally, "having down from [the] head"). It is usually taken to imply a covering of some sort. Isaksson, *Marriage and Ministry in the New Temple*, takes this to mean "having long hair hanging down" (p. 166), bringing it into line with vs. 14.

disgraces his head. Isaksson argues that head coverings in worship were no disgrace for a Jew (cf. Exod 28:36-40; Ezek 44:18; Isa 6:2), but there seems to be nothing in the Old Testament that suggests a requirement for such a covering. The later development of tallith and yarmulke (scarf and skullcap) cannot be used as an argument for first-century usage since the line of evidence is discontinuous. The meaning here is affected by the understanding of "head." In vs. 3 the word has a figurative sense; in 4a it is literal. Ordinary procedure would call for the literal sense in 4b. Isaksson, however, takes the sense from vs. 3; and the man with *something on his head* (or, with long, unbound hair) *disgraces* Christ, who is his "head."

5. *whenever any woman prays or prophesies*. Paul's discussion of the relation of women to public worship is complex. The understanding of 14:29-37 will have to take account of this passage. In that passage "prophecy" is a form of oral communication in worship (="preaching"?); so the participation referred

to here must be more than silent prayers offered in the separated women's section of the synagogue-church.

with an unveiled head. The lengthy discussion in StB, III, 427-434, supports the idea that Paul has in view husband and wife in all this section. Among the Jews of the New Testament period a virgin or maiden was permitted to go about without a covering on her head or face; but when she became married, she was required to have a covering that bound up her hair and reached around her chin. Custom required that she must never go outside her house with an uncovered head. This was so shameful that her husband could use it as ground for divorce without return of the marriage dowry.

disgraces her head. Again the meaning of "head" must be questioned. Here the third clause must be taken into account.

the same as being shaved. If "head" is understood literally, the reference here is sometimes taken to be a mark of adultery or some mourning rite (cf. Weiss); but the evidence for this is weak (cf. Allo). Isaksson (*Marriage and Ministry,* 170) thinks that the allusion is to a Nazirite vow, which a married woman could not assume of her own volition without dishonoring her husband's authority (cf. also StB). *Her head,* then, is her husband as vs. 3 affirms. The way to avoid shame for her husband in the case of a wife praying or prophesying is for her to keep her wifely headdress covering intact.

6. Isaksson's arguments for the existence of Nazirite prophetesses in the early church is forced. He has argued that prophesying *with an unveiled head* (vs. 5) is an indication of assumption of Nazirite status to establish a traditional sanctity; but Paul's assertion that this is *the same as being shaved* (ibid.) would indicate the completion of a Nazirite vow and is intrinsically contradictory. Paul would then be requiring in vs. 6 that the vow be concluded before it is rightly undertaken. He would be arguing (vs. 5) that a woman ought not to pray or prophesy at all; and this is contrary to Isaksson's understanding of the situation and would destroy the obvious parallelism between vss. 4 and 5.

7. *image and glory of God . . . of the man.* Paul is apparently reasoning from Gen 1:27; but cf. COMMENT.

8. *woman from man.* Here the basis seems to be Gen 2:21-23. (Paul is not bothered by problems of E and J sources!) The myth of Aristophanes in Plato's *Symposium* 189-191 has some curious points of comparison but is surely not to be directly related to the apostle's thought here. Isaksson connects the phraseology with 12:15; so *einai ek* means "belongs to" (*Marriage and Ministry,* p. 176).

9. The reasoning again depends upon the Genesis account. This order of creation is stated bluntly in I Tim 2:13. It may be kept in mind that the context throughout assumes the norm of the marriage estate, and it is difficult to separate Paul's argument from this.

10. *Because of this.* The connective reaches back to vs. 7 whether or not the passage be divided as is done here. Verses 8 and 9 are "clarification of tradition" but related at this point to the matter of the veiling and the human image/glory. RSV places vss. 8-9 in parentheses.

authority over her head for the sake of the angels. StB prove conclusively that the angels would never have been thought of in contemporary Judaism as being subject to lust for a human female (III, 437). The traditions according to which spirit beings burned with passion for the daughters of humankind (cf. Gen 6:1-4) always related to evil spirits or fallen angels. M. D. Hooker (*NTS* 10 [1963/64], 410-416) relates *exousia* to the preceding verses: man reflects God's glory and so stands uncovered before him; but woman reflects man's glory and so must stand covered before God to conceal man's glory. The *authority on her head* (Miss Hooker's translation) is then that she can reflect God's glory in worship. The angels, who were present at creation, are the guardians of order in nature and so are concerned with proper respect for God in worship. On angels as observers of the human scene, cf. 4:9. (Miss Hooker slyly suggests that Paul may have had a practical interest: unveiled women might distract precisely men in Corinthian worship.)

There is no other occurrence of *exousia* with *epi* and the genitive in Paul. Indeed, the only such usage in the New Testament is in Revelation, where it occurs at 2:26, 11:6, and 14:18 plus several instances with the accusative without apparent difference in meaning. Since *exousia* in the New Testament usually indicates some power or right exercised, *authority over* seems to be the proper translation. (On the whole verse cf. the extensive literature cited in AGB, 278, and the notes of Foerster in *TDNT*, II, 573-574.)

11. *In any case.* The conjunctive adverb *plēn* interrupts the flow of the argument to make a summary statement. Again RSV places parentheses around vss. 11-12, a questionable decision.

12. *from the man . . . through the woman.* The alternation of prepositions is deliberate, *ek* and *dia*. Presumably, Paul refers to the order of creation in the first instance, the order of nature in the second.

14. *Does not . . . ?* An unusual use of *oude*. It is fairly certain that it introduces a question expecting affirmative answer; so the writer must be thinking of *ou* plus *de*.

nature. In the New Testament practically a Pauline word; most of the occurrences are in Romans.

if a man. On the anticipatory subject before its clause cf. BDF, § 466(1).

wears long hair. The verb and noun occur in the New Testament only in this sentence.

a dishonor. Walker, *JBL* 94 (1975), 94-110, thinks that the variation from "disgrace" in vss. 4-6 indicates a different source-pericope; but certainly Paul's flexibility in the use of vocabulary has been amply demonstrated. The recurrence of *glory* in vs. 7 then provides Walker with a clue for association of the two pericopes editorially—a curiously easy kind of criticism.

15. *covering.* The only other occurrence of the word in the New Testament is in the quotation from Ps 102:27 in Heb 1:12, where it means "garment."

16. The verse actually covers the whole passage and has in mind the particular problem of the local church; but since it establishes a certain attitude to the tradition, it is placed here in that context.

such a custom can refer either to the practices rejected in the passage or to being *contentious*, possibly to both, the latter being an extension of the former.

COMMENT

This is one of several passages in the literature attributed to Paul that have raised the ire of some women, particularly in the "Women's Liberation" movement. A considerable literature has been developing; cf. one such list in "I Corinthians 11:2-16 and Paul's Views Regarding Women," by W. O. Walker, Jr. (*JBL* 94 [1975], 94). The lingering influence of this passage may be seen in the custom of women wearing hats in church (expected until recent times), a practice enforced even for tourists in Saint Peter's, Rome. When women first began to "bob" their hair earlier in this century, there was a wave of hostility against them in conservative circles. In the Middle Ages this passage was employed to justify the idea that women belonged in a category between animals and men, and that while they had souls, they did not have the higher powers of reason, ethical insight, and theological knowledge that men have. This conception led to the denial of educational rights to women and the tacit acceptance of a kind of inferior status for women.

At Corinth some women were assuming leadership roles, and Paul seems to have had no hesitation about working with them. Elsewhere there appears to have been no problem (e.g. Philippi, Colossae/Laodicea), but in Corinth there was some difficulty. Exactly what its nature was is impossible to determine, nor can it be certain how Paul became involved in the problem. His praise of the Corinthians includes a reference to *the traditions;* so perhaps the matter was related to the instruction of practices with Jewish background in a church where pagan influence was so persistent. The immediate difficulty seems to have arisen in connection with public worship, but Paul is concerned to settle the issue on theological grounds.

Accordingly, he addresses himself to the relation between men and women as his understanding of his religious tradition determines it. His fundamental proposition is that there is a line of spiritual subordination. At the top is *God,* who *is the head of Christ. Christ is the head of every man, and the man is the head of the woman.* With the reservations already suggested in ch. 7, Paul considers the married estate normal; so the husband-wife dimension is never far from the surface in the passage, and Paul considers the husband the head in the family relationship if the Colossians-Ephesians tradition be regarded as at all Pauline. He does not develop the implication here, but the identity relationship between Christ and God as the paradigm for the husband-wife relationship is spelled out in Eph 5:22-33.

The basis of Paul's tradition seems to be the Genesis creation stories.

His reading of that material, however, is somewhat selective. He relies heavily upon an interpretation of the J story in Gen 2:21-23, from which he concludes that the original order of creation makes woman's creation secondary to that of man. It is tempting to manipulate the meaning of the vocabulary in the Hebrew: the "man" who was put to sleep was *'ādām;* but when the man awoke, the wordplay on *'īsh,* "male," is put in his mouth. Paul would probably not object to such a treatment of the text. The Eden story, however, is directed toward a marriage state; so it is probable that this relationship underlies this whole passage.

It is most important to note that, whatever strictures he may lay upon worship praxis, Paul affirms an overriding principle of equality. This is a unique insight of his religion, for it is *in the Lord* and because *all things are from God.* This may be considered an extension of "uxorial sanctification," which Paul proposed in 7:12-16. Even though creation tradition places man as head of woman, the mutuality of their relationship is evident in that *the man is through,* i.e. is borne by, *the woman.* Since it is God who gives *all things* unity, his headship is the ultimate paradigm for the human relationship. It would seem that Eph 5:22-33 spells out what is sketched here.

The final clarification of custom is that matters of relation between the sexes and their effect upon worship procedures are not to produce contention; neither Paul nor *the churches of God* countenance this. This seems to be another example of the apostle's firm opposition to divisiveness in the church.

There is no question that women were engaging in prayer and prophecy in public worship in Corinth. It could be concluded from the premise that the wife has her husband as her head that she should not pray or prophesy publicly but should address God through her husband, but Paul does not draw this conclusion. The specific problem that elicits the theological analysis of the relationship between men and women has to do with how women should be attired and particularly how they should wear their hair when taking part in worship leadership. Paul is trying to ensure that the appearance of women in the church concurs with acceptable standards of decency and order, particularly as this is understood from the traditions he recognizes.

It is probable that Paul has in mind married women throughout, and application of his regulations to single women would have to be made with some wresting of detail. It is possible that he is contrasting Jewish-oriented customs with pagan, but all the details are more appropriate if viewed in the light of rabbinic traditions. The heart of his argument seems to be that just as the man stands before God uncovered because of his spiritual subordination to Christ, so the woman should stand veiled because of her spiritual subordination to her husband. Probably her veiling is an indication of her married state, which reflects her relationship to her husband; and this ought not to be put aside for any reason (e.g. a Nazirite vow) because it would be a reflection upon her husband and therefore a breach of the order of things, both spiritual and natural. If the woman rejects this order by praying or prophesying *with an unveiled head,* Paul suggests that she be subjected literally to what she has presented spiritually: *let her be sheared,* or even *shaved.*

His reasoning is based upon the E creation story in Gen 1:26-27, but his reading of the scripture is unfortunately conditioned by the male orientation of his thought-world, *'ādām* means "mankind," but the maleness of the God traditions show clearly in the clause, "in the image of God he created him." When the text continues, "male and female he created them," Paul must have understood this in terms of the J story. It has remained for a more critical age to apply this to the basic equality of the sexes. Probably Paul would have acquiesced in this understanding, but it would have altered his reasoning somewhat. The "image of God" language is from the story in Genesis 1; Genesis 2 says nothing about this. There is no statement in either story that *the woman is the glory of the man;* presumably this is an inference from combining the image language with the rib story. If Paul had not already had traditional beliefs about the relationship, it is doubtful that he would have reached the conclusions he did from the Genesis texts.

A woman who participates in Corinthian worship leadership *ought* to exercise her freedom responsibly. Guardian angels watch over the churches (an idea also reflected in Rev 1:20), and they are concerned about spiritual and natural order. So the wife ought to lead in public worship in such a way (with such traditional decorum) that she will not bring disgrace or dishonor to her husband. Presumably the principle would apply to unmarried women, *mutatis mutandis.*

Paul has expressed his apostolic interpretation of the situation, but he would like the Corinthians to come to the same conclusions themselves. He argues that *nature itself* demonstrates the difference between the sexes with respect to length of hair. His reference must be to common custom, for there is no ànalogy in nature itself that bears out the argument. (Perhaps the reference to *custom* in vs. 16 is an indication of his intent here.) In any case, his analogy is strained. The argument in 12:22-25 seems to suggest that another conclusion might be drawn: since nature gives the woman *long hair for a covering,* additional covering would be inappropriate! But his last word, already considered, is that these matters must not lead *anyone to be contentious;* custom in the churches ought to prevail.

FAULTS AT THE LORD'S SUPPER (11:17-34)

Divisions existing at the Supper

11   17 When I give this instruction, I do not praise you because you assemble not for the better but for the worse. 18 First of all, I keep hearing that when you assemble in church, there are divisions among you; and in part I believe it. 19 For indeed it is necessary that there be factions among you in order that those who are approved may become known among you. 20 So when you assemble together, it is not to eat the Lord's Supper; 21 for each one takes his own supper ahead of time and eats, so that one person is hungry and another is drunk. 22 Do you not have houses for eating and drinking? Or do you despise the church of God and humiliate those who do not have anything? What am I to say to you? Shall I praise you? In this I do not praise you.

The received tradition of the institution of the Supper

23 For I received from the Lord what I also delivered to you, that the Lord Jesus, on the night in which he was being betrayed, took bread, 24 gave thanks, broke it, and said: "This is my body for you; you are doing this for my remembrance." 25 Also in the same way he took the cup after eating supper and said: "This cup is the new covenant by my blood; you are doing this, as often as you drink it, for my remembrance." 26 For as often as you eat this bread and drink the cup, you are announcing the death of the Lord until he comes.

Judgment from unworthy participation in the Supper

27 So whoever eats the bread or drinks the cup of the Lord in an unworthy manner will be guilty of the body and the blood of the Lord. 28 Let a person examine himself, and thus let him eat from the bread and drink from the cup. 29 For the one who eats and drinks is eating and drinking judgment upon himself if he does not discriminate the body. 30 On account of this many among you are weak and sickly, and a considerable number are dying. 31 Now if we discriminated ourselves, we would not be judged; 32 but when we are being judged, we are being disciplined by the Lord in order that we may not be condemned along with the world.

Summary instruction

33 So, my brothers, when you assemble to eat, wait for one another. 34 If anyone is hungry, let him eat at home in order that you may not be assembling to be judged. I will put in order the rest of the matters when I come.

NOTES

11:17. *this instruction.* The verse is transitional, but the reference is to what follows.

I do not praise. Cf. vs. 2. There *hold*ing *fast the traditions* is the basis of praise; here failure to keep a tradition (vs. 23) is the basis of censure.

18. *First of all.* Paul does not enumerate a list of complaints; this immediate matter is of primary importance.

in church. The anarthrous noun must bear a meaning similar to our idiom; Zerwick distinguishes this usage as adverbial (§ 182); cf. Robertson, *Grammar,* 759, 791.

in part. Can be construed as adverbial or accusative of extent (cf. Robertson, *Grammar,* 487 and *Word Pictures,* IV, 163). In 13:9 *ek merous* occurs with much the same meaning.

19. *factions.* These *haireseis* are the outward manifestations of the *schismata* of the previous verse. In Gal 5:20 *haireseis* are "works of the flesh." In Acts the word is used of Jewish "sects" (5:17, 15:5, 26:5) and also of the Christian "way" (24:5,14, 28:22).

those who are approved. The matter is put a different way in 3:13, and cf. Paul's figure in 9:27. The standard of approval is divine.

20. *together.* The phrase *epi to auto* has an adverbial force and is probably not to be understood in a locative sense. This is clear in 7:5, but 14:23 and Acts 1:15 allow the locative possibility. Robertson and Plummer point to "the contrast between the external union and the internal dissension."

it is not to eat. Héring notes that the simple purpose idea is "inadmissible." The Corinthians intended to be eating *the Lord's Supper;* Paul's complaint is that their malpractice renders what they do something other than their intention.

Lord's (kyriakon). The adjective is formed from the title *kyrios,* which is used by the LXX for *YHWH* and applied to Jesus as well as God in the New Testament. The word has a Hellenistic history (cf. Deissmann, *Light from the Ancient East,* 358) where it means "imperial." Its Christian cultic use must have been early. The other occurrence in the New Testament is Rev 1:10, where it refers to the Christian's worship-day.

22. *Do you not . . . ?* The double negative might be rendered, "It isn't that you don't have . . . , is it?"

In this may be construed with the preceding question (so *TR, RSV*, et al.).

23. *the night in which he was being betrayed.* The phrase may be significant for understanding the events leading up to Jesus' death; cf. Walther, "The Chronology of Passion Week," *JBL* 77 (1958), 120, and the references there.

bread, or "a loaf"; cf. 10:16.

24. *gave thanks.* In the customary Jewish meals the first act was thanksgiving over the bread, which was broken by the host and distributed to the guests. *berākōt* include "thanksgivings"; cf. Danby, Mishnah, *Berakoth* 1:1n; also §§ 6-7, especially 6.5.

This is my body. Out of an immense literature cf. Markus Barth, *Das Abendmahl,* Theologische Studien, Heft 18; O. Cullmann and F.-J. Leenhardt, *Essays on the Lord's Supper* (London, 1958); and J. Jeremias, *The Eucharistic Words of Jesus* (New York, 1966). And cf. COMMENT.

for you. The formulary was early accommodated to the liturgical action. From *broke it* the participle "broken" was added (so the Byzantine text, the Lectionaries, and *TR*). From the Lukan tradition (22:19) came the addition "given." Perhaps the most telling of all is the addition "broken in (small) pieces" in the original text of Codex Bezae. The inappropriateness of attributing brokenness to Jesus' body may be inferred from John 19:31-36. Since different words for breaking are used there (note especially the composite quotation from Exodus, Numbers, and Psalms), the liturgical or cultic influence on the variant readings seems to be underlined.

you are doing this. poieite can, of course, be either imperative or indicative. It has almost universally been taken as a command; cf. the Vulgate *facite.* The aspect of the verb is linear, however, which suggests a repetition of the act; and that in turn suggests cultic influence. In the Synoptic records the linear "imperative" occurs only in the Lukan interpolation, 22:19-20. The other commands (*labete* in Mark 14:22; Matt 26:26; Luke 22:17; and *phagete* in Matt 26:26) relate to the immediate action and are aorist. It seems better, then, to take *poieite* as an interpretive instruction than as a command for future repetition. Verse 26, which is patently the apostle's addition to the tradition, gives the justification for the church to make this a halakic prescript. (There seems to be no clue in a conjectural Semitic original that would affect this decision.)

for my remembrance. Both this phrase and the verb in the clause are affected as to meaning by the interpretation of *this;* cf. COMMENT. (For the more traditional interpretation, and especially regarding *my remembrance,* cf. the major treatment in Jeremias, *The Eucharistic Words of Jesus,* 218-255; also J. J. Petuchowski, "'Do This in Remembrance of Me' (1 Cor 11:24)," *JBL* 76 (1957), 293-298; S. K. Finlayson, "1 Corinthians xi.25," *ExpT* 71 (1959/60), 243; H. Kosmala, "'Das tut zu meinem Gedächtnis'," *NovT* 4 (1960), 81-94.

25. *by my blood.* The preposition *en* acquires extensive instrumental significance in the New Testament (cf. BDF, § 195) modeled on Hebrew *b.* In this context the *new covenant* is understood to have been ratified *by* the blood of Christ, which means by his death.

26. *you are announcing.* Again, the verb can be indicative or imperative. It seems probable that *gar* introduces a statement; so the verb is descriptive rather than prescriptive.

27. *cup of the Lord.* It is impossible from the text to decide whether Paul intends *tou kyriou* to go with both *arton* and *potērion.* "Cup of the Lord" occurs in 10:21, but "bread of the Lord" does not occur at all. This suggests that *tou kyriou* in the main clause is to be construed only with *haimatos* and not with *sōmatos.*

28. *examine.* The same root as "approved" in vs. 19; so "check against a standard of approval."

29. The Byzantine text adds "unworthily" after *and drinks* and "of the Lord" after *body,* but neither manuscript nor transcriptional probabilities support these. *if he does not discriminate* obviates "unworthily"; on *body* cf. COMMENT. (It is of questionable significance, but the phrase "body of the Lord" never occurs in the New Testament unless Luke 24:3 be counted.)

30. *On account of this* refers loosely to the preceding three verses and specifically to the failure to *discriminate the body.* The rest of the verse elaborates upon *judgment.*

a considerable number are dying. Barrett suggests possible connections between this and the demons (10:20-22) and/or between this and the misfortune of dying before the parousia (cf. I Thess 4:13-18). Conzelmann warns (p. 203, n. 115) against reversing the sequence and making a principle from it. What is happening in Corinth does not mean that all sickness and death are related to impropriety connected with the Lord's Supper. Since Paul nowhere else elaborates upon this experience sequence (especially in the Thessalonian correspondence), it is best to read it as a part of the total Corinthian problem.

31. *if we discriminated ourselves.* It appears somewhat awkward to maintain the same translation for the verb as that used in vs. 29 (cf. Barrett, who changes to "examine"), but the significance is really the same in each context. One is to subject *the body/ourselves* to such thoroughgoing (*dia-*) judgment (*-krinein*) that the proper significance of the object(s) of scrutiny will be apparent. The condition is present contrary to fact.

32. *condemned.* The wordplay in *katakrinein* is not apparent in translation.

33. *wait for one another.* The simple, practical way the Corinthians can correct the situation is to manifest community in taking food together.

34. *to be judged.* Literally, "unto judgment"; it is clear that it is the Corinthians who are in danger of judgment.

the rest of the matters. Paul seems to have addressed himself to all the problems he has raised about the Lord's Supper. Since we have no way of knowing what other *matters* in this connection have been communicated from Corinth, the meaning of this phrase remains indefinite.

COMMENT

No subject has been more controversial in the church than the meaning of the Lord's Supper. Not only were there deep differences in understanding between Roman Catholic and Reformation doctrines on this subject, but dispute about the precise meaning produced lasting divisions among Luther, Calvin, and Zwingli. Arguments about the metaphysical nature of Christ's body and universal presence have been virulent down to the present day.

Modern efforts toward formulating an ecumenical theology have made slow progress on the question of "transsubstantiation, transsignification, or virtualism."* The source of the disputes is in the idea that Jesus meant to provide a material means for physical or metaphysical consumption of his body—that he could miraculously supply in the sacrament a homeopathic quantum which would convey the full power of a union with his being. So the sacramental elements came to be subject to a special veneration because of their numinous power. The idea has been persistent, even when Christians do not agree on the definition of the relationship between the elements and Christ, since they are united in the conviction that the connection is real and special (note, for example, the treatment by Robertson and Plummer, 248-249).

Unity in the church is likely to remain out of reach as long as there is no consensus in this matter. The taboo view of the elements demands sacred officials to handle them, and the salvation of the recipient is in jeopardy if they are improperly received. This, then, involves discipline. So what should be the very sign and seal of the unity of the church becomes a perpetual cause of its disruption.

Thus the problem in the Corinthian church regarding the Lord's Supper is a critical one for the church in all ages. If (as it would appear) the mistake of the Corinthians was a gentile misinterpretation of essentially Jewish language and the controversies of the later church have been founded on a faulty translation of the first-generation Christian ideas rooted in Jewish social and religious experience, then Paul's explanation of the Lord's Supper furnishes no justification for the complicated eucharistic theologies that were developed.

Divisions existing at the Supper

Traditional interpretations of I Corinthians 11 have been wrong in many particulars because they have not been read with the Jewish practice of the common meal in view. Paul's *instruction* begins with his chagrin, not that the Corinthians are profaning a holy rite, but that they are fragmenting a holy society. In the first four chapters of the epistle he demonstrated how seriously he regards schisms. With apparent resignation he accepts the inevitability of *factions* as a means of testing, but in no way does he approve the division that results from their practice in the celebration of the Lord's Supper.

---

* Cf. *The Common Catechism: A Book of Christian Faith* (New York, 1975), in which "The Sacraments" are treated in Part Five, "Questions in Dispute between the Churches."

What is happening, he says, is that their assembling together is *not to eat the Lord's Supper* but to eat their own. The accepted practice was to bring separate meals to the common place, but they were starting to eat before others arrived so that there was no common supper and no sharing. Since some of the members were very poor, they did not have enough to eat and were hungry after supper while the prosperous were sated, some beyond propriety. It is not the vicious quality of gluttony and drunkenness that occupies Paul's attention at this point but the selfish indifference of each person or family to the needs and situation of the deprived and poor. There is no indication that he is concerned because they have not introduced the meal by a suitable liturgy. They have rushed into the meal upon private impulse and have drunk their own supplies of wine to the point of intoxication; and while Paul introduces the regulatory role of tradition in the next section, his introductory remonstrance has to do with the church's indifference to the communal significance of what they are doing. Those with vigorous appetites and the means to satisfy them without the discipline of restraint imposed by the community setting should anticipate their incontinence by eating and drinking somewhat before they come to church.

To dine alone at church means to decline to join with the church in this great expression of common, Christian, social life; and it therefore manifests contempt for the whole assembly. Some members would be unable to come to the meeting place early because as slaves they could not leave their masters' houses, and the free members who refuse to wait for them really shame them because their late arrival keeps them from full participation in the common life of the church. Paul recoils from this drastic abuse: they *despise the church* by making impossible a communal meal of the whole church. This is the situation which prompts him to cite the traditional origin of the supper practice.

The received tradition of the institution of the Supper

The tradition, which Paul *received from the Lord,* is recalled to show that the present abuses result from failing to continue the Master's practice. The essential agreement with the Synoptic records is evidence that the apostle's claim to dominical continuity is well founded, but it does not prejudice the interpretation of the tradition. Jesus *gave thanks,* then *broke bread, and said, "This is my body for you."* All the church should be together to participate in the thanksgiving and to receive the bread which is broken for the whole company. Since every Jewish meal began by breaking bread, the whole meal is designated by the breaking of the bread. The thanksgiving is meant for the whole meal which followed. Thus the bread as such has no greater importance than it has as the first part of the meal to be distributed. It may be suggested initially, therefore, that identification of Christ with the food at the supper should probably not be confined to the bread if any such identification is to be made. This brings into question at the outset whether the passage can be interpreted to mean that the eating of the bread at the supper is actually a receiving of the body of Christ.

Jesus' words, *This is my body for you*, have been exhaustively analyzed from earliest times. The greatest stress has been laid on the verb *is* with a great amount of attention also upon *body*. It has been disputed whether *is* should be interpreted "is like," "represents," "symbolizes," "stands for," "conveys," or "means the same as"; and many theologians have insisted that it means "is identical with," "is the same thing as," or "has the same substance as." It is remarkable that little attention has been given to the referent of *this* (Conzelmann, for example, does not discuss it). It has been almost unanimously agreed that *this* refers to *bread;* so the sentence is understood to read, "This bread is my body." It is not surprising, therefore, that *discriminate the body* in vs. 29 came to refer to recognizing that the bread is not mere bread but is in some sense the presence and actual body of Christ; and this supports the liturgical and ecclesiastical regulations that developed about this understanding.

The neuter demonstrative *this* occurs also in the second part of the quotation: *you are doing this for my remembrance*. Because of the structure of the clauses *this* can hardly be construed by a single word or phrase of identity. It is curious, however, that it should occur twice where it is not precisely clear what the referent is in either case; so the sense of both clauses must carefully fit together. The word for *do* (*poiein*) is very common in both the Greek Old and New Testaments. In the Old Testament it translates two words (*'āśāh* and *'ābad*) that are often used with various words for feast or meal (Gen 26:30; Exod 12:47,48, 13:5, 23:16, 34:22; Deut 16:13; II Kings 23:21; Job 1:4; Dan 5:1; etc.); and in the New Testament it is used in similar contexts (Mark 6:21; Luke 14:12,16; John 12:2; etc.). In the few instances in which the verb is used with "bread" in the Old Testament it has to do with baking or preparing. The sense here, then, may be connected with a meal or feast. The eating of meals as memorial observances was common among the Jews: Passover and Purim are examples enough. So *this* may be referred to the observance of the supper, and the action of the distribution of bread was the beginning of this meal as it was of common Jewish meals. The meal is participated in by all the assembled company as an appropriate recollection of Jesus Christ.

The reference of *this* to the eating of the meal together is grammatically possible, but the neuter gender cannot be used conversely to "prove" the reference. A common explanation for the neuter is that although *this* refers to *bread,* which is masculine, it has been assimilated to *body,* which is neuter. (The possibility that *bread* may be referred to by a neuter demonstrative because it is an object seems tenuous.) There is no clear case, however, elsewhere in Paul's writings in which he uses *touto* to refer to a masculine noun outside the immediate clause; he regularly uses *touto* to refer to a clause, phrase, implied idea, or, of course, a neuter noun. (Two instructive uses are in Rom 13:11, where *touto* does refer to a masculine noun but is in close apposition, and Philip 1:22, where *touto* refers to an infinitive phrase and is not assimilated to the masculine noun in the predicate. On the other hand, the uses of *hautē* in I Cor 9:3 and II Cor 1:12 suggest assimilation; but the usages of *touto* are too independent to validate a comparison.) This usual general reference of *touto* suggests that in both instances in 11:24 it has to do with the circumstance just described, that is, the dedication of the meal, which in turn draws the disciples together into a table fellowship. This somehow is *for you* the body of Christ, and it is effective for his *remembrance.* Since the festival celebration includes action and idea, the notion is excluded that any particle of food is the body of Christ. (If Paul had wanted to convey that idea, his regular usage would have been to write, "This bread is my body"; cf. *this bread* in vs. 26, where reference to the *body* is pointedly missing.)

It is not possible to come to any helpful conclusion about the nature of the meal from the use of the word *deipnos* for "supper." The word usually referred to a late afternoon meal (whence the appropriateness of the English "supper"). In the Bible it is never used to mean merely an act of eating: it refers to a meal, and its appropriateness for a festal meal is ambiguous. The more common way of speaking of a meal in the New Testament is by the expression "eat bread" (or "break bread"), metonymy for a whole meal (Matt 15:2; Mark 3:20; Luke 14:1; Acts 2:46; II Cor 3:8; II Thess 3:12; etc.).

Paul, then, is not concentrating on the thought of bread as distinct from the rest of the meal; but *bread* is discriminated from *the cup* that is to be drunk. In the Jewish meal the cup had a special significance because it was received with a thanksgiving separate from that offered with the bread that instituted the meal. The latter was thanksgiving for the whole meal; the thanksgiving over the cup, coming at the end of the meal, tied the whole together.

The corporate significance of the meal has already been introduced at 10:16 (cf. *supra,* pp. 250-253). The term "body" was applicable to the Passover societies that were formed for the festival; the group joining in the meal became a new kind of entity with such a close binding connection that all of the persons are members of each other (an idea which Paul develops in 12:12-26). This idea grips his mind, for he elsewhere calls the church the body of Christ (Rom 12:5; I Cor 12:13,27; Eph 1:22-23, 4:4,12,16; Col 1:18, 2:17, 3:15). He thought of the body of Christ as present, active, and purified for his manifestation to the world after he was no longer present in the flesh. The body in which he is now present is the body of believers. Paul regularly refers to the physical, historical existence of Jesus Christ on earth by the term "flesh" (*sarx;* cf. Rom 1:3, 9:5; II Cor 5:16; Col 1:22; etc. The only possible exception is Rom 7:4, and the intent there is possibly a double meaning.) *Body,* then, in this passage may be understood to refer to the church, here recognized in its chief act of common worship, the Lord's Supper.

Paul's regular contrast to "flesh" is "blood" (I Cor 15:50; Gal 1:16; etc.). It is significant, then, that here the contrast is between *body* and *cup.* (In this respect Paul makes a customary Greek distinction: "blood" corresponds to "flesh," which is living tissue, whereas "body" means the entire organism.) *The cup* indicates the means by which believers accept *the new covenant* that is inaugurated by the death of Christ. *Blood* in this context represents Christ's death (cf. Rom 3:25; Col 1:20; etc.; this is in keeping with the Old Testament idea in Lev 17:11,14). So *the cup* refers to the sacrificial destiny of Christ, which brought about a new covenant (cf. cupwords attributed to Jesus: Matt 20:22; Mark 14:36; John 18:11), and one who drinks the cup receives the destiny made possible by the new covenant. Thus the passage indicates that the Supper of the Lord constitutes a body of believers who receive the meal as his followers and who receive the cup as indication of conscious participation in the benefits of the new covenant.

It is not difficult to see how Paul's summary statement in vs. 26 contributed to the cultic-sacramental understanding of the bread and wine: *as often as* easily becomes a rite. The conditional sentences of vss. 24 and 26 are parallel, however; and if the word in 25 refers to the context of the meal, so should 26. The action for Christ's *remembrance* is extended to *announcing the death of the Lord until he comes,* thus specifying the meaning of *the cup* and placing the *remembrance* in the ongoing worship and life of the church. The Passover setting is not to the fore at this point, but Paul is rather emphasizing how each common meal is to become a recollection and proclamation of the gospel.

Judgment from unworthy participation in the Supper

The traditional words of institution are recited as supporting evidence for Paul's reaction against the behavior of the Corinthians at their common suppers. Verse 27, then, resumes the main discussion (*So*); and the eating and drinking *in an unworthy manner* refer to the mistreatment of persons present and not to misinterpretation in liturgical procedures. The indictment concerns injuring the body of Christ by breaking up the unity of the partnership (cf. 10:16-17); and the specific instance is the insult against the poor (11:21-22), which is in fact directed against the church. The erring persons do not accept *the new covenant* (vs. 25), which was brought about by the death (*blood*) of Christ; and thus the guilt is against the church and the Christ who died.

Accordingly, self-examination is enjoined in order to avert judgment that may be incurred by *eating and drinking* with an undiscriminating attitude. If *the body* means the people of the church celebrating the supper together, judgment comes because they do not discriminate the divine nature of this fellowship and are guilty of splitting it apart and mistreating its humbler members.

There is a parallel connection between vss. 29 and 31. There is no reason to differentiate the judgment in the two verses; so the objects of discrimination are evidently the same—*the body* and *ourselves.* Thus, the *body* of the Lord equals ourselves, in this context distinguished by the common participation in eating his supper. Failure to *discriminate* his *body* is the same as failure to *discriminate ourselves,* and this means failure to recognize that people together in the church constitute the very presence of Christ and are to be treated appropriately.

The identity of the church with the body of Christ leads Paul to attribute physical problems of the Christians to the violation of this body. This violation hampers and restricts the redemptive and healing nature of the fellowship wherein the poor are fed, the lonely are befriended, the sick are visited, the grieving are comforted, and sinners are forgiven. Such a redemptive fellowship can produce both spiritual and physical health while the breaking of the fellowship may cause the converse. So serious is this situation in Corinth that Paul posits a connection between it and the death rate there—a relationship that is difficult to interpret except in very general terms.

The judgment is of the nature of *discipline,* not of final condemnation. Condemnation has been removed by the death of Christ, but selfish and sinful perversion of the supper produces damaging results that may serve as corrective influence toward repentance. (Perhaps 5:5 is an extreme example.)

Summary instruction

The particular nature of the whole discussion and the emphasis upon the divisive propensity of the Corinthians is reiterated by the concluding sentences. To *wait for one another* is an evidence of discriminating *the body,* of recognizing that in the common partaking of the supper all the people are assembled as members of Christ's body. Christians are not to allow their selfish appetites to endanger respect for the holy people who are participating in the new humanity. Other *matters* could await a personal visit from Paul; this matter is so urgent that it should be *put in order* at once.

As postscript it may be noted that failure to follow Paul's principal concern in this passage and a false emphasis derived from misinterpretation of its details has produced in the history of the Christian church precisely the fault against which the apostle wrote to the Corinthians.

THIRD QUANDARY:
CONCERNING SPIRITUAL GIFTS
(12:1-14:40)

THE SPIRIT OF GOD AND SPIRITUAL GIFTS
(12:1-3)

12 1 Now with reference to the spiritual gifts, brothers, I do not want you to be ignorant. 2 You know that, when you were pagans, you were led off to the dumb idols whenever you were being led. 3 On this account I am informing you that no one says, "Jesus be damned," when he is speaking by God's Spirit; and no one can say, "Jesus is Lord," except by the Holy Spirit.

NOTES

12:1. *Now with reference to.* Cf. 7:1, 8:1, 16:1.

the spiritual gifts. It is possible that the phrase *tōn pneumatikōn* refers to "persons" rather than "gifts." The discussion that follows is concerned with persons as much as the gifts they receive. The whole section (vss. 12-14), however, deals more specifically with gifts that are distributed to different persons.

2. The verse as it stands in the UBS text has several difficulties that cannot be resolved with final assurance. The combination *hoti hote* is awkward, for *hoti* seems to have no verb unless *ēte* be repeated with *apagomenoi*. *hos an* presents the other principal problem. The translation given here is an attempt to render the text without change except for the repetition of *ēte* understood. Héring, 123-124, lists the theoretically possible solutions.

You know that. The frequent occurrence of *oidate hoti* in I Corinthians is against emendation by elimination of *hoti*.

pagans. ethnē is usually "gentiles," of course; but that translation can be maintained here only by assuming that Paul is thinking of the Corinthians now as adopted Jews, the new Israel. That is quite possible, but the association with idols suggests the present translation. Cf. K. L. Schmidt, *TDNT*, II, 371.

led off to the dumb idols. The figure is that of animals driven to sacrifice. On Paul's traditional view of idols combined with demonic associations, cf. 10:19-21. (On the gender according to sense, cf. Robertson, *Grammar*, 407, 412.)

whenever you were being led. Robertson (*Grammar,* 974) sees this usage as indicating repetition with temporal force (=*hotan*); cf. also BDF, § 367. The idea is that the religious impulses of pagans all lead only to idolatry.

3. *"Jesus be damned"* . . . *"Jesus is Lord."* This verse has been the subject of much writing and many interpretations. Weiss, 294-297, suggests that the Corinthians raised the question because Christians in a state of spiritual ecstasy, presumably caused by the Holy Spirit, had cursed Jesus. The obvious conflict between Spirit guidance and common Christian faith posed for them the problem. Paul resolves the matter by denying that such a curse can be Spirit led. Weiss cites ancient authorities that he claims for this interpretation.

Schmithals (*Gnosticism in Corinth,* 124-130) argues that the curse was a catchword of certain gnostics who separated Christ from Jesus in a kind of docetic pattern and so could consider Jesus insignificant. This view did exist later, but there is no incontrovertible evidence for it this early. Cf. Metzger's note on I John 4:3 in *Textual Commentary.*

The position taken in the COMMENT, which locates the source of these exclamations in controversies with Jewish opponents, is supported by Cullmann, *The Earliest Christian Confessions,* 28-30, and Neufeld, *The Earliest Christian Confessions,* 61-64.

Zerwick, *Biblical Greek,* § 451, finds this an example of Semitic "paratactic thought," in which the first clause is really subordinate in the comparison so that an obvious statement is utilized to demonstrate the main point. There is reason to think, however, that there is ground for the first exclamation even if it is used in this way.

by God's Spirit . . . *by the Holy Spirit.* There is not as yet a refined, theological doctrine of the Spirit. The phrases here are apparently equivalent; and although both are anarthrous, that probably has no significance (in 6:18 "Holy Spirit" has the article). The difficulty of distinguishing locative and instrumental usage with *en* is evident here; linguistic precision must yield to exegetical refinement. *en* might be rendered, "under the influence of."

COMMENT

Here begins the reply to the third major question raised in the communication of the Corinthian church to Paul. It concerns spiritual phenomena manifested in the church. It will at once become apparent that the perplexities are not just theological misunderstandings: there is controversy—which fits the picture of the congregation in Corinth as it has developed so far in the epistle.

Paul adduces a reference to the past to warn them against reliance upon individual or collective impulses that emerge in their church experience. Confidence that the Spirit is guiding the church has prompted some persons to feel that any strong conviction, drive toward action, or emotional outburst occurring in the church is authorized by the Spirit. Paul reminds them that in their recent pagan life strong impulses led them to the worship of lifeless idols. This, he implies, is not irrelevant to their present life as Christians in the church. The turbulent nature of human emotions, especially when connected with excited religious experiences, may lead to ideas and actions that are in conflict with the received traditions and to excessive reliance upon communal feelings. So expressions of the common life that are attributed to the Spirit must be examined to see whether they may not be the product of the old, common, human drives and emotions.

There must be some guidelines by which people may be kept from being *led off* by human impulses under the mistaken impression that these are produced and guaranteed by the Holy Spirit. As an illustration, Paul stresses two extreme exclamations: *no one* under guidance *by God's Spirit says, "Jesus be damned";* and it is impossible to affirm, *"Jesus is Lord,"* without the power of *the Holy Spirit.* The lordship of Jesus thus becomes a standard by which to distinguish human impulse (by implication, misleading) and validation *by the Holy Spirit.*

The affirmation *Jesus is Lord* is undoubtedly one of the earliest credal statements of the church (perhaps from the time when "Christ" was still more a designation of office than a part of a name). The Spirit, then, guides people to make this affirmation and will not influence people to utter the reverse and entirely illegitimate curse.

The idea of cursing Jesus is not hypothetical, even for this comparatively early date. In Paul's defense before Agrippa he says that he "tried to make [the Christians] blaspheme" (according to Acts 26:11); and this would presumably be an abjuration of Jesus. Later in the century there are hints of the same sort of challenge, coming both from within and from outside the church; cf. I John 4:1-6 and Rev 2:13, 3:8, 12:17, 17:14.

Early in the next century cursing and confessing Jesus is well-attested; cf. *Martyrdom of Polycarp* 9:2, 10:1, 12:1, and the *Epistle* of Pliny to Trajan 10:96. The association of confessing under duress by the power of the Spirit is made in Matt 10:17-20.

It needs to be added that when Paul refers to these affirmations, he understands that they are not merely verbal statements though they involve real belief. They are rather commitments of the whole life. The one statement is a rejection of the one who determines what Christian life is; the other means that one accepts the lordship of Jesus Christ and is willing to live by his commandment. The enablement for this latter commitment comes by God's Holy Spirit.

VARIETIES OF GIFTS, DIFFERENT PERSONS, ONE SPIRIT (12:4-11)

12 4 There are apportionments of divine gifts but the same Spirit; 5 and there are apportionments of serving ministries and the same Lord. 6 Also there are apportionments of activities but the same God, who produces all things among all people. 7 To each one is given the manifestation of the Spirit for the common advantage: 8 to one person a message of wisdom is given through the Spirit; to another, a message of knowledge in accordance with the same Spirit; 9 to another, faith by the same Spirit; to another, healing gifts by the one Spirit; 10 to another, miracle-working activities; to another, the gift of prophecy; to another, ability to discriminate among spirits; to another, kinds of tongues; and to another, interpretation of tongues. 11 One and the same Spirit produces all these things, apportioning individually to each one as he wishes.

Notes

12:4. *apportionments*. The word may bear the sense of "dividing" (cf. Luke 15:12), or it may indicate the variety of things under discussion. Here the variety is described in the sequel; so the former idea is appropriate here. The word refers to the process in which God allots what he gives to persons.

divine gifts (*charismata*). Bauer notes: "in our literature only of gifts of divine grace" (AGB, 887a).

the same Spirit. auto bears two references. It points out that the *apportionments* do not make for diversity since they have the same source. It also connects this second step in Paul's discussion with the initial assertion that the Holy Spirit is the power making Christian confession possible.

5. *and . . . and.* On the paratactic style, cf. BDF, § 458.

6. *activities . . . produces.* The words are cognate in the Greek, but the respective English cognates are inappropriate.

all things among all people. A variation of a favorite expression of Paul; cf. 9:22, 10:33, 15:27.

7. *the manifestation of the Spirit* may mean that the Spirit is being revealed or that the Spirit is revealing—i.e. objective or subjective genitive. Perhaps the gifts and their activities are regarded as a revelation of the presence of the Spirit. In any case, it comes to practically the same thing. Bauer observes that "the expression means the same thing as *charisma*" (AGB, 861a).

the common advantage. sympheron could refer to the *advantage* of *each one*, but the mutuality of the Spirit favors the interpretation *common.*

8. *a message. logos* meant the faculty or manner of speaking in 1:17 and 4:20; here it is rather what is spoken, as in 1:18.

through . . . in accordance with. The change of prepositions is probably deliberate (*dia . . . kata*). Wisdom is thought of as coming from God *through* the agency of *the Spirit* (cf. 2:4); but *knowledge,* a human capability, is effective when it is *in accordance with the same Spirit.* So in the next verse *en* probably has the combination of locative and instrumental force referred to in the NOTE on 12:3.

9. *healing gifts,* literally, "divine gifts of healings."

by the one Spirit. There is some textual variation here. It seems more likely that Paul would have introduced the variety (*same . . . one*) than that the scribes would. In any case the unifying power of the Spirit is emphasized, and the phraseology is summarized in vs. 11.

10. *miracle-working activities,* literally, "activities of powers."

the gift of prophecy. As in 13:2 the word is just *prophecy.* It seems necessary to make it clear that the reference is to a divinely given ability and not to a particular message.

ability to discriminate among spirits, literally, "discriminations of spirits." Cf. COMMENT.

kinds of tongues. The plural might indicate that the reference is to the various human languages, which exist in many categories, and which a person might receive power to speak from the Spirit. In Acts 2:4-11 the power of the Spirit gives the apostles ability to speak so that people of various nationalities are able to understand them. The exact nature of that "miracle" is difficult if not impossible to determine, and the reference here may be similar. It seems more likely, however, that the reference is to a kind of utterance which will be discussed in ch. 14, where under spiritual inspiration people utter speech that is not immediately understandable and is presumably addressed to God. What Paul means by *kinds* of such speaking cannot be determined.

Calvin flatly states that *tongue* "means a foreign language" (on 14:2; p. 286 in Fraser's translation, used here and elsewhere in this commentary). His gratuitous remarks about study of languages are of classic moment (on 14:5; p. 287).

interpretation of tongues. If the reference is to "languages," this should be rendered "translation." It is more likely, again, that these *tongues* are unintelligible unless someone receives the additional spiritual gift to interpret them.

11. *individually.* The adverbial use of *idia;* cf. Robertson, *Grammar,* 530, 653.

as he wishes. Although placed nearest to *each one,* the referent is certainly to the *Spirit.*

COMMENT

Having made his introductory point that it is the Holy Spirit who is the very ground of Christian confession, Paul extends the scope of the statement by declaring that the same Spirit makes the various *apportionments of divine gifts* that are at once the power and the problem of the church. The variety of abilities that mark the members of the church are all the result of the Spirit's gifts. These are not natural propensities that people possess from birth or from heredity but gifts that are suitable for the particular life of the church and that the Spirit bestows for the advantage of the church. Different people may receive different gifts because of some appropriate correlation between natural and spiritual ability, but this is not to the fore. The gifts are divine *apportionments,* and the uniqueness of their identity is to be found in the Spirit who gives them.

Parallel to gifts are services or ministries to be performed. Although there is again diversity on the human level, the ministries are rendered in honor of the Lord. There is no explication of what services are meant; but they presumably include missionary activity and teaching such as are enumerated in 12:28-30. *The same Lord* is probably Jesus Christ. *kyrios* without modifiers in this epistle cannot always be so identified, but the usage in the last part of ch. 11 and the emphasis of 12:3 suggest this significance here. "Ministry" is appropriate to Jesus Christ; cf. Mark 10:45 and parallels.

Apportionments of activities refer to the execution of ministries made possible by the gifts. *Activities* is not primarily descriptive of *what* happens but of *why* and *how* it happens. This is because *the same God produces all* that is accomplished in the church. Thus there is here the kind of raw theological material out of which the church developed trinitarian doctrine: gifts are granted by the Spirit, service is performed under the tutelage of Jesus Christ, and God himself "energizes" the entire process.

The passage is elaborating upon a central point, which is put succinctly in vs. 7 and summarized in vs. 11. The schismatic individualism that was plaguing the Corinthian church is wrongheaded. *Manifestation of the Spirit,* whether thought of as the aegis of the Spirit or the exercise of spiritual gifts, is individual only in respect to its diversity and apportionment; its purpose is *the common advantage.* As the apostle began by denying that Christ could be divided (1:13), so now he emphasizes the unifying power of the Holy Spirit. The rest of ch. 12 and ch. 14 will work this out in the context of the church's life.

Here Paul lists spiritual gifts that may illustrate *manifestation of the Spirit. A message of wisdom* has already been discussed in 1:24 and

2:6-13. *A message of knowledge* probably means the ability to present with effective reason the truths of Christian faith; an example is in ch. 8. Wisdom is divinely mediated *through the Spirit;* knowledge is expressed *in accordance* with the Spirit.

Elsewhere, particularly in Romans and Galatians, *faith* is a focal point of Paul's theology. Here it is a particular gift. In the light of 13:2, it seems to be the kind of openness and confidence that enables the power of God to operate through the person who has it. It enables the possessor to perform great and wonderful deeds and to live through hardship. Among the deeds is the particular kind of ability given to one or another to produce healing among the sick. Since many sicknesses are affected by the condition of the mind or spirit (cf. 11:30), persons with the appropriate *divine gifts* may bring confidence and courage, which remove blocks to healing and allow powerful tendencies to healing operating in the body itself to be speeded up. *The same Spirit* that manifests power in other areas of life is effective in the physical realm. The effectiveness does not operate in everyone but the Spirit unites what is diversely done. There are other *miracle-working activities* that are not specified but are in addition to *healings.* Stories in Acts about the apostles and deacons provide the only readily accessible commentary.

The gift of prophecy works in two dimensions: it may be concerned with prediction of the future (e.g. Acts 11:28) or it may be directed to conviction of conscience. In many of the Old Testament prophets these two functions were combined, and John the Baptist both challenged the lives of his hearers and foretold the coming messianic time. In I Cor 11:4-5 and ch. 14 prophecy is an activity in the church, and in contrast with speaking in tongues it is a kind of communication that people can understand and which may convict conscience. The one who prophesies speaks for God and by his Spirit moves people to repentance or appropriate action.

Apparently there was sometimes doubt whether persons were actually possessed by God's Spirit; there may be a reflection of this in 12:3. Some church members, therefore, were given *ability to discriminate among spirits,* i.e. to tell who is guided by the Spirit and who is not. Matters of the spirit can be deceptively elusive; so the discriminatory power is not inherent in ordinary human reason but is possible by a spiritual gift. *Spirits* surely include the spirits of persons and probably also refer to other, perhaps evil, spirits.

Kinds of tongues were a problem in Corinth; ch. 14 deals with it at some length. Though it may cause difficulty, Paul recognizes the phenomenon as a legitimate part of church life; it is a spiritual gift. As he shows in ch. 14, however, it is necessary that there be those with the gift of *inter-*

pretation of tongues. The *tongues,* which speak otherwise unintelligible words of the Spirit, must be translated into a message *for the common advantage.*

These spiritual gifts are all subject to *one and the same Spirit.* The spiritual pride that has appeared in Corinth (4:6,18-20, 5:2, 8:1) is unjustified; for whatever gifts the Corinthians possess come only from divine favor (4:7). It is important to keep Paul's focus in view. The history of the church shows that it is easy to fix attention upon spiritual gifts rather than upon the Spirit, who apportions them.

ANALOGUE: THE BODY AND ITS PARTS
(12:12-26)

The nature of the body of Christ

12 12 Just as the body is one, yet has many parts, and all the parts of the body, though they are many, are one body, so also is Christ. 13 For we also were all baptized by one Spirit into one body—whether Jews or Greeks, whether slaves or free—and we all were given the one Spirit to drink.

Interrelationship of parts of the body

14 And in fact, the body is not one part but many. 15 If the foot says, "Because I am not a hand, I do not belong to the body," it does not for this reason not belong to the body. 16 And if the ear says, "Because I am not an eye, I do not belong to the body," it does not for this reason not belong to the body. 17 If the entire body were an eye, where would be the hearing? If it were all hearing, where would be the sense of smell? 18 But as a matter of fact, God arranged the parts—each one of them—in the body just as he willed. 19 If all were one part, where would be the body? 20 But now there are many parts and one body. 21 The eye cannot say to the hand, "I have no need of you"; or again, the head to the feet, "I have no need of you."

Harmonious function of the body

22 The parts of the body, however, which seem to be weakest are much more necessary, 23 and we bestow greater honor on the parts of the body which we deem less honorable. And our unpresentable parts

have greater presentability, 24 which our presentable parts do not need. But God blended the body together by giving greater honor to the inferior part 25 in order that there may be no division in the body but that the parts may have the same care for each other. 26 And so if one part is suffering, all the parts suffer together; if one part is honored, all the parts rejoice together.

NOTES

12:12. *Just as the body.* This analogue of the body and its parts was common in classical antiquity; cf. the references in Lietzmann, *Handbuch,* 62, and in Weiss, 302. Seneca, for example, writes: "All this which you see in which divine and human things are included is one thing. We are members of a large body (*membra corporis*). Nature announces that we are related since we come from the same things and grow in the same way. This justifies for us mutual love and makes us sociable" (*Epistulae* 95.52).

parts. The analogy seems to require the use of a neutral term. "Limbs" and "organs" are applicable to various parts of the body. "Members" has limited applicability to the body, and it is liable to superficial understanding in its figurative reference. "Parts" has the widest appropriateness and is used throughout this section for *melē.*

13. *For we also.* On *kai gar* cf. BDF, § 452(3).

by one Spirit. Again the difficult use of *en;* cf. last NOTE on 12:3.

given the one Spirit to drink. Since the root idea of "Spirit" in both Hebrew and old Greek was "wind," it is surprising to meet Paul's figure of "drink." John 7:38-39, however, identifies the Spirit with "living water . . . which those who have faith in him were going to receive." Probably the *tertium quid comparionis* is baptism, at least in Paul's thought.

It is advisable, however, to guard against the idea of incorporation into the body of Christ by sacramental means. It is more to the point to speak of "corporate personality." The context is concerned with the operation of the Spirit. Cf. Markus Barth, "A Chapter on the Church—The Body of Christ. Interpretation of I Corinthians 12," *Interpretation* 12 (1958), 131-156.

15. *it does not . . . not.* The double negative is difficult to paraphrase and is best carried over into the translation. KJ and Luther took the apodosis as a question, and more recently JB did so, providing a somewhat awkward rendering.

18. *as a matter of fact,* reading *nuni* instead of *nun* (B A D* et al.). The apparent difficulty of *nun* in the context is offset by its frequency in Paul (note vs. 20).

21. *cannot say.* In Paul's figurative analogy this would, of course, be possible; but he is implying that such a statement would be baseless in the reality of the situation.

22. *weakest*. The form is comparative and may refer to the *much more*. On the use of the comparative for the superlative, however, cf. Zerwick, *Biblical Greek*, § 146, and BDF, § 60(1). The comparatives in vs. 23 may be read in that degree.

23. *honor . . . honorable . . . unpresentable . . . presentability*. The cognates have been brought into the translation at some risk of awkwardness in order to preserve Paul's style.

25. *no division . . . care for*. The figure has been pressed for the sake of the application. So also with the second part of vs. 26.

COMMENT

The nature of the body of Christ

The comparison between a collective group of people and an individual organism, once it is made, is suggestive and somewhat obvious, but the first one who made it performed quite an intellectual feat. The comparison illuminates actual relationships that exist among persons who compose a society, and it also provides a kind of ideal or norm by which members of a society are urged or advised to act in harmony with one another. Both of these uses are in this passage.

Christ exists as a body, the parts of which are all the Christians. The *one Spirit* is related to this as the effective force which, in the act of baptism, brings this body to experiential reality. Diversity of race and social class does not prevent incorporation into *one body,* but conversely the unity of the body does not eliminate the differences among the parts. *Jews* are still Jews and *Greeks* are still Greeks, but they are related together in a common society—and again Paul stresses that it is the one Spirit which produces this. It is as though drinking from a common source of life-giving water had bound them in that life. (Less likely, the drink might be the cup of the new covenant.)

Interrelationship of parts of the body

An analysis of the relationship among parts of the natural body is an only thinly veiled analogue of the church and its members. Several of the parts are singled out for special remark. Their analogical significance is probably not to be pushed, for they first of all are illustrative of the writer's main point. *The foot* might be regarded as servile and lowly since it carries the rest of the body and gets soiled with the dust of the ground. *The hand* is the effective agent of work and social gesturing and might be regarded as more important. *The eye* is perhaps more beautiful than *the ear* and is located frontally in the head. Paul, of course, intends his readers to understand that such attitudes are ridiculous. In a well-organized body different parts perform different functions; and since no one is able to do the work of another, all are necessary no matter how they may differ. This arrangement is by divine appointment.

The analogy is simple, almost to the point of being obvious. In a congregation where there are party quarrels, class rivalries, and quandaries occasioned by sex, marital status, religious background, and spiritual practice, the place of each member ought to be guaranteed by his or her individuality as a creature of God. It is the body formed under the aegis of the one Spirit, which gives significance to the parts in relationship; and this is the presence and working of Christ in, say, Corinth. Moreover, the effectiveness of Christ in this his body is diversified by the functions of its parts, that is, the individual members. Conzelmann pointedly suggests that Paul is opposed to "the practice of individuals' dissociating themselves from the 'body,' that is, against enthusiastic individualism" (p. 213).

An extension of this has to do with a reverse individualism which sees itself as the epitome of the body. No one part, however, can become the whole body or indeed function in its place. *The eye* and *the head* have obvious pride of place in the body and are preeminent in directing its activities, but without the muscular strength of *the hand* and *the feet* they are relatively ineffective in action. So the principle that each person has a place in the function of the body of Christ precludes any one member's assuming the role of the whole. Paul says this *cannot* be, i.e. it is "absurd" (Conzelmann, ibid.).

Harmonious function of the body

This is further illustrated by a line of argument that is not as readily interpreted. Paul seems to be affirming a kind of compensating balance among the parts of the body—and so in the body of Christ. A weak but *much more necessary* part of the body could be the eye or, given first-century knowledge of physiology, the heart or other internal organ. The *less honorable* parts of the body could be the hands, feet, or limbs, which are given various degrees of adornment. The *unpresentable parts* could be feet, the torso, breasts, or genitalia. The identification of analogous parts of the body of Christ is even less assured, but perhaps Paul was only providing a setting for his point: *God* (by the one Spirit) *blended the body* (of Christ) *together*. It is clear that he understands that there is a compensating balance, for the purpose is to eliminate *division* and establish mutual *care*. In the physical body its parts are sensitized by nerves by which feelings of pleasure and pain are registered, and the *suffering* or well-being (*honor*) of one part is variously shared by the whole body through the nervous system. The application of this to the body of Christ is easily made; indeed, the vocabulary of the last verse of the passage is more appropriate to the Christian body than to the physical organism. The relevance to the church in Corinth with its lack of mutual concern needs no elaboration.

FUNCTIONS OF MEMBERS IN THE CHURCH
(12:27-31a)

12   27 Now you are Christ's body and individually its parts. 28 And God appointed some in the church first as apostles, second as prophets, third as teachers, then miracle-workers, then healing gifts, ministries of aid, administrative abilities, kinds of tongues. 29 All are not apostles, are they? Are all prophets? Are all teachers? Are all miracle-workers? 30 All do not have healing gifts, do they? Do all speak in tongues? Do all interpret? 31a But you be zealous for the more important divine gifts!

NOTES

12:27. This verse provides a bridge from the analogue to Paul's functional summary.

28. *prophets*. In 11:4-5 Paul has said that both women and men prophesy in church. In 14:29-38 he will discuss the matter further.

miracle-workers, literally, "powers." The first three appointments specify the persons who perform the roles; here the terminology shifts to the roles. This term recurs at the end of vs. 29; so the personal designation has been used in the translation. There are three words in Paul's writing that may be loosely rendered "miracle"; all occur in II Cor 12:12 (*semeion, teras, dynamis*) and have to do, respectively, with actions that serve as signs or that inspire wonder or that manifest power, as here.

ministries of aid. These deeds that provide help are probably the functions of the deacons in the church; cf. *diakonia* in Rom 12:7.

29. *All are not . . . are they?* Each element in the listing that extends through vs. 30 is a question expecting a negative answer (BDF, § 427[2]). To avoid awkwardness only the first and fifth have been so precisely rendered. On lists of "spiritual gifts" cf. Robertson and Plummer, 283-284.

31a. *you be zealous*. The verb can be either indicative or imperative. Paul may mean that they are seeking greater spiritual status, whereas they should practice the gift they may have. Then the indicative would be the proper translation. G. Iber, "Zum Verständnis von I Cor 12:31," ZNW (1963), 43-52, argues that the Corinthians are seeking charismatic gifts at the jeopardy of the whole body, and Paul is offering love as the corrective measure. Most interpreters, however, infer that Paul is urging them to high aspiration as a setting for his recommendation of the best gift of all. The parallel with 14:1, where the same verb form is almost surely imperative, supports this decision.

the more important. As in vs. 22 this comparative may be used instead of the superlative, but a comparative usage fits the sense of the whole verse better. (The translation is AGB's rendering of *meizona.*)

COMMENT

Paul now converts the lengthy analogue into application as he lists particular functions that various church members perform. The *apostles'* role is missionary and in some degree authority. *Prophets* speak for God. *Teachers* present Christian doctrine and its ethical application (there may be overlap with the role of prophet). The other functions are either self-evident or require further discussion. The *ministries of aid* are nowhere in the New Testament discussed in detail, but they are everywhere assumed (and cf. Acts 6:1-6).

The lesson of the parts of the body applies here, for these roles are individually performed, and God's appointment precludes any monopoly of one function. Each can do what he can do and can receive the benefits of the actions of the others.

It is instructive to compare the two lists of *divine gifts* in vs. 28 and in vss. 29-30. That Paul was not setting up or reflecting a refined protocol is evident, particularly when two other lists are compared, those in Rom 12:6-8 and Eph 4:11-12. It seems clear that apostles and prophets do hold a preeminent place (cf. also Eph 2:20, 3:5); and the sequence "prophets . . . teachers" also occurs in Acts 13:1. In the Romans list prophecy is first, teaching is third, and several more general gifts are added. In the Ephesians list teachers are fifth, and "evangelists" and "pastors" are included. It is also apropos to consider the list of divine gifts in 12:8-10. Five of the nine are in the lists in vss. 28-30, but "prophecy" comes sixth. This relative fluidity added to the lack of such lists in other New Testament books (particularly the Pastorals) suggests that these gifts were widespread and recognized but not precisely locked in a pecking order.

It may be noted that Paul expressly states that all do not speak with tongues, and it may have some significance that this gift and its partner "interpretation" are last in each of the three lists in this chapter. These data are probably related to the fact that there was a problem regarding this gift, which the apostle will take up in 14:2-28. Since ch. 13 is in some sense an excursus, the final verse of this passage may indicate his hope that the Corinthians will aspire to more constructive gifts than tongues and their interpretation.

EXCURSUS: LOVE, HIGHEST OF THE HIGHER GIFTS (12:31b-14:1a)

Worthlessness of all gifts without love

12 [31b] And I am showing you further a more extraordinary way. **13** [1] If I speak in the tongues of human and of angelic beings but do not have love, I have become a resounding gong or a reverberating cymbal. [2] And if I have the gift of prophecy and understand all mysteries and all knowledge, and if I have all faith so that I can remove mountains but do not have love, I am nothing. [3] And if I dole out all my property and if I hand over my body in order that I may boast but do not have love, it does not benefit me.

Characteristics of love

[4] Love is patient, love is kind. It is not jealous; it does not brag; it is not puffed with pride. [5] It does not behave unpresentably; it does not seek its own advantage; it does not become irritated; it does not calculate evil. [6] It does not rejoice at injustice but rejoices over truth. [7] It keeps all confidences, maintains all faithfulness, all hope, all steadfastness.

Permanence of love

[8] Love never fails; but if there are gifts of prophecy, they will be nullified; if there are tongues, they will cease; if there is knowledge, it will be nullified. [9] For we know partially, and we prophesy partially; [10] but when that which is complete comes, that which is partial will be nullified. [11] When I was a child, I used to speak as a child, think as a child, reason as a child. Since I have become a man, I have discarded the ways of a child. [12] For we see now in a mirror indistinctly, but then face to face. Now I know partially, but then I shall know fully just as God has fully known me. [13] But now faith, hope, love endure —these three—but the greatest of these is love. **14** [1a] Strive for love.

NOTES

The relationship of ch. 13 to the context of chs. 12 and 14 remains a difficult problem. The versions manifest an uneasiness in this respect by the paragraphing, which may add 12:31b to ch. 13 (cf. the evidence in the UBS text apparatus). To complete the contextual setting 14:1a has been added here.

Weiss labored with great detail to show how *schwierig* is the transition between chs. 12 and 13 (cf. pp. 309-312). It seems to him that the discussion of love interrupts the connection between the discussion of gifts in 12 and the exhortation in 14 to seek especially the gift of prophecy. This emphasis on prophecy logically develops ideas begun in 12 and is not prepared for or furthered by the "love" chapter. Weiss decides that 13 was an independent, rounded-off paragraph perhaps composed by itself and probably belonging originally to the first of the letters out of which the Corinthian correspondence was edited.

Over against this, it must be pointed out that in ch. 13 love is set as an antithesis to tongues, prophecy, understanding of mysteries, etc. A number of these gifts are specifically mentioned in 12 (knowledge, faith, prophecy, tongues; perhaps doling of property reflects ministries of aid) and 14 (mysteries); only handing over of his body is not mentioned. This close correspondence suggests that 13 was meant to have a specific place in the discussion of gifts.

The repetition of *zēloute de ta charismata* in 12:31 and 14:1 indicates at least that ch. 13 is an excursus. If the first occurrence is taken as an indicative (cf. *supra*, first NOTE on 12:31a), then a progression of thought may be understood; but this is quite uncertain. Schmithals (*Gnosticism in Corinth*, 95, n. 23) suggests that chs. 13 and 14 should be transposed. 12:31a and 14:1a, then, would be eliminated; and 14:1b would follow 12:30 and improve the logic of the discussion. 12:31b would follow 14:40, and ch. 13 would be the climax of the whole section. This is an attractive adjustment, but it founders on the transcriptional question of why 13 would have been transposed to the midst of the discussion and inserted with such admittedly difficult transitional phrases.

Perhaps a mediating conjecture will suffice (like that of Barrett, 297). Chapter 13 was composed by Paul independent of the rest of our I Corinthians; details of this separate existence are not recoverable. Paul inserted it in this discussion at the point where it occurred to him but before he was finished with his discussion of spiritual gifts. This is not out of character for Paul's epistolary practice. Since the letter was occasional and this occurs in the body of a major section, it was not edited by Paul; and it escaped the editorial hand of the collector of Paul's correspondence.

12:31b. *I am showing.* This can be taken as a futuristic use of the present; cf. BDF, § 323.

further a more extraordinary way. eti, taken here with the verb, may be construed with the prepositional phrase, "a still more extraordinary." *Way* is used in Acts to refer to the Christian community and its belief (9:2, 19:9,23, 22:4, 24:14,22); here it designates a distinctive feature of the broader reference. The figure goes back at least to Ps 1:1 (*derek*). Cf. second NOTE on 4:17.

13:1. *tongues.* It is unlikely that Paul means "languages" here. The mention of the same word in the immediately preceding passage and the extensive discussion that follows in the next chapter have to do with "glossolalia." There is a thin line, however, between "tongues" and "languages" as they appear in the early church (cf. COMMENT; also fourth NOTE on 12:10). The early rabbis believed that there were seventy languages spoken by human beings. They held two opinions about *angelic* languages: (a) that the angels understood only Hebrew, except for Michael, who understood all the languages of mankind; (b) that the angels had one or more celestial languages different in range and beauty from human languages (StB, III, 449).

love. The very extensive literature may be surveyed from AGB, 4-6, and in E. Stauffer's article in *TDNT*, I, 21-55. More recently, cf. Furnish, *The Love Command in the New Testament;* and the succinct statement of William Barclay, *The New Testament, Vol. II: The Letters and the Revelation* (Cleveland, 1970), 313-314.

reverberating cymbal. The phrase has been inspired by Ps 150:5. Cf. Goodspeed, *Problems of New Testament Translation*, 160-161.

2. *all mysteries.* The presence of the article suggests "the mysteries," but articles with *knowledge* and *faith* indicate the usage is a special kind of generic (BDF, §§ 252, 275[3]). Cf. pp. 162, 164-165.

faith so that I can remove mountains. The figure is ancient; cf. Isa 54:10. It occurs twice in the gospel tradition: Mark 11:23 // Matt 21:21 and Matt 17:20. It is evidence, as Allo remarks (p. 344), that Paul proclaimed not only the death and resurrection of Jesus but also his "moral teaching."

3. *dole out.* The verb originally meant to feed by putting morsels in the mouth (as of an infant or animal), whence the Vulgate *in cibos pauperum.*

hand over my body. I Clement 55:1-2 gives examples of heathen and Christians who have sacrificed themselves for the benefit of others; in vs. 2 he uses *paredōkan.* Since Clement knows I Corinthians (cf. 47:1-3 and 49), it is reasonable to accept this interpretation. (Cf. Goodspeed, *Problems of New Testament Translation*, 162-165.)

that I may boast. The textual problem is difficult. Nestle and UBS differ. Metzger's summary in *Textual Commentary*, 563-564, covers the options well. Cf. also K. W. Clark in *Studia Paulina*, eds. J. N. Sevenster and W. C. van Unnik (Haarlem, 1953), 61-62. If Clement's understanding of the clause upon which this final clause depends is correct, the idea of "burning" is hardly appropriate. Martyrdom by fire, moreover, faced the Christian communities at a later time; and it would then be easier to explain a change in text. Since Paul is dealing with motive in his stress on love, *boast* seems to fit the context. The impossible reading of the Byzantine text, *kauthēsōmai*, may argue for an original *kauchēsōmai*, of which one letter was changed; or it may be a scribal correction of a possible *kauthēsomai*. Robertson and Plummer's citation of an Athenian tomb with an inscription concerning an Indian who died by self-immolation (p. 292) is interesting but hardly weighty. Against the preference of almost every modern translator except Goodspeed, *that I may boast* commends itself as the best reading.

Paul's ambivalent attitude toward "boasting" is plain in 9:15-16. Among the relatively frequent uses of the term by Paul, cf. especially his comments in II Cor 11:16-30. *kauchasthai* and its cognates is usually rendered by *gloriari* and cognates in the Vulgate; but "boast" is closer to Paul's intention than "glory" in English.

4. *love is kind.* This second *love* may be construed thus with *chrēsteuetai* to form a simple chiasmus with the first clause, or it may be read as the subject of the negatived verbs that follow; the texts and versions differ in punctuation. The first option seems to be preferable stylistically.

5. *behave unpresentably.* The verb can refer to a kind of indecency (cf. 12:23-24) or to disorder (cf. 14:40). The translation is an attempt at compromise, keeping the rendering of the closest previous usage. A comparable decision had to be made at 7:36.

become irritated. paroxynetai is a strong word; perhaps the colloquial "become wrought up" would be fitting.

does not calculate evil. The verb occurs also at 4:1, where it was translated "consider." There is an Old Testament precedent for this statement in Zech 8:17. AGB, "take into account," is surely too neutral. H. W. Heidland, *TDNT,* IV, 289, suggests a Hebrew milieu for the idea but overworks his further explanation.

8. *if . . . if . . . if.* A Pauline usage; cf. BDF, § 446.

9. *partially.* The phrase *ek merous* occurs at 12:27 in connection with the parts of the body of Christ; it is there descriptive of how individual parts relate to the whole. Here it is restrictive; it marks the incompleteness of the function to which it is related. It might be paraphrased, "from a partial perspective."

12. *in a mirror indistinctly.* AGB lists an extensive literature on this figure (p. 313b), and Conzelmann has a full discussion (pp. 226-228). The Old Testament source of the figure is Num 12:8, but it has a much wider use (cf. D. H. Gill, *CBQ* 25 [1963], 427-429). It is used effectively in James 1:23-24. Cf. also II Cor 5:7.

face to face. The phrase is probably not to be taken in a general sense but is to be referred to direct knowledge of God. The reference to Num 12:8 suggests Moses as the paradigm: there the expression is "mouth to mouth"; but it is clear that immediate confrontation is intended (cf. Exod 33:11; Deut 34:10). The same idea occurs elsewhere (e.g. Gen 32:10); but since Paul has been writing about prophecy, Moses as the key prophet provides the appropriate referent. Moses' *face to face* communication with God marks his unique prophetic role.

know fully. R. Bultmann presents a fine summary of the difference between Paul's thought and Gnostic ideas in *TDNT,* I, 710.

God has fully known me, taking the passive as a periphrasis for the divine subject, appropriate to the eschatological context.

13. *the greatest.* Another example of the comparative for the superlative; cf. 12:22.

14:1a. Transitional. Paul's "hymn" is complete with the preceding climax, but it is unthinkable that he would allow it to stand without a paraenetic complement.

COMMENT

Worthlessness of all gifts without love

As the succeeding chapter will show, tongues-speaking was a particularly troublesome problem in the Corinthian church. Paul begins his comparison of gifts by declaring how meaningless this gift is without love. Although *tongues* are a distinctive utterance, they are not to be thought of apart from the phenomenon of language. Like *human* languages they are subject to translation ("interpretation"; cf. 12:30). The tongues of *angelic beings* are subject to interpretation probably only by spiritual gift. (Cf. the cryptic description of another kind of related experience in II Cor 12:2-4.) Unless love animates the communication intended by tongues and their interpretation, the result is of no particular significance. The percussive sounds of *gong* and *cymbal*, employed since very ancient times in Near Eastern cultic and dramatic settings, convey at most an excitement or a mood or a very general contextual idea. Love is the disposition that brings sense out of attempted communication, while the lack of love reduces the vocal sounds to noise.

Love is a key concept for Paul—but perhaps "concept" is a misnomer for what the apostle believes and teaches. His treatment of love in this chapter has been considered hymnic in quality, and its beauty and depth have made it indisputably classic. But love is rather a way of life for Paul. The severity and gravity with which his theology has been treated have obscured the winsomeness that must have been a major factor in his evangelistic success. The personality revealed in the letter to Philemon is evidence of this. Moreover, it is not only where the term is used that love plays a role in Paul's thought. A good example is his recommendation regarding response to the weak person in 8:7-13. (Also cf. p. 229.)

This is why Paul can make love the critical factor in spiritual communication. Without love there can be no depth perception of God, who is love; so persons cannot understand each other in relation to God and the universe without love. The inner significance of the breakdown in communication at various levels today has been reflected by modern art and literature to a considerable degree in that their very forms are chosen for the sake of denying the communication of an intelligible idea of one person to another—since existence is absurd, art and literature must express absurdity. Perhaps this illustrates Paul's point: the only disposition that makes communication possible is love, which must include acceptance of the other person as one who exists in his or her own right, willingness to listen to what the other person is saying, concern to communicate in language the other person can understand, and openness of goodwill aimed at the welfare of the other.

The gift of prophecy has a double function: the ability to foresee the future and predict it, and the power to speak for God to the human conscience. Without love this is abortive. *All mysteries* also have a twofold thrust. One of the competitors of the Christian faith in Corinth was oriental mystery religion (cf. pp. 163-164). Paul, however, would reduce this to a minimal status in comparison with understanding of God's providence, his plans for the future, the concealed meaning of the scriptures, and the questions about the nature of God and his relation to finite reality that human reason cannot discover without revelation. Similarly, *all knowledge* comprises the pretensions of Gnostic wisdom (cf. *supra*, NOTE on *know fully*, vs. 12), theological knowledge about God as revealed, analyzed, and systematized by the human mind, truth recorded in scripture, and information about all reality.

All faith refers to confidence and trust in God that makes a person an open channel for special action of God. It means the sort of power that some people have when their presence conveys healing, assurance, and consolation, the power that others have in getting great works done without being overwhelmed by opposition or difficulty, the ability to sustain serene assurance about life that carries through sickness, pain, disappointment, grief, and death. Such faith is dramatized by the figure of moving mountains, a power attributed to nature's God in the Old Testament but applied to believers by Jesus.

Each of these spiritual gifts is great, and together they are a formidable array of power. Paul boldly asserts that all of these without love are *nothing*. Their motivation, orientation, and purpose are ineffectual unless love gives them God's dimension. This is made even clearer by another illustration: even the ethical laudability of one who distributes his *property* for the needy and makes the ultimate self-sacrifice "but [does] it in pride" (Goodspeed) is utterly valueless unless he has love. All of this Paul puts in the first person to demonstrate that his doctrine represents his very personal convictions.

Characteristics of love

Having made such emphatic pronouncement about the worthlessness of great spiritual gifts apart from love, Paul moves to a series of descriptive statements about love. Nowhere does he provide a definition that would satisfy the Socratic requirement of careful classification according to essence and qualities, but he does pour out a number of short sentences that tell vividly what love does and does not do. It is *patient*—willing to receive slights, injuries, and hardships without complaint, even over a long period of time. It is *kind;* it eases another person's pain, soothes anxieties, fears, and hostilities, and contributes positively to the happiness of others. The root word occurs in the Gospels (Matt 11:30; Luke 5:39, 6:35) and suggests that kindness is characteristic of God, is a concern to eliminate suffering and increase joy. Far from being mere sentimentality, kindness to individuals is a practical demonstration of one's concern to alleviate the miseries and improve the lot of people in general. With all Paul's ability to see theological and ethical issues on a large scale, he was careful of the feelings and needs of person after person in his churches, as witness the personal greetings at the close of his letters, the quite personal letter to Philemon regarding Onesimus, and indeed his concern for personal relationships with the Corinthians (cf. II Cor 2:1-11).

Care for others is evident in that *love is not jealous.* The word Paul uses can have a positive use when it means zeal for something laudable. Here it means zeal for one's own status manifested by envy of the relative success or prosperity of others. Love is genuinely solicitous about the welfare and happiness of others. A counterpart to this is that *love does not brag.* Self-interest is rarely intelligent enough to pursue its own objective with balance; therefore something greater than enlightened self-interest is necessary. Paul has already criticized those who were *puffed with pride* (4:6,18-20, 5:2), and in 8:1 he contrasts *knowledge,* which *puffs with pride,* and *love.* The way of love cuts across the ordinary direction of human movement and directs into an entirely different way.

Love has certain public manifestations, one being "presentable behavior." Chapter 14 will deal with those who are inconsiderate and clamorous in meetings, who violate good manners and ignore other people's desires and feelings in headstrong pursuit of their own objectives. Love takes time to consider how even a good purpose may thwart the feelings of other people. It does not attempt to rush people into decisions, stifle their scruples, or disregard their rights in public assembly. Love combines the tension of the pursuit of good with consideration for those who do not see so clearly or whose effectiveness has not progressed as far in that pursuit. Put another way, love *does not seek its own advantage.* This childish characteristic, if pressed to the point of indifference of the needs of others, causes the breakdown of interpersonal relationships, domestic discord, and the collapse of society. But love takes seriously the needs, sufferings, hopes, and joys of other persons. This goes far to prevent the deep irritation that love avoids. Flashes of anger are sometimes self-righteously valued as courage or hard-hitting honesty. Indeed, Jesus is said to have expressed anger upon occasion (Mark 11:15-17; John 11:33,38); and Paul does not always follow his own teaching (Acts 13:9-11; Gal 5:12). But he does not mean supine acceptance of evil or neurotic repression of natural hostility; he means that love eliminates hasty anger and irritability. He is thinking about an attitude that understands before it condemns and finds better ways to withstand evil than to attack with violence the evil persons. The way of love is under the impulse of God.

Love *does not calculate evil.* It is natural enough to notice and remember every bad thing that another does and to feel judgmental and angry; such an attitude may be just, but it is loveless. But Paul does not mean to ignore evil or to regard it as insignificant. The way of love recognizes the difference between evil and good, but by a miracle of emotional transubstantiation love absorbs evil without charging it against the other person and deals with evil by forgiving it. This can only be done by the power of God; that is, it is a gift. There is no greater illustration of this act of love than the word of Jesus, "Father, forgive them; for they know not what they do" (Luke 23:34). A corollary of this is love's joy *over truth* rather than *injustice.* The injustice may be committed personally, or it may be that of someone else toward which one shows a perverse curiosity and even pleasure. The complacent acceptance of evil is itself a cause of the increase of evil, but love wants truth to flourish. Love is concerned that everyone receive justice and that no one is victimized; so it cannot delight in the failure of justice but *rejoices* at the manifestation of goodness.

Love *keeps all confidences*—the word means "to put a cover over." Paul probably means that love is capable of passing over many things in silence where it would do harm to make them public, and it charitably refuses to attribute to other people evil motives. He writes to a descriptive climax which will lead into the next part. Love trusts in the redeemable possibilities of others and in the overarching goodness of God, who can bring good out of evil. Love stubbornly adheres to the conviction that life has purpose and meaning, that despite appearances God's purpose will be accomplished, and that he is using his people as part of his great plan for humanity. Put the other way round, the only sound basis for hope is love. Love which has been given from God overcomes despair, fear, and hate; and this love has been revealed as a reality in the person of Jesus Christ. The concomitant of this is *steadfastness:* love does not cave in but retains a vital resilience, cheerfulness, and energy. Self-centeredness will surrender to adversity in despair. The gift of love is grounded in God's own love.

Permanence of love

As the issue of all this, *love never fails;* that is, it will never cease to operate and it will never become obsolescent or invalid. This is because it is the purpose and nature of God. Further, love is the only relationship by which human beings can exist together. Love is the irreducible spiritual gift. Paul singles out three other gifts prominent in the Corinthian church: *prophecy, tongues,* and *knowledge.* All of these will cease to function. The milieu in which they operate will one day come to an end and will be superseded by a situation in which they are inappropriate or unnecessary. Love, however, is perpetual and will never be set aside.

All spiritual gifts except love, therefore, can be characterized as *partial*. The prophet has only a fleeting glimpse of God; tongues are a means by which communication is intended in the present order; knowledge is now incomplete, for it is obtained by indirect observation rather than by direct participation in reality. Paul's faith in the future, moreover, emphasizes this incompleteness; for *that which is complete will come*. He does not explain this; it could refer to life after death, to some future stage of human life, or to the new appearance of Christ. Certainly he will develop the thought in ch. 15. At any rate, this completion will displace *that which is partial*.

This is like the experience in which one grows out of childhood and becomes adult. There is a life appropriate to a child; this is manifested in speech, thought, and reasoning power. When adulthood arrives, these characteristics are no longer viable and must be left behind. (The peril of pushing illustrative material is evident when this is juxtaposed with Jesus' statement about children and the kingdom of God; cf. Mark 10:14-15.)

The manners and achievements of both childhood and adulthood, however, are incomplete and fragmentary. It is a future not yet reached that is complete. Already in 3:1 Paul has chided the Corinthians for their immaturity, but the best they could manage would still not be the fullness of reality. He utilizes the figure of a mirror. In the first century these were made of polished metal; and although Corinth undoubtedly could supply the best, the quality of the reflection was far from complete clarity. "To see a friend's face in a cheap mirror would be very different from looking at the friend" (Robertson and Plummer, 298). The reflection of life which is now possible is indistinct; that is, the view of reality, destiny, and true value is not clear because of the indirection of one's viewpoint. People and things may reflect the nature of God, but this is never seen directly. The eschatological vision will be immediate. The best human knowledge is indistinct; the greatest human minds have been unable to penetrate to the inner meaning of being, matter, life, and the cosmos. When this partial view is transcended, we shall see *face to face*. This full view of reality is certain because of the love in which *God has fully known* us.

Paul concludes by singling out the three enduring gifts: *faith, hope,* and *love.* All that he has just written demonstrates that one gift is *greatest: love.* It is at the heart of God's nature, made known by Jesus Christ. It is therefore to be the object of our striving.

SUPERIORITY OF PROPHECY OVER SPEAKING IN TONGUES (14:1b-33a)

Prophecy, tongues, and building up

14 ¹ᵇ Be zealous for the spiritual gifts, but especially that you may prophesy. 2 The one who speaks in a tongue, you see, does not speak to people but to God; for no one hears—he is speaking mysteries in the spirit. 3 The one who prophesies, on the other hand, speaks to people with a constructive, encouraging, and consoling message. 4 The one who speaks in a tongue builds himself up; the one who prophesies builds up a church. 5 Now I want you all to speak in tongues, but especially for you to prophesy. The one who prophesies is greater than the one who speaks in tongues unless he interprets in order that the church may be built up.

Tongues, interpretation, and building up

6 Now, brothers, if I come to you speaking in tongues, how will I benefit you unless I speak to you either by revelation or by knowledge or by prophecy or by teaching? 7 In the same way, if inanimate things producing sound—whether a flute or a harp—do not produce a distinction in their tones, how will anyone know what is being played on the flute or the harp? 8 And indeed, if a trumpet produces an unclear sound, who will prepare for battle? 9 So also if you produce unintelligible speech by the tongue, how will anyone understand what is being said?—for you will be speaking to the air. 10 There are, it would seem, so many kinds of voices in the world, and nothing is voiceless. 11 Then if I do not understand the meaning of the voice, I will be a barbarian to the one who is speaking; and the one who is speaking will be a barbarian so far as I am concerned. 12 So you also, since you are zealous for spirits, keep striving for the upbuilding of the church so that you may excel. 13 Therefore, let the one who speaks in a tongue keep praying that he may interpret. 14 For if I pray in a tongue, my spirit is praying, but my mind is unproductive. 15 What, then, is to be done? I shall pray with the spirit, but I shall pray also with the mind. I shall sing with the spirit, but I shall sing also with the

mind. 16 Otherwise, if you bless with the spirit, how will the one who occupies the place of the uninstructed say "Amen" to your thanksgiving since he does not understand what you are saying? 17 You, indeed, are giving thanks nicely; but the other person is not being built up. 18 I thank God I speak in tongues more than all of you, 19 but in church I would rather speak five words with my mind so that I may instruct others than speak thousands of words in a tongue.

Tongues and unbelievers

20 Brothers, stop being children in your thinking; but be like children in respect to evil; and become mature in your thinking. 21 It has been written in the law,

> "By strange tongues and by the lips of strangers
> I shall speak to this people,
> and even so they will not listen to me,"
> says the Lord.

22 Therefore the tongues are intended for a sign, not to those who believe but to the unbelievers, while prophecy is not for the unbelievers but for those who believe. 23 Then if the whole church assembles together and all are speaking in tongues and uninstructed persons or unbelievers enter, will they not say that you are mad? 24 But if all are prophesying and some unbeliever or uninstructed person comes in, he is convinced by all, he is investigated by all, 25 the hidden secrets of his heart become exposed, and thus he falls prostrate and worships God, as he proclaims, "Truly God is among you."

Tongues, prophecy, and order

26 What, then, is to be done, brothers? When you come together, each one has a psalm, or a teaching, or a revelation, or a tongue, or an interpretation; let all things take place for building up. 27 If anyone speaks in a tongue, let it be two at a time or at most three, and each one in turn; and let one interpret. 28 But if there be no interpreter, let the speaker in tongues be silent in church—let him speak to himself and to God. 29 Let two or three prophets speak and let the others discriminate. 30 But if God gives a revelation to another person who is

seated, let the first be silent; 31 for all of you can prophesy one by one in order that all may learn and all may be encouraged. 32 Indeed, the spirits of the prophets are subject to the prophets; 33ª for God is not the God of confusion but of peace.

NOTES

14:1b. On the connection between this chapter and ch. 12, cf. *supra*, introductory NOTE to 12:31b-14:1a. The use of *de* at the beginning of a new section is no problem in the light of the extensive use of that connective in this epistle. Indeed, the previous three words present a rather stark introduction to a new section; but their elimination as an editorial adjustment leaves an equally infelicitous transition whether or not this be posulated as the original position of ch. 13.

Weiss is correct about the awkwardness of the transition. In ch. 13 love is superior to all the gifts including prophecy; then comes the admonition to *be zealous especially* for prophecy. We are in a dilemma again, however, because of a lack of precise knowledge of the editorial process at the time of the collection of the Pauline corpus and in the century or so before the manuscripts that comprise our earliest knowledge of the text. It would have made a better progression of thought had ch. 13 followed ch. 14, and the whole puzzle may have resulted from an early transposition from that location. There is no evidence for this, however, in the MS tradition nor in the early quotations from the epistle; and examination of Paul's other undisputed correspondence does not suggest confidence in the rearrangement of his material. Indeed, there is ground to think that Paul's mercurial mind often outran the literary orderliness of which he was capable.

2. *speaks in a tongue.* This resumes the subject broached in 12:10,28,30. The use of the dative seems to be a set form. The translation *in* conforms to present-day terminology among charismatic persons (cf. J. M. Ford, *Baptism of the Spirit,* 79-118). Cf. also fourth NOTE on 12:10.

no one hears. It is uncertain whether the person who speaks in a tongue is fully conscious. It may be that he is in something like a hypnotic state of such sort that there is no recollection after the state has passed. On the other hand, the experience may be beyond volitional control and yet be accompanied by full consciousness.

Weiss collects allusions to practices like speaking in tongues from Jewish and Greek writers (pp. 327-329). He stresses that Paul's language plainly distinguishes between the speech of the mind, which is clear and comprehensible, and the speech of the spirit, which cannot be understood. This second kind of speech is analogous to what the Greeks called "ecstasy." Plato describes a poet as one "who becomes inspired and out of his mind, and the mind is no longer present in him" (*Ion* 534B). Weiss quotes Philo in a catena of references to Abraham's experience in Genesis 15: "The best kind of ecstasy is an inspired seizure and madness which the prophetic kind of person uses . . . the experiences of one who is inspired and borne along by God. . . . A prophet does not utter anything from himself, but he echoes all the foreign things of another being . . . he is the sounding organ of God, which is beaten and struck invisibly by him." "Ecstasy, inspired seizure, and madness" occurred when the sun went down. "Whenever the prophet seems to speak, he himself in truth is quiet, but another uses his intellectual organs with his mouth and tongue to relate whatever he will" (*Quis rerum divinarum heres sit* 249, 258, 259, 263, 264, 266). Weiss believes that Philo is describing the same sort of phenomenon as occurred in Corinth. The difference, however, seems to be that the words of the prophets of Israel and of the Greek poets were comprehensible to the hearers and readers. Plato certainly does not refer to divinely inspired gibberish; the poet produces a poem in the normal language even though he himself is not aware of what he is saying. The Corinthian glossolalia seems to be something else.

The classical problem in the early church arose in connection with the Montanist controversy. Tertullian's espousal of the Montanist position brought an articulate interpreter to that side; cf. his *On Fasting, passim; On Modesty* xxi; and *Against Marcion* v viii.

mysteries. Cf. p. 179-180.

in the spirit. The noun is anarthrous in the Greek text. *pneumati* may be treated three ways: (a) "in [his] spirit," i.e. the human spirit of the speaker; (b) "in the [Holy] Spirit"; (c) "to the Spirit." Cf. vss. 14-16 and COMMENT. The variant *pneuma* (G it) is too poorly attested for serious consideration; and in any event, it does not resolve the question.

4. *builds up.* This evaluative standard has already been introduced at 8:1 and 10:23.

5. *unless he interprets.* The poorly attested variant (G), "unless there be one who interprets," raises the question about the identity of the interpreter. The better attested readings imply that the person who speaks in a tongue later interprets what was uttered, and vs. 13 has the same intent. The lists of gifts in 12:10,30, however, seem to differentiate the person who speaks from the interpreter; and 14:26-28 suggests the same. Perhaps the only conclusion is that sometimes one way was followed, sometimes the other.

7. *whether a flute or a harp.* The flute (sometimes rendered "pipe") was used in connection with Greek plays, and it was the instrument in the famous contest between Apollo and Marsyas. This is the only reference to it in the New Testament, but the harp is mentioned three times in Revelation. *aulos* appears several times in the LXX as the translation for three different Hebrew words. *kithara* appears more often, most frequently in Psalms, representing five Hebrew terms (in Dan, *qītārīm*). In two MSS (A S) of Isa 30:32 the words occur together.

8. *trumpet. salpingx* in the LXX represents a number of Hebrew terms, often (and especially in the prophets) *šōfār*, the ram's horn, with which the signal is given to announce the rise of the new moon, the beginning of the Sabbath, the arrival of the new year, and the initiation of feasts. The trumpet came to be as-

sociated with the last day (of judgment), and it is the instrument used by the angels in the second cycle of judgment in Revelation 8-10.

10. *it would seem.* The fourth-class protasis is an adverbial formula (cf. AGB, 837a; BDF, § 385[2]) occurring in the New Testament only here and in 15:37. The contingency must be expressed consonant with the context.

voices. phonōn, "sounds"; but the next verse indicates that Paul has in mind oral communication. Perhaps there is an oblique reference to Ps 19[18]:4,5; cf. also Isa 40:3.

11. *I will be a barbarian.* Héring cites Ovid *Tristia* 5.10.37, 38. Paul could have known that work, but it is just as likely the figure had passed into common usage.

12. *zealous for spirits.* Cf. *supra,* NOTE on vs. 2 "in the spirit," and COMMENT, *infra,* on pp. 307-308. Weiss thinks that the use of the plural represents an irruption of a pre-Christian language that traced spiritual gifts to different spirits, both among Jews and pagans; he cites I Kings 22:19-23 (p. 326). Lietzmann finds an animistic idea behind the usage here, but Conzelmann rejects such an influence. Conzelmann takes *pneumatōn* as equivalent to *pneumatikōn,* which seems to fit Paul's running argument better.

so that you may excel. The final clause may be understood to mean that by *striving for the upbuilding of the church* they will excel in their zeal for spirits; or more simply, it may indicate Paul's wish that they may excel in upbuilding. Perhaps a combination of the ideas is intended: the upbuilding of the church gives a new and eminently desirable dimension to their concern for spiritual gifts. This is in keeping with ch. 12 and anticipates the further argument of this chapter.

14. *For.* The absence of *gar* in P[46] and B and the obvious value of a connective here render the particle suspect. The relational transition, however, is clear enough; and the scribal sense, if admitted, was fair.

my spirit is praying. This may resolve the question about *pneumati* in vs. 2. It seems also to be the locus of the *pneumatōn* of vs. 12. Analysis of Paul's psychology may be frustrating, probably because he thinks with presuppositions combined from Jewish and Greek backgrounds. Here it is important only to mark that he considers prayer in a tongue a genuinely Christian experience but that its irrationality renders it unprofitable for communal church life, which requires that the *mind* be productive. Cf. Conzelmann, 238, n. 56.

15. *What, then, is to be done?* The rhetorical question in diatribe style is often simply *ti oun* (Rom 3:9, 5:15, 11:7). *ti oun estin* occurs also at vs. 26.

I shall sing. In his relatively few references to singing Paul shows a preference for *psallein,* which usually refers to praise accompanied by an instrument. Apparently glossolalia could be related not only to prayer but also to song (a phenomenon that recurs in charismatic circles today). The only other reference to Paul singing is in Acts 16:25 (*hymnoun*). Cf. G. Delling, *TDNT,* VIII, 489-503.

16. *bless.* Probably to be taken as equivalent to "give thanks." This differs from the more general reference in the previous verse in that it has a liturgical

function in the communal worship. It is presented as a part of *being built up*, as the next verse indicates.

the one who occupies the place of the uninstructed. The key word is *idiōtēs* —one whose individuality is stressed, one who is not an official person, the "loner." Outside this context, Paul uses the word in II Cor 11:6, where he applies it to his elocutionary deficiency; and it is coupled with *agrammatoi* in the description of Peter and John in Acts 4:13. Weiss is convinced that the word refers to a special class of persons (somewhat analogous to uncircumcised Jewish proselytes) who had accepted much of Christianity but had neither been baptized nor received the Spirit. He takes the reference to *the place* to mean that certain seats were reserved for those who had not yet been admitted into full Christian communion. These half-Christians would not be able to make the expected response to the thanksgiving. There is, however, no other evidence for the existence of such a distinction in the Christian communities. (Cf. H. Schlier, *TDNT*, III, 217.) Moreover, vss. 2 and 9 indicate that the *idiōtai* are not the only ones who do not understand the things spoken in tongues: other Christians present do not understand either. Baptized Christians who themselves have the gift of tongues do not understand the tongues-speaking of other Christians. If *the place* refers, not to a physical accommodation, but to a function or role, the *idiōtēs* may be anyone who does not possess the gift of interpretation at the moment tongues are being spoken. In vss. 23-24, how-ever, this person is classed with *unbelievers;* and if Weiss' view about an inter-mediary group is rejected, they must be outsiders, nonmembers, at best "inquirers," who participate neither in tongues nor interpretation nor, for that matter, in sympathy for either.

17. *nicely, kalōs.* That is, "well enough" from the standpoint of the speaker and (vs. 2) God.

19. *with my mind,* that is, with the mind productive (vs. 14). Overme-ticulousness in distinguishing this from "in a tongue" gave rise to the textual change *dia tou noos mou.*

20. *be like children.* An unusual verb, only here in the New Testament. The root is used at 3:1 in a pejorative sense, but the figure is used quite flexibly here.

become mature. In 2:6 such persons are in view.

21. *written in the law.* The identification is imprecise; for the quotation is adapted from the prophetic canon, Isa 28:11-12. There is evidence, however, that rabbinic usage allowed the identification of Torah with all Old Testament scripture; cf. StB, II, 462-463. Some of the variation in text may be reflected in Aquila; cf. Conzelmann, 242, n. 17.

Paul interprets the text in a kind of pesher style and refers it to the tongues phenomenon. The original reference of the text may have been to the strange languages of invaders, or it may more immediately refer to the more or less nonsense patter by which children are taught letters (cf. O. Kaiser, *Isaiah 13-39* [Philadelphia, 1974], 242-246).

says the Lord. In no way part of the quoted text, the apostle adds this as the traditional prophetic refrain.

22. *intended for.* This rendering of *eis* prepares for the reversal that is presented in vss. 23 and 24.

those who believe . . . unbelievers. A curiously careful juxtaposition: Paul uses *apistoi* for non-Christians, but he employs the participial phrase for "believers." *pistoi* occurs in this sense in the Pauline literature only in Eph 1:1; Col 1:2; and the Pastoral letters. Perhaps the explanation lies in the ambiguity of *pistos* between "faithful" and "believing"; in the case of the negative term either sense is appropriately descriptive, but here the element of belief is determinative.

23. *the whole church.* An example of the imprecision with which Paul uses terminology—from the modern point of view. He does not mean the entire Christian church, of course, but a full attendance of the local congregation, which would emphasize the bedlam created by general tongues-speaking.

you are mad. H. Preisker's summary of the New Testament usage of the word is instructive (*TDNT*, IV, 361). The examples uniformly reflect "the judgment of unbelief on divinely filled witness."

24. *investigated.* As noted at 4:3-4, there is no satisfactory English equivalent. The translation used there is maintained here for comparative convenience. The four reactions enumerated in this and the following verse are overlapping in meaning.

25. *"Truly God is among you."* The response is approximated in Isa 45:14; Dan 2:47; and Zech 8:23; and Paul is probably adapting the saying with some freedom.

26. *each one has.* TR adds *hymōn.* Correlation is made by the repetition of the verb *echei.* The idea is distributive, not cumulative.

27. *two at a time.* As the sequel shows, this means in one service. The numeration is not to be pushed.

28. *the speaker in tongues.* The subject is necessarily inferred from the context.

and to God. A legitimating concession; cf. vs 2.

29. *let the others discriminate.* There seems to be an implication of the possibility of false prophecy. The problem evidently developed progressively in the early church as may be seen from the discussion in Didache 10:7 - 13:7; in 11:7 the readers are warned *oude diakrineite* while the prophet is "speaking in spirit."

30. *if God gives a revelation.* The somewhat clumsy passive seems to require this rendering; cf. NOTE on 1:5.

who is seated. Standing was the normal attitude for leadership participation, a practice inherited from the synagogue; cf. Luke 4:16.

32. *spirits of the prophets.* Cf. second NOTE on vs. 14.

32-33a are made parenthetical by WH, but the ideas of both verses seem to be appropriate to the context. WH and the English and American Revisers make the paragraph break at the end of vs. 33, but the sense and structure favor the more recent editorial arrangement.

COMMENT

Prophecy, tongues, and building up

In this passage Paul concentrates on one gift, speaking *in a tongue* or *in tongues*. The long treatment indicates that some Corinthians were claiming that possession of this gift demonstrated that they were the only full recipients of the Spirit and that they were spiritually superior to others with different gifts. Whether they claimed that speaking in tongues was an indispensable sign of possession of the Spirit is not stated, but the matter was serious enough to call forth lengthy consideration by the apostle. The theological dimension of the problem is supplemented by liturgical considerations, for there was apparently disagreement on the role and scope of tongues-speaking in worship.

The problem is sharpened for Paul by his belief that this is a legitimate spiritual gift and by the fact that he himself has the gift. He therefore will not treat the practitioners of this gift brusquely, nor will he unceremoniously ban them from the assembly. Yet there seems to be associated with the practice a kind of immoderation which is producing alienation within the church; and outsiders, who should be attracted to the Christian community, are being put off. From Paul's incidental comments it is not hard to conjecture the sorts of consternation, fear, revulsion, or controversy that the situation was producing.

The phenomenon, now prominent in sectors of the charismatic revival today, broke out again about a century and a half after Paul's time when followers of Montanus claimed special inspiration of the Spirit and spoke in tongues. The movement was rejected by church orthodoxy; but it was espoused by Tertullian, who, early in the second century, defended it, largely in reaction to theological and devotional laxity in the church. The relationship of spiritual ecstasy and prophecy at that time is strongly reminiscent of the situation in Corinth as implied by Paul.

Paul's discussion is a serious attempt to deal with the question in such a way as to avoid a split in the church, a danger already present according to his earlier remarks. It is interesting to observe that the quarrels in the church, whatever their theological ramifications, were exacerbated by emotional and aesthetic considerations that surfaced in public worship (cf. chs. 10-11). Paul's correspondence treats theological matters with serious care, but he also considers in detail the minor ethical questions and disturbances over trivial matters that plagued his churches.

Having dealt with the spiritual gift *par excellence,* he returns to the consideration of spiritual gifts as introduced in ch. 12. He will deal with tongues-speaking in some detail, but as a foundation for that treatment he declares *prophecy* to be *especially* important. His reason is that prophecy illuminates the people of the church; by contrast, speaking in tongues is of value only to the person who speaks. Apparently he believes that the primary function of tongues is to express feelings, thoughts, or sentiments too deep for words and to address them to God in vocalization that breaks the bounds of ordinary, rational speech. Perhaps this is what Paul has in mind in Rom 8:26.

The sounds are audible to all, but the meaning escapes cognition. For the auditors there is nothing; the *mysteries* are penetrable only by the *spirit* of the speaker. There is no indication that this process is to be discredited and dismissed, but its exercise and direction must take into account the communal aspect of the exercise of the gift. It is on this basis that prophesying is marked as a more important gift for the church. Calvin (writing on 12:10) says that prophecy means "that unique and outstanding gift of revealing what is the secret will of God, so that the prophet is, so to speak, God's messenger to men" (trans. Fraser, p. 263).

Prophecy addresses the human understanding and provides a *message* that *builds up a church*. It develops loyalty, appealing to the conscience and will; and it helps people confront their reverses and sorrows. Apparently prophecy in these early churches functioned in a role filled now mainly by preaching. (But there seemed to be a greater sense of immediate Spirit direction as the sequel will show.)

It is surprising that Paul regards speech addressed to people more highly than speech directed to God. The reason is the scope of edification; speech in a tongue builds up only the speaker. He seems to be saying that private devotion has its place; but it is not as important as public devotion, which builds up the entire group. The life of the church is more important than the religious development or expression of a single person. Although he does not make the point here, this illustrates the fact that love as the essence of the Christian life can only be expressed in a group of people, and particularly in the body of the church. Paul takes a positive stance toward the devotion of the individual, but he is anxious that this should turn outward rather than inward. The one who prophesies performs a greater function than the one who speaks in tongues since the prophet communicates to other people the mind of God so as to build them up in a social unit that lives as the body of Christ.

The only exception that makes speaking in tongues equal in value to prophecy is when utterances are interpreted. Up to this point the discussion pictures a condition in which glossolalia remains without further treatment, and thus it is private and addressed to God. As such, despite its being a gift of the Spirit, it is of no value to the church. Interpretation gives it such value. Calvin's comment is to the point: "For, if interpretation is added, then there will be prophecy" (trans. Fraser, p. 287).

Tongues, interpretation, and building up

Paul labors the point by using himself as a hypothetical example. Even if he should speak in tongues in their assembly, it would do them no good. He must, rather, provide them a message from God that they can readily appropriate. The emphasis on *prophecy* is elucidated by inclusion of *revelation, knowledge,* and *teaching.* Such communication is a principal purpose of the public meetings of the church.

The apostle's penchant for apt illustration here produces a comparison between musical instruments and oral communication. *Flute, harp,* and *trumpet* were commonly known in the first-century world; but there seems to be no particular reason for his selection of these three. Each produces a recognizable tune or signal, but they must make tones with proper intervals and *distinction,* or no one will appreciate the music or signal. (The trumpet use is evidently that known as "bugle calls" today.) The application is that, if people speak in tongues but not in understandable speech, no one will comprehend what is said; and the people might as well talk into empty *air.*

Now Paul actually compares tongues-speaking with the multiplicity of world languages (further evidence that tongues, in this context, are not unknown, earthly languages). He refers to them as "sounds" or *voices;* the intention is clear from vs. 11. Children born into a region grow up to understand the language of the region, but people outside that territory do not understand the language without extraordinary help. People who do not understand each other in this way are *barbarians* to each other. (The word comes from the term used by the Greeks to refer to those who spoke other languages; apparently their speech sounded like the onomatopoeic "barbarbarbar.") The point, of course, is that, even if vocal sounds make sense to the speaker, they are of no value unless they communicate meaning and ideas to the hearers—and this particularly in the church.

The Corinthian Christians were fascinated with spiritual gifts. Although there seems to be no doubt that Paul traced these gifts to God's Holy Spirit (12:4-11), in the present passage he does not develop that idea. He speaks of the individual's spirit, which seems somehow or other to be a corresponding entity in or of the person. He is not implying that many spirits operate in pouring out the diversity of gifts. There is a somewhat similar use in I John 4:1-3 and in Revelation 1, where each church has a spirit. The individual's spirit is distinguished from his *mind,* which comes into play when interpretation takes place. (This is important in under-standing vs. 32.) The mention of *spirits* here, then, is a kind of accommo-dation to the remarkable power of the Spirit by which numerous people experience effects of the Spirit, each one being particularly aware of his own spirit. Thus Paul can speak of *spirits* without weakening his teaching about the one Spirit.

He reiterates his concern with *upbuilding*. Spiritual gifts are incom-patible with spiritual selfishness. *Upbuilding* may include the membership growth of the church; but the emphasis in this letter is on strengthening the Christian character, unity, and interrelationships of the church body. To this end it is important that tongues-speaking be complemented by in-terpretation that calls into play the mind of the speaker—or, as the case may be, the mind of another person who has a particular gift for inter-pretation. Since Paul says *my spirit* and *my mind,* he may be implying that even when speaking in a tongue is a private devotion, it should not be without exercise of the intelligence. Sometimes the spiritual utterance took the form of song, but the same requirement is laid down: people in the community must be able to perceive and understand.

At vs. 16 there is an interesting though not completely clear insight into first-century worship. A leader pronounces a blessing or prayer of thanks-giving to which the congregation is expected to respond, "Amen." There are present not only baptized, confirmed Christians but also *uninstructed* persons who seem to be interested outsiders, perhaps "inquirers" (more is said about these people in vss. 23-24). Now if the blessing is *with the spirit,* that is, in an uninterpreted tongue, these people are unable to make the response. Such inability would not be critical for Christians, for they have other avenues of spiritual blessing, but apparently this is an impor-tant matter for the *uninstructed*. They fall into the same loss that Paul has already decried: they are *not being built up* even though the prayer is au-thentic from the standpoint of the one who utters it. The purpose of thanks in public is to express gratitude to God for blessings that all in the church have received; therefore thanksgiving in a tongue is not suitable as an outpouring of collective prayer.

Paul's capping argument is his own experience and its significance for him. He has personally practiced tongues-speaking—more than the Corinthians have, he says, although it apparently was not done in their presence. Probably it was usually in private, for *in church* indicates a situ-ation different from that in which he exercised the gift. The New Testa-ment records bear testimony to his speaking *with* his *mind*. This practice in Christian congregations he values more than the most prodigious speak-ing *in a tongue,* for he is building up the church.

Tongues and unbelievers

The luxuriant outbursts of enthusiasm, excitement, inspiration, and miracles are impressive and produce sensational effects. Since these are to be attributed to an activity of God's Spirit, they are regarded with awe and respect. It is surprising, however, that Paul is so persistent in tempering this enthusiasm; and this must be because he suspects that a largely human element enters into the ordinary practice of these gifts. The glorious rays of divine light stream through the prism of human lives and come out refracted into different colors, a diversified spectrum rather than the pure, white, divine light. So he commands them to grow up, to *stop being children in* their *thinking*. Like children they were not exercising critical faculties of discrimination. They were not seeking to put emphasis on the greatest divine gifts and particularly love. Children are fascinated by spectacular novelty; maturer persons learn to distinguish abiding value from temporary excitement. In one respect children are to be imitated: they are innocent of the intricate wiles of *evil*.

Paul cites as commentary a passage in Isaiah that threatens future judgment upon the people of Israel. He appears to take it to mean that the people have refused to listen to the clear message of the prophets and so will be subjected to the strange language of the enemies who are overrunning the land, foreign tongues they cannot understand. This unintelligible speech, then, becomes a sign of God's judgment on the people who do not believe. Paul transfers the idea from the situation of the old Israel to the present condition of the church. The only social purpose for speaking in tongues in a group without interpretation is to strike terror into the hearts of unbelievers who listen to it and thereby perceive the strange, mysterious judgments of God. The purpose of prophecy, on the other hand, is to communicate a message primarily to the believers rather than to the unbelievers. Yet when *the whole church assembles* and there is general tongues-speaking, an unexpected result takes place with regard to *uninstructed persons and unbelievers* who may enter: instead of being stricken by a sense of judgment as they hear the strange noise, they will declare that the church people are insane. Thus the sign meant for judgment misses the mark and produces an opposite result. On the other hand, the prophecy that was meant as a sign *for those who believe* turns out to be a sign *for the unbelievers;* for when a prophet is inspired to speak the message of God understandably, to address various sins of which people are guilty, and to exhibit evils that are being practiced, the unbeliever feels the presence of God reaching into and changing his innermost being. The person responds to this by worship and public confession.

Tongues, prophecy, and order

The issue of the whole matter is to recognize that the expression of all the spiritual gifts must have in view the strengthening of the divine society. The gifts are all inspired by the Spirit, and all have their use. (In this context Paul includes what is presumably another gift, *a psalm.* This suggests that he thinks of all legitimate participation in corporate worship as Spirit-gifted.)

Special instruction, however, is needed to guide the congregation when they speak in tongues. At each particular meeting no more than two or three persons should exercise this gift. The apostle makes the rather obvious recommendation that this be *in turn*—which implies that this procedure was not always followed. (Calvin cites an old proverb, "Too many cooks spoil the broth" [trans. Fraser, p. 301].) He reiterates his earlier stipulation about interpretation. In vs. 13 it was implied that the speaker might also interpret; here it seems more likely that another exercises that gift though it may be one of the tongues-speakers. In any case, *if there be no interpreter,* the would-be speaker is to refrain from public use of tongues though he may continue his devotions in private form. There is no hint given in the passage how anyone could tell whether an interpreter was present or not. Evidently the person who had the gift of interpretation must have been conscious of it. It must also have been possible for the one who was about to speak in tongues to anticipate the speaking and to discover whether interpretation was feasible. All this regulation must necessarily have dampened exuberant excitement that might be merely emotional. Such prerequisites to be taken care of beforehand probably reduced the number of times people would speak in tongues.

Instruction is likewise given to the *prophets* to limit their presentations to two or three persons. Since the prophet was inspired by the Spirit, his message must be received in faith; but down through the ages the believing community has been plagued by false prophets. The problem then becomes one of distinguishing between those who are true and those who are false; and some people in the early church had the gift to *discriminate,* by which they could tell the difference. This mysterious gift is not described and is perplexing; for if true prophets cannot be distinguished without people who have the gift of discrimination, how can the ones who discriminate truly be distinguished? False discriminators could emerge just as easily as false prophets. Spirit-filled communities confront difficulties that arise because they are composed of people who have the weaknesses of human pride.

While one prophet is speaking, a Christian *seated* in the group may receive a divine *revelation* that he feels called upon to communicate to the church. When this happens, the first prophet should yield to the person with the newer, urgent message. It is not specified but is probable that this revelation is of the order of a prophetic message. In Paul's usage *revelation* sometimes is an appearance, visible to the spiritual eye (1:7; Rom 8:19; II Cor 12:1). In other cases it is a message that discloses the nature of the gospel or the judgment of God upon people, or some order to obey (Rom 1:17,18; Gal 1:12, 2:2). In this present verse it is possible that the person seated receives in his mind a strong impression of an idea, an interpretation of the gospel, or some injunction that he feels is imperative for the church to hear. Speakers in the church, however, even when inspired by the Spirit, are to restrain their urgent impulse. They can wait until others get through and allow one person only to speak at a time, this for the good of the assembly. *The prophets* have voluntary control over the prophetic spirit. This means that the word or message that comes from the Spirit to the prophet does not override his will or supplant his intelligence. The prophet understands his own prophetic message and can utter it when the proper time arises. This remarkable restraint reflects a fairly obvious observation about the God who is the source of the prophetic utterance: he fosters *not confusion* but *peace*.

SILENCE OF WIVES IN THE CHURCH
(14:33b-36)

14   33b Just as it is in all the churches of the saints, 34 let the wives be silent in the churches; for they are not permitted to talk. Then let them continue to be subordinate just as the law also says. 35 If they want to learn anything, let them ask their husbands at home; for it is disgraceful for a wife to talk in church. 36 Has the word of God either gone forth from you or drawn near to you alone?

NOTES

14:33b. There is some question about the paragraphing here. WH agrees with *TR* in placing the break at the end of the verse, but most recent editors have begun a new section with *hōs* (Barrett is an exception). There is some awkwardness in the repetition of *ekklēsiais*. Héring and Conzelmann get around this by taking the second occurrence as "assemblies"/"meetings." Sense seems strongly to favor the break as adopted here; custom is directly applicable to the activity of women in the church but is more difficult to relate to God's peace role.

34-35 appear after vs. 40 in some MSS, but the transfer leaves a very awkward text. In case of the transfer, however, 33b would almost certainly have to be construed with 33a. Verse 36, then, would have a somewhat different meaning, perhaps referring to the arrogance of prophets who were willing to sacrifice the peace of the church for the sake of unbridled prophecy.

34. *the wives. gynaikes* is rendered "women" by practically all translators and commentators. It is curious that the position set forth in the COMMENT has been so uniformly overlooked. *TR* adds *hymōn* on very weak manuscript evidence; this pronoun would seem to apply more naturally to "wives" than to "women," but there is no evidence for such an understanding in the tradition.

let them continue to be subordinate. The linear jussive suggests that this is the expected condition rather than that Paul is proposing any radical regulation.

35. *their husbands.* On *idious* used for a simpler possessive, cf. AGB, § 2 (p. 370b). Also cf. Isaksson, *Marriage and Ministry,* 169, n. 1.

disgraceful. The translation used at 11:6 is maintained here.

36. *drawn near.* The only other occurrence of the verb in the Corinthian letters is at 10:11. One translation has been used though perhaps the context here would suggest "come."

As suggested above, the verse is not easy to relate to the context. The correlatives are somewhat awkward however the transition is made. The sense of the verses is better when taken with the passage following. The arrogance of the addressees vis-à-vis the word of God would lead naturally into Paul's high interpretation of what he is writing. The sentence structure, however, supports the accepted paragraphing.

COMMENT

At 11:3 *gynē* is translated "woman" in order not to beg the interpretative question, but the strong possibility is suggested that the word may have its alternative meaning "wife." In the present context it may be inferred that Paul has in mind *wives* throughout the passage, for in vs. 35 these female persons are enjoined to gain church information from *their husbands at home.* This interpretation is strengthened by the exhortation to *continue to be subordinate.* (The same verb is used in Eph 5:24, where wifely subordination is compared to the relationship between the church and Christ.) The reference to *the law* probably has in mind Gen 3:16. Since the societal relation between man and woman in Jewish faith was normally that of husband and wife, Paul probably is thinking of marital subordination rather than some kind of subordination of all females to all males. It is possible, of course, that he might have drawn such a conclusion, but it is important to note that because of his social orientation such a consideration never seems to have come into focus.

The intent of the command, then, is to interdict situations in which wives publicly contradict what their husbands say or think or embarrass them by an interchange of conversation. They may thus be rejecting the authority of their husbands (which was firmly fixed in the sociology of their religion) and thereby be no longer *subordinate*. In 11:5 Paul indicated that women could pray or prophesy in the church; so unless Paul is contradicting himself (or, as some have suggested, there is a non-Pauline interpolation) he here enjoins silence in matters other than praying and prophesying. Since good order is a major emphasis of the context (cf. vss. 26,33,40), he may be referring especially to speaking in tongues or even to any sort of clamorous discussion of controversial issues which have arisen in the assembly.

The advice about asking *husbands at home* suggests that some of the talk Paul is telling them to suppress may have been questioning out loud about what the last speaker said or meant. This would have been all the more likely when tongues-speaking occurred and interpretations were given. It must have happened that on some occasions unseemly, clamorous, shrill, and excessive speaking by the wives threatened the good order of the community services. So Calvin remarks "that the things which Paul is dealing with here are indifferent, neither good nor bad; and that they are forbidden only because they work against seemliness and edification" (trans. Fraser, p. 307).

The *disgraceful* aspect of the wives' actions, then, would refer to shame imposed on the husband by the public conduct of the wife. In his religio-social milieu Paul can hardly be faulted for this attitude. Since the other disorders in the Corinthian church were almost exclusively the result of faults on the part of its male members, the apostle's prejudice is probably compensated by the other emphases he places upon women's rights (as in ch. 7; cf. also Gal 3:8, and, assuming the Pauline authority with Markus Barth [AB, Vol. 34A, ad loc.], Eph 5:22-33).

The summary challenge in vs. 36 could be construed to be addressed to the wives in the context. The tone, however, sounds more general; and indeed the pronoun is modified by a masculine adjective, *alone*. So it is the whole church which is confronted with the questions. *The word of God* did not originate in their church, nor have they been the only ones to receive it. Therefore they ought to recognize that they—both men and women—must not foster disorder in the church: the word of God controls them, not they the word.

INJUNCTION TO PROPER ORDER (14:37-40)

14 37 If anyone seems to be a prophet or a spiritual person, let him recognize that the things I am writing to you are a commandment of the Lord. 38 If anyone ignores this, God ignores him. 39 So, my brothers, be zealous to prophesy, and do not forbid speaking in tongues. 40 Let all things take place properly and in good order.

NOTES

14:37. *a spiritual person.* The flexibility of Paul's terminology may be seen in his use of this word. In 2:12 - 3:3 "spiritual" persons are contrasted to "physically oriented" persons, and the word has a broad frame of reference embracing eminently desirable characteristics. Here it must refer to those who are exercising the spiritual gifts discussed in chs. 12 and 14 (pointedly excepting 13) with prophecy specifically mentioned (in line with the emphasis of 14).

are a commandment of the Lord. There are several variants of the text. Only the western reading, which omits *entolē*, materially affects the meaning of the text; and the UBS properly rejects that reading because of the tenuous support.

38. *God ignores him.* The textual problem is notorious (see Clark, *Studia Paulina,* 62-63), but the decision for the passive indicative against the linear jussive is secure enough. The interpretation of the passive as a circumlocution for the divine subject is supported here by AGB, 11b.

39. *do not forbid speaking in tongues.* The confused state of the text (a "D" reading in the UBS edition) fortunately does not affect the meaning. The details are technical and are adequately presented by Metzger. The linear imperative suggests that there was opposition to tongues-speaking in the Corinthian church; perhaps it was connected with the party disputes.

COMMENT

A prophet or a spiritual person has been illumined and directed by the Spirit; and so he may feel self-sufficient over against anybody else, even an apostle. Paul is quite positive, however, that such a person is not exempt from an obligation to heed and obey what he is *writing;* for his instructions issued about the order of worship and directed to the good of the whole church have the full force of divine command even though they are presented in a common form. Apostolic communication expounding requirements of harmony has a status superior to spiritual impulses.

Verse 38 has been subject to great variety of interpretation, partly

resulting from the uncertainty of the text. The verb can mean "to be ignorant," and the long prevailing translation of the KJ implied that the case of
one who was too ignorant to understand the significance of Paul's authoritative communication was beyond hope or at least beyond the concern of
the Corinthians. Chrysostom thought that the apostle proposed this to
avoid contention (cf. Robertson and Plummer, 327). In this context, however, the verb may be taken to mean "to ignore, disregard"; and it then
refers to persons who deliberately disregard what is best for upbuilding the
church and particularly the apostle's recommendations for that purpose.

The final exhortation emphasizes again the primacy of *prophecy* among
spiritual gifts. The charge to allow *speaking in tongues* is certainly to be
understood as subject to the conditions previously specified. His insistence
throughout chs. 12-14 that the Spirit-source of the gifts demands account-
ability in their exercise is brought to a pointed conclusion, that *all things*
are to *take place properly and in good order.*

EXCURSUS: CONCERNING THE GOSPEL OF THE RESURRECTION (15:1-58)

THE RECEIVED TRADITION ABOUT THE RESURRECTION (15:1-11)

Covering statement

15 ¹Now I am informing you, brothers, about the good news that I proclaimed to you, and which you received, and on which you have taken your stand. ²And you are being saved by means of it if you are holding fast to the message that I proclaimed to you, unless you came to futile faith.

The saving career of Christ

³For I delivered to you with top priority that which I also received: that Christ died for our sins according to the scriptures, ⁴that he was buried, and that he has been raised on the third day according to the scriptures.

First appearances following resurrection

⁵And then he appeared to Cephas, then to the Twelve. ⁶Next he appeared to more than five hundred brothers at one time, the majority of whom remain alive until the present, though some have died. ⁷Then he appeared to James, and next to all the apostles.

Appearance to Paul and the sequel

⁸And last of all, as if to the one untimely born, he appeared also to me. ⁹For I am the least of the apostles, who am not fit to be called an apostle because I persecuted the church of God. ¹⁰But what I am, I

am by the grace of God; and his grace that was for me did not become void; but I worked harder than all of them—that is, not I, but the grace of God with me. 11 So whether it be I or they, this is the way we preach and this is the way you came to faith.

NOTES

15:1. *I am informing.* Bultmann (*TDNT*, I, 718) takes the verb "in a secular sense." The difficulty is that the Corinthians already "know" the substance of what Paul here states. In 12:3 the verb seems to apply to an inference his readers might draw, but in II Cor 8:1 it refers to new information. Probably the expression is parallel to similar ones in 10:1, 11:3, 12:1, etc.

and which you received. The series of relative clauses is in more or less logical order (*tini logō* is "almost like a relative" [Robertson, *Grammar*, 954]). The paratactic structure is better broken up in translation. This verb is part of a chain connecting with *delivered* and *received* in vs. 3: they describe the process of tradition in the early church. On this cf. Dodd, *The Apostolic Preaching and Its Developments,* especially the first lecture.

2. *you are being saved.* Cf. NOTE on 1:18.

you came to futile faith, literally, "you believed in vain." The past aorist of *pisteuein* has almost a technical sense in the New Testament. It indicates, not acquiescence to certain ideas, but a passing from a status of non-faith into the relationship with Christ (by which one is *being saved*). Paul poses the possibility that this can be simulated.

3. *with top priority. en prōtois* may be deliberately ambiguous (so Barrett, who translates "first of all"). It can have a temporal reference ("the first things I delivered") or it can indicate the relative value of the substance ("the things of first importance"). Héring notes and rejects the possibility that the adjective is masculine and refers to the Corinthians ("you were among the first"). It is perhaps superfluous to suggest that the apostle would deliver "first things first." (The example of the phrase in Plato, *Republic* 522C, does not really decide the case.)

according to the scriptures. On the possibility of specific passages of the Old Testament that may have been in mind here and in the next verse, cf. COMMENT. It is likely, however, that Paul here reflects a general conviction developed from the church's treatment of particular portions; cf. especially Dodd, *According to the Scriptures, passim* (this passage is only briefly referred to). Manson thinks that this understanding goes back to Jesus himself; cf. *Mission and Message of Jesus,* 633-634, and *Studies in the Gospels and Epistles,* 22. Cf. also T. Holtz, "Zur Interpretation des Alten Testaments in Neuen Testament," *TLZ* 99 (1974), 19-32.

4. *he has been raised.* The perfect is deliberately and carefully used. Although the time in the past is specified, the continued effect of the action is an essential part of the idea.

on the third day. A part of the kerygma; cf. Luke 9:22 // Matt 16:21 and

Mark 8:31. On the form of the phrase, cf. Beare, *Earliest Records of Jesus*, 139. Also cf. D. Hill, "On the Third Day," *ExpT* 78 (1966-67), 266-267.

5. *Cephas*. He has been mentioned previously at 1:12, 3:22, and 9:5. Since he is here tied into the tradition, the form of the name may be noted. Paul refers to him also in Gal 1:18, 2:9,11,14; the only other use of the name Cephas is in John 1:42. Paul never calls him Simon (Symeon). In Gal 2:7 he uses the name Peter, the name common in the Gospels, Acts, and the Catholic Epistles. One may speculate that Paul utilizes the Semitic form of the name with subtle reference to the spheres of service mentioned in Gal 2:7 (cf. the name change from Saul to Paul).

the Twelve. Metzger, *Textual Commentary*, 567, notes the "pedantic correction" to "eleven" made by some texts, versions, and writers. The phenomenon appears in reverse at Acts 1:26.

6. *have died*, literally, "fell asleep." Cf. NOTE on 7:39; the verb also occurs at 11:30. Although the Greek is aorist, English needs the perfect. The Greek is concerned with their change of vital status; English past punctiliar would be appropriate for narrative.

7. *James*. The COMMENT assumes that this is Jesus' brother. Three other men named James are mentioned in Acts 1:13. Most prominent of these is the son of Zebedee, John's brother; his death is mentiond in Acts 12:2. James, Jesus' brother, appears to have died a martyr's death too. Josephus has one account in *Antiquities of the Jews* XX ix 1; and Eusebius quotes another from Hegesippus in *Church History* II 23.

8. *the one untimely born*. *ektrōma* usually means "miscarriage" but can mean "monstrosity." Conzelmann, 259, n. 95, surveys the literature. It has been tempting for writers to push beyond the evidence. "Monstrosity" is a late use and can hardly apply here. Lietzmann saw that it was the abnormality of Paul's position in the chain of appearances that is in the fore. J. A. Bengel wrote, *articulus vim habet*, i.e. the point of comparison is Paul's status in the appearance-history, not the applicability of the literal figure. Schneider, *TDNT*, II, 465-467, says that "from a spiritual point of view [Paul] was not born at the right time . . . the main emphasis is on the abnormality of the process." Harnack proposed that the apostle is dealing with a term of opprobrium applied by his enemies (ibid.). For discussion of further possibilities, cf. COMMENT.

9. *the least of the apostles*. Cf. Eph 3:8. Contrast I Cor. 4:14-16, 9:1-6, 11:1-2.

fit. Elsewhere the word means "sufficient" (e.g. II Cor 2:16, 3:5); here the idea is "I do not have sufficient qualification."

10. *grace* Cf. COMMENT on 3:10, p. 172. The word is more prominent in Romans and II Corinthians.

all of them. This may mean each one singly or the whole group. The natural meaning of the words suggests that Paul's travels, preaching, founding of churches, and endurance of hardships were greater than all comparable activities of the other apostles. It would suffice for the argument to claim superiority to each individual apostle; but since he attributes the accomplishments to God's grace, he may be making the bolder assertion—which can, indeed, be maintained from the record.

with me. The textual problem is virtually insoluble; the UBS Committee remains uncertain about the article. It is possible to propose a shade of difference in the meaning of the two readings: perhaps the phrase with the article indicates a more exclusive role for *the grace of God.* But even if the reading were sure, such a refinement would be tenuous.

11. *you came to faith.* The aorist, as in vs. 2, indicates not the substance of belief but the basis of the faith relationship (the way of *grace* [vs. 10]).

COMMENT

Covering statement

An excursus on the resurrection occupies the whole of ch. 15, the longest unbroken discussion in the epistle. It is impressive in the original Greek, but no modern translation can compete with the sonorous English rendered by the KJ. The rhythmic sentences, stately language, and triumphant faith compose a majestic anthem that has been heard with awe and conviction by Christians in the English-speaking world for three and a half centuries.

The chapter begins without the formula "with reference to"; so the topic of the ensuing chapter may not have been mentioned in the communication from the Corinthians. Yet it must have been discussed by them, and certain differences of opinion had arisen that required authoritative treatment by Paul. These questions and disputes, like the report of party strife discussed in the early chapters, may have been brought to his attention by *Chloe's people* (1:11). Paul's treatment of the matter indicates that some people in the Corinthian circle were saying that there is no resurrection of the dead (human beings, not including Christ). They must have justified this by arguing that Christ's resurrection was exceptional and that at the reappearing of Christ his kingdom would be composed of those who were still alive. Against the idea that the dead are raised they objected that the decomposed body cannot be restored, that in many instances there is no body to be raised, and that the material body is not suitable for a resurrected existence. It is possible that these people held the Greek belief in the immortality of the soul (as distinct from resurrection of the body), a belief which found a hospitable home as Gnostic ideas developed in the church. This interpretation, however, does not appear to be justified by the language of the chapter.

Paul reminds the Corinthians that he *proclaimed the good news* that he *received* (vs. 3) and that they in turn *received.* This word *received* can refer to a direct revelation from Christ, as in Gal 1:12; but there he is speaking of an immediate revelation. Here the correlation with *delivered* in vs. 3 points to a chain of tradition: Paul *received* the facts that he is relating from Christians who preceded him, and in turn he *delivered* them to the people of his churches. *The good news* (="gospel") is the *means* by which people *are being saved* and *on which* they *have taken* their *stand*. The salvation depends upon *holding fast* to this gospel and believing it in a fruitful and productive manner. Apparently he is afraid that some have come to *futile faith* so that it has no regulative power over their thoughts or lives.

The saving career of Christ

The evangelical details culminating in the resurrection had *top priority* in Paul's message. In this summary account there is evidence that from the very beginning of Paul's Christian experience he accepted the statement that *Christ died* a sacrificial death on behalf of the sins of humankind, which in some way saves them from the guilt and power of sins. The early church affirmed, moreover, that this atoning death fulfilled the scriptures. Many citations from the Old Testament have been proposed to explain how the church became convinced that the suffering and death of Christ were prefigured in scripture, but not all of these are impressive when examined in their contexts. Psalm 22, however (the first line of which is one of the "words" from the cross), has a number of details appropriate to a notable victim of public rejection and suffering. The classic passage is Isaiah 53, the great description of the redemptive suffering of the servant of the Lord. It is possible, also, that the perplexities and difficulties of Moses (experienced from his own family and people) suggested that the "prophet like" Moses (promised in Deut 18:15,18) would have to endure like indignities. The hardships, imprisonment, and neglect imposed upon Jeremiah may likewise have suggested that the ultimate prophet would experience consummate "sorrow" (Lam 1:12,18). The bridge from the Old Testament scripture to this assertion of Paul about the conformity of scripture and the destiny of Christ is, in the last analysis, not clear. Psalm of Solomon 17 contains a summary of the expected messianic deliverance, written not long before Jesus' birth; and there is no indication of belief that the savior would suffer and die. Since the belief that Christ's death took away sins was part of the church tradition that antedated Paul, the genesis of the belief is most reasonably sought in the one great religious genius just before Paul: that is, in Jesus himself.

The second priority datum is that Christ *was buried*. This implies that he was really dead, a *sine qua non* for the proclamation of resurrection. Paul does not pursue the christological implications of this detail, but elsewhere he (and others) used it as a metaphor of baptism (Rom 6:4; Col 2:12; cf. Acts 2:29-31; I Peter 3:18-21).

The third datum, *he has been raised on the third day,* is also *according to the scriptures.* Here there is even less Old Testament scripture to refer to than that hinting at suffering and death. Hosea 6:2 (LXX) says: "He will heal us after two days; in the third day we will rise up and live before him." In the context this is a statement attributed to the people of Ephraim and Judah, who profess their readiness to repent and turn to the Lord, who will heal and restore them. If Jesus identified himself with the true Israel, there is a tenuous possibility of referring this to the Christ; and the cry of hope can tentatively be transferred to him. In Peter's sermon at Pentecost (Acts 2:27) he uses Ps 16:10 to prove that the psalm did not refer to any ordinary man, even David; for men die and suffer corruption; but he referred it to Christ. The original reference to confidence over against premature death is applied to resurrection from the dead. A passage like Isa 54:7, referring to Israel's abandonment to exile, can be transferred to the cross and resurrection if Christ is identified with Israel. Probably *according to the scriptures* must finally be taken as having a general reference; and specific passages supply, not precise exegetical support, but phraseology adaptable to the Christ data believed by the early Christian church.

First appearances following resurrection

The list of people to whom Christ *appeared* alive after his death begins with Cephas/Peter, support for details in the Gospels and elsewhere that Peter held a position of leadership among the apostles. *Then* Christ appeared *to the Twelve.* The number refers to the original band of Jesus' closest disciples. Meticulous accuracy would have required "eleven" here, but the symbolic strength of the number stereotyped its use.

The notable variation from the gospel records at this point is the omission of the role of the women in the first appearances. If one interprets the material in chs. 7, 11, and 14 as evidence of chauvinistic sexual bias on the part of the apostle, then here is additional support for the view. Paul, however, is dealing with known leader-figures and groups and secondarily with weight of numbers of witnesses; so it is precarious to make much of the silence about the women at this point. The questionable viability of women as witnesses in Jewish courts may also have influenced Paul's decision.

The appearance *to more than five hundred brothers at one time* is mentioned nowhere else in the New Testament. The only other sizable groups mentioned in the other records are the hundred and twenty who met to elect a successor to Judas (Acts 1:15) and the unspecified number assembled at Pentecost (Acts 2:1). Since Paul never equates the reception of the Spirit with an appearance of the risen Christ, any identification of numbers here would be questionable. The force of the statement is not only in the number (many as opposed to a relative few) but in the assertion that *the majority* of the number *remain alive* and so presumably can be questioned. The additional detail that *some have died* has at least two points of reference. Witnessing the resurrection did not grant immediate immortality. A more complex meaning of their death is related to expectation of Christ's "return," which Paul will take up later in the chapter. The euphemism of "falling asleep" for "dying" (apparent in the Greek) serves as a preparatory analogue of "waking up," i.e. resurrection.

The next appearance named is to James, the sibling of Jesus. According to the Gospels Mary was the only member of the family that had any faith in the uniqueness of Jesus and his mission. Mark 3:21 contains the remarkable notice that the family at one point thought he had lost his senses, and John 7:5 explicitly states that "his brothers did not believe in him." When Acts, therefore, presents James as a notable leader of the Christian church at Jerusalem, it is fair to question when and how he was converted. Paul supplies the answer by this information about a special post-resurrection appearance. If there was any other direct influence, it is lost to the record. James's new status as a believer offers an indirect proof that there was nothing he could remember from his acquaintance with Jesus in the family that would make such belief impossible.

Then there is an appearance *to all the apostles.* Apparently this includes more than *the Twelve,* and the group cannot be identified with any certainty. They probably include missionaries, and some of them may even be the Seven mentioned in Acts 6:1-6.

Appearance to Paul and the sequel

The final appearance is to Paul himself, *as to the one untimely born.* (For difficulties in identifying this term, cf. NOTE on vs. 8.) If Paul meant the special designation literally, it would seem to mean that he had been born prematurely; and then Christ appeared to him. This could only be if he thought of himself as a kind of stillborn Christian before the vision on the way to Damascus. In such a case he would have been a persecutor of the Hellenists inside the church even though he himself was a Christian, albeit a Hebraist sectarian. Acts 15 shows that Pharisee converts were bitterly opposed to receiving gentiles without circumcision, and it is conceivable that Paul was a Christian of an extremely Jewish type before Christ appeared to him. He could have been a strong legalist even while believing that Jesus was the messiah. This could explain why Acts indicates that "Saul was consenting to" the death of Stephen (8:1) although his role as a Jewish counselor might also explain the mention (especially if this were remembered as a goad to Paul's conscience). There is, however, no substantial support for such an interpretation in Acts.

Probably the "miscarriage" or untimeliness idea is defined in the strictures he makes against himself (evidently the understanding of Ignatius; cf. his usage of the passage in his letter, Romans 9:2). His role as persecutor is most naturally taken to refer to absolute opposition to the Christian church from outside, a misfortune that resulted from the "untimeliness" of Paul's conversion. Though he believed in full and free forgiveness of sins and in the complete emancipation of Christians from the slavery of sin, and though he maintained the genuineness of his apostleship, he never forgot that he had persecuted *the church of God.* The formality of his opposition may be seen in this designation *the church of God;* the intensity of it is evident in its relation to Jesus (Acts 26:15), which might have suggested that he use the phrase "body of Christ." In any case, the burden of this memory—though the sin was canceled and wiped out by the redeeming love of God—remained as a fence against unwarranted self-esteem and pride.

The sequel of the appearance to him, which he understood as a benefit of God's grace, was the appointment and power to carry out an apostle's work. What began *by the grace of God* was continued in the same way, and Paul's apostolic labors were remarkable beyond those of the apostolic band who had been called earlier. Probably this reminder of the extent of his own labors is a part of his running defense against those who compared him unfavorably with the original apostles (as in Galatians 1, 2 and I Corinthians 4, 9). His final words in this section insist again that there is no difference between him and the rest of the apostles about the gospel and Christ's death and resurrection. This is the one way *to faith.* His digression, which came out of his mention of his somewhat irregular place in the chain of witnesses to the resurrection, has worked around to proclamation and ensuing faith, the action of God's grace. This quickly leads back to the main theme of the excursus.

RESURRECTION OF CHRIST AS EVIDENCE FOR
RESURRECTION OF THE DEAD (15:12-19)

15   12 If it is being preached that Christ has been raised from the dead, how are some among you saying that there is no resurrection of the dead? 13 now if there is no resurrection of the dead, neither has Christ been raised. 14 And if Christ has not been raised, our proclamation is worthless and your faith is worthless. 15 Yes, and we turn

out to be false witnesses about God because we testified against God that he raised Christ, whom he did not raise if, as a matter of fact, the dead are not being raised. 16 For if the dead are not being raised, neither has Christ been raised; 17 and if Christ has not been raised, your faith is fruitless; you are still in a state of sin. 18 Then too, those who have died in Christ have perished. 19 If we have hoped in Christ only for this life, we are more to be pitied than all people.

Notes

15:12. *it is being preached.* The christocentricity of Paul's thought shows in the way he puts the subject with the main verb: literally, "If Christ is being preached that he. . . ."

has been raised. The perfect, as in vs. 4, is used here and in 13, 14, and 17.

from the dead. nekrōn is anarthrous throughout this passage. Perhaps "resurrection of dead people" would be more accurate in the sequel, but it would be unnecessarily awkward to try to be consistent throughout. *The dead* has become almost unavoidably traditional. (Although the German has the useful *Totenauferstehung* to replace Luther's *Auferstehung der Todten*, here *von den To[d]ten* remains.)

14. *our proclamation.* For earlier mention of the *kērygma* cf. 1:21 and 2:4.

worthless. kenon suggests emptiness, i.e. nature and content rather than purpose and procedure.

your faith. There is significant support for reading "our faith," but the alternation of these pronouns is a common scribal practice. Here there could be assimilation to *our preaching* or to *your faith* in vs. 17. The similarity of pronounciation of the two Greek pronouns compounds the difficulty. On balance *your* is preferable.

15. *about God.* The Greek genitive is objective. The precise significance of *false witnesses* has been disputed, but the *hoti* clause following seems to set the meaning (cf. Conzelmann, 265-266).

against God. The exact meaning of *kata* is elusive. Perhaps the phrase means about the same as the preceding *tou theou.* The implication of the false witness, however, is that the testimony does not conform to what God has actually done (or not done).

he raised . . . he did not raise. Since the argument turns on the resurrection event, Paul shifts to the past aorist: if there was no event, there is no resurrected Christ (present perfect).

raised Christ. Here *Christ* is arthrous, unusual with this noun as direct object. Three explanations are possible: (a) that the line of argumentation suggested the more formal expression; (b) that in the context Paul really means "the messiah" here; (c) that the variation is by chance. The first seems most likely.

are not being raised. The present here is taken to be linear. It is possible, of course, that it has a futuristic turn; such an interpretation would involve an intensive analysis of Paul's eschatology (some of which must be examined later in this chapter). It may also have aoristic force (since there is no present aorist form in first-century Greek); this implies "the dead [as a matter of principle] are not being raised." The fact that Christ has been raised, however, seems to push Paul into stating what is (as a present experience) going on.

17. *fruitless. mataia* is approximately a synonym of *kenē* (vs. 14).

in a state of sin. Paul uses the somewhat crass metaphor "in your sins." (Cf. also Markus Barth and V. H. Fletcher, *Acquittal by Resurrection*, New York, 1963.)

18. *have died . . . have perished.* Again the problem of the aorist in English. Since the verbs seem to imply the continuing state (in English), the perfect has been used.

in Christ. This pregnant phrase comes close to epitomizing Paul's theology. Weiss renders the phrase from II Cor 5:17 "one with Christ" (*mit Christus eins; Das Urchristentum*, p. 341); and Calvin notes that "Paul calls the Church 'Christ'" (on I Cor 12:12; trans. Fraser, p. 264). For a summary of study, cf. C. A. A. Scott, *Christianity According to St. Paul*, 151-158. Also Bouttier, *En Christ*, and *Christianity According to Paul, passim.*

19. *only.* Does the adverb modify *this life* or *have hoped?* The RSV illustrates the option: the first edition (1946) translated, "If in this life we who are in Christ have only hope"; late editions took the marginal reading of the first edition, "If for this life only we have hoped in Christ." The strong view of hope is overwhelmingly presented elsewhere in Paul's letters: cf. Rom 5:4-5, 8:20-25; II Cor 3:12; Gal 5:5; I Thess 4:13; and, of course, I Cor 13:7,13.

more to be pitied. The comparative often stands for the superlative where the exact relationship is implied (as in 13:13). Here the comparative may stand, but the *all* pushes it to the ultimate degree.

COMMENT

Paul turns from the witness to Christ's resurrection to its implication for faith. He enjoins his readers to reflect upon the obvious logic of denying that the dead are raised. Those who make this denial seem to ignore that the only way it can be true is by affirmation that no one can rise from the dead. In this case *Christ* himself, who lived and died, *has not been raised;* for the universal scope of death made no exception of him. His unique life did not protect him from the end of all human life.

The apostle toys with logic. An old syllogism runs: All men are mortal; Christ is a man; therefore Christ is mortal. But if some Corinthians are proposing a universal negative: No dead men rise from the dead, then the relentless syllogism follows: Christ is a dead man; therefore Christ has not been raised. In his reasoning Paul seems to exclude the possibility that Christ could be an exceptional case. He will not argue that since Christ was divine, he could have been raised from the dead while the rest of mankind are not. Paul assumes that Christ's death puts him in the rank of humanity; and he could not escape the common human destiny, death.

But Paul relentlessly reverses the reasoning. Christ could not have been raised from the dead without the possibility that his resurrection includes the resurrection of the rest of humanity. The syllogism can now read: Christ rose from the dead; Christ is a man; therefore a man rose fom the dead. Or more complexly: If a man rises from the dead, resurrection of the dead is possible; Christ rose from the dead, and he is a man; therefore resurrection of the dead is possible. Paul assumes that Christ in his human nature by being raised from the dead overcame the destructive power of death, and he implies that other human beings receive the same victory. This could be affirmed by a kind of metaphysical argument asserting that the revivification of Christ's human nature introduced a new power into the human nature of those who believe in him so that they, too, are not overcome by death. On the other hand, it may be that God has proved by raising Christ from the dead that he intends to raise other human beings from the dead. Or finally, it may be simply that there was no purpose in raising Christ from the dead if all other persons are to be left to annihilation.

Paul nowhere elaborates on the meaning of the phrase *the dead,* even in his letters to the Thessalonians, who seem to have been unusually concerned about such matters. The metaphor of "sleep" is not developed nor its theological implications explored. Presumably *the dead* include all people since all die (cf. vss. 21-22). The scope of the resurrection, however, is not so obvious. Most of the rest of the chapter will deal with those who are resurrected in the destiny of Christians. His allusions to the fate of others are remarkably few and restrained.

The Corinthians addressed seem also to have ignored another consequence of their argument: the Christian *proclamation is worthless* without the resurrection of Christ, it has no true content and hence no power. Similarly, the *faith* of those who believe the preaching is *worthless,* it is devoid of value and is totally ineffective. This is so because it includes claim and belief about Christ's resurrection, and hence the apostles are perjurers disseminating false testimony. Paul boldly pursues his logic: the testimony is *against God* in that it affirms *God raised Christ,* which is an impossibility *if the dead are not being raised.* His honesty forces him to brand a pious falsehood, no matter how edifying, to be an ultimate lie. If this logical sequence were so, Paul implies that the Christian mission ought to be abandoned; for Christian faith would be ineffectual in dealing with humanity's *state of sin.*

Paul is positive that the resurrection of Christ is a necessary part of God's act of freeing people from sin and guilt. Though Christ's death expressed forgiveness of human sin, the forgiveness does not become effective unless the victim of sin survives. Forgiveness of sins requires that the evil of sin be canceled out, and human hate against God and fellow beings is canceled out by Christ's love expressed in his forgiveness. As long as the victims of human hate and evil are dead, however, the process is blocked. Resurrection turns the evil into good.

The final implication of the fatal logic is that Christian believers who have died *have perished,* they have ceased to exist if there is no resurrection. The ultimate pathos is that a Christian hope limited to *this life* is *to be pitied* in the utmost degree. Paul's thought is that a hope stirred up falsely puts the deluded person into a worse condition than other people who have no hope. Attachment to Christ is truncated and warped unless it is reinforced by confidence that he has overcome death for those so attached. Victories and achievements of a life limited to earthly existence lose their personal significance when they are all to be effaced by universal death. Paul is not deterred by the possibility that he may be subject to the accusation of an eschatological "cop-out"—the "pie in the sky when you die" stigma. Surely he cannot be charged with lack of ethical concern, and his theology makes no concession to the grim history of tyranny and oppression that the church winked at for generations while assuring the victims that they would be recompensed in the future life. Nevertheless, he flatly asserts that Christian hope *only for this life* is pitiable. Perhaps he is thinking of a kind of perpetual misery that seems to be associated with efforts at overcoming the evils in this world; there is a weariness that afflicts many who find how mountainous is the opposition to their efforts. Each generation's victory over evil is set back by the death of the victors, and their descendants often have to repeat the struggle. There is a sense in which each generation starts its moral development from scratch. But perhaps Paul is also thinking about an implication of his understanding of the church as the body of Christ. If those who constitute the visible evidence of that body meet an inexorably final end, then the constant characteristic of faith in Christ is death. In light of the apostle's experience of the risen Christ, this conclusion is unthinkable.

CONSEQUENCES OF CHRIST'S RESURRECTION
(15:20-28)

Christ the "first-fruits" of human resurrection

15   20 But now Christ has been raised from the dead, the first-fruits of those who have died; 21 for since death is through a human agent, resurrection of the dead is also through a human agent. 22 You see, just

as all are dying in Adam, so also all will be made alive in Christ.
23 But each event in its particular order: Christ is the first-fruits, next
are those who belong to Christ in his coming;

Consummation of Christ's reign

24 then there is the end when he delivers the kingdom to the God
and Father, when he nullifies every rule and every authority and
power. 25 For he has to keep ruling until he puts all his enemies under
his feet. 26 Death is being nullified as the last enemy; 27a for "he subjected all things under his feet."

God's ultimate supremacy

27b Now when it says that all things have been subjected, it is clear
that it excepts the one who subjected them all to him. 28 But when he
subjects all things to him, then the son himself will be subjected to the
one who subjected all things to him, in order that God may be the all
in all.

NOTES

15:20. *But now.* An intensive reversal, in "contrast to the preceding conditions" (Robertson, *Grammar*, 1147; cf. his note on "finer shades of thought").
On this passage cf. G. Barth, "Erwägungen zu 1. Korinther 15, 20-28," *EvT* 30
(1970), 515-527.

the first-fruits. The term is derived from the Old Testament sacrificial offering
system; cf. Exod 22:29, 23:19, 34:26; Lev 2:12,14, 23:10-11; and especially
Deut 26:1-11 (LXX adds the term at Exod 25:2-3). The lack of article is apparently not significant; of the nine instances in the New Testament only Rom
8:23 and 11:16 have an article.

21. *through a human agent.* The rhetoric is almost cryptic. Paul may well
have thought "through a man" (*di' anthrōpou*), but his theological understanding warrants the more general expression.

22. *in Adam.* On Adam and the source of sin, cf. Scott, *Christianity According to St Paul*, 49-53. Robertson and Plummer discuss Paul's view of Genesis
1-2 (p. 352); their note regarding the article with *Adam* and *Christō* is hardly
substantiated by Paul's usage elsewhere. On the Adam-Christ typology, cf.
Lengsfeld, *Adam und Christus*, 26-65, and Scroggs, *The Last Adam*, 82-100.
The comparison appears again in vss. 45-49.

23. *each event. hekastos* implies that Paul is thinking of the sequence in

which persons experience the resurrection; but as it turns out, he moves through an *order* of events.

those who belong to Christ. Cf. the note of Zerwick, *Biblical Greek,* § 39, in which he suggests that Paul's theology dictates the meaning of the genitive in this context.

in his coming. parousia carries a lot of theological freight. The phrase could mean simply "when he is present," but it probably contains more eschatological overtone. In the present sequence the *coming* precedes *the end.* Perhaps the order is that suggested in I Thess 4:13-17 and II Thess 2:1. AGB list this reference under the heading, "of Christ, and nearly always of his Messianic Advent in glory to judge the world at the end of this age" (p. 635b). Paul's eschatology ought not to be settled by *petitio quaestionis;* cf. COMMENT.

24. *the end.* J. Leal, "'Deinde finis' (I Cor 15,24a)," *VD* 37 (1959), 225-231, demonstrates that the meaning here is "the final consummation." G. Barth, *EvT* 30 (1970), 515-527, warns against reading an eschatological time-table in this passage; he insists that the emphasis is christological throughout. O. Cullmann, on the other hand, argues for the validity of the time element; see his *Christ and Time* (Philadelphia, 1964), 66-67, 144-148.

delivers the kingdom. Cf. O. Cullmann, "The Kingship of Christ and the Church in the New Testament," in *The Early Church* (Philadelphia, 1956), 105-137; also *Christ and Time,* 150-154. Verse 25 is the precondition of this statement.

the God and Father. The phrase occurs in precisely this form only here and at Eph 5:20 (where there are variants). Usually there is a further modifying gentitive; so perhaps "his" *God and Father* is indicated here. It must be reiterated that Paul does not wrestle with trinitarian niceties.

rule . . . authority . . . power. Cf. Caird, *Principalities and Powers,* for treatment of these terms in Pauline theology. Also COMMENT, p. 163.

25. *his enemies.* Paul, with his Jewish training, does not allow for dualistic speculation. The wording is adapted from Ps 110:1 (LXX, 109:1), a passage often used in the NT and treated as messianic (cf. Dodd, *According to the Scriptures,* 34-35, 119-122; and Hay, *Glory at the Right Hand: Psalm 110 in Early Christianity, passim*).

27a. The citation is from Ps 8:6 [7 in LXX], but it is clearly similar to Ps 110:1. R. Morissette, "La citation du Psaume VIII,7b dans I Corinthiens XV, 27a," *ScEs* 24 (1972), 313-342, examines the quotation carefully and relates it to the Adam-Christ imagery: Christ's resurrection restores and exalts the primitive creation (*all things*).

27b. *to him.* Paul's rhetoric is involved and not easy to follow. The somewhat tortuous use of the pronouns carries along a christological emphasis (cf. G. Barth) which in turn builds to the affirmation of divine sovereignty in the next verse.

28. *the son himself.* There are curious variants. Several fathers read "he himself," and there is fair support for the addition of "also." Although neither of these really changes the meaning, the variations probably expressed sensitivity to implied subordination of the son. (Though some Gnostic thought later made Christ superior to the creator of the material world, there does not appear to be

any evidence for the existence of the idea at this time. Schmithals, *Gnosticism in Corinth,* does not discuss this verse.)

the all in all. The article is textually suspect. The previous three occurrences of *all things* have the article, and it might be expected here. This plus the weight of the few MSS omitting (B A D*) raise a question how the omission came about. The UBS editors straddle with brackets. The translation adopted is traditional with the article added. A literal rendering, "[the] all things among all [people]," is certainly too labored. In any case, the meaning of the sentence does not turn upon the phrase. Héring is inclined to take *[ta] panta* adverbially, "in every respect"; and he is sure *en pasin* is neuter, "in the universe" (pp. 168-169). The context seems to suggest that God becomes *panta,* and the fact that the Bible nowhere teaches pantheism is precisely a guarantee that Paul does not have that in mind here. This seems also to suggest that *pasin* is to be understood personally. (On the lack of reference to the fate of the enemies, cf. Ladd, *A Theology of the New Testament,* 564.)

COMMENT

Christ the "first-fruits" of human resurrection

Paul counters the dismal discussion of life without hope of resurrection with a triumphant assertion of Christ's resurrection. The vigorous clarity of this statement with its striking figure of the first-fruits affirms that all victims of death—past, present, and future—are included in the number of those who enjoy the prospect of resurrection from the dead. He does not attempt to establish anew the fact of Christ's resurrection: it is assumed beyond cavil. But he asserts more than the fact: by his use of the venerable term *first-fruits* he means that Christ is the first one rather than the only one to be raised from the dead. As the first products of the field were used in Jewish sacrificial tradition for special gifts to God that consecrated all the following produce, so the resurrection of Christ is evidence that all whose humanity he shared may now share his resurrection.

There is a certain difficulty when Christ as the first-fruits of resurrection is viewed from the perspective of the Gospel records. There are four incidents mentioned with more or less specificity in which persons are said to have risen from the dead in connection with the ministry of Jesus: Jairus' daughter (Mark 5:35-43); the son of a widow from Nain (Luke 7:11-17); Lazarus of Bethany (John 11:38-44); and "many saints" at the time of Jesus' death (Matt 27:52-53; cf. also 11:5.) Paul's use of the first-fruits figure can be literally consistent with the Gospel records only if he regards *those who have died* as designating Christians who have died since the resurrection of Christ. This is possible. In I Cor 16:15; Rom 11:16;

and 16:5 he means literally the first one(s) in series. Three other resolutions of the problem are possible. (a) A close study of Paul's statements elsewhere about the life, death, and resurrection of Jesus suggests that Paul was unaware of Jesus' having performed miracles of resurrection. He takes the earthly life of Jesus as emptied of divine glory, obedient to the Jewish law, and subject to the common destiny of death (cf. Philip 2:5-8; I Cor 1:22-24; Rom 1:4); and this gives no indication of traditions about resurrections that are noted in the Gospels. (b) Paul's use of "first-fruits" in Rom 8:23 and II Thess 2:13 (accepting the Alexandrian reading) is less precise. It may be argued on this basis that the figure was not intended to be examined for literal applicability. In this case the Gospel records could be treated with relative indifference. (c) Assuming the Gospel traditions including resurrection stories, it may still be demonstrated that Paul's use of "first-fruits" is appropriate. The resurrection of Christ is different from those related to Jesus' ministry. Those persons all died again; Christ's resurrection was the first "permanent" triumph over death. Taking a cue from John, the Gospel resurrection-miracles were "signs"; and they pointed precisely to the one who became the guarantor of life according to the faith of the church (so John 11:25).

The importance of John's stress on "signs" and his emphasis on Jesus' power to give life (5:21,25-29) may be viewed in juxtaposition with Paul's first-fruits figure. In a sense, the Gospel stories tell of resuscitations and recall the Old Testament deeds of Elijah and Elisha. The case of Lazarus seems to be special, however, for three reasons. (a) He had been in the tomb longer than three days, and so according to the thought of the day his soul no longer hovered near the body.* He was (technically) "more dead" than Jesus, who rose *the third day*. (b) John makes the raising of Lazarus the fateful precipitator of the final week of Jesus' career. (c) The case of Lazarus is marked as a "sign" precisely to assure believers that Jesus' resurrection was not exceptional: even though Jesus is divine, it was his intention that his very human followers should share in his resurrection. Thus there is a sense in which Jesus was already the first-fruits of the resurrection before he rose, and his resurrection became the indisputable proof.

Paul moves from this thought to a contrasting parallel between Adam and Christ. The one is a *human agent* through whom *death* became the common human lot; the other a *human agent* of the *resurrection of the dead*. It is not possible to know precisely how Paul understood Genesis 1-2 (cf. NOTES on vss. 20-23 for literature, also on 11:7-9); certainly that

---

* Cf. R. E. Brown, *The Gospel According to John*, AB, vol. 29, second NOTE on xi 17.

is not to be pushed. Death existed before the sin of Adam (even if he was a vegetarian!). Perhaps, as Robertson and Plummer suggest (p. 352), death began with Adam as the penalty of sin; but the transmission is not automatic (cf. Rom 3:23, 6:12-23). The opposite condition is produced by Christ. The ultimate cause of both states is the order and action of God, for it was his will that the two human figures violated and fulfilled.

The scope of the two states is problematical. The result of belonging to humanity is death while the result of belonging to Christ is life. Death as the consequence of Adamic descent is patently universal; and even if Paul is referring to death as the sequel of sin, it is clear that he considers all humanity to be included in this state. On the other hand, there are two distinct possibilities in regard to life because of Christ: all people *will be made alive* because of Christ, or all people who belong to Christ *will be made alive*. The wording of the Greek supports the first alternative, but elsewhere Paul's theology suggests the second (e.g. Rom 6:5-11)—the resurrection achieved by Christ will be available for those who have related to him in a special way, as opposed to its automatic, universal applicability. In any case, the desolate condition of death, the common human lot, is subject to removal because of the marvelous victory achieved through the human agency of Jesus Christ.

The priority of the first-fruits implies that the resurrection of others follows Christ's. They derive the possibility of resurrection from him; and insofar as this is inexorably true, there is a kind of timetable. The association of their resurrection with *his coming,* however, raises questions that have a common denominator in locating a general resurrection at the consummation of the ages, an apocalyptic moment reflected in I Thess 4:14-17. Such an interpretation seems to require either that the dead be in a state of suspended animation approximating nonexistence until the resurrection or that they exist in some intermediate form and state until the resurrection when they resume a bodily wholeness. Verse 18 implies that Paul abhors the idea of nonexistence; the resurrection of Christ means that the dead do not perish. On the other hand, the idea of the survival of the person without the body with a future reunion of the whole finds no confirmation in the writings of Paul.* The inevitable conclusion appears to be that *those who belong to Christ* are raised when they die. (This understanding fits II Cor 5:1-10. It also accords with Jesus' argument about the patriarchs, Mark 12:26-27 and parallels.) The resurrection of the people of Christ, then, occurs after Christ's resurrection but not necessarily at the

---

* Indeed, Rev 6:9 and 20:4 are the only passages which seem to imply such an idea; and as the "souls" in these instances refer to martyrs, they may constitute a special case. Besides, the interpretation of such an apocalyptic context requires special treatment and must be used with extreme care in developing theological ideas.

same time as his final appearing. *In his coming* may be construed with *those who belong to Christ* rather than with *next;* so the sentence will mean that *those who belong to Christ* are to be raised at the end-time *in his coming.* Still to be checked is the balance of the chapter; perhaps a thoroughly consistent view is unattainable.

Consummation of Christ's reign

Subsequent to Christ's *coming* (vs. 23) is *the end.* The Greek *telos* can mean either (a) the goal or final stage toward which everything has been directed, with overtones of completion, success, or attainment; or (b) the finish, coming to a conclusion, even ceasing to be, with the possibility of relating to death or dissolution of the world. The second idea is represented in the New Testament, but it is certainly not the intention here. Paul has the enthusiastic and inspired conviction that Christ is bringing things, not to a destructive disintegration, but to a completion in which the goal of God will be achieved: life, order, peace. The focus is on this intention and its consummation; it comes *in its particular order* (vs. 23), but temporal succession is not to the fore.

The end is characterized by an action: Christ will have nullified all aggregations of opposition to the rule of God and will assign this victory to *the God and Father.* These antagonistic operations are manifest throughout human society. They may be related to some superhuman dominions, but Paul is somewhat cryptic here in this regard. Certainly the forces in human life that confront God are extensive enough without speculation about invisible enemies. (There is, however, a certain personification in *death;* and *under his feet* is figurative; so further consideration of invisible enemies is not precluded in another context.) The rule of Christ in final triumph is primarily to be referred to the collective life of the human race, but Paul would not disregard the personal sense (e.g. Rom 8:24-25). There is a bipolarity in this victory: Christ's rule is in process of controlling *all his enemies,* but the complete subjugation is still to come. Thus the apostle protects his readers from paralyzing pessimism and sentimental optimism. Pessimism overlooks the affirmation that Christ is now *ruling* (and so despairs of the historical process); optimism may treat the victory as already achieved (and so fail to join in the continuing struggle with evil). The life of faith believes that Christ's present rule makes action worth while and puts real power on the side of good over against evil, but it recognizes that the conflict is continuing and commitment allows no respite.

The last enemy is *death.* If *order* in this passage refers to a chronological timetable, death may be scheduled to be eliminated after Christ's enemies have been subjugated, thus at the final resurrection. The verb, however, is linear: *death is being nullified* (in distinction, perhaps, from the aorist *puts,* which seems to stress the event rather than the process). The ultimate enemy of God's people is being abolished as they are dying and being raised in a resurrection to new life. There is nothing here to force the conclusion that death for believers will be abolished at one point in the future. A messianic citation from the Psalter certifies the victory over death by implication (*all things*) but does not bear on the process.

God's ultimate supremacy

The emphasis on the messianic victory leads Paul to emphasize that God himself remains exempt from the subjection under which all things are placed by Christ. This careful statement seems so obvious that it may perhaps hint at some confusion in Corinth that Paul perceives as a dangerous misunderstanding of the relation of Christ and God. *All things* is a universally extensive term, but here it refers only to those things that *have been subjected,* not to the one who *subjects all things,* to the creation and not to the Creator. Paul has not developed a trinitarian doctrine, but his christology is nonetheless a remarkable achievement. Overwhelming as is the work of salvation in the resurrection, it must be seen within the context of the purpose of the Creator God.* Paul meticulously maintains his Jewish monotheistic tradition: therefore *the son himself* is finally *subjected,* a statement that must be read, not from the perspective of a subordinationist christology, but from Paul's position, which is determined to set forth God as *the all in all.*

Nothing is said here about the particular fate of the enemies. What it means for them to be *nullified* (vs. 26) cannot be inferred from this passage. The almost exclusive emphasis is upon those who are raised because of Christ's resurrection and upon the God who effects this triumph in spite of all opposition.

---

* Héring notes (p. 168) how the ancient Greek gods usurped their predecessors in succession.

IMPLICATIONS OF THE RESURRECTION
(15:29-34)

Baptism *"on behalf of the dead"*

15   29 Otherwise, what are those people doing who are being baptized on behalf of the dead? If the dead are not being raised at all, why then are people being baptized on their behalf?

Meaning in Paul's perils

30 Also, why are we undergoing danger every hour? 31 Day by day I am dying—as surely as my boasting of you, brothers, which I maintain in Christ Jesus our Lord. 32 If, humanly speaking, I fought with wild beasts in Ephesus, what benefit is it to me? If the dead are not being raised, "Let us eat and drink, for tomorrow we die."

Summary exhortation

33 Stop deceiving yourselves. "Bad company corrupts good habits." 34 Sober up, as is fitting, and stop sinning; for some are maintaining ignorance of God. I say to you, "For shame!"

NOTES

15:29. *Otherwise.* On this use of *epei,* cf. BDF, §§ 360(2) and 456(3).

baptized on behalf of the dead. M. Raeder ("Vikariatstaufe in I Cor 15:29?" *ZNW* 46 [1955], 258-260) argues that these are persons who are entering the fellowship of the church by baptism in order to share the resurrection with family and associates who had died as Christians. (Cf. also J. K. Howard in *EvQ* 37 (1965), 137-141, who argues the same line and approves Raeder.) It is quite questionable, however, whether *hyper* will bear this interpretation. A practice which appears to have grown out of this reference is attributed to the Marcionites, Montanists, and Corinthians in the second and third centuries. Chrysostom remarks of the Marcionites: "When anyone who is instructed departs this life, they hide a living person under the bier of the dead man and approach the corpse and ask him if he wishes to receive baptism. Then when that one does not answer, the one who is hidden underneath says on his behalf that he wishes to be baptized. Thus they baptize him instead of (*anti*) the one who has departed" (*Catenae* 310; cited by Weiss, 363). (For a modern example, cf. the Mormon practice.) On the use of *hyper* in the sense of *anti,* cf. Zerwick, *Biblical Greek,* §§ 91, 94.

why then. Cf. Zerwick, § 459.

31. *as surely as my boasting of you.* On the asseveration with *nē,* cf. Robertson, *Grammar,* 1150. On *hymeteran* replacing an objective genitive *hymōn,* cf. ibid., 685, and the example from Thucydides in Conzelmann, 277, n. 126. This is the only example of a pronouncement with this adverb-particle in the New Testament. In view of the nature of this epistle it would be tempting to propose that Paul is making an almost joking remark, comparing the uncertainty of his life to the basis of boasting evident in the Corinthian church—but the concluding relative clause makes the whole certainly serious. It is possible to read,

"your boasting," which would then refer to their pride in Paul's accomplishments as their apostle. J. D. Joyce, in "Baptism on Behalf of the Dead. An Interpretation of 1 Corinthians 15:29-34," *Encounter* 26 (1965), 269-277, accepts the poorly attested *hēmeteran* and relates the phrase to a vicarious implication in the baptisms. None of these alternatives is likely.

which I maintain. Literally, "have, hold." If one reads, "your boasting," this clause will indicate that Paul has received their high estimation of his work because it is in *Christ Jesus our Lord;* so they share with the apostle in boasting. The entire sentence, however, seems to be aimed at arguing for the resurrection on the basis of Paul's experience of ultimate *danger* (vs. 30), which is, he would have his readers know, a most solemn experience.

32. *humanly speaking.* The same phrase as in 3:3 and 9:8; but the context seems to require a different translation (whatever interpretation of the verb is adopted). Héring takes the condition as unfulfilled and interprets this phrase to mean that Paul is setting an argument "from a human point of view" without resurrection hope (pp. 171-172), but this creates an unnecessarily awkward sentence and seems to spoil the sequence of the illustrations.

I fought with wild beasts. There is no doubt about the basic meaning of the verb. For the interpretation, cf. COMMENT. Also R. E. Osborne, "Paul and the Wild Beasts," *JBL* 85 (1966), 225-230, and A. J. Malherbe, "The Beasts at Ephesus," *JBL* 87 (1968), 71-80: the former finds a clue in Qumran, the latter places the language in Hellenism; both take it metaphorically of Paul's opponents. There are stories from the second century that bring the experience into close association with Paul's life (cf. *Acts of Paul* in Hennecke-Schneemelcher, *New Testament Apocrypha,* II, 322-387), but there is no detail that can be reliably assigned to the apostle's experience. One wonders where such tortures would have been staged in Ephesus. In the light of the persistent survival of tradition about the location of Paul's prison there, it is strange that there is no shred of local legend.

If the dead. TR followed by KJ takes this clause with the preceding sentence, but the stylistic balance requires taking it with the succeeding quotation.

"Let us eat. . . ." The quotation is taken exactly from Isa 22:13 (LXX). The saying must have been in common use; cf. Luke 12:19-20. Similarly apposite is Isa 56:12.

33. *Stop deceiving yourselves.* Besides 6:9b, the expression occurs in Gal 6:7 and James 1:16.

"Bad company. . . ." The saying may be traced to a fragment (1024) of Euripides but is usually cited as from Menander *Thais* 218. G. M. Lee, "Philostratus and St. Paul," *ZNW* 62 (1971), 121, finds a parallel to Philostratus' *Lives of the Sophists* 502.

34. *Sober up.* The only occurrence of this word in the New Testament. Such paraenetic incursions into arguments are quite Pauline.

as is fitting. dikaiōs, "in a just manner." Their present frame of mind is out of proper relation with Christian faith as Paul understands it. *Ignorance of God* deliberately maintained leads into *sinning.*

"For shame!" The same exclamation that he used in quite different context at 6:5.

COMMENT

Baptism "on behalf of the dead"

The allusion to the idea and/or practice of *baptism on behalf of the dead* is unique in the New Testament in this passage. Practices of heretical Christians in later centuries do not explain the meaning of whatever was being done by some people in the Corinthian church in Paul's time. Close inspection of the language of the reference makes all attempts to soften or eliminate its literal meaning unsuccessful. An endeavor to understand *the dead* as persons who are "dead in sin" does not really help; for the condition offered, *if the dead are not being raised at all,* makes it clear that the apostle is writing about persons who are physically dead. It appears that under the pressure of concern for the eternal destiny of dead relatives or friends some people in the church were undergoing baptism on their behalf in the belief that this would enable the dead to receive the benefits of Christ's salvation. Paul remarks about the practice without specifying who or how many are involved and without identifying himself with them. He attaches neither praise nor blame to the custom. He does take it as an illustration of faith in a future destiny of the dead. Though he gives no indication of the possibility, some of those practicing this unusual baptism may have been among those who were saying that there is no resurrection; they would thus be involved in an incontrovertible contradiction. Since the mention is so unspecific and there is no information from any other New Testament writing (nor, it may be added, in the apostolic fathers), the practice must be considered a curious anomaly, which apparently dropped out of view until revived by some second- and third-century sectarians.

Meaning in Paul's perils

As a second argument to support his teaching about the resurrection Paul proposes that the strenuous and heroic life lived by the witnessing apostles is meaningless unless there is this hope. In the propagating and promotion of faith in the gospel the missionary pioneers were jeopardizing their lives every time they spoke. Paul refers in various ways to his own experiences, e.g. II Cor 4:7-15, Philip 3:10, Rom 8:36-39; and Acts describes a succession of suffering and danger of which he was the victim. These risks are senseless *if the dead are not being raised* (vs. 29). His language is graphic: *day by day I am dying.* The daily dangers are so great that each time he faces the possibility of violent death for the sake of

Christ, he actually gives up his life by denying himself. He underscores the seriousness of his assertion by adding an unusual asseveration in the form of an oath the precise meaning of which is far from transparent. It appears that Paul is insisting that the risks he undergoes as an apostle are deadly serious, as serious as his paternal relationship to his Corinthian friends (cf. 4:15); and these can be accounted for only on the assumption of a resurrection hope.

A somewhat specific illustration is offered, his encounter *with wild beasts in Ephesus*. Elsewhere in his letters or in Acts there is no mention of fighting with wild beasts. In the brutal society of second- and third-century Rome many prisoners were forced to face lions and other animals in the amphitheater before crowds of spectators, and certainly Christians were subjected to such persecution, but there is no reference to such treatment of Christians in the first century. It is not unreasonable that Paul is citing an experience otherwise unmentioned, but the two references to special troubles that he had in Ephesus (II Cor 1:8; Acts 19:23-40) say nothing about *wild beasts*. It is therefore likely that he is using vigorous symbolic language to compare his dreadful experiences in Ephesus to life-and-death struggle with ferocious animals. Perhaps the somewhat enigmatic expression *humanly speaking* is a clue that the language is figurative.

In view of the guarantee of resurrection Paul confidently undergoes such jeopardies. The alternative is the mocking quotation, *Let us eat and drink, for tomorrow we die*. This juxtaposition has seemed to some interpreters to reflect a crassly self-centered outlook. They would affirm that moral values are authoritative and right regardless of belief in a future life, and allegiance to the requirements of justice and truth transcend any and all jeopardies of death. Such moral grandeur has been authenticated by the sacrifice of selfless persons. The acceptance of an absolute authority expressed in moral obligation, however, is itself a testimony to the will of a being who confronts persons with absolute command. Paul dealt most seriously with the impact and obligation of moral law, and he recognized its universal manifestation in human hearts (so especially Romans). But his experience took him further: he was convinced that perfect obedience to law is impossible for unaided human will, and he found deliverance from this disability in his faith relationship with Christ. His experiences convinced him that the life of moral vigor and faith is required, but he also believed that the requirement demands the conclusion that there is a destiny of life after death, which makes sense out of the anomalies and mysteries of this life—a Pharisaic view which he found fortified by God's revelation in Christ. He recognized the constant temptation for people to accept the selfish way, meeting physical needs and enjoying physical experiences without thought about morality, faith, or the future. The mere statement of this temptation refutes its underlying basis. The idea of succumbing to a life limited to the experiences and achievements of the present is fundamentally impossible for Paul, yet he will admit that it makes bizarre sense if indeed this life is all there is.

Belief in a resurrection may also be scoffed at as appeasement of victims of injustice and discrimination through assurance of a happier life in the future. In this view faith is regarded as an actual evil since it diverts attention from the causes of human misery, from tyrannical powers and oppression. The church has on occasion endeavored to soothe suffering people by pointing them to a future happiness that will compensate for present anguish. Paul's position, however, affirms that the certainty of the resurrection offers a proper and effective motive for sacrificial living dedicated to the establishment of an international church dominated by the spirit of love. The struggle to set up this divine fellowship on earth may require the risk of safety, ease, and even life; and so the struggle can be carried out on an effective scale only if those engaged in it are buoyed by the living hope of the resurrection. There is no human experience to demonstrate that the struggle to establish a really redemptive society based on love rather than force or balance of power can be effectively carried out without the deep and living acceptance of the resurrection hope in Christian faith. Even though the efforts of the believing church have not been uniformly successful, the example of the church in the first three centuries proves that such a faith can be effective against the power of human world empire.

Summary exhortation

Paul's presentation has moved from descriptive argument to exhortation. Those who hold a view about the resurrection contrary to his are *deceiving* themselves. Here he indulges in a quotation from Greek secular literature, a rarity in his letters. Whether he had read the line in Menander's play, or whether it had, like many of Shakespeare's lines today, become a common saying, it is impossible to know. He had no interest in making a show of Greek wisdom, but there is no reason to believe that he did not read Greek literature or that he would have been unappreciative of its esthetic qualities. The point of the quotation in this context seems to be that even with the best personal intelligence and independence of mind constant association with those who deny by thought and practice the fundamental assumptions of Christian faith—such as the resurrection—may promote corrupt conformity with the life style of this world. This leads to a kind of intoxication of mind that issues in sin; so Paul strongly enjoins the sobriety *fitting* the faith. Rejection of the resurrection is *maintaining ignorance of God*.

This passage by its diatribe-like questions and assertions implies that denial of the resurrection involves denial of the basis for religious practice, sacrificial living, or serious acceptance of moral duty. This raises the further question: what is being denied in denial of the resurrection? It may be the Hebrew idea of the resurrection of the body in distinction from the Greek philosophical belief in some kind of immortality of the soul. On the other hand it may be the view reflected in II Tim 2:17-18 that the resurrection has already taken place in whatever change had occurred when people become Christian believers (an idea that may be implied in the Fourth Gospel). It seems necessary to affirm that Paul is attacking the notion that nothing of a personal life survives death. The questions in this passage are hardly directed toward the idea of an impersonal soul entering a happy state of eternal reality. They seem rather to presuppose that those in error are either (a) like the Sadducees, who believed in God but rejected any kind of life after death, or (b) like the Epicureans in their doctrine that human personality dissolves into atoms at death, or (c) proponents of a special variation of Christian belief. Paul seems to presuppose that his opponents destroy the point of serious Christian living, and this would issue from belief that death ends all for each person. These persons, then, actually believe that Christ was raised from the dead, but they deny that individuals who die are raised, and they may combine this with a belief that some kind of resurrection has already taken place. They could believe that Christ rose in order to prepare to enter the righteous rule of God on earth. Those who are alive when this takes place will participate. They had no idea how either the souls or the bodies of any who died could survive (cf. the discussion to follow on vss. 35-49); so those who die before the final triumph have no hope.

Paul argues that it is necessary that all believers participate in the life which God has prepared for his people. This can be sustained either by the belief in a future resurrection to take place at one time or by the belief that individuals are raised to new life immediately after death. It is impossible to make an incontrovertible choice between these two readings of the apostle's teaching. He does use the present tense repeatedly in this chapter to refer to the resurrection, and this may indicate a process or series of actions. On the other hand in I Thess 4:16-17 he seems to be dealing with a future, single event. (It is perhaps instructive that these same Thessalonians were concerned precisely about those who were dying before the eschaton [4:13-15].) This supports the view that the earliest Christian generations who were looking for the return of Christ had no doctrine about people who would die in their generation; apparently they thought he would return before anybody died. Paul developed his answer to the Thessalonians that those who die "ahead of time" will be raised specially so they will not miss the coming of the Lord. Unfortunately, Paul left no systematic consideration of this matter; and his remarks seem to be directed to those who have peculiar problems—and his answers are probably *ad hominem.* As time went on and he began to consider the doctrine of the resurrection more carefully, he could affirm that believers are raised as soon as they die. There is no necessary contradiction between the two positions. The early enthusiasm of the Christians had to be adjusted to the fact that people kept on dying (and this must have been evident to Paul as many as fifteen years before the Thessalonians heard the gospel!). Paul redirects the doctrine of resurrection from faith in a remote future action to application to the experience of each person after death. The succeeding passage supports the view that after the earliest formulations of faith questions about the resurrection kept arising to require refinement in new detail.

THE NATURE OF THE RESURRECTION
BODY (15:35-49)

Analogies

15   35 But someone will say, "How are the dead being raised? With what kind of body are they coming?" 36 Foolish person! What you yourself sow does not come to life unless it dies; 37 and what you sow is not the future body but a bare grain, whether of wheat or of some other variety. 38 Now God gives it a body just as he willed, and to each of the seeds he gives a particular body. 39 All flesh is not the same; but people have one kind of flesh, cattle have another, birds another, and fish another. 40 Also there are heavenly bodies and earthly bodies, but the glory of the heavenly bodies is one kind, and that of the earthly is another kind. 41 There is one glory of the sun and another glory of the moon and another glory of the stars, for star differs from star in glory.

Scriptural and theological description

42 This is the way it is with the resurrection of the dead. There is a perishable sowing, an imperishable raising; 43 there is a sowing in dishonor, a raising in glory; there is a sowing in weakness, a raising in power. 44 A body is sown in natural life, it is raised a body in spiritual life. If there is a natural body, there is also a spiritual body. 45 And this is what has been written, "The [first] person [Adam] became a living, natural being"; the last Adam became a life-making spirit. 46 But the spiritual is not first, rather the natural is—then the spiritual. 47 The first person was earthy, from the earth; the second person is

from heaven. 48 Just as the earthy one was, so also are the earthy people; and as the heavenly one is, so also are the heavenly people. 49 And in the same way as we have borne the likeness of the earthy one, we shall also bear the likeness of the heavenly one.

NOTES

15:35. *someone will say.* A diatribe device, but Paul is undoubtedly facing a question that had reached him from the Corinthian community. The immediate section is vital to his consideration of the whole matter of the resurrection. Cf. Dahl, *The Resurrection of the Body, passim;* also the essay of Evans in The Clarendon Bible volume, 136-140; Schep, *The Nature of the Resurrection Body,* esp. 189-200; R. Morissette, "La condition de ressuscité. I Corinthiens 15,35-49: structure littéraire de la péricope," *Biblica* 53 (1972), 208-228.

With what kind of body. The second question narrows the first and represents a kind of justification for the more general query. This specifies the focus of the inquiry.

are they coming. The verb *erchomai* carries the same ambiguity as the English verb "come" with regard to present/future signification. If the regular recurrence of *egeirontai* is interpreted as literally present, there is no convincing evidence for taking this verb otherwise.

36. *Foolish person!* Dahl, *The Resurrection of the Body,* 80, n. 4, notes that wisdom for Paul is more spiritual than intellectual. The implication of the interjection is not that the objectors are ignorant but that they will not see how everyday facts illustrate Christian truth.

you yourself. The emphatic pronoun *su* underscores the foolishness of the addressee, who should recognize personal experience that supports Paul's point.

unless it dies. Paul's statement is not to be pushed from a botanical standpoint. As a matter of fact, the practical disappearance of the sown grain supports the analogy rather well.

37. *bare grain.* The adjective is meant to contrast the state before planting and after growth, but here as elsewhere *the future body* is treated with reserve, and its differentiae are not elaborated.

38. *just as he willed.* The past aorist suggests that the process of germination and growth is in accordance with a divine plan. Cf. COMMENT for possible connection with Gen 1:11 (there is no word association).

39. The literary structure of the Greek cannot be reproduced in English without an unwieldiness that is not in the original. *Flesh* is repeated four times. In this context it is not completely distinct from *body* (vs. 38), but its specificity is observed (cf. Conzelmann, *An Outline of the Theology of the New Testament,* 189).

40. *glory.* It is always an open question whether *doxa* should be translated consistently or by a variety of words. "Splendor" would be a good alternate here.

41. Again a reference to Genesis 1 is possible. Probably Paul's argument ought to be taken in stride and not pushed in detail.

42. *This is the way it is. houtōs kai* introduced more than a simple comparison: it marks a major step in the reasoning.

There is a . . . sowing. Through vs. 44 the passive *speiretai* is repeated. The subject appears to be "one who passes through human life and death and the resurrection." It seems best to vary the clauses according to the rest of their contents. Perhaps TEV is correct in rendering this verb "bury," but the references certainly include the life characteristics of the one buried and therefore allude to somewhat more than the wretched estate of death. (It is possible that *sowing* could hold a reference to conception, but in the context this is unlikely.)

44. *in natural life, psychikon.* The Greek word almost defies translation. Cf. E. Schweizer, *TDNT,* IX, 662-663 (and inevitably the whole article, pp. 608-666); Pearson, *The Pneumatikos-Psychikos Terminology,* 7-9 (he deals with the whole fifteenth chapter, pp. 15-26; and the entire study merits attention in this context); Hatch, "On Psychological Terms in Biblical Greek," in *Essays in Biblical Greek,* 94-130, the seminal study. The interpretation must turn on the quotation from Gen 2:7 in the next verse.

a body in spiritual life. The awkward circumlocution for *spiritual body* seems to be required by the difficulty with the meaning of *natural body.* On a possible connection between Paul's idea of "body" here and in chs. 11-12, cf. B. Schneider, "The Corporate Meaning and Background of 1 Cor 15,45b . . . ," *CBQ* 29 (1967), 450-467.

45. *what has been written.* Paul adapts Gen 2:7c (LXX) to support his point. *ho anthrōpos* is supplemented by rendering the Hebrew it translates, *hā'ādām,* by the proper noun. He also infixes *prōtos* in order to anticipate *eschatos* (which in vs. 47 becomes *deuteros*). He does not develop the theological implications of this idea in this context; after all, he is dealing with another question. But he does treat it elsewhere: cf. II Cor 5:17 and especially Rom 5:12-21.

became a life-making spirit. Conzelmann raises a question about when this took place (pp. 286-287) and opts for the resurrection as against "at his creation before all time" or at the incarnation (n. 56). This appears to be a theological plaything: the apostle's point is broader. Paul doubtless argues according to his context, and here it is the resurrection. In Romans 5, on the other hand, the context is Christ's death; and it is his righteousness that gives life. In Rom 6:5-11 the resurrection is again introduced; but if Paul is to be pressed into a schema, the relationship of Christ to the Holy Spirit must be resolved (cf. Hamilton, *The Holy Spirit and Eschatology in Paul;* but more remains to be done in this area). The Johannine treatment is broader: in John 5:21-29 the *life-making* power of the Son is at work in his earthly ministry (a phase of the evangelist's "realized eschatology").

On the Adam-Christ idea, cf. the extensive bibliographical data in Lengsfeld, *Adam und Christus,* and Scroggs, *The Last Adam.* Conzelmann has an excursus on "Adam and Primal Man" (pp. 284-286); and this concept is related to "Son of man" research in F. H. Borsch, *The Son of Man in Myth and History*

(Philadelphia, 1967), 240-256. Cf. also W. G. Kümmel, *The Theology of the New Testament* (Nashville, 1973), 155-157; and Caird, "The Christological Basis of Christian Hope," in *The Christian Hope*, 9-24.

46. *the spiritual . . . the natural.* Schneider, *CBQ* 29 (1967), 456, takes the neuters to indicate a corporate concept, developed from the two individuals. Paul has already given a summary statement of this in verse 22. Schmithals's note on this verse (*Gnosticism in Corinth*, 169-170) is important: the inimical implications of the Gnostic belief vis-à-vis the Christian gospel are vital to an understanding of the vigor of Paul's rebuttal.

47. *earthy, from the earth.* The language is strongly suggestive of Gen 2:7a (LXX: *choun apo tēs gēs*).

the second person. The addition of "the Lord" undoubtedly arose from theological considerations but has no substantial textual support.

49. *we have borne.* The past aorist points to the condition, not the continuity of the experience.

likeness. eikona is the LXX word from Gen 1:26-27 (cf. I Cor 11:7).

we shall also bear. The textual evidence is somewhat stronger for a hortatory aorist (the difference is the length of the "o" vowel). Editorial considerations, however, suggest the decision for the future. *The likeness of the heavenly one* is hardly to be achieved by exhortation, and *lectio difficilior* must yield to the common understanding of Paul's theology. Theodoret (fifth century) writes: "He has said 'we shall bear' in a predictive, not a paraenetic, sense."

COMMENT

Analogies

Paul has digressed slightly, and he now returns to the main theme of this part of the letter by addressing a primary problem that some putative opponent is raising. If resurrection is a reality, what is the form in which it takes place? Apparently the query is not a desire for truth but rather an expression of doubt regarding the resurrection belief. The present tense is taken to indicate that the objector is unable to understand how dead people can be raised since they are now invisible. Moreover, the idea of resurrection is absurd because one cannot conceive how or in what fashion those who are raised may be equipped with a body—it seems to be meant as a kind of *reductio ad absurdum*.

The repeated use of the present tense in this passage appears to have an emphatic point; it is not used as a future. The early Christians seem to have entertained a transitional eschatology. The Jewish community had built up a fairly stable and detailed system of eschatological beliefs including expectation of a coming messiah who would overcome the enemies of God and of the people of Israel and who would awaken the dead. After he achieved the world-wide kingdom of God, there would be a final judgment and assignment of the righteous to the heavenly regions and the evil to the torture of Gehenna. Some statements of Jesus employ phraseology drawn from this conventional system though other statements imply divergence from it. Paul likewise draws upon the ideas and terminology of the old viewpoint in various passages, but he has to make significant changes in view of his belief that the messiah has already come, been put to death, and been raised from the dead. This revelation through Jesus seems to require at some point the displacement of the old system or its radical transformation; at other points it appears possible to splice into the system ideas based on Jesus' career without seriously altering the basic Jewish expectation. In this excursus the older system may be reflected in vss. 22 and 52: the future tenses seem to indicate that there will be a coming resurrection probably at the time of Christ's return. Since Jesus did not establish a world-wide kingdom either before or immediately after his resurection, and since there was no visible resurrection taking place, some Christians were anticipating Jesus' speedy return so that he might successfully perform the messianic functions not yet accomplished. Jewish thought anticipated the resurrection of the dead at this return.

Other Christians (cf. II Tim 2:17 and perhaps Matt 27:52-53) seem to have believed that Jesus' resurrection had accomplished the resurrection of the messianic community. Akin to this is the idea in the Gospel of John that the resurrection occurs when people believe and faith eliminates death.

Paul appears to have ideas that were compatible with most of these views. The one feature of contemporary Jewish eschatology that he omits is the future kingdom of the messiah after the resurrection; for this he substitutes the belief that Christ is ruling now on earth (15:25). The return of Christ he takes to involve the reception of all the living and dead saints into a heavenly fellowship. His stress on a transcendent, eternal, spiritual life elevated altogether beyond the conditions of this world means that he need not affirm that the actual dead bodies are reanimated and brought back to life as presently experienced. In two strong statements Paul expressly rejects such a revival: 15:50 and II Cor 5:1. The eternal kingdom unites all believers in a realm occupied by people with a new kind of body that is not afflicted with the frailties and perishability of the bodies in this world—*spiritual bodies*. Presumably, then, the resurrection can take place as soon as the old body is abandoned. In any case, the resurrection body is invisible to those who are still in the *earthy* body of *flesh;* so Paul can argue that *the dead are being raised.* Yet he has to correct the opponents' idea that the resurrection must be a visible, physical appearance; for obviously if it is visible and physical, no resurrection is taking place; and it is at least debatable whether it can ever take place.

Paul adduces some analogies to demonstrate that his opponents have restricted and inflexible minds and do not take into account numerous, logical possibilities that are actually suggested by phenomena in the visible universe. The first comes from plant life: the full plant is not sown in the ground to be recovered in the same form as it was when sown; rather *a bare grain* is sown and, according to Paul's understanding, dies. Then in due time a plant appears, and it is of quite a different form from the grain though it produces in the end many grains of the same variety as the grain that was sown.

This continuity and cycle of life is attributed to God's will. The apostle affirms a doctrine of continuous creation: in accordance with an original, divine decision a body is produced by an act of God each time a seed dissolves in the ground. The seeds dies; but the same kind of body is given over and over to a *particular* seed. The idea conforms to the statement of Gen 1:11, which declares that God wills that each plant will bear *according to its kind*. Paul's botanical knowledge is about as primitive as that of Genesis; but later systems (occasionalism; continuous creation) have given his view some appearance of sophistication.

Another analogy is found in the resources of nature, which are more prolific than the opponents have imagined. Within the visible biological realm are four great divisions: *people,* beasts (*cattle*), *birds,* and *fish;* and these differ not only in appearance but in the *kind of flesh* of each. (The modern view that forms proliferate in complication does not invalidate the point but could be used to strengthen it.) The tremendous variety and divergence of forms shows that numerous possibilities are open to God.

Like Immanuel Kant, Paul transfers his vision from the earth to the sky and points out that the myriad bodies there differ from each other and from the earth. Presumably he has in mind that *the heavenly bodies* shine with their own light while *the earthly* ones have only reflected light. He gives no further indication of his astronomical thought,* and obviously his data are critically limited. Since his express purpose is only to show that many possibilities are open in the realm of reality, his analogy provides a valid illustration.

Scriptural and theological description

While the analogies of nature, to which Paul has referred, present a regular sequence confirmed by the experience of all observers, the resurrection of the dead is really different; for the reappearance of dead people on earth is in no way a regular datum of experience. For Paul, however,

* Many ancient philosophers believed that the sun, the moon, and the planets were inhabited by perfect minds. Physical observation and reason were able to deal with the orderly movement of these bodies but hardly with their composition and properties.

this difference does not annul the analogy: the illustrations he has given justify for him the conclusion that a new body takes the place of the old one which is buried in the ground, and a new and radically different glory succeeds the pale and doubtful glory of life on this earth. The repeated use of the present tense (*is a sowing*) refers to the repeated burial of people as they die. The correlative statements about *raising,* then, point to a similar, continuous succession of resurrections. *Perishable* probably refers to the decay to which a corpse is subject; the risen body is free from such decay.

Sowing in dishonor may allude to the Jewish conviction that a corpse is a source of uncleanness to anyone who touches it. The Greeks had a powerful urge to bury dead bodies and to preserve them from the ravages of carrion birds and from disintegration. The stench of a decaying body was very strong in the nostrils of ancient peoples (cf. John 11:39) and was to many a sign of the repulsiveness of death. The apostle therefore could imply that death is not to be regarded as a somewhat honorable, peaceful sleep but a degrading experience imposed by a bitter enemy. Over against this, however, is the glory of the resurrection with an implied luminosity opposite to the darkness characteristic of earth. The imperishable state is free from sickness, infection, and attendant conditions of dishonor.

This suggests another pair of opposites, *weakness* and *power.* The buried body represents the lowest possible condition with the absence of energy, movement, resistance, discipline, freedom, even consciousness. No person escapes this lapse into absolute weakness. The contrast suggests that for every faculty, ability, and skill that has succumbed, a new power will exceed the one lost—as much as the glory of the resurrection exceeds the condition of death.

The summary pair of opposites is *natural body* and *spiritual body.* There is some difficulty in delineating Paul's meaning in the word *psychikos.* Its derivation carried the idea of that which characterizes life in this world beyond the mere fact of biological existence. The apostle regularly uses it to designate that which contrasts to the supernatural world (characterized by *pneuma,* "spirit"); so there is no contradiction here. It is not a living entity that is buried but one that is identified with the *natural* world. It is the body composed of the natural elements without any supernatural or divine qualities. By contrast the body which is raised is *spiritual:* either it is composed of spirit, or it is under the rule or power of God's Spirit, or it is both. The body that *is sown* is subject to the course of nature; the body that *is raised* is subject to the operation of the Spirit. Paul sums up with an axiomatic statement derived from the argument from analogy which he has employed.

(Again the verbs are in the present tense on both sides of the contrast. The burial of natural, human beings occurs as they die one after another; and the consistent conclusion from the language would be that the resurrection occurs time after time as persons die and are raised.)

Now Paul caps his discussion with an allusion to scripture, as he so often does. From Gen 2:7 he draws the reference to God's breathing into the newly created human being the breath of life so that *the person became a living, natural being* (using the noun *psychē,* cognate to the adjective mentioned above). This is a characteristic possessed by humans by virtue of having been created by God, and all succeeding persons receive this same mode of natural existence. But a new creation has taken place effected through *the last Adam,* a tour de force derived from Paul's interpretation of the Genesis passage. This person (Christ) became *a life-making spirit.* In the apostle's thought Christ's power to make people alive is associated with his resurrection (Rom 1:4). (He does not have occasion to address Christ's power to make alive during his earthly career, a theme developed by the Fourth Gospel.) This life-making power is accomplished by the Spirit, and those he makes alive also become spirits with spiritual bodies.

Paul pushes this comparison. The separation of *the first Adam* at the beginning of the human race from *the last Adam* thousands of years later becomes the pattern of human experience: natural life in a flesh and blood body takes place first; after the death of this body the spiritual body emerges. From this presentation of the precedence of the natural life it may be inferred that Paul did not believe that "souls" have existence prior to birth. This means he would not accept a doctrine of reincarnation, which would affirm that an immortal, spiritual personality enters this life when a person is born; for that would imply that the spiritual life is first and then the natural. This view was common enough in the contemporary world; it had a basis in Platonic thought, and was a part of Gnostic belief. Against this Paul affirms that the beginning of each person's existence is at conception and birth, so that the natural existence is the first. Spiritual existence comes later. (His understanding of what happens at conversion to Christian faith is not at all in view in this discussion.)

Human life originates in no glorious substance but *from the earth.* Again the reference is to Gen 2:7, where God created *of dust from the ground.* (Whatever interpretation is given the Genesis passage, it is ultimately true that human, physical substance is composed of elements drawn from the earth; but Paul's argument is on a quite different plane.) The most humble material was employed to produce the first humanity; the second creation has its origin from heaven, whence came Christ (cf. Philip 2:6-7) to bring a new nature to humanity. By natural generation human beings after *the first person Adam* participate in the same *earthy* material. Those who by spiritual generation are given a new nature by *the last Adam* participate in his heavenly being. As the first Adam had successors, *earthy people,* so Christ has successors, *heavenly people;* and the contrast of the successors is based upon the contrast of the two Adams.

The likeness of the earthy one is the body, which persons have in this life as a kind of burdensome garment; it is like the body of the first person, originating from earth and going back to earth (Gen 3:19). In contrast to this, *the heavenly one* came into this world, for the time empty of the divine glory; and by the resurrection he returned to the realm from which he came with a risen body, free from earthy composition and dependence. Those who belong to him by faith will likewise *bear* a heavenly body like him (cf. II Cor 5:4). Here Paul employs a verb in future tense (the first such occurrence since 15:22). No timetable is suggested: he is rather drawing the logical implication from his insistence that this experience contrasts to the *earthly* life; the resurrection is ahead for each of his addressees.

THE "MYSTERY" OF THE
END (15:50-57)

15   50 Now this I am saying, brothers, that flesh and blood cannot inherit God's kingdom; neither does the perishable inherit imperishability. 51 See, I am telling you a mystery: we shall not all die, but we shall all be changed, 52 in a moment, in a blink of an eye, at the last trumpet; for the trumpet will blow, and the dead will be raised imperishable, and we shall be changed. 53 It is indeed necessary that this which is perishable be clothed with imperishability and this which is mortal be clothed with immortality. 54 When this which is perishable is clothed with imperishability and this which is mortal is clothed with immortality, then the saying that has been written will take place:

> Death has been swallowed by victory.
> 55 Where, death, is your victory?
> Where, death, is your sting?

56 The sting of death is sin; the power of sin is the law; 57 but thanks be to God, who is giving us the victory through our Lord, Jesus Christ.

NOTES

15:50. *flesh and blood.* Paul may mean the material substance of bodies, composed of flesh and blood; or the phrase may have a quasi-technical significance, referring to humanity. If he means the former, then certainly *God's kingdom* is future. If he means the latter, then he seems to be referring to the natural human being in other terms. The other two uses of this phrase in the Pauline literature, Gal 1:16 and Eph 6:12, suggest the second option (cf. also Matt 16:17 and Heb 2:14).

inherit God's kingdom. In 6:9b-10 he has specified categories of deviant persons who will *not* "inherit God's kingdom." As these are characteristics of flesh-and-blood people, presumably the two references are mutually supportive. The verb is future in 6:10, and the implication of 15:24 is also clearly future. In 4:20 and here, however, futurity is not explicit; and the kingdom references in the epistle are hardly usable in setting up a putative temporal program for the concept.

does . . . inherit. Again the emphasis is upon the stipulation, not upon any sequence of experience.

51. *we shall not all die, but we shall all be changed.* There are five textual readings for these clauses, and the MS evidence is significantly distributed. Clark, *Studia Paulina* 63-64, seems to favor the strongly attested reading (Aleph Aᶜ C 33 et al.), "We shall all sleep, but we shall not all be changed"; and he argues for its contextual appositeness. Metzger, however, cogently insists (p. 569) that the familiar reading of B, *Byz* et al., "best explains the origin of the others"—the most reliable criterion, after all, for resolving difficult textual alternatives. The fact that Paul did die suggests that the first clause is primitive, and the second clause is supported by the following verse and the schema of I Thess 4:17.

52. *the last trumpet.* Cf. NOTE at 14:8; also I Thess 4:16 and Matt 24:31. On the cognate verb used with impersonal subject, cf. BDF, § 129.

we shall be changed. The emphatic subject is expressed, strongly implying that Paul expects to be in this group.

53. *immortality.* It is significant that Paul stresses the necessity of being *clothed with* immortality. For many Greek philosophers immortality was a natural endowment of humanity, and the immortal soul was thought of as clothed with flesh (so Plato *Phaedo*). This was also a consideration of Gnostic thought; cf. The Gospel of Philip 23: "Some are afraid lest they rise naked. Because of this they wish to rise in the flesh, and they do not know that those who bear the flesh [it is they who are] naked" (trans. R. McL. Wilson [New York, 1962], 87)—I Cor 15:50 is quoted in this section! For Paul *imperishability* and *immortality* are acquired with resurrection.

54. There is some textual confusion about the two temporal clauses. The well-attested omission of the first clause may well be a scribal oversight occasioned by the repetition of key words in the context.

Death has been swallowed by victory. The quotation is from Isa 25:8, but the textual situation is complex (Conzelmann marshals the evidence in detail, p. 292). The reading is not that of LXX but seems to be closer to that of Theodotion. A. Rahlfs denies that there was a pre-New Testament Theodotion text (*Septuaginta* [Stuttgart, 1935], xxvii), and it hardly seems likely that Theodotion would have been influenced by textual variants originated by Paul. The rendering of *lāneṣaḥ* by *eis nikos* is perhaps easy to explain, but *katepothē* is difficult. Perhaps Paul merely recognized that the LXX, which reads "death swallowed," had to be amended, which he accomplished by making the verb passive. No finally satisfactory solution is available. (Again a past aorist must be translated by the present perfect; the emphasis is on what happened, not on the time of its happening.)

55. *Where, death, is your sting?* The quotation is patently from Hosea 13:14, ("O Death, where are your plagues?" [RSV]), but explanations of the variation are even harder to come by than in the citation from Isa 25:8. Perhaps it is enough to suggest that Paul adapts *dikē* to *nikos* in the previous quotation and substitutes a second *thanate* for *hādes,* which he never uses. Scribes, as might be expected, produced textual variants by accommodating to the LXX.

57. *is giving.* The linear participle seems to have been chosen deliberately. Though Paul recognizes the future dimension of the Christian *victory,* he affirms its present reality *through Jesus Christ.*

On the whole subject of Paul's eschatology, Scott's summary (*Christianity According to St Paul,* 236-243) is succinct and comprehensive. It is instructive to compare Johannine eschatology: the tension between present and future is evident, but more emphasis is given to the present (cf. Brown, AB, vol. 29, CXV-CXXI).

COMMENT

Paul works into a summary climax of his discussion. His statements, analogies, and arguments may be put in traditional terms: unchanged human beings are not ready to take their place with the people who are under the reign of God. (This kingship theme is one of the persistent threads which give a certain unity to the Judaeo-Christian scriptures.) *Flesh and blood* decay, and life in the heavenly kingdom is not subject to decay; so a *perishable* being cannot take a place in the immortal realm. If this were so, he would have to agree with his opponents that the idea of the resurrection of the body is absurd. But of course the doctrine of the resurrection he is expounding is not contradictory nonsense.

Thus he moves from argument from analogy and theological observation and announces his subject as *a mystery,* that is, something that is not discovered by processes of human reason but is made known by special, divine disclosure. Neither reason nor analogy could demonstrate that some people would not die and that a bodily change would take place in those who have not died when the eschatological moment arrives. The pattern of Paul's thought seems to be that the age will end before he and many of his addressees die, and therefore a radical change will have to take place in those who come to that time while still in perishable flesh and blood. Assuredly those who die undergo a change which fits them for the life beyond death. The resurrection allows no time for this alteration; so the change of those who do not die will be sudden; and its speed of occurrence is emphasized by illustrative phrases, especially the traditional blowing of *the trumpet.*

The picture of the end in I Thess 4:13-17 is more detailed; apparently the Thessalonians were particularly troubled by eschatological questions. There the suddenness and grandeur of the moment are stressed, and mention is made of "God's *trumpet*." The resurrection occurs before the change of the living, the reverse of I Corinthians 15. Paul's freedom in giving a different order in the two passages suggests that a sequence of "events" ought not to be an interpretative focus; "before" and "after" are not of primary importance. It is important that the experience—whatever and whenever it is—is future for each of Paul's readers. The resurrection will be appropriate to the condition of each person at the end.

To the *perishable-imperishable* terminology Paul adds *mortal-immortality* and employs the figure of clothing. A similar usage is employed in II Cor 5:3. It is a bold conception: persons are *clothed* with the resurrection body, imperishable and immortal. In Greek thought it was common to think of the natural body as an impedimentum which the "real" person utilized for a time. Paul develops his inherited Jewish thought by implying that the concept of "body" is essential. The person who is characterized as *perishable* and *mortal,* that is, subject to the ravages of death, receives *imperishability* and *immortality,* the clothing of resurrection, and is no longer at the mercy of death. This newly constituted body is invisible to the human eye but is visible to other spiritual bodies, and this is the outcome of the *mystery* Paul is telling. In Rom 13:14 the clothing figure is employed with reference to the relationship between the believer and *the Lord Jesus Christ;* so again a caveat must be entered against focusing upon a sequential timetable. The point is that perishable existence is replaced by imperishable, immortal life.

Entry into the new condition is the victory over the final enemy (note 15:26). All other enemies of life such as weakness, sickness, suffering, strife, and hatred may be overcome; but the ultimate enemy death cannot be defeated except by participating in the resurrection; and this can occur only through the power of the resurrection of Jesus Christ. Paul finds a prophetic declaration of this in Isa 25:8, which he renders as a triumphant declaration of Christian destiny. To this he adds a taunting paean from Hosea 13:14. The *victory* which *death* seems to achieve is doomed to disappear. The *sting* which is inevitably felt when *death* comes will prove to be a thing of this life, displaced by the resurrection.

At this point Paul inserts what seems like an amazing anticlimax: the real *sting* and *power* of the ultimate enemy are based on *sin* and the *law.* The sequence would be simpler if vs. 56 were omitted as a theological gloss of later editors, but there is no evidence for such an emendation. At one stroke these affirmations place this excursus in the context of Paul's broader theological understanding. *Sin* means failing to meet the purpose of God and missing the life he has ordained; it is a kind of alienation or estrangement from God that takes away trust and fills people with guilt and fear. Without this, death would have no sting. Sin, moreover, would have no power if there were no awareness of God's purpose revealed by *the law;* for the law is the agent that fills with guilt. Sin and the law, therefore, cause people to approach God with shrinking and terror; "thus conscience does make cowards of us all."* The fallacy of the reassurance of Epicurus, that death is only a sleep and has no terror, is found in the guilty conscience, which is not assuaged by the persuasion that life merely ceases. Doctrines about death as a physical event are ineffectual if they do not deal with the moral dimension. The real *victory* over law, sin, and guilt is given by God *through our Lord, Jesus Christ.* Having received his forgiveness, one no longer need fear death—or anything else. The greatest miracle of all is that a guilty sinner is innocent, and this innocence is a gift given by divine forgiveness worked out by the death and resurrection of Jesus Christ. By faith in him one knows that one is forgiven and has life imperishable and immortal. Just as the fear of death and punishment is lost, so the assurance of the gift of life in resurrection is gained. For this Paul thanks God (cf. Rom 7:25).

* Shakespeare, *Hamlet*, III i 83.

EXHORTATION (15:58)

15   58 So, my beloved brothers, continue firm, immovable, always excelling in the work of the Lord since you know that your labor in the Lord is not void.

Notes

15:58. *continue. ginesthe* could be indicative expressing natural result but is probably linear imperative, an exhortation to "keep becoming" what Paul implies they already are to a degree.

excelling. The linear ("present") participle continues the force of the imperative.

since you know. The participle *eidotes* is circumstantial; i.e. its function is different from the preceding one.

in the Lord. The position of the phrase in the Greek sentence (last) is emphatic. It can be read as modifying the preceding *not void* and should then be rendered, "because it is in the Lord." Paul, however, probably thinks of all the Christian's *labor* as being *the work of the Lord.*

COMMENT

The sublime statement of resurrection doctrine comes to a solid, ethical result (cf. I Thess 4:18). Freedom from guilt and the sting of sin together with assurance of life immortal should issue in stable, trustworthy, consistent life, which excels in doing the Lord's labor. This should pour forth naturally in the life of triumphant faith. Paul seems to have some assurance that this is a reasonable expectation from the Corinthians (for a contrary experience, cf. II Thess 3:6-13). He offers encouragement by reminding them that their work is not meaningless but will have abiding results. For the apostle, belief in the resurrection does not mean a transfer of interest to the future life only; it is the basis on which life is lived now, with profound confidence because it is *in the Lord*.

PERSONAL MATTERS
(16:1-24)

CONCERNING THE COLLECTION FOR
JERUSALEM SAINTS (16:1-4)

16 1 With reference to the collection for the saints: do just as I directed the churches of Galatia. 2 The first day of every week let each of you put aside at home savings appropriate to your prosperity so that there may be no collections at the time I come. 3 Now when I am there, those whom you approve by letter I shall send off to take your gift to Jerusalem; 4 and if it is suitable for me to go too, they will travel with me.

NOTES

16:1. *With reference to. . . .* The collection of personal notes with which the letter is concluded contains two items considered presumably because of inquiry originating with the Corinthians. The second (vs. 12) has to do with Apollos. This reference to *the collection for the saints* is dealt with briefly, perhaps because general information about the subject was widely known in the Pauline churches. Cf. Acts 11:29-30; Rom 15:25-28; II Cor 8; Gal 2:10.

the churches of Galatia. Identification of these has long been a thorny problem; cf. the major commentaries and Feine-Behm-Kümmel, *Introduction,* 191-193. It is not necessary to press for a solution in the present connection, for Paul's directions in any case are not recoverable.

2. *The first day of every week.* Jews were forbidden to handle money on the Sabbath; so perhaps the arrangement to lay aside money on the first day of the week was a convenience to avoid offense. There is no mention of a worship service in this instance. The shift in Christian practice from keeping the Sabbath to observing the first day came early; cf. Acts 20:7 and Rev 1:10. By the beginning of the second century it was established; cf. Didache 14:1; Ignatius *Magnesians* 9:1; Justin Martyr *Apology* 57. The explicit specifications of the first day of the week as the time of Jesus' resurrection in each of the Gospels may also bear upon the evidence. This command of Paul, then, may be a clue regarding the shift; but the evidence is inconclusive.

3. *by letter.* The editors disagree whether this phrase belongs with *approve* or with *send off;* the comma in UBS is not really helpful. The letters are probably for the identification and recommendation of the bearers when they take the collection to Jerusalem. Since Paul expects to be in Corinth, the letters would hardly be addressed to him. Messengers played an important role also in first-century Judaism: they were the living link among the diaspora communities around the Roman empire. They would have to be reliable people, and they would carry papers confirming their role. Curiously, if the list of travel companions in Acts 20:4 reflects the arrangements made in response to Paul's plan, there is no Corinthian representative in the party.

4. *if it is suitable*. Acts 20:2-3 appears to refer to Paul's coming to Greece in connection with these intentions, and the rest of the chapter recounts the return portion of the "third missionary journey." There is no information to supplement the plans offered here. Cf. also the next section of this chapter.

COMMENT

The rest of this epistle contains "loose ends," the matters following one another in casual sequence. The Corinthians knew that Paul cherished an ongoing project of making a financial collection for the needy *saints* at Jerusalem, and they must have inquired how he wanted them to go about it. There are numerous hints, particularly in Acts and Galatians, that the church leaders in Jerusalem and Paul maintained a somewhat uneasy fellowship; and while there is no reason to doubt that Paul's Christian, philanthropic motivation was unassailable, he certainly must have been aware how politic the successful accomplishment of the collection would be in the life of the developing church.

His directions are apparently standard; at least, what he tells the Corinthians is said to be the same as the churches of Galatia had heard. Every Lord's Day (Sunday) *each* church member is to *put aside* an amount of money commensurate with the financial gain of the previous week. There is no indication given whether this is meant to be a tithe (no such prescription occurs in the New Testament); but it is implied that it is proportional and substantial. It seems this is to be done on a family basis and the funds kept *at home*. Perhaps lack of appropriate organization or of adequate banking facilities dictated this provision. Paul anticipates that he will be occupied with other concerns when he comes to Corinth; he does not want the collection to preempt time that should be devoted to matters that require apostolic attention and decision.

Paul will not himself carry the collection to Jerusalem; a delegation approved by the Corinthian church will do that with Paul's apostolic concurrence. They will carry letters, probably from the giving church, possibly from Paul. Certainly the gift would go under double auspices. Not only did the principal missionary figures travel throughout the circuits of the first-century churches, but there were deputations from one local church to another and particularly, it seems, from the newer congregations to the longer established groups, especially in the principal cities.

Paul expects that after his visit to Corinth he will be heading for Jerusalem. If his schedule is *suitable,* the delegation from Corinth would join his company—a possibility that does not seem to have worked out (according to the record in Acts 20).

TRAVEL PLANS (16:5-9)

16　5 I shall come to you when I pass through Macedonia, for I am passing through Macedonia; 6 and possibly I shall stay with you and even spend the winter so that you may send me on my way wherever I am going. 7 Indeed, I do not want to see you now in passing, for I hope to stay on with you for some time if the Lord permits. 8 But I shall stay on in Ephesus until Pentecost; 9 for a great and productive door has opened to me, and adversaries are many.

NOTES

16:5-9. On Paul's travels and activities in this period, see pp. 17-19, 89-91.

5. *I am passing through Macedonia.* The same resolve is noted in Acts 19:21-22.

6. *even spend the winter.* The advantages provided by Roman imperial policies and developments still did not eliminate the natural hazards of "off-season" travel in the first century. Cf. Acts 27:9-12.

7. *if the Lord permits.* The specific explanation of *possibly (tychon)* in the previous verse. Such a proviso must have been common in early church communication; cf. Acts 18:21 ("God willing"); Heb 6:3 ("if God permits"); and the rationale in James 4:13-16.

8. *until Pentecost.* Robertson and Plummer suggest that Paul is not determined to celebrate the festival at Ephesus but is indicating that he will *stay on* perhaps six or seven weeks if he is writing after travel has become possible in the spring. Ogg (*Chronology,* 136-139) thinks that Paul did not leave Ephesus until "late summer"; but he did *spend the winter* in Greece. He left the following spring (Acts 20:6) and hoped to celebrate Pentecost in Jerusalem (20:16).

9. *a great and productive door.* The figure is fairly common in the New Testament (e.g. Acts 14:27; II Cor 2:12; Col 4:3; Rev 3:8). Ogg considers (*Chronology,* 136-139) how this phrase may be related to Artemisian festivals.

and adversaries are many. There is no verb. The idea may be concessive ("though there are"), but it is more straightforward to take it as an additional reason why Paul is impelled to *stay on in Ephesus* (vs. 8).

COMMENT

Having introduced the subject of his projected travel in connection with the collection, Paul offers additional details of his intentions. He intends to return to *Macedonia,* where he would probably visit the churches at Philippi, Thessalonica, and Beroea; and this would bring him to Greece late enough in the traveling season (spring-summer-fall) that he might reasonably expect to *spend the* following *winter* in Corinth. That city would be a natural departure point *wherever* he decided to go—he has indicated in vss. 3-4 that one option would be to return to Jerusalem, which, as it turned out, he did.

He does not want, however, to make a quick visit. Depending on the disposition of providence, he intends to make a protracted visit. The reasons for this are not difficult to deduce: the problems of the Corinthian church seem to demand his personal attention (cf. 4:18-21).

At the same time, there is good reason to remain in Ephesus. Its status as the principal city of western Asia Minor renders it strategic for the propagation of the gospel, and Paul declares that he is faced with unusual opportunity. The city was a center for the worship of Artemis; her temple there had been one of the seven wonders of the ancient world and was magnificently rebuilt after it burned in 356 B.C. This was a fertility cult (not of the Graeco-Roman Artemis/Diana), and the prominence of idolatry made it a prime target for Paul's efforts. Acts 19 contains stories of the hectic confrontation that took place, and I Cor 15:32 hints at the dangerous strength of his *adversaries.* Difficulty and danger are not deterrents but rather incentives to his determination: Paul will use the *door* before he visits Corinth again.

RECOMMENDATION OF TIMOTHY (16:10-11)

16   10 If Timothy comes, see that he has no cause to be afraid as far as you are concerned, for he is doing the Lord's work the same as I. 11 So let no one scorn him. Send him on his way in peace so that he may come to me, for I am expecting him with the brothers.

NOTES

16:10. *Timothy*. Cf. Introduction, pp. 36-37.

11. *let no one scorn him*. This curious defense of Timothy may be echoed in I Tim 4:12. The verb there, however, is *kataphronein*, perhaps not quite as strong a negative implication as here. While the Pastoral note reflects the idea in the Corinthian letter, it certainly is not a literary echo.

in peace. Though *eirēnē* occurs often in the Pauline writings (usually in the sense of *šālōm*), this phrase occurs only here and in 7:15. (Elsewhere only in Acts 16:36; James 3:18; II Peter 3:14; and notably Luke 2:29.) The phrase and equivalents are fairly common in the Old Testament.

COMMENT

In Paul's dealings with Corinth and Ephesus, Timothy plays an important role. Paul has already mentioned Timothy's going to Corinth (4:17), and in the context he expresses concern about church members there who overestimate their position. He gives evidence of some uncertainty whether Timothy is equal to the responsibility, and he arms him with an apostolic injunction. He was determined, however, that Timothy take a leadership role in the churches. The letters to Timothy hint that he achieved this with some difficulty (e.g. I Tim 5:23; II Tim 1:4-7).

The movements of Paul and his associates are not easy to trace in exact detail. Apparently Paul tried to have his trusted lieutenants in important fields where he himself could not be. In the present situation Acts 19:22 states that Timothy and Erastus went to Macedonia (and Greece?) while Paul stayed in Ephesus. Acts 20:4-5 states that Timothy and others (he is the only one named without geographical identification) went ahead of Paul on his later return from Greece and Macedonia. I Tim 3:1 locates Timothy in Ephesus while Paul is traveling in Macedonia, but precise schedules cannot be determined. Paul did expect to meet him before he journeyed to Corinth; so the data are not necessarily contradictory even if incomplete.

The dynamics of interpersonal relationships in the early church are intriguing. The information in the texts is unfortunately less than is needed for conclusive analysis. It does seem clear, however, that Christian conversion was no guarantee that persons would be tractable, reliable, and cooperative. So Paul's excursus on the change wrought by the resurrection is a practical as well as a theological climax.

PROJECTED VISIT BY APOLLOS (16:12)

16   12 With reference to brother Apollos: I urged him strongly to go to you with the brothers; yet he was not at all willing to go now; but he will go whenever he finds opportunity.

NOTES

16:12. *brother Apollos;* Greek, "Apollos the brother." The use of *adelphos* in the early church is intriguing but not precisely clear. The proper name followed by the article and *brother* occurs also in 1:1 and occasionally elsewhere in the epistles (three times with "Timothy": II Cor 1:1; Col 1:1; Philem 1). As often in Paul and always in other epistles there is a further modifier ("my," "beloved," etc.). In two of the accounts of Paul's conversion in Acts, Ananias addresses him as "brother Saul" (9:17, 22:13). In the present context the designation is important as it establishes beyond doubt a collegiality that might have been in question after remarks in chs. 3 and 4. The plural, "brothers," occurs often in address to the Christian fellowship. Here *with the brothers* is the same phrase that in the previous verse designated a deputation that was coming from Corinth to Ephesus. Since the reverse movement is indicated here, it may be inferred that there was some relatively regular movement between these two Christian centers (and presumably other centers). The communications from Corinth which prompted this correspondence probably arrived in such a way. (A note in *JB* suggests that the phrase *with the brothers* may also be taken to mean that they are with Paul *expecting* Timothy. This would clear the group to go to Corinth—without Apollos.)

COMMENT

The last matter from Corinth to which Paul addresses reply has to do with Apollos, whose leadership role is implied earlier in this letter and elsewhere. Apparently the query was "When is Apollos coming?" or "Why hasn't Apollos visited us (lately)?" Paul's answer includes a bit of self-justification and implies that guidance of the Spirit did not always bring about unanimous decisions among the Christian leaders. Paul had tried to get Apollos to accompany a recent embassy from Ephesus to Corinth, but Apollos did not find the journey timely. No reason for his reluctance is given, but it does not seem to be a matter of any importance so far as Paul is concerned, for he assures the addressees that his colleague will go when the time is right.

The movements suggested here do not match those given in Acts 18:24-20:2, but apparently the writer in Acts was not enough interested in Apollos to follow all his journeys. It is clear, however, that Apollos was well enough known in both Ephesus and Corinth to justify both the desire of each community to have him visit and his determination to prolong his stay in one or the other.

CONCISE EXHORTATIONS (16:13-14)

16   13 Keep alert; stand fast in faith; behave in manly fashion; be strong. 14 Let all your affairs be conducted in love.

NOTES

16:13. *Keep alert.* The verb indicates keeping awake. The implication is figurative, but the figurative overlaps the literal sense. Often there are eschatological overtones; cf. I Thess 5:1-10; Rev 3:2,3. About half the occurrences in the New Testament are in the synoptic gospels (three times in the so-called "little apocalypse").

stand fast. BDF, § 73, discusses this verb formation.

in faith. RSV translates, "in your faith," a legitimate rendering of the article in the phrase *en tē pistei.* The literal translation, "in the faith," would suggest that there existed in the church at this time a body of data to which Christians were expected to give unwavering assent. When such a situation came into being is a moot problem of New Testament historical study, but decisions are reflected in translations. For example, comparable phrases in II Cor 1:24 and 13:5 are translated "your faith" (RSV); but the same phrase in Titus 1:13 is rendered, "in the faith," presumably reflecting a decision that Titus is from a much later period. Similarly, cf. Rom 11:20 and Gal 1:23 with I Tim 3:9, 5:8, and II Tim 3:8. This is not the place to pursue this problem. It certainly must be raised, however, inasmuch as the translation here practically disregards the article (cf. Rom 4:19 and Titus 2:2, RSV!). On the shades of meaning that *pistis* may bear and its connection with the Hebrew words deriving from *'mn,* cf. Burton, *Epistle to the Galatians,* 475-485.

COMMENT

Short series of concise exhortations occur in several of Paul's letters (II Cor 13:11-12; Philip 4:4-6; Col 4:5-6; I Thess 5:14-21). Apparently the paraenesis of the early church regularly included summary directions how the believers might conduct their lives. Such instruction would not be strange to those whose background was influenced by either the Jewish synagogue or Greek philosophy.

The exhortation to *keep alert* could have been part of the tradition Paul received, for it is reported from Jesus' teaching, Mark 13:35,37, 14:34,38, etc. Paul has already (15:1) indicated a relationship between the received tradition and steadfastness. This is a characteristic of *faith;* and the overlap of "belief," "trust," and "faithfulness" is evident in such a reference. *Behave in manly fashion* and *be strong* are echoes of a pair of Old Testament exhortations, which occur in almost exactly this form in Ps 31:24[30:25, LXX] and similarly in Deut 31:6; II Sam 10:12; and Ps 27:14. The final paraenetic word in the series is a practical summary of what he has written in beautiful detail in ch. 13.

APPRECIATION AND COMMENDATION OF CORINTHIAN LEADERS (16:15-18)

16 15 Now please, brothers—you know the household of Stephanas, that it is the first fruits of Achaea and they exerted themselves in service to the saints — 16 you in turn are to yield to such persons and to everyone who cooperates and works hard. 17 And I am happy for the presence of Stephanas, Fortunatus, and Achaicus, because these men made up for your absence, 18 for they put my spirit and yours in a fresh relationship. So give recognition to such men.

Notes

16:15. *please*. Cf. first Note on 1:10. Since this imperative looks to what follows rather than back at the preceding verses, the connection is grammatically loose; but cf. *infra* on vs. 16.

the household of Stephanas. Whether *oikos* (and its equivalent here, *oikia*) includes children and even infants has been a moot question for centuries; cf. K. Aland, *Did the Early Church Baptize Infants?* (London, 1963). Since the reference here indicates that the *oikia* rendered *diakonia*, it is highly probable that only adults are in focus (ibid., 88). Paul, however, with his Jewish training and understanding would naturally think of the family as a unit; so the baptism issue cannot be settled one way or another on this evidence. Again, as in the case of the husband and wife, the practical outworking of Paul's thought and doctrines comes into view; and the implications of his background and religio-social situation must be pursued with full knowledge that the results will fall short of final proof. (On Stephanas, see pp. 16 and 80-81 in the Introduction.)

first fruits of Achaea. Attempts to discover how (or whether) Stephanas could actually be the first convert in Greece (was he among the Athens converts mentioned in Acts 17:34? Cf. Grosheide, 402) are hardly worth while. *aparchē* is anarthrous, and it is at least debatable that Paul considered the first fruits in this case to include more than one person and/or family group. Conzelmann points out that Rom 16:5 suggests special importance attached to the role of "first baptized" (p. 298; the reference in the first edition reads 6:5).

in service. The use of *diakonia* is not to be taken as evidence that such an office had been formalized in the mid-first-century church. Certainly it is not included specifically in the list of God-appointed persons in 12:28.

16. *you in turn are to yield.* On *hina* with the subjunctive as an imperative, cf. BDF, § 387(3). There is a continuity of thought from *parakalō* in the preceding verse. In the other use of this construction in this epistle, 7:29, there is such a carry-over possible from *touto de phēmi.*

17. the *presence. parousia,* of course, can refer to the "coming" of these men (Conzelmann is sure it means "arrival" [ibid., p. 298]); but the following remarks seem to emphasize what they did by being there rather than by arriving. The relative movements of persons and groups between Ephesus and Corinth at this time (e.g. vis-à-vis 1:11) seem to be beyond reconstruction: probably Conzelmann's despair over the second part of the verse (p. 299) should also be applied to this part.

18. *put . . . in a fresh relationship.* The verb primarily means to "cease" or "cause to rest"; to "refresh" derives from this. The use of the term here suggests that the representatives of the church allayed some tension that existed between Paul and the Corinthians.

COMMENT

In picking up loose ends at the end of his letter Paul remembers to say a good word for certain leaders who were playing a significant role in the life of the Corinthian congregation. *Stephanas* was mentioned near the beginning of the letter (1:16—almost as an afterthought), and his *household* is singled out here. Apparently the adult members of the whole family group were engaged in particular *service* to the Christian community, but the nature of the service is not specified. This family also had the distinction of having been in the first group of converts in Greece.

The apostle gives his approval to a kind of hierarchy of service in the church. Natural leadership is to be recognized, and this is to include more than casual acknowledgment: the membership is to *give recognition to such* people. Two characteristics of this serving leadership are identified: cooperation and hard work.

Stephanas must have come to mind because he is with Paul at Ephesus. Two others, *Fortunatus* and *Achaicus,* are not mentioned elsewhere in the

New Testament literature. These three somehow *made up for* the *absence* of the rest of the Corinthians: either they represented the whole group, whom Paul missed; or they performed the services which he feels are due because of his apostleship (cf. the clearer example in Philem 13). This makes Paul *happy,* and a *fresh relationship* is established between him and the people of his church (cf. Philem 20). Perhaps this is the positive side of what is more negatively presented in ch. 9.

GREETINGS FROM ASIAN CHURCHES AND LEADERS (16:19-20)

16   ¹⁹ The churches of Asia greet you. Aquila and Prisca along with the church at their house send special greetings in the Lord. ²⁰ All the brothers greet you. Greet one another with a holy kiss.

NOTES

16:19. *Aquila and Prisca.* The same couple joins in the greetings in Rom 16:3 (and cf. II Tim 4:19). There is some detailed information about them in Acts 18:1-3,18,26 (cf. also pp. 81-82, 84-85 in the Introduction; also Munck, AB, 176). It has been intriguing to eisegetes to note that in four of the six times the couple is mentioned the wife is named first. (Cf. von Harnack's ideas, cited in Robertson and Plummer, 398.) At most it can be inferred that she was a person of outstanding qualities in Christian leadership and service. Luke regularly uses the diminutive form of *her name, Priscilla;* and it is not surprising that *TR* substitutes that form here. There is a western textual addition that indicates Paul lodged with the couple in Ephesus, but that would seem to be an extrapolation from Acts 18:3.

at their house. The phrase *kat' oikon* is unusual. Twice in Acts (2:46, 5:42) it is distributive, but here it has a relational meaning (AGB, 408b, § 6). Rom 16:3-5 also mentions a church in the house of "Prisca and Aquila"; on the problem of the destination of Romans 16, cf. Manson, *Studies in the Gospels and Epistles,* 230-239. Conzelmann thinks that *the church at their house* can refer either to a Christian assembly at the private house or to the "household as a church" (p. 299). Calvin thinks "a particular Christian household" is intended, and he is enthusiastic about the significance of this (trans. Fraser, p. 356). It is likely, however, that, even though the home played a role as community model, it is the Christian assembly for worship and fellowship that is in view here; cf. H. D. Galley, "Das 'Haus' im Neuen Testament," *Evangelisch-Lutherische Kirchenzeitung* 15 (1961), 201-205.

20. *a holy kiss.* This early Christian practice is mentioned identically in Rom 16:16 and II Cor 13:12. In I Thess 5:26 it is specified for "all the brothers" (cf. the restrictions in the Apostolic Constitutions, ii 57 and viii 11). A "kiss of

love" commended in I Peter 5:14 indicates that the practice was widely used in the church; and Justin Martyr, Clement of Alexandria, and Tertullian still know of it (cf. Héring, 186). It may have had a place in first-century liturgy, but there is no evidence for this (e.g. in Didache, 9-10).

COMMENT

Paul includes a series of greetings both general and personal. *The churches of Asia* are those in the Roman province which occupied the western section of Anatolia. The principal churches will be those to which the seven letters of Revelation 2-3 are directed. These seem to have formed a kind of "circuit" with Ephesus as the hub. It was doubtless very important for the congregations of the young church to receive a reinforcing sense of solidarity one with another.

Special greetings from Aquila and Prisca are appropriate because of their earlier relationship with the Corinthian church (Acts 18:1-3). As incidental information it is mentioned that they host a house church in Ephesus. There is no indication that any of Paul's churches utilized buildings other than private homes for their services (cf. Rom 16:5; Col 4:15; Philem 2). The addition of greetings from *all the brothers* seems redundant, but perhaps it is intended to include Christians in Ephesus who were members of local congregations other than the particular one just mentioned.

The exhortation to employ *a holy kiss* in greeting has some special significance that is now not quite clear. A greeting kiss is known in the Old Testament (e.g. Exod 4:27), and there is the notorious example in Mark 14:45. The designation *holy* indicates that this greeting has a special purpose related to the Christian fellowship. It may have had some use in liturgy although there is no set form this early. It is at least a visible sign of the kind of affection that Paul wants to prevail in the church.

PAUL'S PERSONAL GREETING, MONITION, AND BENEDICTION (16:21-24)

16 21 Paul's greeting—in my own hand! 22 If anyone does not love the Lord, let him be damned! Come, our Lord! 23 The grace of the Lord Jesus be with you. 24 My love be with you all in Christ Jesus.

NOTES

16:22. *does not love the Lord.* The only other Pauline use of *philein* is in Titus 3:15, and probably no difference from *agapan* is intended. Cf. C. Spicq, "Comment comprendre *philein* dans I Cor xvi,22?" *NovT* 1 (1956), 200-204; he finds this verse to contain a liturgical formula rather than a curse, i.e. it describes the condition of one who rejects the lordship of Christ, and it is thus parallel with 12:3. W. F. Albright and C. S. Mann, "Two Texts in I Corinthians," *NTS* 16 (1969/70), 271-276, reconstruct an Aramaic original which would read, "If anyone loves the Lord, let it be, 'Come, our Lord'"; and they manage to find the same formula behind 12:3.

Come, our Lord! There is general agreement that the Aramaic words should be divided, *marana tha;* but Conzelmann warns that this does not decide the meaning (p. 300); cf. also the extensive literature in AGB, 492. The interpretation as a perfect ("our Lord has come") can be justified: since the Lord has come, anyone who does not love him is under a ban. But then it is difficult to explain why the Aramaic formula would be preserved for such a context. The imperative seems better (cf. J. A. Emerton, "MARANATHA and EPHPHATHA," *JTS* 18 [1967], 427-431; also the presumed translation at Rev 22:20; so Cullmann, *The Earliest Christian Confessions,* 56); but even so it is not certain whether it is an eschatological prayer or an invocation for the Lord's witness to the ban formula (C. F. D. Moule, "A Reconstruction of the Context of *Maranatha,*" *NTS* 6 [1959/60], 307-310; he cites II Tim 4:1). The exclamation occurs in a eucharistic context in Didache 10:6, which Albright and Mann (*NTS* 16 [1969/70]) think derives from this verse and Rev 22:20. The discussion of *kyrios* and its relationship to this invocation in G. Dalman, *The Words of Jesus* (Edinburgh, 1909), 327-330, is still worth study.

23. *the Lord Jesus.* TR with some early support adds "Christ," but this is almost certainly added under the influence of the benedictions in most of the other Pauline letters.

23, 24. *be with you.* The missing copula may be read "is," but the benedictory character of the passage suggests the jussive.

24. *in Christ Jesus.* A liturgical "Amen" occurs in most MSS, and there are some other variations, but it is likely that these are additions.

Most MSS include subscriptions; but these, of course, were not part of the original letter. There are at least a dozen forms, the earliest being simply "To Corinthians A." The form in which it is found in most of the medieval manuscripts (so, of course, *TR*) includes the mistaken information that the letter "was written from Philippi" and adds the names of Stephanas, Fortunatus, Achaicus, and Timothy as bearers. A number of manuscripts, however, including the third corrector of Vaticanus locate the origin of the letter in Ephesus. These details are interesting with reference to the history of the text but add nothing to its exegesis.

COMMENT

In four other epistles there are passages that are ostensibly from Paul's own hand (Gal 6:11; Col 4:18; II Thess 3:17-18; Philem 19—the exact extent in each case cannot be determined). It appears that Paul usually employed a secretary to write out his letters (cf. Rom 16:22); but near the end of his dictation he often took a pen and added some words: *in my own hand!* Indeed in II Thess 3:17 there is a claim that this personal message is a "sign in every epistle," but that may be taken with some latitude since such a "sign" does not occur in several of the letters that are certainly genuine.

This personal message begins with what, in its present form, is a kind of liturgical "ban-formula." It may be taken as an echo of 12:3. There one who curses Jesus is declared to be speaking without the Spirit of God. Here one who *does not love the Lord* (Jesus presumably) is himself placed under a curse (*anathema*). Then by a traditional interjection in Aramaic the presence of the Lord is involved (*marana tha*), perhaps to witness the ban, more likely to reestablish his eschatological presence with his church. By the end of the first century such exclamations had taken a place in the formal liturgical practice of the church; this may be seen more clearly in Rev 22:7,17,20.

The epistle concludes with two benedictions. The first is common in Paul's writing: *The grace of the Lord Jesus be with you;* and its use in one form or another is not peculiar to him (cf. Rev 22:21). In II Cor 13:14, where Paul uses what has come to be known as a "trinitarian" formula, his benediction begins with "the grace of the Lord Jesus Christ" rather than "the love of God"; and in I Cor 1:3 grace is "from God our Father and the Lord Jesus Christ." Since Paul orients his theological thought in Christ (1:4-9), it is natural that this should be reflected in his most solemn words.

His final benediction is personal: *My love be with you all in Christ Jesus.* This is the only place in his letters where Paul expressly passes his love to his readers. It is certainly appropriate here (a) after the strenuous rebukes and vigorous exhortations which he has directed to the Corinthians and (b) in the light of his declaration that love is the crown of all spiritual gifts. Since love has its origin in God's Spirit, Paul's love, personal as it is, still is *in Christ Jesus.* The life, message, and mission of the apostle can only be understood and explained from a christological perspective.

INDEXES

INDEX OF AUTHORS

Aalen, S. 250
Aland, K. 262
Albright, W. F. 68, 155, 366
von Allmen, J. J. 135, 207
Allo, E. B. 134, 238, 260, 291
Aratus 75
Aristotle 75, 148
Augustine 202

Baljon, J. M. S. 177
Bammel, E. 105
Barclay, W. 134, 291
Barré, M. L. 210
Barrett, C. K. 134, 135, 149, 214, 219,
   222, 223, 239, 268, 290, 311, 317
Barth, G. 328, 329
Barth, K. 166
Barth, M. 31, 135, 267, 284, 313, 325
Batey, R. 136
Baudraz, F. 134, 214
Bauer, W. (Arndt and Gingrich) 9, 50,
   82, 133, 141, 177, 206, 215, 218, 223,
   225, 239, 247, 261, 279, 288, 291, 292,
   302, 312, 314, 329, 364, 366
Bauernfeind, O. 67
Beare, F. W. 135, 318
Bengel, J. A. 120, 318
Benko, S. 71, 136
Betz, H. D. 15
Beza, T. 39
Blass, F. 133, 144, 148, 158, 159, 177,
   194, 215, 238, 240, 250, 259, 261, 267,
   277, 279, 284, 285, 287, 290, 291, 292,
   302, 335, 350, 361, 363
Bornkamm, G. 46, 48, 136
Borsch, F. H. 343
Bouttier, M. 135, 137, 325
Brown, R. E. 151, 331, 351
Bultmann, R. 103, 137, 218, 292, 317
Burrows, M. 38
Burton, E. D. 69, 135, 141, 148, 218,
   361

Cadbury, H. J. (cf. also Foakes-Jackson
   and Lake) vii, 59, 77, 80, 82, 95,
   137, 254
Caird, G. B. 136, 157, 329, 344
Calvin, J. 27, 134, 194, 214, 269, 280,

306–307, 310, 312, 325, 364
Caragounis, C. C. 238
Chrysostom, J. 223, 315, 335
Clark, K. W. 291, 314, 350
Clement of Alexandria 73, 74, 365
Conzelmann, H. 37, 39, 70, 119, 120,
   134, 137, 145, 163, 178, 185, 190, 194,
   199, 200, 212, 219, 226, 239, 247, 268,
   271, 286, 292, 302, 303, 311, 318, 324,
   335, 342, 343, 350, 363, 364, 366
Cullman, O. 136, 267, 277, 329, 366

Dahl, M. E. 136, 342
Dalman, G. 366
Danby, H. 186, 228, 267
Daniel-Rops, H. 137, 250
Davies, W. D., & D. Daube 114, 137
Deissmann, A. G. 88, 119, 133, 141,
   192, 199, 266
Delling, G. 302
Dibelius, M. 8, 37, 39, 65, 135, 137
Dodd, C. H. 62, 137, 317, 329
Dressler, H. H. P. 250
Duncan, G. 33
Dungan, D. L. 137, 211, 218, 239

Ellis, E. E. 137
Emerton, J. A. 366
Enslin, M. S. 22
Epicurus 353
Epictetus 200, 206
Euripides 336
Eusebius 318
Evans, E. 134, 342

Feine-Behm-Kümmel 21, 33, 120, 355
Finegan, J. 119, 133, 141
Finlayson, S. K. 267
Fletcher, V. H. 325
Foakes-Jackson, F. J. (cf. also Cadbury
   and Lake) 49, 57, 58, 71, 74, 77, 81,
   82, 88, 97, 135
Foerster, W. 199, 238, 250, 261
Ford, J. M. 136, 223, 224, 300
Forestell, J. T. 105
Fuller, H. R. 45
Furnish, V. P. 136, 291

Galley, H. D. 364
Gill, D. H. 292
Goodspeed, E. J. 31, 137, 291, 294
Grant, R. M. 23
Grosheide, F. W. 134, 162, 214, 363
Gunther, J. J. 119, 136

Haenchen, E. 8, 46–50, 65–68, 77, 80, 82, 91, 92, 94, 99, 135
Hall, E. 175
Hamilton, N. Q. 137, 343
von Harnack, A. 318
Harrison, E. F. 31
Hatch, E. 137, 343
Hay, D. M. 137, 329
Hegesippus 318
Heidland, H. W. 292
Hennecke, E. 133, 336
Héring, J. 21, 27, 98, 115, 120, 134, 137, 157, 158, 163, 178, 184, 199, 200, 214, 223, 224, 238, 239, 266, 276, 302, 311, 317, 330, 334, 336
Hill, D. 318
Hippolytus 157
Holtz, T. 317
Homer 118–119
Hooker, M. D. 178, 261
Howard, J. K. 335
Hurd, J. C. 64, 121, 136, 224, 254

Iber, G. 288
Ignatius 35, 164, 323, 355
Isaksson, A. 136, 259, 260, 312

Jackson, J. J. 250
Jeremias, J. 267
Josephus 318
Joyce, J. D. 335

Kaiser, O. 303
Kant, I. 346
Kelly, J. N. D. 38, 42, 44, 135
Kierkegaard, S. 47
Kittel, G. 133, 185
Knox, J. 31, 32, 135
Kosmala, H. 267
Kümmel, W. G. 8, 21, 120, 121, 223, 344

Ladd, G. E. 137, 330
Lake, K. (cf. also Cadbury and Foakes-Jackson) 57, 77, 98, 135
Langkammer, H. 231
Leal, J. 329
Lee, G. M. 336
Leenhardt, F.-J. 267
Lengfeld, P. 136, 328, 343

Liddell and Scott 50, 133
Lidzbarski, M. 84
Lietzmann, H. 121, 134, 156, 223, 284, 302, 318
Lightfoot, J. B. 69
von Loewenich, W. 8, 137
Longenecker, R. N. 137, 238
Luther, M. 27, 86, 269, 284, 324

Malherbe, A. J. 336
Mann, C. S. 55, 68, 366
Manson, T. W. 16, 137, 138, 218, 220, 223, 317, 364
Menander 336, 339
Metzger, B. M. 28, 83, 84, 94, 113, 135, 138, 144, 191, 199, 212, 219, 245, 246, 277, 291, 314, 318, 350
Meyer, H. A. W. 20, 46, 134, 157
Michaelis, W. 82, 114, 179
Miller G. 156–157
Moffatt, J. 138
Morissette, R. 329, 342
Moule, C. F. D. 366
Munck, J. 24, 50–53, 55–58, 62, 91, 93, 95, 135, 138, 155, 162, 364
Musonius Rufus 206

Neufeld, V. H. 136, 199, 231, 277
Nunn, H. P. V. 133, 154

Ogg, G. 16, 49, 115, 138, 357
Origen 155, 156, 157, 164
O'Rourke, J. J. 71
Osborne, R. E. 336
Ovid 302

Pausanius 119
Pearson, B. A. 105, 136, 343
Petuchowski, J. J. 267
Philo 86, 106, 119, 152, 245, 300–301
Philostratus 336
Phipps, W. E. 207
Plato 85, 195, 197, 260, 300–301, 317, 350
Pliny 278
Plummer, A. 21, 22
Pope, M. H. 170
Preisker, H. 304

Raeder, M. 335
Rahlfs, A. 350
Ramsay, W. 69
Reicke, B. 38
Rengstorf, K. H. 141
Richardson, C. C. 45, 133
Robertson, A. T. 133, 135, 219, 238, 239, 240, 259, 266, 276, 277, 280, 317, 328, 335

Robertson, A., and A. Plummer 119, 121, 134, 149, 178, 214, 219, 237, 239, 266, 269, 287, 291, 297, 315, 328, 332, 357, 364
Robinson, H. S. 119, 136
Ropes, J. H. 193
Ross, J. M. 178

Scharlemann, M. H. 136
Schep, J. A. 136, 342
Schippers, R. 105
Schlatter, A. 67–68
Schlier, H. 303
Schmidt, K. L. 98, 141, 276
Schmithals, W. 54, 119, 120, 136, 152, 178, 227, 237, 251, 277, 290, 330, 344
Schneider, B. 343, 344
Schneider, J. 246, 318
Schweizer, E. 343
Scott, C. A. A. 103, 138, 325, 328, 351
Scott, E. F. 98
Scroggs, R. 136, 328, 343
Seneca 284
Sevenster, J. N. 291
Shakespeare, W. 339, 353
Socrates 73, 294
von Soden, H. 233
Spicq, C. 366
Stählin, O. 178
Stauffer, E. 291
Stendahl, K. 38

Strabo 118–119
Strack, H. L., and P. Billerbeck 4, 135, 185, 196–197, 206, 208, 228, 245, 246, 250, 260–261, 291, 303
Stumpff, A. 169
Suetonius 81

Tertullian 301, 305, 365
Theodoret 344
Thrall, M. E. 134
Thucydides 335
Tillich, P. 233
von Tischendorf, C. 229
Tyndale, W. 158, 175

van Unnik, W. C. 291

Walker, W. O. 261–262
Walther, J. A. 155, 186, 267
Weiss, J. 21, 50, 120, 135, 138, 178, 206, 227, 233, 238, 260, 277, 284, 290, 300–301, 303, 325, 335
Wendland, H.-D. 135, 223
Wilder, A. N. 221
Wood, J. 155
Wright, G. E. 119

Zerwick, M. 134, 148, 194, 215, 219, 266, 277, 285, 329, 335
Zwingli, U. 269

INDEX OF SUBJECTS

Abraham 6, 54, 104, 300
Achaea 14–15, 25–26, 81, 85, 90, 107, 151, 363
Achaicus 17, 89, 363
Acts of Paul 336
Adam 78, 328, 331–332, 343, 348
Adoption 78
Adriatic 97
Aegean 15, 70, 92
Aeon 37, 164
Agabus 9, 61, 93
Agrippa 9, 95
Alexander 37, 41, 42
Alexandria 6, 55, 83, 84, 86, 96, 152
Allegory 86, 105
Altar 71, 74, 75, 229
Ambassador 141

Ananias 57, 58
Anathema 9, 111, 113, 277, 278, 367
Ancyra 14, 69
Angel(s) 53, 114, 142, 145, 164, 175, 181, 194, 233
Antioch (Pisidia) 40, 49, 56, 61, 62
Antioch (Syria) 8, 13, 54, 59, 60, 62, 63, 64–68, 84–85, 111, 114
Anti-Semitism 83, 105
Aphrodite 119
Apocalyptic 193, 194
Apollo 144, 301
Apollos 17, 18, 46, 83–88, 114, 150, 152, 169, 171, 172, 177, 178, 181, 355, 360–361
Apologetics 93, 116
Apostatize 93

Apostle 5–8, 18, 21, 24, 37, 42, 43, 48,
    50–51, 53–55, 58–60, 61, 63, 64, 68,
    85, 87–88, 101, 107, 114–116, 122,
    141, 142, 146, 148–150, 163, 177–178,
    179–182, 185, 188, 201, 202, 206, 207,
    237, 240, 241, 288, 318, 321–323
Apostolic Constitutions 364
Apostolic decree 63–64
Apphia 32
Aquila (see Prisca)
Arabia 7, 59, 100
Aramaic 94, 144
Archaeology 46, 74
Archippus 32
Aretas 7, 50, 57, 59
Aristarchus 29
Artemis 90, 119, 357–358
Ascension 54
Asia Minor 11, 18, 30, 32, 34, 39, 40,
    55, 65, 66, 69, 87, 96, 121, 365
Asiarchs 49
Assistants 177
Astrology 72
Athens 14, 15, 34, 70–74, 77, 80, 81,
    115, 200, 233
Athletics 243
Atomism 72
Atonement 96
Attica 81
Augustus 119
Authority 21, 102, 260–261

Babylon 74
Balkan Peninsula 26, 41
Ban 103, 105, 188, 192
Baptism 15–16, 58, 63–64, 70, 82,
    84–85, 86–87, 148, 150–151, 163, 189,
    199, 200, 201, 214, 245, 284, 321, 335,
    337
Barnabas 8–9, 11–13, 29, 48, 53, 56,
    58–64, 66–68, 114, 238
Belief 81, 86, 88, 163
Bernice 95
Beroea 71
Bishop 36, 38, 174, 175
Blasphemy 71, 90
Blessing 104, 142, 143, 207, 251
Blood 59, 64–66, 251, 267, 273,
    349–351
Boasting 161, 239, 242, 291–292,
    335–336
Boaz 213
Body 199, 200, 203, 204, 250, 253,
    267–274, 284–288, 323, 345, 352
Boeotians 149
Bread 250, 271–272
Brother 58, 59, 60, 61, 63, 83, 90, 99,

    108, 121, 149, 150, 169, 183, 191, 192,
    196, 197, 198, 216, 238, 321, 358, 360,
    364–365
Burial 61

Caesar 9, 34, 71, 95, 97, 99, 143, 233
Caesarea 33, 39, 58, 93, 94, 95, 96
Canon 119, 121
Carpus 42
Cauda 97
Cenchreae 16
Centurion 96–97
Cephas 7, 9, 12, 17, 58–59, 114, 148,
    150, 181, 241, 318, 321
Charity 161
Chloe 149, 319
Chrestus 82
Christology 62, 76, 324
Christophagy 251
Christosomatosis 252
Chronology 60
Church(es) 8, 37, 38, 40, 43, 51, 53,
    54, 56, 60, 62, 64, 65, 66, 67, 70, 84,
    89, 92, 99, 100, 107, 109, 111, 112,
    113, 114, 120, 121, 141, 142, 143, 145,
    148, 150, 157, 161, 163, 166, 171–174,
    177, 179, 181, 182, 187, 189, 192, 194,
    195–197, 201, 206, 208, 212, 213, 217,
    234, 245, 273–274, 281, 306–311,
    312–313, 320, 322–323, 337, 355–356,
    359, 364–365
Cilicia 8, 55, 59, 100
Circumcision 3, 10, 13, 17, 43, 50, 51,
    52, 63–66, 68–69, 93, 114, 215, 216
Claudia 41, 42
Claudius Caesar 60, 81
Claudius Lysias 94
Cnidus 96
Collection 60, 61, 101, 121, 356, 358
Colossae 29, 32, 42, 87, 100
Commandment 84, 195, 241
Condemnation 119, 120, 274
Conscience 232, 234, 255, 257, 282
Conversion 82, 83, 85, 94–95, 101, 108,
    142, 149, 151, 172, 216
Corinth 12, 15, 17–18, 23–26, 34, 41,
    43, 50, 53–54, 64, 81–82, 86–88, 90,
    102, 112–114, 119–121, 142, 149, 150,
    162, 165, 173, 175, 189, 192, 202, 203,
    207–208, 240–241, 301, 319, 325–326,
    335, 354, 356, 358, 359, 363–365
Cornelius 63–65
Corruption 61, 93, 146
Cosmology 109
Courts 73, 121, 177
Covenant 52, 273–274

Creation 74, 75, 76, 77–78, 79, 115, 165, 175, 203
Crescens 40, 42
Crete 43–46, 96
Crispus 16, 82
Cross 61, 66, 117, 150, 152, 156, 159, 160, 162–165, 166, 170, 202
Cults 75, 119
Cup 268, 250–253, 273–274
Curse (cf. also Anathema) 104
Cynic(s) 72, 119
Cyprus 11, 49, 56, 61, 84
Cyrene 55, 56, 96

Dalmatia 41
Damaris 81
Damascus 7, 50, 56–58, 101
David 6, 61, 148, 213
Day of the Lord 144, 146
Deacon 36, 37, 172
Dead Sea scrolls 38, 85, 148
Death 41, 57, 72, 77, 78, 80, 90, 93, 100, 104, 109, 110, 111, 116, 118, 144, 152, 159, 160, 162, 164, 165, 175, 181, 186, 188, 189, 192, 273, 324–327, 330–334, 335–337, 350–353
Deity (deities) 62, 72, 73, 75, 76
Delphi 81
Demas 29, 41, 42
Demetrius 41, 90
Demon (demonic) 37, 121, 157, 164, 250, 252–253
Devil 175, 188, 207
Devotion 151
Diakonia 38
Diaspora 84, 93
Dietary laws 54, 65
Diogenes 119
Dionysius the Areopagite 81
Disciple(s) 41, 54, 58, 60, 69, 86, 88, 90, 96, 102, 151
Discipline 20, 202
Divorce 18, 102, 209, 213, 214, 218, 260
Drunkards 190, 191

Earth 74
East 34, 74, 91
Ecstasy 75
Egnatian Way 70
Egypt 75, 84
Elder(s) 43, 51, 52, 56, 62, 63, 68, 92, 93
Elijah 331
Elisha 331
Elymas 61
Emanations 76

Emperor 95, 108
Enemy 144, 329, 333
Epaphras 29, 32
Epaphroditus 35
Ephesus 17, 18, 28, 33, 36–38, 40–42, 49, 84, 86–87, 89, 90, 92, 94, 100, 120, 121, 149, 336, 338, 357–358
Epicureans 72, 73, 202, 340
Erastus 41, 42, 90
Eschatology 105, 172, 174, 180, 191, 208, 220–222, 224, 225, 246, 297, 325, 329–334, 340–354
Essenes 38, 85, 86, 179, 208
Eternal life 37
Ethics 72, 110, 117, 142, 187, 189, 196, 200
Ethnarch 7, 57
Eubulus 41, 42
Euodia 35
Evangelism 35, 44, 55, 62, 64, 81, 87, 98, 100, 120, 151, 192, 213
Evangelist 58, 92
Evil 39, 41, 146, 188, 189, 195, 200, 295, 296
Evil one 191, 207
Evil spirits 37, 88
Excommunication 21, 185
Exodus tradition 196, 245
Exorcist(s) 88
Extirpation 186, 188

Fair Havens 44, 96
Faith 41, 47, 49, 66, 77, 103, 104, 106, 112, 116, 117, 145, 146, 158, 163, 169, 172, 175, 184, 282, 291, 294, 297, 324, 326, 361–362
False (teaching) 11, 23, 26, 37, 54, 186
Famine 60
Fasting 61
Father 76, 113, 182, 185, 187, 224, 233, 245, 247, 329, 333
Feast days 61, 92
Felix 9, 94, 95
Festus 9, 94, 95
Fetters 39
First day of the week 91
Fire 173–175
Flesh 59, 170, 186, 188, 199, 203, 219, 342, 345–346
Food 55, 163, 169, 170, 245, 250–257
Foolishness 159, 160, 163, 165, 166, 167, 175, 181
Forgiveness 61, 106, 110, 113, 142, 146, 197, 198, 201
Form criticism 47, 77
Fornication 18, 63, 64, 185, 203, 206, 208

Fortunatus 17, 366
Forum of Appius 97, 99
Fraud 195, 197
Freedom 105–106, 110, 117, 121, 202, 204, 215, 217, 241, 255–256
Friendship 146

Gaius 16
Galatia 14, 18, 24, 41, 50, 51, 53, 67, 69, 89, 113, 114, 158, 216
Galileans 54
Gallio 81, 83, 120
Gamaliel 57
Gauls 14, 69
Guardian 179
Gehenna 345
Genealogy 43
Gentile(s) 5, 40, 50–52, 53, 58, 61, 63, 64–67, 68, 69, 78, 80, 82, 84, 92, 93, 96, 98, 100, 101, 103, 105, 106–107, 109, 114, 119, 142, 143, 160, 174, 179, 185, 216, 245, 249, 276
Gift(s) 19, 26, 181, 196, 207
Glory 79, 112, 117, 151, 161, 164, 175, 186, 200, 202
Gnostic(ism) 37, 53, 152, 157, 164, 200, 202–203, 207, 348, 350
Gods (heathen) 62, 71, 73, 76, 84, 90, 97, 112, 119, 144, 159, 165, 203
Golden calf 55, 246, 248
Gospel 7, 8, 12, 19, 26, 27, 28, 34, 35, 37, 47, 53, 54, 58, 65–66, 68, 70, 74, 77, 79, 80, 84, 95, 99, 101–103, 105, 106, 107, 110, 112, 114, 115, 116, 118, 142, 144, 146, 150, 151, 158, 161, 163, 165, 166, 170, 172, 179, 181, 192, 197, 201, 202, 216, 241–242, 243, 319–320
Gospels, the 164
Governor(s) 39, 94, 95, 99, 107
Grace 103, 110, 141, 145, 173
Grave 61, 146
Greece 14, 64, 90
Greek(s) 42, 56, 70, 84, 87, 93, 119, 159, 160, 197, 257, 285
Greek language 74, 93, 284
Guilt 79, 113, 161, 141, 142

Hagar 105
Hallucination 111
Harlotry 185
Headdress 122, 258–264
Healing 57, 62, 88, 91, 97, 112
Heart 78, 177, 224
Heaven 27, 117, 194, 348–349
Hebrew 4, 53, 54
Hellenist(ic) 3, 4, 55, 58, 59, 193, 199, 215, 322

Heresy 37, 54, 73, 92
Hermeneutic 104
Hermes 62
Herod 61
Hierapolis 29, 32
Hierodules 119
High priest(s) 57, 88, 148
Hippolytus 157
Holy, holiness 61, 142, 161, 175
Holy of holies 174
Holy Spirit (cf. also Spirit) 33, 53, 54, 55, 58, 60, 66, 80, 86, 87, 91, 204, 277–283
Homilies 72
Honor 151
Hope 106, 109, 146, 159, 238, 297, 325, 327
Horace 107
Hostility 161
Human race 74, 75
Husband(s) 36, 109, 206–214, 225, 259, 262–264, 312–313
Hymenaeus 36, 41, 42
Hypocrisy 67, 68

Iconium 14, 40, 62, 69
Idol, idolatry 18, 63–65, 71, 76, 79, 89, 102, 115, 120–122, 190, 227–235, 246–256, 276
Ignorance 76, 78, 79, 80
Illyricum 26, 88, 100
Image of God 79
Immaturity 170
Immorality 119, 185, 187, 189, 190, 194, 195, 200, 203, 208, 246, 248
Immortality 350–353
Imprisonment 37, 38, 41, 45, 46, 63, 92, 98, 100, 117
Incest 18, 20, 121, 185–188
Inspiration 96
Institutes of Gaius 186
Intermarriage 69
Interpretation 86, 107
Isaac 104
Isis 119, 144
Israel 53–55, 58, 61, 98, 104, 141, 142, 179, 192, 196, 245, 276, 301, 321
Italy 81, 96

Jail 70
James (apostle) 93
James the Just 7, 9, 12, 13, 51, 52–54, 59, 64, 65, 114, 241, 318, 322
Jerusalem 7, 12, 18, 24, 25, 26, 28, 38, 39, 43, 49, 51, 52, 54, 56, 58, 60, 61, 63–66, 68, 70, 80, 85, 88, 89, 92, 93, 95, 100, 105, 106, 107, 121, 356–357

Jesus' teaching 85, 98, 142, 195, 213, 215, 216
Jewish Christians 51–55, 57, 64–66, 91, 216, 262
Jews, Judaism 4, 17, 27, 35, 40, 41, 50, 51, 53, 54, 56, 58, 59, 61, 62, 68, 70, 71, 74, 81–84, 86, 87, 90, 91, 93, 98, 100, 103, 104, 105, 107, 109, 113, 115, 116, 119, 142, 143, 148, 149, 160, 165, 185, 186, 187, 189, 192, 213, 352
John 12, 54, 63
John the Baptist 61, 84, 85, 87
Joy 112, 144, 175
Judaism (see Jews)
Judas 164
Judea 19, 50, 52, 53, 59, 60, 63, 110
Judge(s), judgment 76, 79, 83, 94, 103, 144, 165, 167, 179, 180, 188, 192, 194, 195, 196, 197, 268, 273–274
Julius Caesar 81, 118
Julius (centurion) 96
Justification 10, 48, 61, 66, 103–104, 116, 117, 146, 151, 161, 179, 193, 196, 197, 201, 202
Justus 31
Juvenal 107

King 57, 70, 95, 99, 148, 179
Kingdom 78, 110, 112, 160
Kingdom, messianic 148
Kingdom of God 87, 98, 99, 103, 117, 179, 195, 197, 200, 230, 329, 350, 351
Knowledge 144, 151, 159, 161, 175, 230–232, 296–297

Lais 119
Lamb (Passover) 186, 189
Laodicea 30, 32, 87, 100
Law 3, 13, 26, 36, 43, 45, 49, 51, 52, 57, 61, 63, 65, 68, 78, 79, 82, 85, 93, 95, 97, 100, 103, 104, 105, 109, 114, 117, 149, 186, 188, 196, 201, 202, 213, 236–237, 303, 312, 352–353
Lawsuits 18, 35, 121, 195, 197
Laying on of hands 57, 60, 61, 84, 85, 87
Lazarus 331
Laziness 201
Leather worker 82
Leaven 186, 188, 189
Letters 56, 142
Liar 45
Life 76, 104, 106, 109, 110, 146, 159, 160, 170, 172, 174, 175, 204, 325, 327
Linus 40, 42
Lion 39
Lord 39, 41, 57, 58, 74, 84, 87, 100, 101, 104, 109, 142, 143, 144, 146, 148, 149, 161, 164, 167, 175, 179–181, 185, 188, 199, 201, 202, 202–204, 213, 215, 216, 237, 240, 241, 242, 253, 263, 268, 270, 273, 277–278, 281, 303, 314, 336, 353–354, 357, 366–367
Lord's Day 356
Lord's Supper 18, 110, 122, 192, 246–247, 251–253, 265–275
Love 65, 102, 104, 106, 107, 109, 110, 112, 144, 160, 170, 175, 197, 201–204, 227–228, 229–230, 290–297
Loyalty 114, 115, 150, 151, 203
Lucian 107
Lucius 60
Luke 29, 40, 42, 47, 48, 50–52, 54, 57, 60, 61, 63, 65, 66, 67, 68, 69, 73, 74, 77, 79, 80–82, 84, 85, 87–89, 90–93, 95, 98–100, 105, 115
Lycaonia 62, 115
Lycia 96
Lydia 70
Lysias 94
Lystra 14, 27, 40, 62, 69

Macedonia 5, 15, 18, 20, 24, 25, 34, 37, 38, 42, 70, 82, 89–91, 107, 112, 113
Magic 88, 89
Magistrate 70
Malta 39, 44, 97
Manaen 60
Mandaeans 84
Manna 245, 247
Marcion 30, 335
Marriage 18, 37, 102, 109, 110, 121, 122, 179, 181, 185, 186, 187, 188, 202, 205–226, 263
Mars Hill 73
Marsyas 301
Martyr 35, 36, 99
Mary 322
Master 37, 43, 109, 115, 149, 181
Meat 37
Mediator 197
Mediterranean 43, 55, 64, 88, 92, 96, 107, 243
Megara 148
Melchizedek 86
Mercy 104
Messenger (cf. also Angel [s]) 36
Messiah 52, 58, 62, 82, 84, 85, 98, 104, 115, 148, 159, 160
Miletus 39, 91–93
Milk 163, 169, 170
Mind 150, 166–167, 302–303, 307–308
Ministry 60, 93, 163
Miracle(s) 55, 85, 88, 91

Mishnah 112, 186, 224, 228
Mission(ary) 14, 38, 54, 57, 59, 61, 62, 63, 64, 69, 70, 81, 84, 99, 100, 106, 118, 121, 179
Monotheism 14, 73, 105, 107
Montanist(s) 301, 305, 335
Morals 119
Moses 3, 6, 52, 53, 55, 61, 85, 93, 103, 148, 236, 245, 292, 320
Mother 185, 186
Mourning 185, 187
Murder 66
Myra 96
Mystery 28, 75, 105, 114, 156, 161, 163, 164, 167, 177, 179, 306, 351, 352

Naassenes 157
Nabataea 57
Naples 97
Nazarite 93, 260, 264
Neighbor 104
Nephew of Paul 94
Nicopolis 45
Noachic covenant 66
North Africa 96
Nympha 32

Oath 7
Obedience 104, 106, 143, 163, 230
Octavia 119
Offering 24, 25, 89, 90, 91, 107
Office 151
Onesimus 16, 28, 149, 295
Onesiphorus 39
Oracles 51
Ordination 62
Origen 30, 156, 164
Orosius 81
Orphans 38, 116
Overseers 37

Paganism 6, 69, 78, 109, 119, 201
Palestine 15, 54
Pamphilia 11, 61, 66
Pantheon 62, 119, 165
Papyri 88, 144
Parable 177, 180, 187
Paradise 117
Paraenesis 246, 336
Passover 186, 187, 188, 189, 192, 250–252, 272, 273
Pastoral epistles 36–46, 207, 304
Patriarchs 62, 104, 196
Patriotism (Jewish) 56
Pauline letters 31, 56, 59, 60, 64, 68, 77–80, 87, 89, 98, 100, 103, 106, 108,
110, 112, 142, 144, 149, 157, 162, 191, 215
Paulinist 38
Peace 63, 141, 212, 216, 311
Pedagogue 104
Peloponnesus 81
Pentecost 17, 62, 91, 357
Perga 61, 66
Pergamum 87
Persecution 40, 55–58, 90, 100, 111, 112, 182, 242
Perversion 113, 115
Peter (cf. also Cephas) 13, 48, 52, 54, 55, 62–65, 66, 68, 69, 85
Pharisee(s) 11, 51, 63, 94, 322
Philadelphia 87
Philemon (person) 28, 31, 42, 149, 295
Philetus 42
Philip 55, 56, 62, 85, 92
Philippi 15, 27, 33, 34, 35, 49, 70, 101, 112, 114
Philosopher(s), philosophy 71–75, 85, 115, 116, 119, 162
Phoenicia 84
Phoenix 96
Phrygia 69
Phygelus 42
Piety 54
Pilate 34, 61
Pilgrims 52
Pillars of Hercules 45
Pillars of the church 65
Pleasure 72
Pneumatic ubiquity 188
Poetry 76, 199
Politarchs 49
Polytheism 72
Polygamy 185, 187
Poor 38, 63, 91, 100, 110, 116, 119, 122, 146
Poseidon 119
Poverty 112, 113
Praetorium 33, 34
Praise 112, 181, 204
Prayer 54, 60, 105, 113, 144, 209, 259, 263
Preacher(s), preaching 15, 17, 28, 33, 40, 44, 51, 54, 55, 56, 57, 59, 62, 64, 65, 70, 73, 77, 79, 80, 82, 83–85, 87, 88, 90, 91, 95, 97, 98, 101, 102, 105, 107, 111, 114, 117, 119, 121, 142, 151, 155, 162–165, 171, 173, 193, 201, 324
Prejudice 149, 170
Pride 149, 160, 161, 175, 181, 185, 186, 187, 189, 295
Priest 148, 149

Prisca (Priscilla) 17, 41, 81–82, 84, 85, 87, 120, 142, 303, 364–365
Prisoner(s) 70, 95, 96, 97, 99, 107, 142
Proclamation (cf. also Preacher) 19, 54, 61, 85, 101, 102, 104, 144, 151, 155, 159, 162, 171, 173, 199, 324, 326
Proconsul 34, 61, 81, 82, 107, 119
Procreation 76
Profane 105
Promise 104
Propaganda 55, 100
Prophet(s), prophecy 45, 60–63, 65, 87, 88, 92, 95, 104, 115, 148, 158, 218, 259, 263, 287, 288, 290, 300–311, 314, 315
Proselyte(s) 8, 51, 53, 107, 187
Prostitution 63, 185, 200, 202, 203
Pseudonymity 32, 36, 40, 42
Publius 97
Pudens 41, 42
Punishment 188, 202
Purificatory rites 54, 93
Puritan 116
Purity 189
Puteoli (Pozzuoli) 97

Quarrel(s) 146, 150
Qumran 85, 336

Rabbi(s), rabbinic(s) 26, 66, 68, 103, 106, 113, 141, 152, 178, 185, 187, 196, 208, 241, 245, 263, 291, 303
Ransom 200, 204
Reason 72, 77, 171, 289, 345, 351
Reconciliation 21
Redemption 84, 104, 146, 160, 161, 164
Remnant 104
Repentance 76, 79, 84, 87, 185, 186, 189
Resurrection 18, 54, 61, 62, 70, 73, 76, 77, 80, 94, 95, 98, 110, 116, 118, 121, 145, 162, 179, 202, 233, 317, 319, 321–332, 334, 335, 337–349, 351–353, 354
Revelation 58, 60, 63, 72, 74, 77, 79, 82, 101, 102, 103, 107, 109, 111, 113, 115, 116, 117, 144, 161, 164, 165, 167, 179–181
Rhegium (Reggio) 97
Rich 119, 195, 197
Righteousness 76, 80, 144, 145, 161, 201
Roman people 26, 70, 81, 83, 88, 94, 95, 99, 119, 161, 209, 216
Rome 15, 27, 28, 33, 34, 35, 39, 42–45, 56, 71, 82, 89, 92, 95, 97, 98, 99, 100, 106–108, 109, 111, 115, 186, 195

Rufus 42
Ruler of this world 164, 165
Ruth 213

Sabbath 82, 355
Sacrament 84, 186, 189
Sacrifice 62, 75, 148, 252, 330
Sadducees 94, 340
Saints 18, 25, 43, 60, 89, 107, 142, 144, 193, 194, 196, 355–356
Salome 44
Salvation 54, 63, 103, 104, 112, 116, 117, 144, 154, 159, 160, 165, 167, 174, 175, 179, 186, 189, 214, 256, 317, 320, 334, 337
Samaria 56, 85
Sanctification 142, 201, 213
Sanctuary 80
Sanhedrin 39, 211
Sardis 87
Saronic Gulf 81
Satan 15, 27, 36, 41, 88, 112, 114, 164, 186, 188, 191
Saul (Paul) 6, 56–58
Savior 61
Scandal 146
Sceva 89
Schism 17, 92, 121, 150, 187
Scourging 93, 109
Scribe 55
Scripture(s) 3, 70, 82, 84, 86, 106, 116, 151, 179, 317, 320–321
Sect 63, 98
Seed of David 62
Seer 61
Septuagint 143, 154–156, 157, 158, 169, 185, 199, 206, 210, 225, 238, 266, 301, 350
Serapis 144, 232
Sergius Paulus 49, 61
Sermon 62, 72
Servant(s) 36, 54, 172, 173, 181
Service 80
Seven (the) 55, 84, 85, 322
Sex 72, 185, 202, 203, 206, 208, 209, 223, 224, 246–248
Shipwreck 26, 27, 39, 97, 111
Shrines 90
Sidon 96
Sign(s) 84, 85, 88, 159, 160, 309
Silas 63, 68, 70, 71, 72, 82
Simeon Niger 61
Sin(s) 61, 78, 79, 104, 106, 110, 112, 113, 116, 142, 144, 159, 160, 161, 170, 185, 188, 192, 196, 199, 201, 203, 320, 325–327, 352–353
Sinai 105

Sister 107, 214, 238
Slave(s), slavery 37, 43, 109, 115, 142,
    146, 149, 161, 177, 201, 204, 215, 216,
    217, 243, 283
Smyrna 87
Solomon 105
Son of David 62
Son(s)of God 6, 58, 76, 78, 101, 102,
    109, 111, 145, 146, 148, 159, 163, 170
Sophists 152
Sosthenes 82–83, 142
Soul(s) 72, 348
Spain 33–34, 92
Spirit 13, 55, 60, 70, 76, 84, 85, 86–88,
    92, 93, 98, 102, 106, 109, 110, 113,
    117, 148, 149, 156–159, 161, 163,
    164–167, 170, 171, 174, 175, 179, 180,
    181, 183, 194, 199, 201, 203, 276–285,
    343–348
Spirit, human 157, 200
Spiritual gifts 18, 65, 87, 110, 114, 144,
    165, 196, 287, 294, 300–303, 305–311
Stephanas 16, 17, 80, 151, 362, 363,
    366
Stephen 42, 55–57, 59, 62, 84, 85, 99,
    322
Stepchildren 187
Stepmother 185–188
Steward(s) 55, 60, 114, 117, 242
Stoic(s) 72–77, 85
Stoning 26, 40, 56, 59, 62, 109
Suffering 70, 112, 159
Superstition 72
Symbolism 72, 148, 187
Synagogue 55, 61, 70, 72, 82–84, 85,
    100, 119, 142, 362
Synoptic Gospels 62, 211
Syntyche 35
Syracuse 97
Syria 8, 17, 59, 74, 90, 120
Syrtis 96

Table fellowship 65, 68, 114, 192
Taboo 170
Tarsus 6, 57, 58–60, 100
Teach, teaching 60, 63, 73, 77, 83, 85,
    87, 93, 94, 98, 103, 111, 113, 115, 142,
    307
Teacher(s) 60, 61, 288
Teacher of Righteousness 86
Tearful letter 20, 24
Temple 54, 56, 71, 74, 75, 80, 90, 93,
    94, 104–106, 119, 170, 174, 203–204
Temptation 209, 247, 249
Tent maker/making 82, 107
Tent of testimony 55
Tertius 33

Tertullian 30
Tertullus 39, 94
Testing (cf. also Temptation) 173, 209
Thanksgiving 111, 112, 113, 117, 118,
    144, 257, 302, 308
Theater 90
Theological hatred 62
Theology 77, 185, 189, 195, 201
Theophilus 99
Thessalonians, Thessalonica 14, 15, 26,
    27, 41, 49, 70, 101, 102, 113, 326
Thirty-nine stripes 26
Thorn in the flesh 27, 112, 163
Thrace 45
Three Taverns 97, 99
Thyatira 88, 100
Timothy 15–16, 18, 20, 24, 28, 34–38,
    40, 42, 43, 68, 69, 72, 82, 89–91, 179,
    183, 359, 360, 366
Titius Justus 82
Titus 8, 9, 10, 19, 20, 22, 24, 41,
    42–44, 46, 91, 112
Toleration 82, 98
Tomb 61
Tongues 87, 88, 102, 114, 280, 288,
    291, 300–311, 315
Torah 230, 238, 252, 303
Tradition(s) 4, 5, 63, 68, 71, 105, 151
Trial 94–95, 99
Tribes of Israel 87
Tribune 93–94
Trinity 76
Triumph 145
Troas 20, 22, 41, 70, 87, 91, 92, 113
Trophimus 39, 93
Trumpet 301–302
Trust (cf. also Faith) 163
Truth 75, 95, 103, 104, 117, 144, 149,
    152, 166, 181, 189, 296
Tübingen school 68
Turkey 69
Twelve, the 48–49, 54, 56, 59, 87, 154,
    241, 322
Tychicus 30, 31, 41, 42, 45
Typology 245, 246
Tyrannus, school of 87
Tyre 92

Unknown god 74, 77
Unleavened bread 186, 188, 189
Unrighteousness 79
Utopia 148
Uxorial sanctification 213, 263

Vice(s) 192, 201
Victory 41, 144
Viper 97
Virgin(s) 102, 210, 219–224

Vision 57, 96, 99, 110, 111
Vulgate 267, 291, 292

Wages 172
Way 87, 94
We 91, 96, 99
Wickedness 119
Widow(s) 37, 38, 55, 102, 116, 186, 187, 210, 211, 225–226
Widower(s) 210, 211
Wife, wives 37, 102, 109, 187, 206, 208, 209, 259–264, 312–313
Wild beasts 90
Wilderness 55
Wisdom 55, 74, 85, 102, 151, 155–167, 170, 174–175, 183, 280–281
Witnesses(es) 61, 62, 85, 88, 99, 173, 323

Woman (cf. also Wife) 18, 43, 62, 70, 102, 108, 122, 185, 220, 258–264
Wonder(s) 61, 88
Word (also *logos*), words 72, 76, 156, 158, 159, 179, 183, 280, 313, 350
Works 115
Worship 66, 71, 73, 78, 79, 82, 90, 110, 119, 162, 173, 235, 258–264, 273, 305
Wrath 181

Yahweh 88, 105, 143, 196
Yeast (cf. also Leaven) 186

Zeal 4, 5, 71, 287, 300, 302
Zealot 5, 52, 57
Zenas 46
Zeus 62

INDEX OF SCRIPTURAL AND OTHER REFERENCES

Gen 1 343
1, 2 328, 331
1:11 342, 346
1:26–27 264, 344
1:27 260
2:7 78, 343, 344, 348
2:21–23 260, 263
2:24 200
3:16 312
3:19 349
6:1–4 261
9:20, 21 238
15 300
18:1–15 251
20:4, 6 206
26:8 246
26:30 271
32:10 290
39:17 246

Exod 2:1–2 206
4:27 365
6:7 230
8:19 231
9:14 231
10:2 230

(*Exod*)
12:15 186
12:23 246
12:47, 48 271
13:5 271
13:7 186
13:21–22 245
14:19–20, 21–29 245
16:4, 35 245
17:5, 6 245
18:11 230
18:13–26 196
20:4–6 228
21–23 196
22:29 328
23:16 271
23:19 328
25:2–3 (LXX) 328
28:36–40 259
32:6, 28 246
33:9–10 245
33:11 292

(*Exod*)
34:22 271
34:26 328

Lev 2:12, 14 328
17:11 251, 273
17:14 273
18:8 185
20:9 251
23:10–11 328

Num 12:8 292
14 246
14:14 245
18:20–24 239
20:7–11 245
21:4–9 246
25:1–9 246

Deut 4:35, 39 232
6:4 232
13:3 230
16:13 271
16:18–20 196
17:7 191
18:1–4 239

(*Deut*)

18:15, 18 62, 320
19:19 191
20:6 238
22:21, 24 191
24:7 191
24:15 238
25:4 238, 241
26:1–11 328
28:30 206
29:6 230
31:6 362
32:21 250
34:10 292

Josh 22:31 231

I Sam 20:12 (LXX) 158
25:15 196
29:4 186

II Sam 1:16 82
10:12 362
19:22 186

I Kings 5:4 186
8:27 106
11:14, 23, 25 186
22:19–23 302

II Kings 23:21 271

I Chron 21:11–16 246

Ezra 7:25 196

Neh 8:9 185

Job 1–2 186
1:4 271
5:13 170

Ps 1:1 290
8:6 329
16 62
16:10 61, 321
19:4–5 302
19:7–11 105
22 320

(*Ps*)

23:5 250
24:1 254
27:14 362
31:24 362
50:6 196
78:15, 16, 23–28, 30, 31 245
93:11 (LXX) 170
94:11 170
102:27 261
110 231
110:1 329
115:3–8 232
116:13, 17 250
119 105
138 231
139:1–18 230
150:5 291

Prov 6:29 206

Isa 5:19 231
6:2 259
13:16 206
22:13 (LXX) 336
24:4 185
25:8 350, 351, 352
28:11–12 303, 309
29:14 154
30:32 301
33:22 196
40:3 302
40:13 159, 167
40:18–20 79
44:9–17 79
45:14 304
52:15 157
53 320
54:7 321
54:10 291
55:8–9 165
56:12 336
64:4 157
65:17 157
65:24 230

Jer 1:5 5
3:16 157

(*Jer*)

9:24 (9:23, LXX) 156

Lam 1:12, 18 320

Ezek 3:17–21 82
44:18 259

Dan 2:22 157
2:47 304
5:1 271
7:22 194
10:2 185

Hosea 6:2 (LXX) 321
6:3 231
13:14 351, 352

Amos 8:8 185
9:12 143

Hag 2:11–14 213

Zech 3:1 186
8:17 292
8:23 304

Matt 5:31–32 212, 217
5:39–42 197
5:39, 41, 43–45 217
6:24 253
7:1–2 146
7:23 230
7:24–25 173
10:17–20 95, 278
11:5 330
11:30 295
13:33 186
15:2 272
15:11, 17–18 232
16:6, 12 187
16:17 350
16:21 317
17:20 291
18:18 186
19:5–6 200
19:9 212
20:22 273
21:21 291

(*Matt*)

21:28, 31 99
22:30 224
22:41–45 62
24:31 350
24:38 224
25:34 158
25:45 235
26:26 267
27:52–53
  330
28:5 156

Mark 3:20 272
3:21 322
4:11 164
5:35–43 330
6:3 241
6:4 178
6:8 212
6:21 271
7:15–20 232
8:6 212
8:15 186
8:31 317
9:35 171,
  178
10:11–12
  212
10:14, 15
  297
10:17–27
  195
10:19 195
10:32–34 92
10:43 171
10:45 281
11:15–17
  295
11:23 291
12:26–27
  332
12:29 232
12:35–37a
  62
12:40–44 38
13 361
13:35, 37
  362
14:22 267
14:34, 38
  362
14:36 273
14:45 365
15:21 42
16:6 156

Luke 1:7 156
2:29 359
3:22 247
4:14 156
4:16 304
5:14 212
5:39 295
6:35 295
7:11–17 330
8:29, 56 212
9:21 212
9:22 317
9:49–50 89
9:51–18:14
  92
10:7, 8 239
12:19–20
  336
12:42–47
  180
13:20–21
  186
14:1 272
14:12, 16
  271
15:12 279
16:1–8 177
16:18 212
20:41–44 62
22:17, 19–20
  267
23:29 225
23:34 296
24:3 268

John 1:3, 10 234
1:42 318
3:14, 15 246
4:2 151
5:21, 25–29
  330
5:21–29 343
5:37 247
6:31, 49 245
6:45 158
7:5 322
7:38, 39 284
8:58 234
11:7–10 92
11:25 330
11:33, 38
  295
11:38–44
  330
11:39 347
12:2 271
12:31 164

(*John*)

13:27 164
14:30 164
16:11 164
17:15 191
18:11 273
18:33 34
19:23 164
19:31–36
  267
20:22 84
20:23 186

Acts 1:1 99
1:4 212
1:8 156
1:13 318
1:15 266,
  321
1:22 240
1:26 318
2:1 322
2:4–11 280
2:27, 29–31
  321
2:29–36 62
2:34–36 231
2:36 164
2:46 272,
  364
3:20–22 148
3:23 246
4:6 41
4:13 303
4:30 148
4:36, 37 238
5:9 55
5:17 266
5:42 364
6 216
6:1 38, 55
6:1–6 171,
  288, 322
6:3, 8–9, 13–
  14 55
6–8 85
7:2–53 55
7:58 57
7:60 42
8 56
8:1 56, 57,
  322
8:3 57
8:4 145
9:1–2 56
9:2 85, 290
9:3–6 57

(*Acts*)

9:4, 7 57
9:10–30 58
9:17 360
9:22 115
9:23f 49
9:29 3
10:38 156
10:43 148
11:18 65
11:19–24 56
11:22–26 60
11:27–28 9
11:27–30 60
11:28 60
11:29–30
  355
12:2 318
12:19 158
13:1 288
13:1–3 60
13:4–12 61
13:9 58
13:9–11 295
13:13 66
13:13–41 61
13:14 – 14:28
  40
13:23 62
13:32–41
  115
13:42–52 62
14:1–7 62
14:4 48
14:8–18 62
14:14 48
14:15–17
  115
14:19–28 62
14:27 357
15 11, 13,
  65, 121, 322
15:1–2, 4 63
15:5 63, 266
15:19–29 93
15:6–20, 21–
  35 63
15:29 254
15:36–41 66
16:1 40
16:1–3 10
16:3, 4 69
16:5 40
16:6 69
16:9–12 91
16:11–12 70
16:13–40 71
16:17 85

(*Acts*)

16:25 302
16:36 359
17 79–80,
  162
17:10–15 71
17:11 158
17:15–34 71
17:18 200
17:24–29
  106, 115
17:31 233
17:34 16,
  151, 162,
  363
18:1 81, 357
18:1–3 364,
  365
18:2 81
18:3 82, 178,
  238, 364
18:4, 5–17
  82
18:12 83
18:12–17 81
18:17 142
18:18 364
18:18–22 84
18:23 69
18:24 152
18:24–28 84
18:24 – 20:2
  361
18:26 364
18:27, 28 85
18:34 178
19 89, 358
19:1a 85
19:1–7 85,
  86
19:7 87
19:8–10 88
19:9 85, 290
19:11–13, 18–
  19 88
19:21–22 89,
  357
19:22 42, 89,
  359
19:23 85,
  290
19:23–40
  338
19:33 41
20 357
20:1 90
20:2–3, 4
  356

(*Acts*)

20:2–6 91
20:4–5 359
20:6 357
20:7 355
20:7–12, 13–
  17 91
20:16 60,
  357
20:18–38 91
20:28–29
  241
20:29–30 92
21 52
21:1–6, 7–14
  92
21:15–16 93
21:20f 52
21:20–21 51
21:27–36 93
21:37 – 22:30
  94
22:4 85, 290
22:13 360
23:1–10, 12–
  35 94
24:1–23 94
24:5 266
24:6b–8a 94
24:10–21
  115
24:14 85,
  266, 290
24:17 89
24:22 85,
  290
24:24–27 95
25:1–12 95
25:13 – 26:32
  95
25:14 9
26:5 266
26:11 278
26:15 323
26:28 95
27:1 – 28:16
  96
27:7–8 43
27:9–12 357
27:24 99
28 99
28:15 99
28:17 94
28:17–22 98
28:22 266
28:23–28, 30,
  31 98
28:31 195

Rom 1 78, 112, 116
1:3 62, 148, 273
1:4 80, 233, 331, 348
1:7 142
1:9 157
1:11 99
1:16–17 165
1:17, 18 311
1:18 41, 79
1:18–23 235
1:19–23 3, 78
1:23 79
2 117, 146
2:4 79
2:7 118
2:11, 13 215
2:14–15 78
2:14–15, 26 3
2:16 103, 144
2:23–24 192
3:9 302
3:23 332
3:25 273
3:29–30 10
4:19 361
5:3–5 117
5:4–5 325
5:5 228
5:8 229
5:12 239
5:12–21 78, 343
5:13 79
5:15 302
6:4 321
6:5–11 332, 343
6:12–23 332
6:23 172
7:4 273
7:5–11 104
7:11 169
7:12 103
7:22–25 150
7:25 353
8 5, 110
8:1 146
8:1–17 171
8:10 157
8:18 118

(Rom)
8:19 108, 311
8:21 118
8:23 328, 331
8:24–25 333
8:26 306
8:29 163
8:35 228
8:36–39 337
8:38 164
8:38–39 175
9–11 104, 245
9:3 149
9:5 273
9:22–24 239
10–11 214
10:19 250
11:7 302
11:16 214,
11:20 361
11:25 164, 245
11:25–33 180
11:26 104
11:34 159, 167
12 5
12:2 144
12:5 250, 273 328, 330
12:6–8 288
12:7 38, 287
12:8 38
12:11 84
12:15 219
13:1 164
13:10 229
13:11 272
13:14 352
14:5 150
14:17 98, 195
15:8 171
15:13, 19 156
15:15–28 355
15:18 145
15:18–19 88
15:19 26
15:20 44, 171, 173
15:23–24, 28

(Rom)
92
15:24 33
15:25 25
15:25–26 60, 180
15:25, 26, 31 142
15:27 146
15:30 228
15:30–32 91
16 42
16:3 42, 364
16:3–5 364
16:5 331, 363, 365
16:16 364
16:18 169
16:22 32, 367
16:23 42
16:25 164

I Cor 1 121, 163, 201
1:1 83, 360
1:1–3 141–143
1:1–9 141–146
1:2 196, 256
1:3 367
1:4, 7 17
1:4–9 143–146, 367
1:7 311
1:9 215, 250
1:10 362
1:10–11 121
1:10–17 147–152
1:10–4:21 147–183
1:11 363
1:11–13 114
1:12 170, 207, 241, 318
1:13, 15 245
1:14 16, 82
1:16 363
1:17 163, 280
1:18 145, 232, 280, 317
1:18–2:16 152–167

(I Cor)

1:18 – 4:13
  18
1:21 324
1:22–24 331
1:23 232
1:24 281
1:25 157
1:26 250
1:29, 31 186
2, 3, 4 199
2:1 16, 169,
  180
2:1–5 102
2:4 145,
  179, 324
2:4–6 85
2:6 303
2:6–13 282
2:7–8 164
2:11–16 155
2:12 – 3:3
  314
2:14 177,
  237
2:15 195
2:21 159
3 360
3:1 297, 303
3:1–2 163
3:1–23 167–
  175
3:3 238, 336
3:4 170
3:5–6 17
3:6 241
3:5–11 17
3:9 229
3:10 318
3:13 266
3:16 179
3:16–17 105,
  200, 203
3:19 215
3:21 186
3:22 318
4 323, 360
4:1 114, 292
4:1–21 176–
  183
4:3–4 158,
  167, 304
4:6 254, 282,
  295
4:7 186, 283
4:9 233, 261
4:9–13 18,
  102

(I Cor)

4:14 197
4:14–16 318
4:15 17, 113,
  338
4:16 114,
  256
4:17 291,
  359
4:18–20 185,
  282, 295
4:18–21 358
4:20 98, 195,
  280, 350
4:21 229
5 24
5:1–5 194
5:1–8 18,
  184–189
5:1 – 6:20
  184–204
5:2 282, 295
5:4 148
5:5 157, 246,
  274
5:9 18, 120,
  207
5:9–13 190–
  193
5:10 212
5:10–11 199
6 35
6:1 254
6:1, 2 142
6:1–8 186
6:1–9a 193–
  198
6:1–11 18
6:3 233
6:3–6 167
6:5 179, 336
6:6 212
6:7 206
6:9 118
6:9–10 98,
  192
6:9–20 187
6:9b 336
6:9b–10 350
6:9b–20
  198–204
6:10 195
6:11 148
6:12 199,
  254
6:18 277
6:19 106,
  169

(I Cor)

6:20 215
7 38, 102,
  121, 202,
  262–263,
  313, 321
7:1 227
7:1–7 205–
  209
7:1–40 205–
  226
7:5 24, 186,
  195, 266
7:6–12 207
7:8 205, 207
7:8–9 210–
  211
7:9 240
7:10–12 142
7:10–16
  211–214
7:11 210
7:12–16 102,
  263
7:15 216,
  359
7:17–24
  214–217
7:23 200
7:25 205
7:25–35 210,
  217–222
7:26 205,
  207
7:29 363
7:35 210
7:36 292
7:36–38
  222–225
7:39–40
  225–226
7:40 102,
  166, 185
8 102, 121,
  191, 254,
  255
8, 9 254
8, 10 102
8:1 205, 254,
  282, 295,
  301
8:1–3 227–
  230
8:1–7, 10–11
  226
8:1 – 10:33
  18

(*I Cor*)

8:1 – 11:1
227–257,
254
8:4 79
8:4–13 230–
235
8:7–13 256
8:7–15 293
8:13 255
9 122, 254,
323, 364
9:1–6 178,
318
9:1–15 102
9:1–27 235–
243
9:3 272
9:5 318
9:8 336
9:9 250
9:13 105
9:15–16 292
9:16 12, 110
9:17–18 172
9:19–22 256
9:22 115,
256, 257,
279
9:27 266
10 102, 122,
305
10:1 317
10:1–15
244–249
10:4 173
10:11 312
10:14 233
10:16 146,
267, 272
10:16–17
274
10:16–22
249–253
10:19–20
233
10:19–21
276
10:20–21
121
10:20–22
268
10:21 268
10:23 121,
229, 301
10:23–29
253–256

(*I Cor*)

10:24, 28–29a
256
10:30 – 11:1
256–257
10:33 279
11 187, 216,
305, 321,
343
11–12 174,
203, 250
11:1 113
11:1–2 318
11:1–16 18,
122
11:2–16
258–264
11:2–34
258–275
11:3 245,
312, 317
11:4, 5 287
11:5 313
11:6 312
11:7 78, 344
11:7–9 331
11:16 256
11:17 207
11:17–34
122, 265–
275
11:18 122
11:20–22
120
11:22 256
11:25 251
11:30 282,
318
12 167, 202,
203, 207,
300, 302,
306, 314,
343
12–14 18,
281, 315
12:1 205,
245, 317
12:1–3 276–
278
12:1 – 14:40
276–315
12:3 280,
317, 366,
367
12:4–11 87,
279–283,
307
12:8 145

(*I Cor*)

12:8–10
288
12:10 300,
301
12:12 325
12:12–26
272, 283–
287
12:12–27
251
12:12–30
200
12:13 245,
273
12:22 292
12:22–25
264
12:23–24
292
12:27 273,
292
12:27–31a
287–289
12:28 300,
363
12:28–30
151
12:30 293,
300, 301
12:31 288
12:31b –
14:1a
289–297
13 5, 110,
162, 229,
314, 362
13:2 180,
231, 280,
282
13:7 325
13:8, 9 231
13:13 325
14 295, 314,
321
14:1 288
14:1b–33a
298–311
14:2 179,
280
14:3–5 229
14:5 280
14:12 229
14:14 157
14:14–19
209
14:23 266

(*I Cor*)

14:26–28
301
14:29–37
259, 287
14:33 142
14:33b–36
311–313
14:34 102
14:37–40
314–315
14:40 292
15 5, 18,
110, 145,
221, 297
15:1 17
15:1–11
316–323
15:1–58
316–354
15:1, 2 239
15:2 145
15:3 259
15:5 208
15:5–9 48
15:8–9 178
15:9 242,
256
15:12–19
323–327
15:20–28
327–334
15:24 164
15:27 279
15:29–34
334–341
15:30 19
15:30–32 17
15:32 90,
358
15:33 119
15:35–49
341–349
15:37 302
15:42–43
118
15:45 78
15:50 98,
118, 195,
273
15:50–57
349–353
15:51 164,
180
15:58 221,
353–354
16 25, 89

(*I Cor*)

16:1 18, 142,
205
16:1–4 18,
60, 355–357
16:1–24
355–367
16:5 19
16:5–9 357–
358
16:8, 9 17
16:10 89
16:10–11
179, 358–
359
16:12 18,
205, 360–
361
16:13–14
361–362
16:15 80–81,
151
16:15–18
362–364
16:16 142
16:17 17
16:19 42,
142
16:19–20
364–365
16:21 32
16:21–24
365–367

II Cor 1:1 142, 143,
256, 360
1:3–10 118
1:8 19, 90,
245, 338
1:9 19
1:12 272
1:15 19
1:15–24 90
1:16–2:1
19
1:23–2:11
240
1:24 361
2:1–4 112
2:1–11 295
2:2 23
2:4 19
2:5 23
2:5–11 20,
114
2:9 120
2:12 357

(*II Cor*)

2:12, 13 20,
90, 113
2:13 22, 112,
120
2:16 318
3 5, 318
3:8 272
3:12 325
4:7–15 337
4:8–12 115
4:13 157
4:17 118
4:17–18 116
4:18 108
5:1 118, 345
5:1–5 116
5:1–10 332
5:3 352
5:4 348
5:7 292
5:14 228,
229
5:16 156,
273
5:17 325,
343
6:2 144
6:4–10 115
6:9–10 117
6:14–7:1
120
6:16 105,
169
7 22
7:5 112
7:5f 24
7:6–7 43
7:7–8 24
7:12 22,
120
7:13 120
7:14 20
8 25, 355
8:1 317
8:4 146
8:6, 8 43
8:20–25 325
9 25
9:1–5 60
10–13 21–
24, 120
10:1–6 171
10:7–11 22
10:10 240
10:13–16 26
10:14–16
171

(*II Cor*)

10:15 99
11, 12 23
11:3 169–170
11:4*f* 23
11:4–5 23
11:6 303
11:8, 9 25
11:12–15 114
11:13 23, 54
11:13, 14 21
11:13–15 23
11:16–30 292
11:18–23 27
11:20 23
11:22 23, 54
11:22–29 4
11:23–27 40
11:23–28 26
11:23–29 63, 115
11:32 59
11:32–33 7, 50
12, 13 22
12:1 311
12:1–8 27
12:2–4 393
12:2–5 27
12:6, 7 239
12:7 329
12:7–10 112, 115
12:10 117
12:11 23
12:12 88, 287
12:18 23, 43
12:20 21
12:21 185
13 22
13:5, 11–12 361
13:12 142, 364
13:13
(Greek) 33, 146
13:14 33, 367

Gal 1 103
1, 2 323
1:1 101, 142

(*Gal*)

1:4 144, 218
1:6–7 103
1:6–9 103
1:8 9, 114, 142
1:8–9 112
1:11, 12 7, 220
1:11–22 58
1:12 311, 319
1:13 256
1:13–14 4
1:15 5
1:15–16 101
1:16 273, 350
1:16–17 7
1:17 8
1:18 8, 318
1:19 8, 241
1:20 8, 59
1:21–24 8
1:23 361
2 103
2:1 8, 60
2:1–10 9, 64
2:2 9, 60, 311
2:3 10, 43
2:3–6 239
2:4 10
2:5, 6 12
2:6 178
2:7 17, 318
2:7–10 12
2:9 7, 318
2:10 355
2:11 13, 318
2:11–13 54
2:11–14 254
2:13 10
2:14 318
2:20 112
3:1–2 13
3:2 158, 165
3:3 170
3:8 312
3:10–13 104
3:11 215
3:16 104
3:24–25 104, 179
3:27 245

(*Gal*)

4:8 233
4:13–14 14
4:13–15 115
4:14 53
4:19 113
4:21–31 104
4:24–26 105
5:5 325
5:9 189
5:12 45, 295
5:13–26 171
5:18 166
5:20 169, 266
5:21 98, 195
5:22 229
5:22–25 166
5:23 240
6:1 157
6:6 145
6:7 336
6:11 367
6:13 51
6:18 32–33

Eph 1:1 142, 304
1:5 163
1:9–10 180
1:22–23 273
2:3 214
2:20 173, 288
2:21 105
3:1–12 180
3:5 288
3:8 318
3:16 156
4:4 273
4:11, 12 288
4:12 273
4:16 250, 273
4:17–19 78
4:18 79
5:5 98, 195
5:20 329
5:22–33 262, 263, 313
5:24 312
5:32 180
6:12 350
6:12–17 241
6:16 191
6:19 180

Philip 1:1 36, 38
1:3–7 113
1:6 144
1:12–13 33
1:12–18 99
1:15 33
1:15–18 112,
  114
1:18 33
1:20 33
1:22 272
1:27 33
2:1 146
2:5–8 331
2:6 233, 348
2:12–18 36
2:17 348
2:19 36
2:19–21 34
2:25–30 35
3 4
3:2–7 3
3:8 112
3:10 146,
  337
3:14 111,
  118, 243
4:2–3 35
4:3 43
4:4–6 361
4:4–16 26
4:10 35
4:12 156
4:18 35

Col 1, 2 116
1:1 142, 360
1:2 304
1:7 30
1:8 32
1:15–20 233
1:18, 20, 22
  273
1:24 31
1:26 163,
  164, 180
2:1 245
2:12 321
2:15 164
2:17 273
3:15 250,
  273
4:3 31, 357
4:5–6 361
4:7 32
4:9 29
4:10 11, 29,
  35, 61

(Col)
4:10–11 31
4:11 98, 195
4:12 30
4:14 29, 31,
  42
4:15 32, 365
4:16 31
4:17 32
4:18 32, 367

I Thess 1:5 14, 179
1:1–10 15
2:1–7 15,
  101
2:7 113
2:12 98, 195
2:13 102
2:13–16 105
2:14 256
2:14–16 104,
  118
2:17, 18 15
4:13 245,
  325
4:13–15 340
4:13–17 329,
  352
4:13–18 268
4:14–17 332
4:16–17 340,
  350
4:18 354
5:1–10 361
5:2 144
5:3 246
5:14–21 361
5:26 364

II Thess 1:5 98, 195
1:6 215
1:9 246
2:1 329
2:3 170
2:4 105
2:7 164
2:7–10 180
2:13 331
3:3 191
3:6 185, 259
3:6–13 354
3:7–10 26
3:12 272
3:14 190–
  191
3:17–18 367
4:1 256

I Tim 1:2 36, 43
1:3, 3–20 37
1:13, 16 37
1:20 41, 42
2:8–15 37
2:11 37
2:13 260
2:14 170
2:15 259
3:1 359
3:9 361
3:14–15 37
4:12 36, 359
5:1–10 37
5:8 361
5:18 238
5:23 359
6:2 215
6:5 195
6:9 246

II Tim 1:1 142
1:2 43
1:4–7 359
1:5 213
1:7 156
1:8 38–39
1:15 41
1:16, 17 39
2:9 39
2:13 146
2:17–18 340
3:10–11 40
4:1 366
4:6–8 41
4:10 9, 30
4:10–12, 13
  41
4:16 39, 41
4:17, 18 39
4:19 42, 364
4:20 39, 42
4:21 41

Titus 1:4 9, 43
1:5–9 43
1:10–12 44
1:12–13 45
1:13 361
2:1–10 43
2:2 361
3:1–11 43
3:15 366

Philem 1 360
2 365
9 28
10 28, 179

(Philem)

13 28, 364
16 149
19 28, 367
20 364
24 42
24–25 29

Heb 1:2 234
1:12 261
2:4 156
2:14 350
4:14 148
6:3 357
9:9 218
11:10 173
11:38 246

James 1:16 336
1:23–24 292
2:1–7 197
2:19 231
2:24, 26 232
3:18 359
4:9 185
4:13–16 357

I Peter 2:4–6 173
2:23 197
3:7 206
3:18 194
3:18–21 321
5:14 365

II Peter 1:12–14, 16–
18 42
3:1–2 42
3:14 359
3:15–16 42

I John 17 320
4:1–3 307

(I John)

4:1–6 278
4:3 277

II John 10 192

Jude 6 194

Rev 1 307
1–3 142
1:10 266,
355
1:20 164,
264
2 365
2:13 278
2:14, 20 64
2:24 157
2:26 261
3 365
3:2, 3 361
3:8 278, 357
6:9 332
8–10 302
10:7 164
11:6 261
12:9–10 207
12:17 278
13:2 40
14:4 220
14:18 261
17:5, 7 164
17:14 278
20:4 352
22:7, 17 367
22:19 178
22:20 366,
367
22:21 367

2–4 228

Ps Sol

I Macc 1:11–15 3
1:15 215

II Macc 4:9–16 3

Sir 1:10 157

Wisd Sol 3:8 194
18:20–25
246

Jub 24:29 194

I Enoch 38:5, 95:3
194

Test Naphtali
VIII 8 206

Didache 9–10 365
9:4 250
10:6 366
10:7 – 13:7
304
11:7 304
14:1 355

Gospel of Philip
23 350

RABBINIC
Abodah Zarah 254
Berakoth 1:1n, 6–7
267
Pesahim 8:3, 4, 7 251
Sanhedrin 10:1 4
Chullin 2:18, 20 228

QUMRAN
1QM 2:1–6 148
1QS 9:11 148
1QSa 2:11–12 148

KEY TO THE TEXT

Chapter	Verses	Section	Chapter	Verses	Section
1	1-9	Introductory	11	17-34	V B
1	10-17	I A	12	1-3	VI A
1	18-31	I B	12	4-11	VI B
2	1-16	I B	12	12-26	VI C
3	1-23	I C	12	27-31a	VI D
4	1-21	I D	12	31b	VI E
5	1-8	II A	13	1-13	VI E
5	9-13	II B	14	1a	VI E
6	1-9a	II C	14	1b-33a	VI F
6	9b-20	II D	14	33b-36	VI G
7	1-7	III A	14	37-40	VI H
7	8-9	III B	15	1-11	VII A
7	10-16	III C	15	12-19	VII B
7	17-24	III D	15	20-28	VII C
7	25-35	III E	15	29-34	VII D
7	36-38	III F	15	35-49	VII E
7	39-40	III G	15	50-57	VII F
8	1-3	IV A	15	58	VII G
8	4-13	IV B	16	1-4	VIII A
9	1-27	IV C	16	5-9	VIII B
10	1-15	IV D	16	10-11	VIII C
10	16-22	IV E	16	12	VIII D
10	23-29	IV F	16	13-14	VIII E
10	30-33	IV G	16	15-18	VIII F
11	1	IV G	16	19-20	VIII G
11	2-16	V A	16	21-24	VIII H